The intrepid
Election Observer
Each Mission is an Adventure

Jos Tesselaar

The intrepid Election Observer

Each Mission is an Adventure

Aspekt Graphics

The intrepid Election Observer

© Jos Tesselaar
© 2023   Uitgeverij Aspekt | Amersfoortsestraat 27
         3769 AD Soesterberg
         info@uitgeverijaspekt.nl | www.uitgeverijaspekt.nl

Omslagontwerp: Lisa Dijkhuizen
Binnenwerk: BeCo DTP-Productions, Epe

ISBN: 9789464629668
NUR: 906

Alle rechten voorbehouden. Niets van deze uitgave mag worden verveelvoudigd, opgeslagen in een geautomatiseerd gegevensbestand of openbaar gemaakt, in enige vorm of op enige wijze, hetzij elektronisch, mechanisch, door fotokopieën, opnamen of enig andere manier, zonder voorafgaande toestemming van de uitgever.

Voorzover het maken van kopieën uit deze uitgave is toegestaan op grond van artikel 16B Auteurswet 1912 j° het Besluit van 20 juni 1974, St.b. 351, zoals gewijzigd bij het Besluit van 23 augustus 1985, St.b. 471 en artikel 17 Auteurswet 1912, dient men de daarvoor wettelijk verschuldigde vergoedingen te voldoen aan de Stichting Reprorecht (postbus 882, 1180 AW, Amstelveen). Voor het overnemen van gedeelte(n) van deze uitgave in bloemlezingen, readers, en andere compilatiewerken (artikel 16 Auteurswet 1912), dient men zich tot de uitgever te wenden.

CONTENTS

1. MOZAMBIQUE - 1994 'These are the first elections ever'.................... 13
2. GUATEMALA - 1995 'One candidate kills with arms; the other with poverty'.. 27
3. GUATEMALA - 1996 'Keep your car windows closed at all times'.......... 37
4. PISA - 2005 'Eastern European countries are now EU members'....... 42
5. VENEZUELA - 2006 'Democracy is fine, as long as Hugo Chávez wins'......... 48
6. NIGERIA - 2007 'They cannot read or write, but they can shoot'......... 67
7. PAKISTAN - 2008 'Benazir Bhutto has just been assassinated'............... 92
8. BOLIVIA - 2009 'The president is also chair of the coca growers'..........118
9. BOLIVIA - 2009 'Bolivia is a great country that lost all its wars'........134
10. KYRGYZSTAN - 2010 'So this what ethnic cleansing looks like'................151
11. SUDAN-Reg - 2010 'You are obliged to stay at Khadaffi's hotel'...........174
12. SUDAN-Ref - 2011 'Without a common enemy, they'll fight each other'.......186
13. NICARAGUA - 2011 'The Sandinistas copy the tactics of Hugo Chávez'......199
14. RUSSIA - 2012 'Phantom polling stations: they really do exist'.........211

15.	KENYA	- 2013	'The slums are no go areas for our observers'.	232
16.	HONDURAS	- 2013	'Thank you, observer, for being here'.	253
17.	EGYPT	- 2014	'Belongs our interpreter to the Muslim Brotherhood?'.	273
18.	MOZAMBIQUE	- 2014	'Democracy, but the winner is always Frelimo'.	308
19.	GUINEA	- 2015	'Ebola is still there; don't go to hospitals or funerals'.	330
20.	PERU-First	- 2016	'There is a Peru above and a Peru below the table'.	349
21.	PERU-Second	- 2016	'The Peruvians are nice as well as corrupt'.	365
22.	NETHERLANDS	- 2018	'Hostile Environment Awareness Training'.	378
23.	GEORGIA-First	- 2018	'Georgians are even more rude than the Dutch'.	389
24.	GEORGIA-Sec	- 2018	'You'll find the Stalin Museum at the Stalin Avenue'.	406
25.	MOZAMBIQUE	- 2019	'You're suffering from the Stockholm Syndrome'.	417

FOREWORD

When I tell people that I'm an election observer, I know what their first question will be: 'How does one become an election observer?' My answer is invariably the same: 'It's very difficult to get on the list, but once you're on the list, it's nearly impossible to get off it'.

Not much of an answer, I have to admit. The truth is that it was very easy for me to become an election observer. In the summer of 1994 I read an advertisement in a Dutch national newspaper.

The Dutch ministry of foreign affairs wanted to enlist a sizeable number of Dutch observers for the upcoming elections in Mozambique. Since my wife and I had been aid workers in Mozambique for three years, I knew the country quite well and I spoke Portuguese. I was recruited.

After the year 2005 it became more difficult to enter the ranks of election observers, as the EU and the OSCE preferred to field experienced observers instead of 'tourists'. Therefore, countries like Germany and The Netherlands effectively stopped recruiting new observers for a number of years.

I thoroughly enjoyed my 20 observation missions. Each mission is an adventure, whereby the most important question always is: who is going to be my partner? Observers in the field customarily work in pairs.

I am not a very social person, but the truth is that I spend more time with my partner, than I would ever spend with my wife. My wife goes to work during the day and goes to her bridge club in the evening. My partner, on the contrary, is always with me: seven days a week and also seven evenings a week.

Observers work every day and every evening, including Saturdays and Sundays. And since we are usually based in the same guesthouse in a province where neither of us know anyone, we are forced to have breakfast, lunch and dinner together.

Apart from doing interviews together, we are also obliged to write our Weekly Reports together. A potential source of mutual irritations. To summarize: if you have a horrible partner, you have a horrible mission.

Since most of my colleague observers are still active in the field, I mention them only by their first names. Public officials, like ministers and ambassadors, are mentioned by their full names. This is a work of non-fiction, therefore all names are real names.

This book is about elections, but also about interpersonal and intercultural relations. Not only is there a cultural clash between Europeans and people in the Third World, there are also great differences between people from western and eastern Europe, as well as between people from northern and southern Europe, Africa and North and South America.

Even though I wrote this book from the perspective of a journalist, my profession, it is also about me, doing my best to act as a social person. I see it as my job, to be social. That's what I get paid for. The physical hardships of working in the tropics are a minor headache, compared to the social hardships. Believe me.

I have worked in provinces in Egypt and Mozambique, where it was 42 degrees Celsius every day. That's so hot, that you cannot even sit outside after dark, without sweating profusely. It was even hotter in the most eastern province of Nigeria, where it was 46 degrees every day, and there was no electricity. In Russia, east from Moscow in the middle of winter, it was -22 degrees every day.

This book takes you around the world, while you stay comfortably at home. You are not bitten by mosquitoes, you are not sweating your butt off every day, you don't have to work with horrible French people. I endured all the hardships. I hope you enjoy it and that, in the process, you will learn a thing or two.

Jos Tesselaar
Enkhuizen
The Netherlands

INTRODUCTION

Back in the 1990's, election observation was still in its infancy. It was very much a learning process. In fact, it was only in the year 2000 that the EU developed a comprehensive observation methodology, that was subsequently also adopted by the OSCE and the Carter Centre.

The new methodology includes long-term observation and a central (core) team of specialized experts. Not only Election Day is observed, but also the preparations leading up to it, as well as post E-Day developments.

The EU and the OSCE have divided the world into two parts: the EU observes in Third World countries and the OSCE observes in the ex-Soviet states. The Carter Centre observes in a number of Third World countries.

Regional observation organizations are active in Africa and Latin America. Some embassies field their own observers. Domestic observers are deployed—sometimes in very large numbers—in nearly every democratic country.

Since the year 2000, EU Election Observation Missions are organized with military speed and precision. First, an agency is selected to handle all administrative and logistic matters. This 'Service Provider' then travels to the Third World country where the elections will be observed.

The Service Provider rents an entire gangway in an expensive hotel in the capital city. Local guards are recruited and placed at the entrance to the gangway. Then the beds are removed from the rooms and replaced by office desks. Computers and other office equipment are installed. At the same time, local staff are recruited: secretaries, interpreters, drivers.

Next, the Core Team experts arrive. The number of experts varies between four and twelve, depending on the size of the EU Election Observation Mission. There are usually one or two electoral experts, political experts and legal experts. They work in close cooperation with local counterparts.

The overall head of an EU EOM, the Chief Observer, is nearly always a member of the European Parliament who visits the country twice: at the start of the mission and around E-Day. In the case of OSCE missions, The CO is usually an ambassador of an OSCE member state.

The de facto head of an EU EOM is the Deputy Chief Observer, who is in charge of day-to-day operations for the duration of the mission. Since LTOs and STOs are deployed to remote places, they always work in pairs. This not only improves their security situation, but also improves the quality of their work.

One week after the arrival of the Core Team, the Long-Term Observers arrive at the same hotel. This means that the Core Team has only one week to make preparations for the three days of briefings for the LTOs.

The Core Team also prepares an LTO Manual and a Deployment Plan for the LTOs to the provinces. LTOs remain between four and ten weeks in the country. The Short-Term Observers spend around two weeks in the country. Their main job is to observe E-Day. They are also briefed for three days.

At the end of the mission, everything happens in reverse. First, the STOs are debriefed and leave the country. Then the LTOs do the same. Finally, the Core Team leaves the country, after which the Service Provider wraps up the pending administrative and logistical issues.

An EU EOM produces two reports: the Preliminary Statement is published within two days after E-Day. It contains the major conclusions and recommendations of the mission. Two months later the Chief Observer and the Deputy Chief Observer return to the country, to hand over a much more elaborate Final Report to the Government and the Election Commission.

What are international observers allowed to do and what not? This is defined very clearly in a 2005 UN document entitled *Declaration of Principles for International Election Observation*. The organization of the elections is entirely the responsibility of the host country. International observers are not allowed to interfere. They do have the right to ask questions, though. They also have the right to observe the elections without restrictions.

Before an EU EOM is fielded, the host country must officially request the EU to do this. A Memorandum of Understanding is then signed between the country and the EU. Most Third World countries are quite happy to invite an EU EOM.

For many countries it is the only way to attract attention from the international media. Without an EU EOM, it is quite likely that CNN and BBC World will not bother to send camera crews to cover the elections.

In addition, an EU EOM usually means more positive relations with the EU and EU member states, resulting in increased development aid and investments. For semi-dictators, it may feel that an EU EOM legitimizes their hold onto power. So they are also happy to invite the EU to observe the elections.

An EU EOM costs between half a million and one-and-a-half million euros, depending on the size of the mission. Within the available budgets, the EU can field around twelve EU EOMs every year.

The EU finances its own missions. Each observer signs a contract with the EU. The OSCE, however, doesn't have much money. This means that observers working for OSCE missions are financed by their own countries.

As a result, observers on EU missions all receive the same daily allowances, while on OSCE missions there are enormous differences in remunerations between observers from western and eastern countries. A potential source of friction.

Chapter 1

MOZAMBIQUE - 1994

'Mozambique is now a democracy, where the old communist party always wins the elections'

Dozens of aspiring election observers assembled in a conference room at the Dutch Ministry of Foreign Affairs in The Hague. We were briefed on our upcoming mission. The very first elections in the history of Mozambique were to be held on 27 and 28 October 1994.

None of us had any observation experience, but nearly everyone had lived in Mozambique. I recognized quite a few faces. We were all looking forward to go back to the country where we had spent such a good time.

After our three years in Mozambique, my wife and I worked for UN agencies in Bolivia, Ecuador, Pakistan and The Gambia, where life was definitely more comfortable. But—like all old Mozambique hands—we really cherished our time in Maputo, the capital city. In spite of all the hardships.

Mozambique had been a communist country since its independence from Portugal in 1975. Frelimo, the liberation movement, had transformed itself into the only political party that was allowed. The communist system was an exact copy of the Soviet Union.

That meant that not only the political system was communist; the economy was also communist. A capitalist economy in Africa means that there is little production; a communist economy in Africa means that there is no production at all.

Immediately after independence, the new Frelimo government under president Samora Machel nationalized all private properties. From then on, large industrial and agricultural enterprises were led by inexperienced bureaucrats who lived in Maputo, in the far south of the country. The prices of products were also determined by bureaucrats in Maputo.

As a result, all production in the country came to a full stop. Bureaucrats did not have a clue as to how to run a business. And prices were soon out of bounds with market realities. A fisherman, for example, was forced to sell his catch at a very low price, in order to 'provide cheap food for the population'.

But the fishermen could only buy petrol for their boats on the black market, at very high prices. That meant that the costs of going out to sea were much higher than the profits. As a result, not one fish was caught anymore. The same applied to agriculture. Instead of cheap food, there was no food at all.

To make matters worse, the overwhelming majority of the Portuguese, who ran the economy during the colonial days, had left the country. They had taken most of their machinery with them. What they could not take with them, they destroyed in their anger and frustration.

But even worse was to come for Mozambique, as an insurgency, named Renamo, spread throughout the country. Renamo was sponsored by white Rhodesians, in retaliation for Frelimo's support of Robert Mugabe's 'freedom fighters'.

In the west, Robert Mugabe was heralded as a Marxist-Leninist liberator. In reality, he was a scrupulous dictator, who lead his country onto the brink of catastrophe. Mugabe belonged to the Shona people, who comprise 82 per cent of the population.

His main domestic competitor, Joshua Nkomo, belonged to the Ndebele, also known as Matabele, who comprise only 14 percent of the population. Since in Africa it's quite inconceivable that someone would vote for anyone belonging to another tribe, this meant that Mugabe would always win the elections.

Even so, Mugabe felt threatened by his rival. In the 1980s, Mugabe employed the services of the ex-communist dictator of Ethiopia, Haile Meriam, to slaughter thousands of Matabele tribesmen in Zimbabwe. Mugabe's killing squads had been trained by North Koreans.

It took Mugabe only a few years to completely destroy the second strongest economy in Africa, after which a quarter of the population of Zimbabwe migrated to South Africa, in search of jobs and food. While Mugabe and his cronies became millionaires, Zimbabwe was transformed into a pitiful country.

It always surprised me that African leaders are not interested in developing their countries. Mugabe was only interested in remaining in power. While ordinary Zimbabweans were starving, his wife went shopping in Paris or London. Three times per year. The Zimbabweans did not call her First Wife, but First Shopper.

After Mugabe had taken power, Renamo continued its armed struggle in Mozambique, supported by South Africa's apartheid regime, in retaliation of Mozambique's support the ANC. Mozambique was now suffering under a communist system in Africa, combined with a civil war: a recipe for disaster. There was no production in Mozambique and in many areas it was too dangerous to travel.

Luckily, Maputo has a sea port and a railway to South Africa. The entire population of one million people could therefore be fed by the World Food Program. This had a strange twist to it, since WFP was funded by the western capitalist countries and Japan. So the population of a communist city was saved from starvation by capitalist aid money.

This was the situation when my wife and I arrived in Maputo in September 1983. The first half year we travelled once a month to Swaziland, the neighbouring country that later changed its name to Eswatini, to do our shopping. But after several westerners had been abducted by Renamo, the UN and all western embassies forbade their staff to travel outside Maputo.

As a result, for the next two and a half years we were confined to a besieged city. We were only allowed to travel by airplane or by boat, but there were hardly any boats and very few flights.

Every year, my colleagues and I would say that things could not get worse. We were wrong. Things did get worse every year. Even the dollar shop was a joke: only three things were for sale there: chocolate bars, whiskey (tax free, since I possessed a UN Laissez Passer) and sardines in cans. I never really liked whiskey, but I resold Johnny Walker red label to obtain local currency at forty times the official rate.

For twelve tax-free Johnny Walkers, I received a huge plastic bag filled with meticais. I didn't bother to count it. It lasted for three years, since there was hardly anything to spend the money on. And after Mozambique, I never ate sardines in cans any more.

In the mid-1980s, there were nearly four thousand aid workers in Maputo. They had money, but the shops were empty. To ensure that they would not leave, the government allowed South African companies to fly in consumer goods, even though this was in defiance of UN regulations from New York, which expressly forbade doing business with South Africa, because of the apartheid system.

In the meantime, more than 250,000 Mozambicans left their country and headed for South Africa. Why did they risk being eaten by lions in the Kruger Park? And why did not one ordinary South African ever move to Mozambique, the socialist paradise?

Anyway, South African businessmen are inventive: to make the UN officials in New York happy, the South Africans printed P.O. Box addresses in Swaziland on their invoices. We would send a telex to South Africa and order anything we wanted. The South Africans flew the goods in for us in small aircrafts: straight from South Africa.

In the end, everyone was happy: the UN in New York, because on the invoices it said that the goods came from Swaziland. The Mozambican government, since the aid workers would not leave the country. The aid workers were also happy: they could import anything they wanted, as long as they paid for it in hard currency. It was cheap anyway, because the South African rand had lost a lot of ground against the dollar.

The Mozambican government also opened a petrol station where you could only pay in dollars. This was the only petrol station that always had petrol. Bad news for the locals, who did not possess dollars. But even this petrol station was problematic, since it ran on electricity, which was in short supply. No electricity meant no petrol.

In spite of all the hardships, Maputo really was paradise for western aid workers. The Portuguese had constructed beautiful wide avenues, on which there was no traffic, except for us foreigners and the happy few of the communist leadership. There were still beautiful restaurants, with well-trained staff.

Since there was no production in the country, the restaurants had neither food nor drink, but we found a solution: we ordered meat and vegetables from South Africa and we delivered it to a restaurant in the afternoon. In the early evening, we went to that same restaurant with a group of friends, where the cooks had prepared our food for us.

We brought our own beer, soft drinks, ketchup and mayonnaise, since the restaurant had none. But we had a marvelous time. And we gave a handsome tip to the restaurant staff, so they were also happy. It was a win-win situation.

I used my abundant local currency to learn horseback riding. The evening lessons, including a fully saddled horse, cost me less than a dollar per hour. The lessons were provided by a Portuguese guy and his Swiss girlfriend.

The only problem was that the horses were getting old. For some reason, no horses had been born since independence. The saddles were also getting old, stiff and worn out. But as we say in Holland: 'Don't look a gifted horse in the mouth'.

We also played football. There were hundreds of South Americans in Maputo, who had fled the fascist regimes in countries like Argentina, Chile, Brazil and Uruguay. They were now employed by western aid agencies. Like Europeans, they loved football. We played in a sports hall, that had been built by the Portuguese just before they abandoned the country.

While we, aid workers, had a great time, the country was going down the drain. Outside the major cities, where WFP food could not be delivered because of the civil war, people were starving from hunger. All elephants and other wildlife in the game parks were killed and eaten by the local population.

Prolonged scarcity has a profound effect on your psyche. To this day, my wife and I still experience a lasting result of our time in Mozambique. Even more than thirty years later, both of us still have a hang-up about the petrol in our car.

In Mozambique, we were obliged by the UN to always keep our tank at least half full, so that in an emergency situation we could reach the border with either Swaziland or South Africa in a protected convoy. To this very day, my wife and I get nervous when the level in our tank falls below half full.

In the autumn of 1986, a few weeks after my wife and I had moved to Bolivia, the Russian airplane of president Samora Machel crashed just across the border in South Africa. Apparently, the Russian pilots had been drunk. The minister of foreign affairs, Joaquim Chissano, became the new president.

A few years later, the Soviet Union collapsed and Nelson Mandela was released from prison. He would later marry Samora's widow, Graça Machel, who remained a leading figure within the Frelimo party. The world had changed. In Mozambique, communism was replaced by democracy. But it was going to be democracy with a twist, since the same party would always win the elections.

The country was in such a bad shape, that these first elections had to be funded and organized entirely by the UN. To gain credibility, the UN requested hundreds of international election observers on the ground. And so it happened that in the summer of 1994 I read an advertisement in a Dutch national newspaper, the Volkskrant.

At the time, I was working with my brother Peter in our family greenhouse. Peter grew roses, but during the dark winter months, roses don't grow much. A good excuse for me to go back to Mozambique. Since I had lived in Mozambique for three years and therefore spoke Portuguese, I was recruited immediately.

I was looking forward to going back to Maputo and catching up with old friends. But things don't always move in the expected direction. At the briefing at the Ministry of Foreign Affairs in The Hague we were told that we would be flown to Johannesburg in South Africa, since all hotels in Maputo had been fully booked by journalists and observers.

So we landed at the international airport in Johannesburg. At the time, it was still called Jan Smuts airport, after the apartheid president. Twelve years later, in 2006, it would be renamed Oliver Tambo airport, after a leading ANC figure.

We were taken by bus to an expensive downtown hotel. There we were briefed by UN staff on our upcoming mission. I noticed a problem that would haunt me—and the other Dutch observers—on all my future missions. My name plaque was placed in front of me on the table, but instead of 'Jos Tesselaar' it read 'Johannes Tesselaar'.

The reason for this is that in The Netherlands we have full Christian names in our passports. All of us. So my observer friend 'Kees' has 'Cornelis' in his passport. No one in Holland ever calls him Cornelis. My observer colleague Ineke faces the same problem. Her full passport name is Catharina, but in Holland everyone simply calls her Ineke.

Observation Missions are required to use our full passport names, in case a visa or a security permit is needed. And since our full passport names also appear in the LTO Manual and STO Manual, most colleagues only know us by our full passport names.

In any case, in Holland nobody ever calls me Johannes. A Dutchman who is called Jan also has 'Johannes' in his passport. The same for someone who is called Hans or Hannes. Or Johan. Johan Cruijff also had 'Johannes' as his passport name.

Johannesburg (not named after me, nor Cruijff) was one of the most dangerous cities in the world. In fact, we were warned not to walk alone in the city center, not even during the day. Several observers went out onto the streets anyway.

Surprise, surprise: several of them got mugged. A group of young men would surround you and then put a knife to your throat. You had to hand over all your valuables. It happened to one of the Dutch observers.

He had worked in Mozambique for an ultra-leftist Dutch NGO called the Eduardo Mondlane Foundation, who had wholeheartedly supported the communist regime. He later told us that he fully understood that poor Africans had robbed him, since he was rich and they were poor. In my opinion, someone who puts a knife at your throat is a criminal. But who am I?

Anyway, I was told that I would be sent to Lichinga, the capital of Niassa province in the far north-west, bordering Tanzania and Lake Malawi. And my partner would be a Chinese military man, who had been in Mozambique for six months on a peacekeeping mission.

A few days later we found ourselves in a chartered Russian airplane. Before we took off, the pilots had to solve a little mechanical problem. We were not told anything, but we saw one of the pilots walking on the right wing, with a screwdriver in his hand. I learned later that as an observer you get used to these kinds of things.

We finally took off and the plane landed first in Beira, Mozambique's second largest city, to drop off a number of observers. Then the plan flew on to Pemba, a coastal town in the far north-east, to drop of yet another bunch of observers.

Finally, when it was already getting dark, Lake Malawi came into view and the plane touched down at the airstrip of Lichinga. A nice little airport, thanks to those horrible Portuguese colonizers.

The downtown hotel did not have enough rooms for all of us. After twenty years of neglect, the hotel was not really comfortable either, so we were taken to a school, several kilometres out of town, where field beds had been made available for us.

There were not enough beds though, so the UN staff asked if anyone would prefer to stay at the rundown hotel in town. I volunteered, since I preferred to be able to walk around the centre of town in the evening.

Lichinga is literally the coolest provincial capital in Mozambique, since it sits on top of a plateau, at an altitude of 1,360 meters. The evenings are pleasantly chilly. I walked around the town centre. The roads were full of potholes, there were very few street lights and there was hardly any traffic.

Houses and shops had not been painted since 1975. It felt like a communist town. But then I noted a little restaurant with an outside terrace. I asked the waiter if he had any beer. His answer surprised me. ,,Of course", he said. ,,What kind of beer do you want?"

They also served meat and fish. And vegetables. Capitalism had definitely arrived in Mozambique, but the country would need a long time to recover from communism. The waiter explained to me that all the food and drink were imported from nearby Malawi.

That evening I met a few expatriates who lived in Lichinga. They told me that communism indeed belonged to the past. But the country was still facing enormous problems. Poverty, illiteracy, bureaucracy. For the last twenty years, things had gone backwards instead of forwards.

People had become used to not taking any private initiatives, since under a communist system this is not allowed. It would take many years to get the country back on its feet again.

The next day we were briefed by UN staff. I met my Chinese partner, a major in the Chinese Army. China had joined the international peacekeeping forces in Mozambique. He was a cheerful fellow. He spoke decent English but hardly any Portuguese.

We were told that each team would be provided with a vehicle, commissioned from EU-funded development projects. There was a little problem though: there were plenty of cars, but not enough drivers.

Some teams would have to drive themselves. Were there any volunteers? My Chinese partner explained to me that he was not allowed to drive in Mozambique, since he was not insured.

I did not know if I was insured, but I didn't care: I had brought my international driving license with me, just in case. So I bravely volunteered to drive our Nissan land cruiser. Not knowing what lay in store for us in the Mozambican countryside.

They gave us a detailed map of Metarica district. It would take us about four hours to get there: the first two hours we would be heading west, on the highway to Pemba, a decent asphalt road. After that it would be dirt roads. They also gave us forms to be filled in on Election Day. And money for petrol. That was about it.

In later days, observers were equipped with laptops, BGANs, mobile phones, satellite phones, HF radios and VHF radios. On top of that, our vehicles are equipped with tracking devices, panic buttons and even remote control. But back in 1994, these futuristic gadgets were not yet available.

To make matters worse, we were told that in our district there was not even a fixed telephone. But we didn't need to worry, because in case of an emergency we would be able to use an army radio. We were told that in our district there was no hotel and no restaurant. There was not even a decent shop.

The good news was that military peacekeepers had set up camp in the very centre of the district's main town. Two majors from Ghana had been camping there for several months. We were welcome to stay with them. They would have army rations for us.

After six years in Africa, I knew what we could expect from our two military hosts. I explained to my Chinese partner that they would be very happy to see us, especially if we brought a few beers with us. So before setting out to our village we drove to a shop and bought six crates of beer.

„Is that not too much?" my Chinese partner asked. „Trust me", I replied. „It's probably not enough." We also bought fresh bread and some vegetables. And plenty of mineral water.

Finally, we left Lichinga behind us in our UN vehicle, with the blue UN flag flapping cheerfully in the wind. The asphalt road, leading us to the west, was a pleasure to drive on. Two hours later, we turned to the right onto a dirt road.

Even this dirt road was not bad, at least for the first hour. After that, the road got smaller and more rugged. And I noted that we were descending. That meant that the temperature was rising.

At first, the bridges over the rivers were normal bridges. Then we came upon our first makeshift bridge, made of logs. It was just wide enough for our car, but it would be tricky to get across. I told my Chinese partner that one of us had to get out of the car, walk to the other side, and guide the driver from there.

Since I was driving, he had to get out of the car. He did a good job. He signalled to me when I drifted off too much to one side. The crossing took a bit of time and I was relieved when I finally climbed the opposite bank. By now, my partner was sweating profusely.

In the days to come, it would become routine for us to cross rivers this way. Each time, my Chinese partner had to get out of the car and cross a bridge under the burning sun, while I stayed behind the wheel in the air conditioned Nissan.

Finally, we arrived safely at the main town of Metarica district. The central square was in fact a sandy football field. We drove over to the far side, where four large army tents had been erected. The two majors from Ghana were waiting for us. They had been informed over their radio of our arrival. They were happy to see us. Especially after I showed them the beer.

The military camp was well equipped. It had its own generator, since there was no electricity in the entire district. They even had their own fridge, to keep our beer cold. They also had plenty of army rations and mineral water, so we would not starve from hunger or thirst.

There was a catch though: army rations, in those days, were horrible food. The two Ghanaians had found a solution to this problem: they exchanged canned army rations for fresh chickens. Apparently, the local population liked army rations. Some local women even prepared the chickens for them.

It was a miracle that they had managed to achieve all this, since they could not communicate with the local people. The Ghanaians did not speak one word of Portuguese and the local people did not speak one word of English. All communications had to be done by hand signals.

The Ghanaians asked me if I could translate for them. ,,Of course", I said. We went to see the mayor and the police chief of Metarica district, who were also happy that finally they could talk to the peacekeepers.

In fact, the locals did not have a clue as to what the Ghanaian majors were actually doing in their district, since there were no security issues at all in the region. My translation made everybody happy.

Just before darkness I washed myself in the little 'shower room', made of elephant grass. In the tropics, it makes sense to clean the dirt and the sweat off your body before nightfall. Malaria mosquitoes attack after dark. That evening I sat at a campfire with three majors. All around us, it was pitch dark.

We ate chicken, freshly prepared by local women, with maize meal and a hot red sauce. Great food, especially since you are allowed to eat it with your hands. After that, we drank a few cold beers. I quickly realized that I should have brought more beers. The six crates would only last us a few evenings.

So there we were in our military camp: three majors and me. The two Ghanaians were happy that, after several months, they could finally talk English to some other people. My Chinese partner had long conversations with them about the differences between communism and capitalism.

Funnily, the two Ghanaians, coming from a capitalist country, were in favour of communism. The Chinese major was the opposite: he explained to the Ghanaians that a communist economy does not work at all.

The next couple of days, my Chinese partner and I visited different parts of the district, mapping out the schools where people would vote. We observed the training of polling staff by UN-staff. Every evening we would sit around the campfire with our newly found friends from Ghana.

On Saturday evening, the Ghanaians even took us to the local 'disco', which turned out to be somebody's back garden with a portable cassette player that ran on batteries. Great fun and great dancing, but neither food nor drink. These people were really poor.

The next morning my Chinese partner and I got up very early from our field beds in the sleeping tent. It was Election Day. My very first E-Day. We had planned a route, aided by our map. When we arrived at the first Polling Station, we could not believe our eyes. At six o'clock, enormous queues were already lining up.

It was obvious that the Mozambicans were keen to vote, for the very first time in their history. Voting took place at schools which, in a poor country like Mozambique, were simple constructions without any luxury. Sometimes even without furniture.

Most of the polling staff were teachers, since they could at least read and write. They had been trained by the UN and all materials had been delivered by the UN. Voting went on reasonably well, all two days, apart from some minor problems.

The secrecy of the vote was compromised in some instances. It wasn't the fault of the polling staff, though. In their polling manual, a drawing had been included as to how the polling booths should be positioned. But the drawing was ambiguous.

Therefore, some polling staff concluded that the open side of the polling booths should face the room, instead of facing the wall. When we pointed this out to them, they showed us the drawing in the manual, which indeed was not very clear.

In later years I realized that I had made a mistake in Mozambique: as international election observers we are not allowed to interfere. We are allowed to ask questions, but that's the limit. But in the 1990's these guidelines were not yet drawn up.

In fact, it was only in the year 2005 that the UN published guidelines as to what election observers could do and could not do. Added to this, my Chinese partner and I had no means of communication with the UN electoral office in Lichinga.

The two Ghanaian majors possessed an army radio, but they were only allowed to use it twice a day, at fixed hours. Not only was the quality of the transmission quite bad, but on the other side of the radio there was another military man from Ghana.

I couldn't understand a word he was saying. And even if we could convey a message, what was this military man going to do with it? He had no contact with the UN electoral office, except in case of a real emergency.

All of this did not really matter, since there were no major disturbances to report. The two E-Days progressed just fine. People queued all day in the full blaze of the hot tropical sun. Not only because they were fed up with communism. We learned from our conversations with local people that everyone in the district was sick and tired of the civil war as well. Everybody wanted peace.

We observed the closing and counting in a polling station in our own town. No problems, apart from the fact that there was no electricity. The UN had included lamps in the electoral kits for the polling stations, but the batteries sometimes didn't fit or ran out of power rapidly. Luckily, Africans are resourceful. Someone would bring a candle or his own flashlight.

The polling staff announced the results before midnight. We went back to the two Ghanaian majors. We discussed with them if we could transmit the data on our observation sheets via the army radio, but they advised against it. If we used the radio at night, the Ghanaian army would think that something was horribly wrong with us. We agreed, also because of the fact that there was nothing of interest to report.

The next morning we said goodbye to our Ghanaian friends. They were actually crying when we left their camp. They could not talk to anyone over there, but as they had explained to us: they were in it for the money. They were paid much more than back home in Ghana. Therefore, they were going to sit it out.

On the way back we fell into our routine again. My Chinese partner had to cross every bush bridge on foot and then guide me over the wobbly logs. Thank God we didn't face a mechanical problem, out there in the middle of the hot bush.

And we had enough petrol, since the only petrol that was available in the district was sold in bottles along the road. As an old Africa hand, I knew that this petrol could be dirty or even mixed with water. But everything went fine.

Close to midday we finally entered Lichinga, where the air felt pleasantly cool. We drove straight to the UN electoral office. We were told that most other teams had already reported in. We handed them our duly filled in sheets. We were told that the UN had already declared the elections 'free and fair' in Maputo.

As expected, Frelimo, the ruling ex-communist party, had won with a landslide. We didn't care anymore. My Chinese partner and I agreed that it had been a great adventure for us. And in any case, it had been a very good experience for me.

We were flown back to Johannesburg for a debriefing by the UN, but this time we would change planes in Maputo. I hoped I would finally see the city again, but after the usual delays, we could only spend one hour at Maputo airport.

The airport hadn't changed much, except that there were some small shops now. I wanted desperately to call my Dutch friends Erick and Marianne de Mul on the phone. He was the UN chief in Mozambique.

There were no public telephones, but I asked an Indian shopkeeper if I could use the phone in his shop for five dollars. He happily agreed. Marianne was surprised that I was so close to them. Erick said that he would come to the airport, but I explained that there was no time. My plane would be leaving for Joburg any minute.

Things do not always go the way you want them to go. As Johan Cruijff used to say: 'The player can be fast, but the ball is faster'. The good news was that now I was an election observer. I was looking forward to my next mission.

Chapter 2

GUATEMALA - 1995

'One candidate will eventually kill us with arms; the other with poverty'

After my mission to Mozambique, my name appeared firmly on the list with election observers of the Dutch Ministry of Foreign Affairs. It is not easy to get on the list, but once you're on it, you're on it for eternity. It felt as if I was one of the chosen few.

Since I spoke Spanish, I was invited to go to Guatemala, where elections were to be held in November 1995. It would be rather complicated elections for president, national deputies, provincial deputies, Central American parliamentarians and mayors. There were 19 candidates for the presidency. The Partido de Avanzada Nacional (PAN) and the Frente Republicano Guatemalteco (FRG) were the most likely winners.

My wife and I had visited Guatemala in 1988, when we stayed with our friends Erick and Marianne de Mul for a week. We visited all the major tourist sites, including Tikal, the legendary Maya city. I liked Guatemala and it would be good for my Spanish. Apart from that, some other Dutch friends were still living there: Jo and Sylvie Mertens. I decided to pay them a surprise visit.

The candidate for PAN was Alvaro Arzú, the ex-mayor of Guatemala City. The candidate for FRG, Alfonso Portillo, had been handpicked by Rios Montt, the former strong-man of the country, who was hated fiercely by western leftist intellectuals, since they considered him to having been a fascist dictator.

It is easy to judge when you're living in a comfortable, well-organized western country, but it is not so easy when you live in a poor, chaotic Third World country. Like one peasant told me: „We only have two options: one candidate will eventually kill us with arms and the other candidate will eventually kill us with poverty. So whom should I vote for?"

What's my opinion on the matter? Well, since I'm a journalist, I always make a distinction between facts and opinions. As Clint Eastwood used to say: 'Opinions are like assholes; everybody has one'. I can think whatever I want, but I don't live in Guatemala.

This was to be an EU Election Observation Mission. My first EU EOM actually, since Mozambique had been a UN-led mission. So on 5 November 1995, at Schiphol Amsterdam Airport, I waited in line for the KLM counter with Paul Haarhuis, the Dutch tennis player who had won several grand slams in the doubles, with his partner Jacco Eltingh.

We flew with five Dutch observers to Mexico City and then on to Guatemala City, where we met the other 45 observers at hotel El Dorado for two days of EU briefings. The briefings were coordinated by the Spanish embassy, because Spain was chairing the EU at the time.

One of the proposed Dutch observers did not show up at the last minute. Apparently, he had just been released from hospital. His name was Peter Rehwinkel and he was a prominent member of the Dutch parliament for the Labour party. A few years later he would be appointed mayor of Groningen, the biggest city in the north of The Netherlands.

I have to explain one thing here: there's only one democratic country in the world, where the mayors are not elected but appointed: my own country. Even stranger: 90 per cent of all Dutch mayors are active members of the largest national parties. They are politicians. So why are they not elected then, like in the rest of the world?

In Venezuela the mayors are elected. In Mozambique as well. Even in Pakistan the mayors are elected. In these countries, the governors of the provinces are also elected. Not in The Netherlands. Like the mayors, the provincial governors are members of the large national parties, but they are appointed.

How democratic is my own country? Have I the right to be an election observer? Anyway, the parliamentarian was replaced by young Ronald, who worked at the Ministry of Foreign Affairs and had been based at the Dutch embassy for Central America. The other Dutch were Cynthia, Liesbeth and Marijke.

Liesbeth was quite a character. She dressed herself in multi-coloured poncho's and identified herself with the suppressed people of Guatemala, even though she had never lived there. She had only participated in a few short missions to the country.

I always thought it a bit strange that western leftist intellectuals identified themselves with poor Latin Americans. After all: they have nothing in common and usually they never meet one another.

But who am I? On several occasions, Liesbeth would comment on my 'conservative views'. I don't consider myself to be a rightist, but I try not to be too politically correct either. I prefer to keep an open mind.

Liesbeth was not the only observer of our mission who was preoccupied with the poor and suppressed Guatemalans. I always found it a bit hypocritical when westerners, living a safe and comfortable life in Sweden or Austria, loudly claimed to be supportive of the poor in Third World Countries.

Nevertheless, quite a few EU observers were in favour of Arzú and against Portillo. This was all the more remarkable, to say the least, since EU observers are supposed to be impartial and neutral at all times.

Fourteen years later, I would meet one of the Dutch observers again at the Dutch Ministry of Foreign Affairs, when we were briefed on our 2009 mission to Bolivia. To my embarrassment, I did not recognize Cynthia at all. But she convinced me by divulging a number of details about our 1995 Guatemala mission.

I have a bad memory for faces. In fact, I had totally forgotten about Par, my Swedish partner during the 1995 Guatemala mission. In 2009 I ran into him just outside our hotel in La Paz, the capital of Bolivia. Par was the political expert of the EU Core Team, while I was a Long Term Observer on that same mission.

Luckily, he did not recognize me at first, either. ,,Where have we met before?" he asked me. I recalled a few EU missions. ,,Were you with me in Venezuela, in 2006?" I asked. He said no. ,,Maybe in Nigeria, 2007?" Again he answered no. Than it dawned on him. ,,You were my partner in Guatemala, in 1995. Didn't your father grow flowers in greenhouses?" I said yes.

So Par had been my partner in Guatemala in 1995. He was a very serious Swede, like most Swedes. Or am I prejudiced here? In Holland, we can hardly tell the difference between one Scandinavian and another, but when you work in an international environment, the differences become quite obvious.

Years later, during my Honduras mission of 2013, my partner would be Jon from Norway. Jon explained to me that the Norwegians really hate the Swedes, because 100 years ago Norway was the poorest country in Europe. Consequently, Norwegians emigrated to America or worked in Sweden, where they were mercilessly exploited by the Swedes.

Nowadays, the roles are reversed, since Norway is now the richest country in Europe, thanks to their North Sea oil. Because of this, Swedes now travel to Norway to find work. But the Norwegians have not forgotten their years of poverty.

As a Dutchman, it is hard to understand the animosities between two Scandinavian neighbours. In The Netherlands, we profoundly disliked the Germans for several decades, after having been occupied by them during the Second World War, but we only really hated them after we lost the World Cup final of 1974 in West-Germany against West-Germany. This caused a severe national trauma in Holland.

The hatred ended when we beat them in the semi-finals of the 1988 European Cup, yet again against West-Germany in West-Germany. After this match, we beat the Soviet Union in the finals, but for every Dutchman and Dutchwoman the victory over West-Germany in the half finals was much more important. Since then, we don't hate them anymore.

In fact, on a personal level, the Germans are just like us. The Dutch are descendants of Germanic tribes. Many words in Dutch are quite similar to words in German. The main differences lie in the grammar, which makes it difficult for them to learn proper Dutch and for us to learn proper German. But we understand each other quite well.

With our other neighbours, the Belgians, we don't have any problems, even though they are not descendants of Germanic tribes. They are descendants of a Gaelic tribe: the Belgae. This explains why Belgians love to eat and drink well, while the Dutch prefer to work hard and efficiently, with one exception: me. I am lazy and I like to eat and drink and smoke a cigar. So I am more like the Belgians.

It is a bit more complicated than this, since Belgians don't exist. Those of them who speak French we never meet, since they live to far from our borders and also since they don't speak Dutch and we don't speak French anymore. The Flamish speak our language, albeit with a funny accent, which sounds quite pleasant to our ears.

We don't have problems with the Flamish, but the Flamish really hate the French speaking Belgians. Should there ever be a referendum, undoubtedly 90 per cent of the Flamish would vote for full independence from their French-speaking country folk. That would be the end of Belgium. So there will never be a referendum.

The briefings in hotel El Dorado in Guatemala City were relaxed. The EU joined forces with the OEA. I visited the beautiful colonial city of Antigua with the other Dutch observers. Nowadays, the EU calls this 'tourism' and it's forbidden. I call it 'history, archaeology and culture'. The EU always proclaims that observers should learn about the history and the culture of the guest country.

All EU observers were taken to the *Tribunal Supremo Electoral* and to the *Casa Presidencial*, where we had to listen for nearly two hours to a speech by president De Leon Carpio. The *Casa Presidencial* is situated behind the presidential palace. The president preferred not to work in the palace itself, since this is where Guatemalan presidents were traditionally assassinated.

Not very far from the presidential palace, Rigoberta Menchú had bought herself a fancy house from her Nobel Prize money. She was famed all over the world because of her human rights activities. Just three days before our visit to the palace, her 15 months old nephew had been abducted. It was not clear if the kidnappers wanted money or if they wanted to intimidate her for political reasons.

I found out that the WHO office of my Dutch friend Jo Mertens was just a few hundred meters from our hotel in Guatemala City. I walked over there, hoping to surprise him, but his secretary informed me that he was not in town. In fact, he was out of the country, on official business.

I asked the secretary if she could call Sylvie, Jo's wife. Sylvie picked up the phone instantly. She could not believe that I was standing in her husband's office. That evening, Sylvie picked me up from the hotel. She took me to their house, inside a compound that was protected on all sides with barbed wire and German shepherd dogs, to keep the criminal gangs out.

We had a pleasant evening, reminiscing about the years that we spent together in Maputo. Jo and Sylvie's two young sons were also present. They were very happy with the Dutch liquorice and the Dutch Santa Claus sweets that I had brought for them. Sylvie was very happy with the Dutch magazines, newspapers and cheese. Since I had been an expatriate myself, I knew what expatriates missed most from back home.

After the briefings, Par and I stepped in our Toyota land cruiser, that had been commissioned from an EU development project. With a driver, this time. His name was José Manuel. I liked him and he liked me. In Guatemala, a driver is called 'piloto'.

To my surprise, Par refused to speak English with me while we were in the car. He insisted on speaking Spanish, in order not to be offensive to our driver. I learned later that this is quite normal behavior for Swedes.

We headed north, to the town of San Marcos, not far from the border with Mexico. It was quite a drive, past Chichicastenango and the lakeside town of Atitlán. Many North Americans live there. Because of that, the locals call it Gringotenango.

Pensión Pérez in San Marcos was very basic but clean and the staff was friendly. Luckily, tortillas with refried beans and chilli peppers are one of my all-time favourite foods. I can eat it three times a day.

Since we were quite high up in the mountains, the climate was pleasantly cool, even cold at night, like the *altiplano* in Bolivia. There was a fixed telephone in our hotel. The EU EOM did not hand out mobile phones in those days yet and internet was still a thing of the distant future.

Three OAS observers were already based in the hotel: Greg (or Craig) from the US, Bjerte from Norway and Rebecca from God knows where. They briefed Par and me on the political and electoral situation in the province. Decent folks.

They joined us for breakfast too. All of them found it quite interesting that I filled my thermos flask with fresh coffee, for the road. ,,Is that a typical Dutch thing?", they asked me. I explained that two things were really important to me: coffee during the day and beer in the evening.

From our base at the hotel, we visited the nearby electoral districts, both higher up in the cold mountains and down towards the hot and humid tropical coast. I preferred the coolness of the mountains.

Observers spend many hours in cars. During one of our conversations, I found out that Par received a daily allowance from his Swedish government that was much higher than the allowance that I received from my Dutch government. This problem was tackled by the EU in later years.

Nowadays, all EU-observers sign a contract with the EU, so we all receive the same allowances. On OSCE missions this is different. Since the OSCE does not have money, all OSCE observers are paid by their own governments. As a result, on OSCE missions there are enormous differences in allowances, especially between eastern and western European nationals.

One day, Par and I were interviewing representatives of the electoral body in San José Ojetenan, a small town, very high up in the mountains. They asked me which country I was from. When I said 'Holland', they told me that a Dutch priest was living in the small house next to the church. At first, I did not believe it, but they persisted. So I told Par that I was going to check it out.

I walked around the church, but all I saw were some chickens. There was a small house, that appeared to be empty. I decided to knock on the door. I was about to walk away, when the door opened. An elderly priest looked at me and asked who I was in Spanish. I answered in Dutch.

At first, he was speechless. Finally he replied, also in Dutch, but with a funny accent. It turned out that he was actually Flemish. Father Cesar Maes invited me in and told me that he had lived in that remote town for 25 years. He told me that I was the very first Dutch speaking person to visit him there.

Every 5 years, he was allowed to take six months home leave in Flanders, so his Dutch was still good. It was quite emotional for him, though, to be able to speak Dutch after such a long time. He told me that during 1981-83, the years of the worst violence in Guatemala, he had lived in Mexico and the US, because his name appeared on a death list of the army.

I promised him that I would visit him again and give him my bottle of Beerenburger, a typical Dutch liquor, and also my remaining Dutch old cheese. Those are the rewards you get as an observer: you get to visit places that ordinary tourists would never visit and you get to meet interesting people that you would otherwise never meet.

Par and I visited about eight municipalities in the hot, coastal region of San Marcos province. One of the mayors told us that he had received death threats. He showed us an anonymous letter. Later, in the car, I joked that finally we had something to report. Par told me that I should not make fun of death threats. Do Swedes have any sense of humour at all?

Since we were living high up in the cool mountains, we were not used to the tropical heat of the coastal region. We were sweating our butts off. When you're a tourist, the tropics are pleasant, but when you have to work, it's a sweaty business.

The coastal region has advantages though: in the town of Tecúh Umán I ate a nice *ceviche*. And people who live in hot areas are usually more outgoing and cheerful than people who live in the cold. In Macatán our driver, José Manuel, wanted to buy a cheap bed cover at the local market. I joined him.

When we returned to our car, a Danish man of about fifty years of age approached me. He told me that he had been kicked out of Mexico. He had no money and no passport. I had the impression that he was a drug trafficker, so when Par arrived I told him that we could not take this Danish guy in our official mission car. For once, Par fully agreed with me.

In Guatemala, like in many Latin American countries, it is not allowed to buy or sell alcoholic beverages on the day before Election Day and on the day itself. It's called *Ley Seca*: 'Dry Law'.

But in most countries this law is not enforced on the ground, so people are not really bothered about it. When you really want a drink, you can get it anywhere, which was surely the case in the rather remote San Marcos region. I purchased a few beers in any case.

Finally, it was Election Day. We got up very early and drove to a nearby polling station. After that we visited polling stations in several towns and villages. We did not observe any major incidents. The only problem was that the mountainous dirt roads were very bad, so we spent more time in the car than in polling stations.

We observed in San José Ojetenan, where I handed my bottle of Beerenburger and my Dutch old cheese to my new friend, the Flamish padre. Once more, he was happy that he could speak Dutch with me, even though I did not have much time for him.

In the town of Tacamá there were 21 polling stations, with 600 voters each. When we arrived there, at 15.00 hours, only 3,000 people had voted. The reason for this low turnout was that there were no local elections for mayors over there.

When you are a candidate for the position of mayor, it is tempting to organize transport for the people that will vote for you, since it is in your direct interest. In the case of national elections, nobody is going to pay for transport. The national candidates reside far away, in the capital city.

We observed the closing and counting in Ixchiguán, a small town high up in the mountains. There were several polling stations in one polling center. It took them quite some time to count all the votes, but towards midnight all PSs had finished counting, except one. Par and I decided to stay, until this last PS would also finish.

This turned out to be a bad decision, since the representatives of several parties could not agree on a few disputed votes, so they counted all the votes over and over again. Still, they could not agree. The situation was not helped by the fact that there was no electricity.

The party agents and national observers that were present became tired and quite agitated. It is not easy for some twenty persons in a small room, to check each and every vote by the flickering lights of candles and torches. It went on and on, all because of an ongoing disagreement about just a few votes.

Luckily, Par and I could take turns. While one of us staid in the room, the other took a stroll around town. It was getting colder and colder, but I found a little family restaurant that was still open. Tortillas and refried beans were all I needed, to warm up and lift my spirits.

Finally, at around two o'clock in the morning, the polling staff and the party representatives agreed on the results. We woke up our driver and drove back to our hotel over the horrible dirt road. The sun was already rising when we finally arrived there.

We went to the post office to transmit our forms to the EU-representatives in Guatemala City by fax. Compared to Mozambique, this was an enormous technological step forward.

The next morning we had breakfast with Greg and Rebecca in Pensión Pérez. They had also observed that there had not been major problems in our region during E-Day. Just a few death threats, but that seemed to be the national sport all over Guatemala.

A few incidents had been reported though. In Tecúm Humán a group of people had entered a polling station and burned 5 of the 17 ballot boxes.

As expected, two candidates emerged as the clear winners of the presidential elections: Arzú and Portillo, but neither of them obtained more than 50 per cent of the vote, so there would be a second round, just a few months later.

The debriefings in hotel El Dorado in Guatemala City were a minor event. By now, the election results had come in from all over the country. All in all, it had been a rather peaceful event, by Guatemalan standards. And I was now a seasoned EU observer. In my own mind, in any case.

Chapter 3

GUATEMALA - 1996

'Keep your car windows closed at all times'

Just two months after the elections in Guatemala, I received a call from the Dutch Ministry of Foreign Affairs. There was to be a second round of the presidential elections on 7 January 1996, between the numbers one and two of the first round: Alvaro Arzú (PAN) and Alfonso Portillo (FRG). Was I interested in returning to Guatemala?

And so on 2 January 1996 I found myself on a plane to Guatemala yet again. This time with three Dutch observers who had been there during the first round: Marijke, Ronald and myself. We were joined by two additional Dutch observers: Annelies and another Ronald. We stayed at the same hotel El Dorado. It felt like coming home.

This time, my Dutch friend, Jo Mertens, was in town. He took me in his car to the archaeological museum in Guatemala City. He told me to keep the windows of the car closed at all times.

A female colleague of his had been waiting for a red traffic light, when a boy stuck his hand through the open window and tore her earring straight from her ear. I don't wear earrings, but I kept my window closed anyway. I always listen to good advice from the locals. The museum was quite interesting, but we were the only visitors.

My partner on this mission would be Armando, a Spaniard, and we would be deployed in Puerto Barrios, at the hot Caribbean coast. He worked at the Spanish Ministry of Agriculture and was rather talkative.

Armando had hardly ever been to Latin America, so our driver, Luís, and I explained a few things to him. For example, that in Guatemala City everyone carries a weapon. Armando was shocked. We also explained that in Guatemala you can simply buy a driver's license.

„Then how do they learn to drive?" Armando asked. Luís just laughed. Luís was born in Honduras and had never been to Puerto Barrios. Armando complained several times about the driving skills of Luís. I had seen worse driving over the years, so I was not really concerned. But on the whole, Armando was OK.

The only problem with Spaniards is that they talk very fast and their Spanish is not as clear cut as the Latin American Spanish. So I had to really pay attention to what Armando was saying. But I found it interesting to see yet another part of Guatemala. The trip to the Caribbean coast took us five hours. Halfway along the road we passed a sign that said: Copán, 15 kilometres.

Copán is one of the five most important Maya sites, together with Tikal in Guatemala and Chichen Itzá, Tulum and Palenque in Mexico. But Copán is situated in a remote part of Honduras. Very few westerners have ever visited it.

I asked Armando if we could try to cross the border and visit Copán, if only for one hour. He was not enthusiastic about crossing an international border, so we decided to skip it. A bit further on, we passed other Mayan ruins. We visited this *Parque Archeologico de Quiriga.* Not as well-known as Tikal or Copán, but still quite interesting.

It has an authentic feel to it, since there are hardly any tourists over there. Little did I know that a few years later, in 2013, I would be based in the Honduran province of Copán as an observer. I would visit the Copán ruins several times.

Armando and I drove on to Puerto Barrios, with its hot and humid climate. Luckily, we found a hotel with a fully functioning air conditioning. Hotel Mar Brissa was situated in a rather remote area, so we could only get there by car.

But it was a good hotel at a decent rate. We travelled around the area by car and also by boat, since some parts of that region can only be reached by boat. At one point, we even set foot in Belize, the neighbouring country across the river.

We took the 'ferry' to the town of Livingston. There were 15 seats on board and the captain was a huge black man called Júni. A cheerful guy. In Livingston there were two voting centres with a total of twenty polling stations. Very quiet town. No cars. Many inhabitants were black. In addition, several old-fashioned hippies strolled around the streets over there.

With Júni at the steering wheel, we sailed up the *Río Dulce*, the Sweet River. Don't ask me why it's called sweet. We passed through a green canyon and Armando and I visited a *Biotopo*, that could only be reached via a small jungle path. A popular place for Dutch rucksack tourists, as I learned from the register.

At one point, Armando confided to me that during the first round, two months previously, his partner had been a Danish feminist and that he really hated her guts. So Par, my Swedish partner, had not been so bad after all. In later years, I would learn that some observers are really horrible people. They can turn your life into hell.

I learned that, on average, in a group of twenty observers, one would be horrible and one would be very nice. The remaining eighteen would be quite decent. I call this 'The Law of Tesselaar'. This law would prove itself to be true, over and over again.

Since most missions consisted of around forty LTOs, two would be very good and two would be very bad. The others were just simply OK. On the whole, I have been quite blessed with my partners over the years. Until my ill-fated Mozambique mission of 2019. My 20th mission. Unfortunately, the 'Law of Tesselaar' proved to be accurate.

As always, I carried a thermos flask with freshly made coffee with me while on the road. Armando was constantly looking for *Té de Manzanilla*, herb tea. It became an obsession for him. In Puerto Barrios it's nearly impossible to find it, but after a few days Luís, our driver, managed to obtain some. After that, Luís was Armando's best friend.

Everything went fine. On E-Day, for the first time in my career as an observer, I was interviewed by a local television station. It happened quite unexpectedly: someone tapped me on my shoulder, I turned around and the next thing I saw was a big TV-camera in front of my face.

The interview went fine, as far as I can remember. In any case: I trusted that nobody in Guatemala City would ever see it, as it was a local TV-station. And in those days, people did not have access to internet yet.

There were a total of 60 polling stations in Puerto Barrios. We visited as many as we could. On the whole, people were friendly towards us. No problems here. Since this time there were only two candidates, closing and counting went much faster than in San Marcos.

At 19.00 hours most polling stations had finished. Armando and I filled in our forms and faxed them to the EU representatives in Guatemala City. The next morning, we drove straight back to the capital.

At 15.00 hours we were back in hotel El Dorado in Guatemala City. I managed to sleep one hour before heading to the debriefings. It was merely a formality. The EU-press briefing had already taken place in the morning.

Luckily, there had hardly been any disturbances in the country. The leftist Arzú had won the presidency with just 51 per cent of the vote, thanks to the capital city. The rightist Portillo had won in nearly all other departments, but obtained an overall 49 per cent of the vote.

I met Par, my old partner. He had observed yet again in San Marcos, but this time all by himself, without a partner. He hadn't changed a bit. He was still his old serious himself. Are all Swedes like this? Or am I prejudiced?

I did not have enough experience yet to conclude this with any kind of certainty, but I had noticed that the Swedes are really quite different from the more easy going Danes and the rather formal Norwegians.

During later missions this proved to be very true. When you're not a Scandinavian, all Scandinavians appear to be the same. But over the years I learned that in fact the Danes have more in common with the Dutch than with their nearest neighbours, the Swedes. The Danes have the same sense of humour that we have.

The Swedes are much more politically correct. And the Norwegians are unbelievably formal and polite. Even more so than the English, as I would find out during later missions. I haven't even mentioned the Finnish yet. They speak a language that is entirely different from all of the above. In fact, as I understand it, Finnish is quite close to Hungarian.

But enough of Scandinavia. I had now participated in three observation missions. I had developed a real taste for it. Each mission is an adventure. And it suited me fine, since I had ten years of experience in Third World countries and I spoke seven languages, albeit not all of them fluently.

But from 1998 until 2006 I was unable to do another mission. As an elected member of the town council in my home town, Enkhuizen, it was simply impossible for me to be abroad for any period of time.

Chapter 4

PISA - 2005

'Eastern European countries are now EU members'

From 1998 until 2006 it was impossible for me to go on missions. As an elected member of the town council of Enkhuizen, I simply could not be absent for more than a week.

My hometown, Enkhuizen, is a medieval town with only 18.000 inhabitants. That means that there are 17 members in the town council. There are always lots of political parties, which means that a coalition of three or four parties has to be formed, to obtain a majority in the council.

Usually, the coalition parties possess 9 seats and the opposition parties 8 seats. This means that if only one member is absent, the vote could be lost. The town council usually meets once a month, but extra meetings can be convoked at any time.

Because of this, I could not go on missions. Even so I duly filled in the forms that the Dutch Ministry of Foreign Affairs sent once every three years to all its observers. The objective is to keep the contact details of the observers up to date and also to make sure that the observer is still available. If you do not submit your form, you're simply taken off the list.

In fact, the Dutch list (and also some others, like the German list) was too long. The EU preferred experienced observers instead of freewheeling 'tourists'. This meant that The Netherlands stopped recruiting new observers for a number of years. It did not affect me, as my name appeared on the existing list.

What I did not know was that a new observation methodology had been introduced by the EU in the year 2000. Before that, all observers had simply been short-term observers, focusing on E-Day.

In the year 2000, long-term observation was adopted, not only by the EU, but also by the OSCE and the Carter Centre. From then on,

Election Observation Missions would consist of a Core Team, Long Term Observers and Short Term Observers.

Long Term Observers are usually in charge of a province. Their main task is to interview anyone in that province who has anything to do with elections and to report to the Core Team on a weekly basis. LTOs are also tasked with preparing everything for the arrival of the STOs to their province. And to supervise the STOs as long as they remain in the province.

The main job of STOs is to observe E-Day. All in all, STOs are away from home for about two weeks, while LTOs are away from home for anything between four and ten weeks. Consequently, the member states introduced a separate list for LTOs. At some point, the Dutch list for STOs contained around 800 observers, while the list for LTOs contained only about 50.

Since LTOs are away from home for such a long period of time, a person with a regular job cannot become an LTO. The only people who can be deployed as LTOs are in fact pensioners, self-employed persons and freelancers, like me.

But even for these last two categories it's difficult to be away for an extended period of time, since one loses not only income, but also valuable contacts. Apart from this, many people don't want to be separated from their loved ones for an extended period of time.

The list of LTOs, being so much smaller than the list of STOs, meant that an LTO had a much better chance of being selected by the Dutch Ministry of Foreign Affairs than an STO. In addition of being a small list, it was made up of several language compartments: the Spanish speaking, the Portuguese speaking, the French speaking and the Russian speaking.

English is spoken by everyone, so English is not really a criterion. There were just about enough Spanish and Portuguese speakers, like me, but there were not nearly enough French and Russian speakers.

I know this now, but I didn't know all this in June 2005, when I received the forms from the ministry. In fact, I thought I could just as well tear them apart, since I had been invited for only two missions over the last eight years.

Apart from that, I remembered that the remuneration for my three missions in the 1990s had barely been enough to cover my expenditures.

I had almost forgotten about the forms when, nearly two months later, to my surprise, I came across them at the bottom of a pile of documents on my desk. The ultimate returning date had almost expired, so I decided to fill them in and send them back to the ministry straight away.

What did I have to lose any way? I also decided to make a little change, not realizing that this little change would have tremendous consequences.

The little thing that I changed was that, instead of being available for short missions, I filled in that I was available for long missions. This prompted an immediate reply from the ministry. I received an invitation for the LTO course that would be held in Pisa, Italy, in the autumn of 2005.

First I decided to pay a visit to the Academic Medical Center in Amsterdam, to renew my vaccinations. I always went to the AMC. They have a special section for tropical diseases, staffed by experienced doctors who have worked in the tropics themselves. They know what they are talking about.

They asked me where I would be going to, but I said that I didn't know that yet. Then they asked if it was for work or for pleasure. I replied that I worked as an election observer. I knew what the next question would be, since it was always the same one: 'How does one become an election observer?'

The doctor reviewed my vaccination booklet and advised me to renew several of the vaccinations. She typed it in on the computer, turned the screen to me and asked: ,,Is everything correct?" I looked at the screen. It appeared to be correct, except for one detail: behind my name my age was written between brackets.

I was about to say that they had made mistake with my age, since it said 51. But then it dawned on me that I really was 51. I could hardly believe that I was that old. I didn't feel that old. But there it was, undeniably and mercilessly, in big letters on the computer screen. How time flies.

In November 2005 I flew to Italy, together with two other Dutch aspiring LTOs, a women and a man, both in their fifties, like me. We had to change planes at Milan's Malpensa airport, but the airport was covered in dense fog for most of the day. Consequently, our connecting flight to Pisa was delayed.

One of the charms of traveling is that you meet all kinds of people. People that you would normally never meet. In the bus from the airplane to the transit hall, I thought I recognized a familiar face. I could hear from his accent that he was an American.

Than another man opened a piece of paper. It said 'VPRO Television' at the top and it contained a list of names. I recognized the first name. It was Chad Hedrick, the world champion all-round speed skating of 2004. He was standing next to me!

People in other parts of the world might not understand this, but in Holland speed skating is the second most important national sport, after football. Speed skaters are heroes, no matter where they come from. Chad Hedrick was a hero in Holland. It's like standing in a bus, next to Mohammed Ali or David Beckham.

That's how important speed skating is in my country. A few months after our encounter in the bus, Hedrick would win the gold medal at the 5,000 meters speed skating at the Winter Olympics in Turin, Italy. He was now not just a hero but a legend in The Netherlands.

Anyway, we only arrived in Pisa in the evening. We had missed the opening session of the LTO course, but we met some of the other observers. It was raining, so we were huddled together inside a tiny coffee bar.

The others talked about their missions as STOs. All of us had done at least three missions as STOs, but mine had been many years previously. The others had met one another during recent missions.

„Where were you deployed in Ethiopia?"

„Who was your partner?"

„Yes, I remember him well."

I felt like a novice, even though I had more Third World experience than most of the others, since I had worked as an aid worker for the UN for ten years. Still, I desperately wanted be a member of the in-crowd. I knew that I had to do missions. I could not wait for the LTO course to start.

It did the next morning. It was in a school building. There were 40 of us, seated in a great square. That first day, something struck me. For eight years I had been a local politician and a local journalist. I had been very local.

Of course, I read the newspapers and I watched the news on television, but I had never fully realized that the EU was not the same western European EU anymore.

All of a sudden, there were observers from Hungary, the Czech Republic, Slovakia, Lithuania and many more eastern European countries. They had shredded their communist past. Now, they were democrats and capitalists, just like us!

I learned another lesson the hard way. We didn't have to pay for our hotel ourselves, but to cut the costs, two observers had to share a room. I found myself in the same hotel room with Jan, the other Dutch male observer.

Apart from not having any privacy and having to wait your turn to take a shower in the morning, you have to put up with someone who makes funny noises in the middle of the night.

For some reason, he didn't like me and I didn't like him. There were little irritating conflicts: it was warm in the room, so I wanted to open a window. But he was against it, because of the noise from the street below. But, as Johan Cruijff always said: 'Every disadvantage has its advantage'.

This proved to be a good lesson for me. From now on, I would pay extra money from my own pocket, just to have a hotel room all to myself. Also because I like to take a nap, if possible. You cannot take a nap if someone is likely to burst into your room at any moment.

Pisa is a pleasant, medieval town. The world famous leaning tower was closed to the public at the time, but the organizers of our training course had managed to obtain special tickets for us. During a lunch break, a group of us, including me, believe it or not, climbed all the way to the top, just like Galileo Galilei had done four centuries earlier.

The next day, we were taken to a training camp of the Italian special forces in the middle of a forest. It must have been quite a sight for the young and very fit soldiers, to watch 40 elderly men and women stumble out of a civilian bus.

Initially, we must have looked a sorry lot, but after their commander had explained to them that we, observers, worked all by ourselves in distant provinces in countries like Afghanistan, Pakistan, Sudan, Nigeria and Palestine, the Italian soldiers treated us with a lot of respect.

Soldiers always live in compounds with other soldiers from their own country. Their own cooks prepare their national dishes. They watch satellite television with national channels in their own language, while the air-conditioning cools the air. They keep their distance to local people, while observers meet locals all the time. We quickly earned the respect of the Italian military men and women.

The training camp provided us with realistic experiences. We learned how to recognize booby traps, how to avoid landmines and how to behave when our car was stopped by masked men armed with Kalashnikovs.

We also practiced what to do after you had been kidnapped (your main objective is to stay alive, until you are liberated). We learned what not to do after you had been kidnapped (don't irritate the kidnappers unnecessarily).

And we learned what to do when the special forces arrive to liberate you from the bad guys (lay down, flat on the ground, and stay down, until it is absolutely certain that the good guys have taken out all the bad guys).

In the evenings, I took long walks around Pisa, all by myself. It's quite enough for me to have to spend all day with the same people. I hereby admit that I am not a very social person. If I can escape in the evening, I will.

But I must also admit: the five-day course, organized by NEEDS, was really useful, not only the contents itself, but also the contacts with the other observers. I would meet quite a few of them again and again over the coming years. Except one. Thank God, I never met my roommate Jan again.

Chapter 5

VENEZUELA - 2006

'Democracy is fine; as long as Hugo Chávez is the winner'

In March 2006, just after the municipal elections in The Netherlands, I had my last meeting with the town council of Enkhuizen. My party, a local party called New Enkhuizen, had won the elections for the third time in a row, so it was with a good feeling that I said farewell to local politics. It was time for something else.

A few months later I received an invitation from the Dutch Ministry of Foreign Affairs. Was I interested in participating in the EU Election Observation Mission to Venezuela as a Long Term Observer? I was more than ready, but the invitation had been sent to a number of prospecting Dutch LTOs. First I had to be selected by my own government.

A few weeks later I received an email from the ministry. I had been selected and proposed to the EU in Brussels. All 28 EU member states, plus Norway, Switzerland and Canada, could propose LTOs for observation missions. This means that normally there are too many candidates for a mission.

Again I had to wait a couple of weeks. The waiting was agonizing, because it was the first time for me. In later years I got used to it. It's just the way it is. You have to go with the flow and just hope for the best.

To my relief, I was also selected by the EU. In the 1980s I had lived in Mexico, Bolivia and Ecuador, so I spoke quite decent Spanish, but it was a bit rusty now. To be honest, I had hardly spoken any Spanish at all in 17 years and I knew that in Latin America we would not get interpreters. Therefore, I frantically started practicing my Spanish.

I was also invited by the ministry for a briefing in The Hague. There, I met Paul and Nico, the other two Dutch LTOs, both older than me. Together with several ministry officials we were briefed on

Venezuelan politics and elections by a Venezuelan university professor, who happened to be visiting The Netherlands. I was pleased that my Spanish was still good enough to understand what he was saying.

An Election Observation Mission is implemented with military precision. There is very little time for preparations, so every step has to be done by professionals. Each EOM has a complicated administrative and logistical component. Therefore, the EU contracts a specialized administrative office, called 'Service Provider', to handle the administration and logistics of a mission.

The service provider in this case was IOM, the International Office for Migration, based in Brussels, next door to the EU. IOM has experience in servicing EU missions. They also have offices in many Third World countries.

So IOM sent me my flight tickets. On 17 November 2006 I had to fly to Lisbon for briefings by IOM. That was fine with me. I had never been to Portugal, but my wife and I had lived in Mozambique for three years, so I spoke decent Portuguese. The airport of Lisbon has the appearance of a Third World airport: chaotic and shabby.

Lisbon itself gives you the odd feeling that you have left Western Europe, but not yet entered Africa. The roads are quite bad, the buildings are quite rundown and public transport is not the best in the world. I noted one great improvement, though: I did not have to change money. Like the Netherlands, Portugal had adopted the euro as its currency.

The briefings were held in a meeting room in our hotel, Holiday Inn. In fact, there were no briefings. Just a few organizational remarks. Then each of us was called forward, to sign our contracts.

That was the real reason why all of us were assembled in Lisbon. There was another reason: we would all be on the same plane to Venezuela. For logistical reasons, Core Teams prefer all LTOs arriving on the same plane.

Together with Paul and Doloroza, a Swedish LTO, I visited several parts of Lisbon. During diner in a small restaurant, Paul and I discussed the political situation in Venezuela. To our surprise, our Swedish colleague urged us to be cautious, since people might be listening in.

We told her that we were talking in English and anyway: we were still in Portugal. She repeated that it would be better to be cautious. Weird. Yet again: I don't understand the Swedes. Or am I biased?

At Caracas airport a giant of a man is waiting for us near our suitcases. He looks Latino. He just stands there and doesn't say a word. I get the impression that he is one of our drivers.

I found out later that his name was Pedro, that he was actually Portuguese and that he was our logistical expert. Little did I know that he would be the logistical expert on most of my Latin American missions. And that he was the biggest idiot on the planet.

Why do they keep recruiting nitwits over and over again, while there are many decent people around to do the job? To make matters worse: with each mission Pedro came to like me more. He would always scream my name with great enthusiasm. An unrequited love story.

Caracas sits at an altitude of 1,000 meters, but the airport is situated at sea level, so it takes about an hour to climb up to the city. We were all cramped in an old, rented bus. The first thing Manuel, our Spanish security expert, told us was to close all the curtains, so that highway robbers could not see that we were westerners.

But we arrived at hotel Caracas Palace without any incident. It appeared that the hotel had been reopened especially for us, because it smelled of fresh paint and there was hardly any other guest.

Caracas is rife with crime. In fact, Venezuela boasts the highest crime rates in Latin America, together with Colombia, Honduras and El Salvador. Not only rich people are abducted for ransom money, it happens to the poor too. Even so, during the briefings we were told that we would not get police escorts.

We were also told that all observers had to remain in their hotels after dark during the entire mission. The good news was that we would receive extra hazard pay, to compensate for the extra costs. Since we were not allowed to go out in the evening, we were prohibited from having dinner at cheaper restaurants.

That first evening in Caracas, Paul asked me to join him onto the terraced roof of the hotel next door. I was not sure if we were allowed to leave our own hotel, but he persuaded me to join him anyway.

So there we were, just before midnight, having a nice cold beer at a rather chilly rooftop terrace in Caracas. I thought Paul was a decent chap, but later on in the mission it appeared that it would be a rough ride for him.

To my surprise, Paul told me that he had never been to Latin America before. He didn't speak one word of Spanish, but he had lived in Angola for 17 years, so he was fluent in Portuguese. To make matters worse, he had the misfortune that his partner was a women from Spain.

I generally like Spaniards, but I had learned from my second mission in Guatemala that they speak very fast and very educated Spanish, so you really need to concentrate on what they are saying.

Anyway, towards the end of our mission, during my very last day in Yaracuy province, Paul called me. He told me that he had had a terrible time with his partner. At one point, she had even called the Core Team, to complain about Paul's language deficiency.

Since all LTOs were required to speak Spanish, the CT could have decided to send Paul back to Europe. They did not. Instead, they sent him an interpreter. But his Spanish partner kept on talking so fast, that the interpreter could not possibly keep up.

In the end, Paul received the utmost negative evaluation: 'Not Recommended for Future Missions'. Since Paul lived in Brussels and had many contacts there at the EU, he protested fiercely to this verdict after his return home. It became an infamous incident: to this day, many LTOs still talk about it.

At the beginning of the mission, Paul, Nico and I were invited by the Dutch ambassador. The embassy was just a few hundred meters from our hotel, so we walked over there. He was a nice guy and gave us a lot of information about Venezuela.

The ambassador told us that Hugo Chávez was a leftist populist, but at the same time also a realist. He had heard that Fidel Castro had confided to Hugo Chávez that it would be a bad idea to introduce communism in Venezuela.

By now, Fidel apparently realized that, as an economic system, communism didn't work. Fidel also confided to Chávez that it was too late now to change things in Cuba. He and his brother Raul didn't want to lose control.

So in Cuba, the people would continue to live in 'controlled poverty'. Education and health care were free of charge, but of poor quality, while the average Cuban had to survive on a pitiful 30 euros per month.

The Venezuelans, at least, had a choice. But what a choice! The other candidate to the Venezuelan presidency was Manuel Rosales, a rightist populist and not the brightest fellow on the planet. In the end, what's better: a leftist or a rightist populist?

I met my partner, Milan, from the Czech Republic. He was much younger than me, but he had a lot of experience as an LTO. In fact, he came straight from another EU EOM in Nicaragua. And before that, he had done yet another mission. He told me that he had not had time to wash his cloths, so he had only one clean shirt left.

Milan had lived as a Jesuit missionary in Bolivia for a year. Thanks to this, his Spanish was a bit better than mine. But his religious career was short lived. Milan fell in love with a woman and married. And then he became an election observer.

Having done three missions in a row, he had not seen his wife and infant son in nearly three months. He was in it for the money. We were all earning the same amount of money, but for Eastern Europeans one euro had much more value than that same euro had for Western Europeans. For us, it was a decent salary; for them it was a fantastic salary.

The briefings were the same as always: you just had to sit it out. The problem was that all of us were suffering from jet leg. Paul fell asleep several times. I stirred him a few times, but then I gave up. At one point, Paolo, our Italian Observer Coordinator, came over to Paul.

,,You cannot sleep here, in full view of everybody. Better go to your room." Paul obliged. An hour later, all of us went outside to the swimming pool, for the customary group photograph. Everybody was on it, except Paul.

Milan and I were deployed to the province of Yaracuy. It was only three hours by car, but for some reason they gave us air tickets. So first we had to take the dangerous road down to the airport and then pay for our excess luggage. We had a lot of excess luggage, since each

LTO team is provided with a mobile office and all sorts of communication devices.

In the departures hall there's no air conditioning, so we were sweating our butts off. Then we had to pass through security at the airport. After all that, you still have to wait several hours, before your flight takes off. If it takes off, because you never know with airlines in Latin America.

Luckily, we were not the only LTO team at the airport. We had company. And we could eat sushi there. Milan was a bit embarrassed: he was very skilled in the use of modern electronic equipment, but he was absolutely hopeless with chopsticks. I was the opposite.

Since there was no airport in our province, we flew to the city of Barquisimeto, in the neighbouring province of Lara. First we had to wait for all our luggage to arrive on the arrivals belt. Then we had to go outside into the hot sun, to try to find our driver and his car.

We found them, but instead of one, there were two drivers: Jesús and Osvaldo. I told them that we were not allowed to have anyone in our vehicle, apart from ourselves and the driver.

Milan took me apart and said that I should not be so harsh, but I insisted on playing by the rules of the mission. Osvaldo than told us that he would be our interpreter, but this was impossible: on Spanish speaking missions all observers are required to speak Spanish.

So first we had to enter the city of Barquisimeto, to drop off Osvaldo. I had never heard of Barquisimeto before, but it is a big city, with nearly one million inhabitants. We got stuck in the traffic.

After that, we still had to drive one hour to San Felipe, the capital of Yaracuy province. I made a mental note to request permission from the Core Team to return to Caracas by car, which would be much faster, much cheaper, much easier and much safer.

We told Jesús that Hostel Colonial had been reserved for us, but he said he knew a much better hotel for the same price. We decided to check out the other hotel first. It was called Río Yurubí and it was situated in a quiet residential area, several kilometres from the city centre, which did not matter since we were not allowed to leave the hotel after dark anyway.

It seemed a very nice hotel. I checked out the presidential suite on the second floor at the back, overlooking the swimming pool. I managed to get a nice discount, since we would be staying long-term and since our four STOs would also be staying there. Milan opted for the smallest room of the hotel, to save money. So both of us were happy. The only problem was that the hotel was fully booked for one more night, because of a conference.

It was almost dark when we arrived at Hostel Colonial, that had been booked for our first night. At least: that's what we had been told by the Service Provider of our mission. At the reception, they didn't have our names. And they had never been contacted by anyone from the EU. Thank you, Pedro!

But they had rooms available for one night. It was not a bad hotel, it had a nice terrace, but it didn't appear to be very safe. Our rooms were at street level and the doors were quite thin. The next morning, at breakfast, Milan told me that he hadn't slept at all. ,,I was afraid armed bandits would storm into my room at any moment", he said.

So we moved to Hotel Río Yurubí, which had an indoors restaurant, but during the evenings I preferred the roofed half-open terrace on the first floor, where basic food and beer was served. Milan usually purchased food in La Galeria supermarket and ate it in his room, to save money.

On later missions I noticed that observers from eastern European countries usually tried to live as cheap as possible. There was a good reason for this: after decades of communism, the economies of eastern European were lagging far behind western Europe. In fact, eastern Europe was economically at the level where western Europe had been in the 1950s.

To give one example: Milan's wife had a full-time job in Prague, but earned only 600 euros per month: three times less than a western worker would earn in a similar job. In other words, in the eyes of an eastern European one euro would be worth at least three times more than it would be in western European eyes.

We went to work, interviewing officials at the local electoral committee, the mayor, chief of police, army chief, representatives of political parties, people from human rights organizations. We observed training sessions of polling staff. We also visited other parts of the province.

Since I was a rookie, I was grateful that Milan took the lead. He managed our petty cash expenditures, because I did not have a clue as to how to do that. He sent the morning and evening security SMSs to the security expert in the Core Team.

This is an obligation on every EU EOM: every morning, each observer team had to transmit their traveling plans for the day. Every evening, they had to send an SMS, confirming that the team was back safely at the hotel. Before dark.

Milan took the lead in the conversations, not only because he had more experience as an observer, but also since his Spanish was slightly better than mine. We worked well together. We had the same work philosophy. This surfaced when Jesús, our driver, arrived late, not once, but twice.

We told him in unison: ,,If you're late for a third time, we'll fire you." We told our driver to pick us up at ten o'clock the next morning. We waited and waited. He arrived finally at 11.30 hours. He told us that he had been obliged to attend a wedding all night. We fired him straight away.

Some observers would give the driver one more chance, but Milan and I were of the same mind. We had told the driver clearly what the consequences would be. The only problem was that we would be without a driver for the next couple of days. We were obliged to take taxis. But we did not come back on our decision to fire Jesús.

Just then, on a Sunday, all observers were allowed to take a day off, to compensate for all those evenings that we had been confined to our hotels. We asked the receptionist to call a taxi. We drove up to *La Misión*, an old mission post just outside San Felipe, which over the years had been transformed into botanical gardens.

Since I come from a family of small farmers, I had seen more than enough flowers and plants for the rest of my life, but Milan photographed every tropical flower along the path. It was a nice break for both of us, though. And Milan took the opportunity to attend mass in the small mission church. Once a Jesuit, always a Jesuit.

Our next driver turned out to be Osvaldo, the guy that we dropped off in Barquisimeto. He was OK, though. One day he told us, to our surprise, that his best friend earned more than a million dollars per year. I thought that I had misunderstood him, since Venezuelans speak less clear Spanish than Bolivians or Peruvians. But a few days later he repeated it.

It turned out that it was true: his friend was a professional baseball player. He played for one of the top teams in the US. Venezuela is the only country in Latin America where football is not the major sport. Venezuelans loved baseball. And they loved to go shopping in Miami. During the good days, at least. Knowing this, it's quite weird that the leftist president Hugo Chávez hated the US so much.

The interesting part of election observation missions is that, as an observer, you live for a number of weeks in places that you would otherwise never visit. And as an observer you meet all kinds of interesting people, with interesting stories. In my own country I would never meet anyone with a friend who is a professional baseball player.

Milan quickly realized that my English was much better than his and since our Weekly Reports had to be written in English, I would do all the typing. I was happy that I could make myself useful. As a journalist, I was used to typing with ten fingers anyway. I would later notice that many observers typed with only one finger.

We wrote our WRs in his cramped little room, because our mission laptop stood in his room. He used the laptop to contact his friends on the internet and to Skype with his wife and little son. Until then, I had never used Skype in my life.

We were a good team. Milan would sit next to me and dictate what to type. It worked well. While I was typing, he had time to go through his notes. There was something else with which I made myself useful: contacts with the media.

Many observers try to avoid journalists at all costs, since we are always told at briefings that we are not allowed to tell journalists what we have observed. The EU was very strict on this. If you made a serious mistake, you could end up on the black list for the next five years.

There is a reason for this. In 2005, during the LTO course in Pisa, they gave us an example of an interview that went totally awry. An election observer was interviewed by CNN, somewhere in the jungle of a tropical island. The observer told CNN that he had observed fraud, since the indelible ink was absent in the polling stations. The interview was broadcast all over the world.

The next day, however, the truth was made public: the truck that carried the indelible ink had suffered a mechanical breakdown in the middle of the jungle, where the driver's mobile phone did not have a signal. So there was no fraud. I'm not sure if this was a true story, but it was used to explain why observers must always be very careful in their dealings with the media.

In any case, an EU EOM operates as a mission for the country as a whole. I fully agree with this, because if every observer would comment on every incident, there would be lots of incidents going around. Each journalist could then select any juicy story and it would be total chaos.

The observations of an EU EOM are published in two reports: the preliminary report, published 48 hours after E-Day, is basically a five page summary of the conclusions and recommendations of the mission. The final report, published about two months after E-Day, contains all the observations of the mission in much more detail, with elaborate conclusions and recommendations. It's usually between 100-150 pages.

All observers are trained in dealing with the media. We can tell journalists lots of things, but not what we have observed. Which, of course, is the main thing journalists are interested in. And professional journalists are both clever and persistent.

If an observer would make a mistake with the media and it would become known to the Core Team, the observer could expect a call from the Observer Coordinator and a negative remark on his final evaluation.

Each LTO receives an evaluation at the end of the mission. This evaluation is very important for future missions, so observers don't want to ruin their evaluations. The best way to make sure that you don't make a mistake with journalists is to avoid journalists.

I am not afraid of journalists, because I am a journalist myself. I know how they work, I know how they think. And I know exactly what I can say or not say. Still, you have to be very careful with newspaper journalists, because in the end they can write whatever they want to write. As an observer I can control what I say into a radio or television microphone, but I cannot control written articles.

Provincial journalists love to interview international observers, especially in areas that are not visited by tourists. As observers we are easily recognizable, since we wear visibility jackets. And we cannot avoid the journalists, since we visit the same events: political rallies, manifestations, training sessions for polling staff, and so on.

Which is OK, since—this may sound a bit contradictory—the EU wants the whole world to know about its EOMs. Observers are therefore encouraged not to avoid journalists. We are allowed to give them factual information, like how many observers are deployed by this EOM and in which countries we have observed previously.

In San Felipe we were on local TV nearly every day. Every time we visited the provincial electoral commission's office, one or two radio or TV teams would bump in on us within half an hour. Someone in the office probably tipped them of.

I suspected it was the director himself who did this. We were later told by several interlocutors that he was a stern Chávez supporter. It was important for Chávez to show the world that international observers gave credibility to his election victory.

Milan was not at ease when we were approached by members of the media, so I volunteered to do most of the talking. One day, we were invited to join the live breakfast show on local TV. A full hour, with four guests: the director of the provincial electoral commission, the police chief, the army chief and an EU observer.

Luckily for Milan, one of us had to travel to the airport of Barquisimeto, to pick up our four Short Term Observers. So Milan happily left for Barquisimeto and I did the breakfast show. It was exhausting, since my Spanish was not that great yet and we had to answer in turn.

I had to listen very carefully to both the questions and the answers of the other participants. But it went reasonably well. Afterwards, the network even presented me a DVD of the entire show.

I went back to the hotel and awaited the arrival of Milan and the STOs. Luckily, they were a good bunch. Many STOs have little or no observation experience, but in this case it was quite OK. Three of them had done at least one observation mission and all of them spoke decent Spanish.

And all were positive of mind, which for me is always the most important factor. Henry (UK) was 58 years of age. Ana Rita (Portugal) and Alberto (Spain) were both 34 years of age. Johanna (Austria) was the youngest, with her 27 years. In turns, they would ask me how one becomes an LTO. I always gave the same answer: 'Only the best and brightest can eventually become LTOs'.

That same afternoon, all six of us observed the visit of president Hugo Chávez to San Felipe. It was crowded at the corner of Av. Caracas with Av. Libertad, but when people spotted our EU-visibility jackets, they invited us to a quiet spot along the road, behind the fence of a college. Balancing on top of a felled log, we saw Chávez passing by at less than fifteen meters.

When he spotted us he waved at us. He clearly had charisma. And, being a leftist populist, he knew exactly what the audience wanted to hear from him. He was a good speaker.

Chávez knew that he was going to win the elections, because he always won the elections. He had invented a very clever system to perpetually win elections: he simply bought the votes of the poor. And since the poor formed 65 percent of the population, a clear majority was always guaranteed.

The poor received welfare benefits (*bonos* in Spanish) for old age and for each child. In addition, projects were developed in their neighbourhoods, like schools, electricity, water pumps and so on.

Before each election, Chávez would send his party militants to all local communities, explaining to them that if they did not vote for Chávez, they would lose all their benefits. So Chávez cleverly used both the carrot and the stick: it worked very well for him.

The only problem was that most of the billions of dollars that Venezuela earned with the exportation of oil went into subsidies, welfare benefits and imported consumer goods. The money was not used for investment in productive activities, so when oil prices dropped, the Venezuelan economy went down the drain.

Ninety per cent of the food was not produced locally, but imported. There was no money left for the police either, turning Venezuela into one of the most dangerous countries in the world.

In addition, Chávez transferred hundreds of millions of dollars to his leftist presidential friends in Nicaragua, Bolivia and Ecuador, to buy the allegiance of Daniel Ortega, Evo Morales and Rafael Correa. He needed their allegiance for his favourite hobby: USA bashing.

Chávez also shipped oil to his friends in Cuba, arguably not the most democratic country in the world and after more than fifty years of communist dictatorship, the Cuban people were the poorest in Latin America. In exchange for oil, the Cubans sent thousands of medical doctors to Venezuela.

A few of them had arrived in San Felipe. The locals were not happy with them, since the Cuban doctors were not really motivated to treat Venezuelans free of charge. The doctors were mainly interested in acquiring capitalist consumer goods, like refrigerators and air conditioners, to take back with them to Cuba.

Years later, after Chávez' death, the Venezuelan economy collapsed completely. Inflation became rampant. In what was once the richest country in Latin America, with a thriving middle class, people had to queue for several hours to buy toilet paper. Millions of Venezuelans fled to neighbouring countries.

Chávez' successor and party member, Nicolás Maduro, blamed everything on capitalist conspiracies. Maduro managed to win the elections once again, but a few years later 'Venezuelan Socialism' had reached the end of the road. After the opposition gained the majority of seats in parliament, Maduro simply ruled without parliament.

But back in 2006, Hugo Chávez was still very much alive and the economy was still functioning. I enjoyed my time with the STOs, especially in the evenings. I had gotten used to being on my own at the hotel's half open terrace, since Milan usually ate cheap supermarket food in his room. For an entire week I was joined on the terrace by one or more STOs.

Especially Henry, from Dorset in the south of England, came to join me. He had been a career diplomat all his working life and he was of my age: in his fifties. The others were in their thirties. Younger people have other interests than older people.

Luckily the terrace was roofed, because every evening, at exactly 21.00 hours, it started to rain. A short but violent tropical downpour, that made so much noise that normal conversation became impossible. The rain hit the roof with so much noise that you could not even hear the omnipresent TV-sets anymore. Which was fine with me, since I don't like baseball at all.

One of the STO teams ran into problems with their driver, so we gave them our car and driver. The STO teams had to travel to outlying districts every day, while Milan and I remained in town, where it was much easier to take a taxi. There were no problems, except that one evening when we returned to our rooms, Alberto discovered that his door was unlocked. He was sure that he had locked it, when he left his room.

His room was next to mine, so I told him to check out his entire room, while I waited for him in the gangway. After a few minutes he returned. Everything was OK. Apparently, either the cleaning lady or he himself had forgotten to lock it. But since the regional newspapers reported every day on a number of abductions and homicides in our province, I did not want to take any chance.

There was also a curious incident. One morning, Henry arrived five minutes late for our daily STO briefings in our 'office' at the outdoor swimming pool. Milan, whom I had come to know as a gentile character, reacted furiously. „We are six people. When one arrives too late every day, we cannot work properly."

Henry mumbled an excuse. Later, Henry confided to me that he had felt 'like a schoolboy', but that Milan had been right, of course. This was a good lesson for me. I decided to arrive always on time for meetings. Better safe than sorry.

The day before E-Day was a Saturday, the 2nd of December. My birthday. I always try to keep it a secret, since I'm terrified that my colleagues will burst out singing 'Happy Birthday' in a busy restaurant. This would definitely be the worst thing that could possibly happen to me. But there was a problem: since I did not possess my own laptop, I used our team's laptop, which was in Milan's room.

My wife had given our team's email address to several family members and friends. As a result, Milan noted a significant increase in emails from Holland addressed to me. He could not read Dutch, of course, but he could figure out enough. So on the 1st of December he asked me if the next day would be my birthday.

I decided to tell him the truth: yes, the 2nd was my birthday. There was no escape. I would have to make the best of it. I would have to buy a cake and champagne for all six observers. So on Saturday morning, Milan and I set out to try to find a liquor store.

We found one, but it turned out that it was closed because of the '*Ley Seca*', the 'Dry Law': in many Latin American countries it is forbidden to sell alcoholic beverages just before and during E-Day. But there is a solution to every problem. Since we were foreigners, the owner would be quite happy to sell a bottle of champagne to us.

He lifted the iron outer gate a little bit: we had to crawl under it, to enter the store. Later that afternoon I offered cake and champagne to the other observers. They sang for me. Thank God we were the only customers in the hotel's restaurant.

E-Day went without problems for us. Voting is done electronically in Venezuela, which meant that the counting went very fast. We did not observe major fraud or problems in our province. After the results of our polling station had been transmitted to Caracas, Milan and I returned to our hotel.

Both STO teams arrived within an hour. Elated, as usual, at the end of E-Day. It is always the most exciting day for observers. The next morning, all six of us assembled at the swimming pool, to write our final report. As always, I did the typing. The others gave their input in turns.

After I had finished, I turned the laptop to Henry, the English STO, to check my English. After that we had lunch at a small hotel annex restaurant in the countryside, just outside San Felipe.

They had lots of parrots there and also six German shepherd dogs, to deter potential criminals. Venezuela is a grim country. When we walked to the half open restaurant, the dogs were sleeping calmly in the grass. No doubt, they had been trained to take on the bad guys, should they ever try to enter the premises.

I sat opposite Johanna, the Austrian STO. At 27 years of age, she was one of the youngest STOs I would ever meet. She was extremely thin. Her bare arms and pulses looked unbelievably fragile. I wondered if she suffered from anorexia. I didn't have the courage to ask her. She ate normally, though.

We handed our evaluations of the STOs to each of them. There was a problem, that I regret to this very day. Over the years, LTOs had developed the habit of giving all their STOs a 'Highly Recommended' evaluation, thus inflating the term 'Highly Recommended'.

The EU had therefore, for good reasons, decided that from now on, only a maximum of ten per cent of the STOs and LTOs would be eligible to receive a 'Highly Recommended'. On this mission, Milan and I had specifically been instructed that only one of our four STOs could receive a 'Highly'.

The others would be evaluated simply as 'Recommended'. Unless they had performed below standards: then they would receive a 'Recommend But', meaning that they needed to improve certain things. A 'Not Recommended' could only be given to an observer who had seriously breached the Code of Conduct.

Anyway, I told Milan that in my opinion all STOs had done a decent job and that it would be awkward for the others if one was to receive a 'Highly'. For some reason, Milan disagreed with me. He said: „For some STOs it's important to receive a 'Highly', because they want to be LTOs in the future. We are entitled to provide one of them with a 'Highly', so let's do this."

I then asked him who would be the lucky one. Johanna had done a decent job, but as a beginner, she still had to learn many things. That left Alberto, Henry and Ana Rita in the race for one 'Highly' evaluation. I couldn't make a choice. I thought all three of them had done a good job. For some reason, Milan preferred to give the 'Highly' to Ana Rita. So we did.

After lunch we visited the shrine of María Lionza, near the town of Chivacoa, about one hour drive from San Felipe. There, next to an idyllic little river in a forested area, devotees came from all over Venezuela to request a miracle. God knows that nowadays Venezuela needs a miracle.

The cult of María Lionza is in fact a mix of indigenous, Catholic and African beliefs. An estimated 30 per cent of all Venezuelans have made the pilgrimage. María Lionza is depicted as a muscular, naked woman sitting on a tapir. She has a statue in Caracas.

On the way back I received the unexpected call I wrote about at the beginning of this chapter. It was Paul, the Dutch LTO. I was quite shocked to hear about his problems with his Spanish partner. It was a good lesson for me, though. I realized that not all partners are like Milan. After this mission, I never met Paul again, but in spite of his flaws he was quite a character.

The next day, we drove the STOs over to the airport in Barquisimeto. Milan and I took the opportunity to visit the city. We spent a few hours in the biggest mall I had ever seen. Shop after shop, filled to the roof with consumer goods. Back in 2006, the Venezuelan economy was still going reasonably strong.

Thank God, we received permission to drive back to Caracas in our own car. A pleasant voyage of less than four hours, much safer and much more comfortable than the airplane, with the added advantage that we saw something of the Venezuelan countryside. Back at the hotel in Caracas, we were greeted enthusiastically by our own STOs. They were still there!

During a reception, later that evening, I chatted with Henry, who had been our STO. ,,Why did Ana Rita receive a 'Highly', instead of me?" he asked me. I felt ashamed, since he was right: Henry and also Alberto had done an equally good job. I decided never to make this mistake again.

After the debriefings, we flew back to Europe. At Caracas airport I spent the last of my local currency on a bottle of Hugo Boss perfume. At Lisbon airport I was taken out of the line at the security checkpoint. ,,You are not allowed to carry liquids", the security lady said angrily. I replied that I did not have any liquids.

But she insisted and pointed at the inner pocket of my coat. She was right. I had totally forgotten about that stupid rule, since in Venezuela nobody cares if you take liquids on a plane or not. It's only in Europe and the US that people are paranoid about liquids. I had to hand over my Hugo Boss.

Apparently, some years earlier, a Muslim planned to make an explosive devise by mixing certain liquids. This plan never materialized. It never happened. Even so, for the next twenty years, 380 million Christians were not allowed to carry liquids in their hand luggage on airplanes in the EU.

For me, this meant that I could not take shampoo, shaving foam nor tooth paste in my hand luggage to countries where the risk of losing your suitcase is very real. In fact, it would lose my suitcase several times on future missions.

Back home, I fell literally from the hot tropics into the icy European winter. I had completely forgotten that my wife and I had ordered new front windows for our house in the centre of Enkhuizen.

Since it was an old, medieval house, the windows had to be tailor made. It took nearly half a year to produce them and they were installed the day after my return from Venezuela.

So on the 14th of December 2006, workmen arrived at 07.30 hours to take out the old windows. My wife left for work and the rest of that day I was shivering with our dog in a house that was completely open on one side. It was below zero outside as well as inside. Luckily, they managed to put in the new windows that very same day.

What a homecoming! But on that very day I decided what my future would be. It had been a relatively short mission in Venezuela, just over four weeks, but I had learned a lot, mainly thanks to Milan. I knew now for certain that I wanted to do more missions.

Each mission is an adventure. And the only thing that is really important is your partner, since you have to work and live with your partner for seven days a week. And also seven evenings a week, because we are always working.

In comparison, back home I hardly ever saw my wife. During the daytime she worked in the Dutch prison system and in the evenings she went to her singing group or bridge club. When you're not together, you cannot fight.

But during a mission I could not escape my partner. The good news is that each mission comes to an end. You don't have to live with your mission partner for the rest of your life.

Since my wife's surname is Govers, as a child she was called Goofy. Because of that, she collected Goofy's. I tried hard to find a Goofy in San Felipe and Caracas, but to no avail: no Goofy on this mission. The good news was that, even without a Goofy, my wife still wanted me back.

Chapter 6

NIGERIA - 2007

'They cannot read or write, but they can shoot'

I had hardly recovered from my Venezuela mission when I received an invitation for yet another mission: Nigeria. Many people would hesitate to go there, but my wife and I had fond memories of it.

In 1982, after we finished our studies, we hitchhiked from The Netherlands to Zimbabwe. It took us seven months to reach Harare. We crossed the whole of Nigeria, but not all of it by car. The first stretch, from the border with Niger to the city of Kano, we got a lift from a bunch of Germans who planned to sell their old cars for decent money in West-Africa.

We were stopped at so many police roadblocks that my wife and I decided that it would be more convenient to take the train from Kano to Lagos. In Nigeria, the police are notoriously corrupt. And sometimes drunk. They will harass you, until you hand them some money.

As a result, we spent three days in a hot, overcrowded train, without beds and without air conditioning. We arrived in Lagos at 04.00 hours. Nobody left the station, even though the doors were not locked. Outside, the station square looked ominously dark and deserted. At first light, taxis arrived. Only then, people started leaving the station, including ourselves.

In Lagos we stayed a few days at the house of Dick, a Dutch expatriate, whom we had met at the Central Hotel in Kano. He offered us free air tickets to Port Harcourt, in exchange for carrying his oil company's monthly administration in our hand luggage. We gratefully accepted. From Port Harcourt we hitchhiked to the border with Cameroun.

So, in fact, we had not seen much of Nigeria, but what we had seen was not too bad. And Nigeria is not only the most populous country in Africa, but also an important oil exporter, so a mission in Nigeria would look good on my CV.

On top of that: I love Africa and I had not been there for 13 years, so I decided to apply for the mission. I was duly selected by the Dutch government and after that by the EU.

The EU had decided to make good use of the UN security system, for the protection of the EU observers. Should something go terribly wrong, like a coup d'état or ethnic clashes, the UN would take care of us. The EU paid a lot of money to the UN for this service. But there was a catch: apart from receiving money, the UN insisted that all observers should be extensively instructed as to how the UN security system worked.

This meant that, while I was still in Holland, I had to complete two internet courses: Basic Security in the Field and Advanced Security in the Field. Each of these courses took about three hours.

The problem was that I needed a fast internet connection. At home, my wife and I still used an old fashioned and extremely slow telephone connection, so on a Sunday afternoon I had to spend six hours on the modern PC of my political friend Hans Langbroek.

He was quite amazed at the number of things we, observers, were required to learn. Not only how the UN security system worked, but also what to do in case we were abducted or stopped by masked men at a makeshift roadblock. And how to detect booby-traps and landmines.

We also learned how to avoid malaria and stress. In fact, these two courses gave me a lot of stress, since some of the answers were quite ambiguous. You had to pass a number of intermediate exams, before getting to the final exam.

If the courses were interrupted, you had to start all over again. At the end of each course you obtained a diploma with your name on it, but this diploma could not be saved on your computer. It could only be printed.

Luckily, Hans had a printer that worked. I was also fortunate that I knew the UN system quite well, after having worked for the UN as an aid worker for ten years. I imagined that some observers would have had even more stress than me, while trying to complete the two courses.

Anyway, a few days later I found myself once again at the Dutch Ministry of Foreign Affairs in The Hague, this time for a briefing by the ministry's Nigeria expert. The other two Dutch LTOs were also there: Kees and Monique.

They had participated in lots of missions and I was a novice, but I gained a bit of their respect during the briefing, since—to my own surprise—I happened to know the Dutch ambassador in Abuja: Van der Wiel. I immediately realized that I knew that name. But from where?

In a blink it flashed through my mind. „Is his first name Arie?" The three of them looked at me in astonishment. After all, I was the rookie. I explained that I had known Arie van der Wiel in Mozambique, in the 1980s, where he had been the first secretary of the Dutch embassy.

I also told them that I ruined Arie's farewell football match. It was customary to let the person who was leaving the country win his last football match, but my team mates and I decided otherwise. With our combined Dutch-Latin American indoors football team we beat the Dutch embassy team fair and square, thus spoiling Arie's farewell, much to his chagrin.

The briefing went well. I was quite familiar with Nigeria's history. After the Biafra war, the Nigerians decided that both the country's presidency and vice-presidency should be rotated between northerners and southerners, to avoid tensions between the Muslim north and Christian south.

After the briefing, Kees and I took the tram to the Nigerian embassy, to apply for our visas. We found ourselves in a small room with some fifteen Nigerian men. Outside was The Netherlands, inside we got our first taste of Africa.

We had to fight our way to the counter, since it was blocked by several tall Nigerians, who were constantly arguing amongst themselves and with the embassy man behind the counter, both in English and in local languages.

We finally managed to hand our passports and visa forms to Henry, one of the embassy's staff. We were then told that we had to pay for our visas, but we could not pay at the embassy: we had to pay at a bank and return to the embassy with the receipt. The embassy was about to close, so we decided to take a taxi to the bank.

By the time we returned to the embassy, the consulate was indeed closed, but luckily our newly acquired friend Henry was still there. He accepted our payment slips and told us to come back in a couple of days. He then added: 'You're doing a good job. Please make sure the elections are free and fair'.

I was about to explain to Henry that we don't use the phrase 'free and fair' anymore. Instead, we use a booklet called 'International Standards for Democratic Elections' as our reference. Elections are never completely free and fair, not even in my own country.

To give an example: a few days before E-Day in The Netherlands, the leaders of the biggest political parties are invited to electoral debates on national television, but the leaders of small parties are not. There is a reason for this, since there are far too many parties, most of which will not obtain seats in any case.

Even so: it is not fair. Also, national parties are subsidized, but local parties are not. In any case: the phrase 'free and fair' is not unambiguous, so we don't use it anymore.

But I didn't explain any of this to Henry, the Nigerian embassy guy. It was getting late. We went home. A few days later I returned to the embassy, hoping that my passport had not gone lost. It had not. It contained a nice visa, filling an entire page. And so, a few weeks later, I found myself on board of a British Airways plane heading for ….. London.

There are direct KLM flights between Amsterdam and Abuja every day, but either to save a bit of money or because they wanted all LTOs to arrive on the same plane, I was forced to travel via London. Worse than that: via Heathrow, one of the most complex airfields in the world, to put it nicely.

Luckily, I was not alone. Monique and Kees were with me on the plane. Our plane landed and then parked at some distance from Terminal 4. For the next half hour, nothing happened. No explanation was given. Finally, a bus arrived and we were allowed to enter the building.

We had to pass through the usual security checkpoint, where we even had to take off our shoes. A few years earlier, Richard Reid, a converted Muslim, had attempted to blow up a plane with a bomb that had been hidden in his shoe. Because of this, from then on all 380 million Christians in Europe had to take off their shoes at Heathrow.

We were much too early. We drank a cappuccino in one café and we drank a cappuccino in another café. One by one, the other LTOs arrived. I hardly knew any of them, but Kees introduced me to them. At one point, he pointed at a blond women: 'That is Hanna; she will be your partner'.

Just before we left home, the Core Team had sent us the deployment plan for the LTOs. I was deployed to the most eastern and least important province: Adamawa state, bordering Cameroun. The provincial capital was called Yola. My partner, Hanna, was a 43 year old judge from Poland.

We had a brief conversation. Hanna told me that she had had several Dutch LTOs as her partner on previous missions. One of them had been Kees. She liked the Dutch, she told me. And she had a lot more experience than me. That sounded good.

Around midnight, our BA flight finally departed. When we arrived in Abuja, the sun was just coming up. Like on most of my missions, I did not sleep that first night on the plane. By the time we arrived at the Hilton Hotel, I was totally awake anyway.

The Hilton Hotel turned out to be a gigantic bastion, surrounded by high walls. Outside reigned chaos and criminality. At least: that's what we were told. We could not verify it, because we were also told that it was forbidden to leave the hotel.

To add insult to injury, we were not allowed to enter our rooms until twelve o'clock. Since I was a rookie, I was a bit surprised by all this, but in later years I would learn that these things would happen on nearly all missions.

You just have to accept it and go with the flow. That's what experienced LTOs do. Kees and Monique were undaunted. They did not complain. They just sat down and drank a cup of coffee. I was a rookie. I didn't realize it then, but within a few years I would be just like them.

It was an integral part of our missions. The leaders of the missions have a special phrase for it: 'Thank you for being flexible'. That means that LTOs accept whatever shit is thrown at them. Without complaining. It's what makes an LTO different from ordinary human beings. It's what makes us say proudly: 'I'm an LTO'.

The next morning, the briefings would start at 08.30 hours. I was one of the first to arrive in the conference room. A man with white hair was standing there. I immediately recognized him, even though the last time I had seen him was in the 1970s, on a black and white television screen. His name was Max van den Berg and he was the Chief Observer of our EU EOM. He was a member of the European Parliament for the Dutch Labour Party.

The Chief Observer of an EU EOM is nearly always a member of the European Parliament. The Chief Observer does not remain with the mission all the time, but usually arrives for a week or so at the start of the mission and then again, around E-Day, for another week or so. So most of the time the Deputy Chief Observer is the actual leader of the mission.

I introduced myself to Max van den Berg. I had never seen him in the flesh, but he had been quite a political character in the 1970s. He had been widely regarded as an ultra-leftist member of the Dutch Labour Party.

His nickname had been: 'Rasputin of the North', but the real Max van den Berg, the one that I met, turned out to be a pleasant fellow. In the 1980s and 1990s he had been the director of the Dutch volunteers aid organization, so he was well informed on the Third World.

With 66 LTOs, this was a large mission. We were briefed for two days. I sat next to my partner, Hanna. All LTOs had received a mobile phone. On the second day, the security expert of the Core Team asked each LTO to send him an SMS, to check if the phones worked.

This was a problem for me. I had never sent an SMS in my life! I had never possessed a mobile phone. There was a reason for this. I had been a local politician for eight years and a local journalist for many more years.

If I carried a mobile phone, people would call me continuously, to complain about a street light that was not working or a loose stone in the pavement. People could contact me on my fixed phone at home, which I thought was reasonable enough.

But on these missions the mobile phones are the most important tools. In Venezuela, Milan took care of most communications, but this time I could not escape. I decided to wait till the end of the briefings and then ask a colleague to explain to me how to send an SMS.

To my embarrassment, just before the briefings ended, the security expert announced that he had received SMSs from all LTO teams, except two. He mentioned the team numbers. One of which, of course, was ours.

Hanna looked at me in surprise. Or in anger. Or both. I handed her my phone under the table and whispered that she had to transmit my SMS for me. Dutifully, she obliged, thus saving the day for both of us.

In Nigeria there are 35 provinces, called states. LTO teams were deployed to 32 provinces. The three provinces in the oil producing delta were not covered. It was too dangerous there. Westerners were continuously under threat of being abducted for money.

An extra LTO team was deployed to Lagos. Thank God I did not have to work there. Apart from being a dangerous place, the Lagos team would spend most of their time being stuck in the traffic.

Each team was briefed on its particular Area of Responsibility by Heinz, the Political Expert. Our province, Adamawa state, was definitely not the most exciting place in Nigeria. Nothing much happened there.

But I made a mental note of two remarks: the bad news was that Adamawa state was characterized by the ominous words: 'Very Hot'. To add insult to injury, Heinz added: ,,You're going to suffer. It's 46 degrees Celsius, every day. And there's no electricity".

The good news was that it was the only Nigerian province with an American university. I told Hanna that this meant that there would probably be Americans, who would be very happy to see a western face for a change, since tourists, for sure, would avoid Adamawa state like the plague.

Monique, Kees and I were invited by the Dutch ambassador. We had to ask permission from our mission's security expert. He said: 'OK, but only if the embassy picks you up in an armoured vehicle'. The armoured vehicle turned out to be a fortified Mercedes. You needed all your strength just to open the heavy door. It would be the only time we left the hotel. We only saw a bit of Abuja by night.

We had a pleasant time at the ambassador's residence. Arie van der Wiel claimed that he had forgotten about our last football match in Maputo, but his wife remembered it. We reminisced about our time in Mozambique. All old Mozambique hands have fond memories of the country, in spite of all the hardships.

Arie also told us that, just before we arrived, the previous Dutch prime minister, Wim Kok, had been staying in the same Hilton Hotel that we were now staying in. All though he was a member of the Dutch Labour Party and considered to be a socialist, he had joined the board of Shell, the very capitalist Dutch-British oil company, which was quite active in Nigeria.

The next day, Hanna and I set out early for our duty station. EU observers had to comply with UN rules and regulations and the UN had put most national airlines on a black list. There was an airport near Yola, but only two or three national airlines were operational there. All of them appeared on the black list.

So we had to travel—luckily—by car. Even though it would take us two days to get there, I still preferred a car to the hassles of an airplane. In our land cruiser we had a lot of space in the back for all our stuff. And our driver, Musa, lived in Yola. This meant that he would know his way around over there.

We set off with four LTO teams, all bound for eastern provinces. We would all stay overnight at the same hotel in Gombe. But once on the road, we soon lost track of the other teams. No problem: we were not obliged to travel in convoy, which is a complicated procedure in any case, but especially in Africa, where traffic and road conditions are not entirely up to European standards.

On top of that, each team was accompanied by a police escort in a separate car. Our escort turned out to be two pleasant chaps in their late twenties. They belonged to the Mopols: mobile police forces and they were armed with Kalashnikovs. Ezekiel and Ayuba would always be at our side while we were on the road, which had the advantage that we were not stopped at the omnipresent police roadblocks.

The moment the police at the roadblocks noticed our police escort, they waved us on. Mopols were known to shoot first, ask questions later. They were therefore respected by all their police colleagues. Ezekiel and Ayuba even took their AK-47s inside restaurants, whenever we invited them for lunch. As our interpreter would later explain to us: ,,They cannot read or write, but they can shoot."

We passed through the city of Jos. I made our driver stop at the entrance to the city, where Hanna had to make photographs of me standing under the sign 'Welcome in Jos'. I explained to our police escorts that my name was Jos. They thought I was joking.

Jos is the coolest place in Nigeria, literally, since it sits at the Jos Plateau, at around 1,000 meters altitude. It cools off in the evening. In Jos you'll find the Jos Museum, the Jos School and even the Jos Church. All named after me.

We continued our journey to the town of Gombe, where we met the other three teams at the designated hotel. The drivers and the police escorts slept in a cheaper hotel. I did not know it at the time, but I would meet several of the other LTOs on future missions.

The team that would travel on to the north eastern city of Maiduguri consisted of Dimitra from Greece and Wlodzimirz from Poland. Dimitra would later be the observer coordinator on my ill-fated 2010 Kyrgyzstan mission, where I found myself in the middle of an ethnic war.

I would meet Wlodzimirz on most of my English speaking missions, either as a colleague LTO or as security expert. Since nobody could pronounce his name, we all called him, affectionately, Wlodek.

They did not know it at the time, but Dimitra and Wlodek were lucky to be in Maiduguri as early as 2007. Just a few years later, Maiduguri would be a household name all over the world, because of the infamous Boko Haram assaults.

The team that stayed in Gombe consisted of Peter from Austria and Analisa from Italy. The next morning, I noticed that three teams were having breakfast together, but Peter and Analisa were sitting at different tables. Far apart. Not a good sign, I thought.

It seemed to me that Peter had a defiant character, but I was wrong. I learned this when our paths crossed yet again in Kyrgyzstan in June 2010. After I had been evacuated by military helicopter from the city of Osh, Dimitra told me that I had to travel to the province of Naryn, to become Peter's new partner, since his first partner had left him.

Peter actually turned out to be a fine partner. He had not been the one creating problems. His partner, Analisa, had been the bad apple. This taught me that sometimes things are not what they seem to be at first glance.

While on the road to Yola, I received a call on my mobile phone from the Nigerian secret police. This came as a total surprise to both Hanna and me. How did they get my number? It appeared that I had made a little mistake, when I filled in the obligatory form at our previous hotel in Gombe.

I had forgotten the name of the province where we were deployed. They just wanted to check if we were safely on our way there. I said yes. I told Hanna that apparently the secret police already knew everything about us.

We arrived in Yola, to find out that the best hotel was undergoing a major renovation. It would be closed for a year or so. So we had no choice: we had to check into the only other reasonable hotel. It did not look good.

That evening, we faced serious problems. The generator that was supposed to generate electricity failed most of the time and—worse—there was no Wifi. This meant that we had to use the BGAN, or better said: Hanna had to use the BGAN, since I had never used it before.

The BGAN is a device that has to be pointed at a satellite, so it has to be out in the open. To make matters worse, the cable that connected the BGAN to our mission laptop was only two meters long, so the laptop had to be in the open as well.

Many LTOs complained about this. Successfully, because on later missions the LTOs would be equipped with connecting cables that were ten meters long, which meant that you could place the BGAN outside, while you remained indoors with the laptop.

But for now, Hanna had to sit in an open space. It was about eight o'clock and already dark, but it was still unbelievably hot. We were sweating like idiots. This attracted mosquitoes, of course, and since Hanna was busy with the BGAN and the laptop, I tried to fend off the flying insects, but both of us got bitten several times.

A BGAN is a complicated device. First, you must point the BGAN at a satellite. This means turning it in all directions, until finally the red lights turn green. Then you must fiddle with the software on the laptop. All this takes at least half an hour.

Finally, if you're lucky, you can connect to the internet, but since it is a very slow connection, it takes ages to download an email with attachments. And if there is an interruption of just one second, you have to start all over again.

That first night, I didn't sleep at all. The tiny bed bent through all the way to the floor. And since the generator went off all the time, my old-fashioned airco also went off all the time. Every time, I had to get up to switch it on again. I was sweating like an idiot. In the room next to me I could hear Hanna moving around all night as well. She didn't sleep either.

The next morning I went to the dining room, for the most horrible breakfast I had ever had in my life. The sun had just risen above the horizon, but it was already unbearably hot and the fan did not work. Hanna did not show up, but while I waited for my half-boiled egg and surrogate coffee, I was joined at my table by a big fellow.

He introduced himself as being a member of the secret police. He even handed me his card. I gave him my card: I knew now that they knew everything about us anyway. And Yola is a small town. There would be no escape for us. The man appeared to be friendly. He told me that we could always call him, should we run into any kind of trouble.

When Hanna arrived, we decided to pay a visit to the American university, to find out if any of them would be away on holidays, so that we could rent a decent house. Both of us desperately wanted to get out of that horrible hotel. But first we introduced ourselves to the provincial office of the Election Commission. And we paid a visit to the UN representative, since he would be our UN focal point in Yola.

He was a Nigerian and worked for Unicef, the children's fund.

The American university occupies a huge part of the town of Yola. We managed to pass the security at the entrance and made our way to the main building. From our air-conditioned car to the air-conditioned entrance was only ten meters, but it was ten meters in the burning midday sun. Hanna and I were sweating profusely under our EU visibility jacket.

The president and vice-president of the university were an American couple, Michael and Elspeth Smith. We were led into the office of Elspeth, the vice-president, who immediately took pity on us. Inside her room it was freezing cold, but we were dripping wet from our own sweat.

The first thing she did was to offer us an ice cold Coca Cola. And a bottle of mineral water. I drank it all at once. We explained our problem. Elspeth fully agreed that the hotel was abominable. She said she would help us. There were several options.

Some university staff would indeed go on home leave within a few days, but there was also another hotel in town. Elspeth accompanied us to the other hotel. It turned out to have a nice little restaurant and terrace, with a view of the river. But the rooms were even more basic than in our first hotel.

Then a thought crossed her mind. The university owned a guesthouse in a small side street in town, that was used by visiting consultants. Were we interested? You bet we were. The guesthouse was fantastic. I couldn't believe my eyes.

It had a huge central room, with an enormous TV with some 800 channels. The large kitchen was well-equipped with a gas oven, microwave, two fridges, pots and pans. There were four bedrooms, one of which was currently occupied by an American software consultant.

Back at the university, we were introduced to this consultant. His name was Jordan and he had to consent to having us as his house mates. Jordan agreed immediately. He was in his late thirties and came from Ohio. I told him that my wife has worked for Care in Mozambique and that her boss, Terry, had been born in Cincinnati, Ohio.

To Jordan's surprise I mentioned some (in)famous people who also came from Cincinnati: Doris Day, Jerry Springer and Charles Manson. ,,I didn't know that Charles Manson came from Ohio", Jordan said.

Jordan was happy with our company in the huge but otherwise empty guesthouse. It was his first time in Africa. We told the vice-president that we were very happy with the guesthouse, but that we wanted to pay for it and that we needed payment receipts that we could show to our mission.

That was a little problem, since nobody had ever paid for it. She asked how much we wanted to pay. I looked at Hanna and said: 'Let's pay the same rate as we paid for the hotel: 35 dollars per person per day'. Everybody agreed.

And so Hanna and I were saved by the bell. Each room of the guesthouse had a large, modern airco. Outside, two large diesel generators took turns in generating electricity. It was a very safe place, with a high wall all around, topped with barbed wire. There was a permanent guard at the gate, who also operated the generators.

But before we could move in, there was a little problem. As EU observers, we had to comply with UN safety regulations. Our first hotel had been approved by the UN, but our new guesthouse had to be inspected. And the UN was far away, in the capital Abuja.

Thank God, Matt, our security expert on the Core Team in Abuja, had a solution. ,,Take the local UN representative to the guesthouse. If he approves it, you can stay there." So we drove up to the UN representative, who came back with us to the guesthouse.

He noticed immediately that the guesthouse was much safer than the hotel, so we were allowed to stay. Hanna and I could not be happier. We drove back to the hotel, to pick up our stuff. I was so happy that I threw everything hastily in a couple of bags.

It was only later that evening that I realized that I had forgotten my alarm clock in my hotel room. Along with several underpants. It took me three days to find a shop that sold alarm clocks, but I couldn't care less. The guesthouse was our saviour.

Especially after Jordan explained to us that the guesthouse had excellent Wi-Fi. No more outdoors nightmares with the bloody BGAN. Well, that is not entirely true: a few weeks later we decided to test the BGAN in broad daylight, just in case we should need it on E-Day, when we would be on the road all day.

So we set up our laptop and the BGAN on a public table, out in the open at midday. It was good that we did it, because we found out that there were two problems: because of the bright sun we could not see anything on the screen, so we could not program the software.

And then, when I touched the laptop, I burned my finger. At 46 degrees Celsius and under the burning sun, the laptop functioned like a greenhouse. I told Hanna it was going to explode! Just in time, we put everything back in the air-conditioned car. That would definitely be the last time that we used the bloody BGAN.

From then on, we worked well. As LTOs, we were supposed to interview people for our Weekly Reports, but also to prepare the way for our STO teams. We were supposed to map routes for the STOs and to brief them, but the problem was that Yola was the only town of any significance in Adamawa state.

Outside Yola, the countryside was very interesting, but in the villages we could not obtain any information that would be useful for our WRs. On top of that, our Core Team had difficulties in obtaining specific legal information in Abuja.

Apparently, our mission's legal expert was not on speaking terms with the judges of the high court over there. So nearly every day our legal expert called Hanna with certain legal questions. After all, she was a judge in her native Poland.

This meant that I had to accompany Hanna to the judicial premises in Yola nearly every day, where she discussed all kinds of incomprehensible legal issues with the regional judges. She liked it, but to me it was abracadabra. I am just a plain and simple economist, turned journalist.

As a result, we only made three visits outside the town of Yola. Not that this was a problem, for we were told quite early on by the Core Team that we would not get any STOs in any case. We were too far away from Abuja and the STOs were, like us, not allowed to travel by plane. No STOs meant that we did not have to write an STO manual either. Hurray!

The few trips we made outside Yola revealed something interesting. At every village where we planned to visit the local representative of the Election Commission, we were met by a well-dressed young man who claimed to be working for the secret police.

They were waiting for us, with their motorbikes, at the entrance of the village, but we had never told anybody where we were going. Not even our drivers. Weird. It became even weirder when one of them told us: ,,We were expecting you".

When I thought about it later, it seemed quite conceivable that the secret service simply deployed young men with motorbikes to every major village, where they would be on standby permanently. Big brother is watching you. The secret service guy would not only direct us to the office of the EC in the village, but would also join us during our meetings with local electoral officials.

The first time this happened, I asked the guy to please get out of the room. To my surprise, Hanna, my partner, corrected me. She said that this was the custom of the country and we were guests in the country. A few weeks later, Hanna had changed her mind completely: by then, she was the one demanding that the secret service guy should leave the room, while I thought: 'Well, who cares'.

Apparently, the secret service believed that Hanna and I sided with the opposition, because they sent emails to the EU in Brussels, explaining that we were staying at a guesthouse that belonged to the American University. And the owner of the AU was Atiku Abubakar, the vice-president of the country, who challenged Umaru Yar'Adua, of the ruling PDP party, at the polls.

Since we were staying at Abubakar's guesthouse, we were perceived to be prejudiced against the ruling president, according to the anonymous email, that could only have been sent by the secret service.

A few days later, one of our local interlocutors told us that the Hilton hotel in Abuja, where our CT was staying, was owned by president Olusegun Obasanjo of Nigeria. Apparently, in Nigeria, hotels are owned by politicians. But where can we, observers, stay then? We have to stay somewhere.

In general, it is quite true that ruling parties have much to lose during elections and that EU EOMs are often critical of ruling parties, who will do anything to remain in power, including illegal actions. It is also true that opposition parties, since they are in a much weaker position, are much more positive towards EU EOMs, since nobody else will come to their aid.

At this point it has to be explained that Nigeria is probably the most corrupt country on the planet. Corruption is endemic. Everyone who can be corrupt, is corrupt. It is not seen as a negative thing. It does not mean that the people are not nice. The reason why people enter politics is simply to put money in their pockets.

Political parties have no ideology. They just want to win the elections, so that their followers can stuff their pockets, instead of the followers of other political parties. As several Nigerians told us: 'It's better that I put public money in my pocket than that someone else puts public money in his pocket'.

Abubakar had started as a lowly customs official, but after a number of years, as if by miracle, he had become a millionaire. By the time he became vice-president, he was a billionaire. Hanna and I visited Yangwe, the village where he was born, not far from Yola. What we saw there was appalling: a gigantic modern villa, surrounded by high walls.

The rest of the village consisted of poor houses and very bad dirt roads. Extreme richness, surrounded by extreme poverty. It's a shame, really. But Abubakar had at least done one thing that was certainly beneficial to his fellow Nigerians: he had financed the American University. The students came from all over Nigeria.

So almost daily we paid visits to the judicial premises in Yola. Sweaty business. There was no electricity in Yola, except for one hour per day, and there were just a few generators in the judicial premises, so the fans hardly ever worked.

On top of that, the judges kept the curtains at their windows closed, to prevent people from peeping inside. As a result, with 46 degrees Celsius outside, it was even hotter inside the cramped, little offices.

Our Core Team recognized the problem with the extremely hot weather in our province. We were granted permission to buy mineral water for ourselves and our drivers, police escort and interpreter and pay for it from the mission's petty cash. Limitless amounts of mineral water free of charge for all of us.

So every other day we bought several boxes with bottles of mineral water. We kept the boxes in the back of our car. This meant that, after the car had been parked in the hot sun for a while, the mineral water would be close to 60 degrees Celsius. But we had no choice: we had to drink the hot water, in order not to dehydrate.

As LTOs, we are supposed to present ourselves to the governor, mayor, chief of police, army chief and whoever else is important in our province. So we went to the Governor's House. An assistant told us that we had to send an official written request to the governor, if we ever wanted to meet him.

I told Hanna to forget about it, but she replied sternly: ,,It's important that we meet the governor." So we wrote an official letter. A week later, we were welcome. We had an appointment at 11 o'clock sharp, so we decided to leave our mineral water in the car. This turned out to be a mistake. We were let into the office of the governor's Director of Protocol, who was not there. In fact, there was nobody there.

We waited and waited. It was hot inside the empty office, there was no fan and we had no water. I should have gone back to the car, to get some mineral water, but it was quite a long walk and we expected to be called into the governor's office at any moment. This did not happen.

I noticed that Hanna was struggling with the heat. I took a notebook from by bag and waved it in front of her face, to cool her off a bit. It didn't help. Her eyes went blank. Then she collapsed. It was the first time in my life that I saw a human being collapse, because of dehydration.

I assisted her back to our car and forced her to drink some of the hot mineral water. In the car, thank God, we had airco. We drove back to our guesthouse, to recuperate. All of a sudden, an unmarked vehicle pulled up beside us. I opened my window.

It was the Director of Protocol himself. He yelled at me: ,,The governor will see you now." I yelled back: ,,My partner doesn't feel well. We'll return some other day". I turned to Hanna: ",,I am not going back there." This time she agreed: ",,Neither am I. I have had enough."

All in all, we had a good time in Yola. We were welcome to have lunch at the university restaurant. It was cheap and it had air-conditioning, so we could cool off a bit. Teachers and students ate there. Since it was a buffet, we didn't have to wait for a waiter.

It was quite funny that there were two counters: one said 'Nigerian Food' and another one said: 'Expatriate Food'. The food was all right. The chief cook was, in fact, a Croatian, with whom Hanna communicated in their Slavic languages.

In the beginning, we queued for the 'Expatriate Food', which was usually chicken curry. I like chicken curry, but after a week or so, I decided to queue for the 'Nigerian Food', for a change. The Nigerians behind the counter were flabbergasted: a white man, queuing for African food.

It was clearly a sight they did not see every day. I asked them to fill my plate with mealy meal and beef with a hot, red sauce. It was delicious and what's more, like all Nigerians I ate it with my hands, to Hanna's horror. When we returned for another lunch, a few days later, the staff smiled as they remembered me as the only white person who would be queuing for African food.

On Sunday, Hanna, as a good Polish catholic, decided to go to St. Mary's Church, which gave me a few hours to wash my clothes by hand. I was enjoying a few hours on my own, but then she called me. I was invited to have lunch with the parish priests. Since we had given our drivers and police escort a day off, I had to walk nearly a kilometre under the scorching sun.

But lunch was delicious: African food. Yet again I ate it with my hands. So did the priests. Then Hanna told me that the secretary of the parish was interested in becoming our interpreter. I was not enthusiastic. We already worked with two drivers and two police escorts.

The more people, the more complicated it becomes to organize everything. On top of that, all educated Nigerians speak English. But we met Thomas, the secretary, and he seemed to be a cheerful fellow, so we decided to hire him as our assistant/interpreter. We later found out that Thomas had in fact been born in Jos, but had lived in Yola for the last 24 years.

In our province the people spoke Hausa/Fulani amongst themselves. As it was, Thomas would become more our assistant than our interpreter. He gave us a lot of valuable background information, that we used in our Weekly Reports. And he was pleasant company. We laughed a lot in our car.

It was not a problem that our interpreter was a Christian and that our driver was a Muslim. In Adamawa state there were no tensions between Christians and Muslims, because the leaders on both sides instructed their followers to remain calm and respectful. Boko Haram, very active in Borno state, just north of Adamawa, never got a real foothold in our state.

Hanna and I were welcome at any time in the American Club. The first evening there, we sat outside at the swimming pool, but we soon found out why everybody else was sitting indoors. Even at 8 o'clock in the evening, in the pitch dark, it was too hot to sit outside. You were simply dripping with sweat. From then on, we ordered our hamburgers or pizzas indoors, where the airco was buzzing pleasantly.

Thanks to Jordan, our guesthouse mate, we quickly made new friends. Curiously, several of them were Egyptians. The American university employed quite a lot of Egyptians. They managed the university's finances and administration.

There were also teachers from several European countries. Most of them were very happy to have a chat with us, since all in all there were very few expatriates in Yola. And no tourists, even though the border with Cameroun was less than twenty kilometres away.

The guesthouse had a big kitchen. One Sunday afternoon we had been working on our administration and Weekly Report, when Hanna announced that she would cook rice for the three of us. We could not find any rice, though. She asked me to go out and buy some.

By now it was 16.00 hours and still unbelievably hot. I had to walk several hundred meters to the little shops. They sold several kinds of rice. I did not know what kind of rice Hanna wanted, so I bought three different kinds. When I returned to the guesthouse, I was sweating profusely.

An hour later, Jordan and I were watching TV in the enormous living room. The TV made a lot of noise, so I could not understand what Hanna was asking me. Jordan's ears were younger than mine. He understood her.

He turned to me: ,,I thought you bought rice already", he said. I nodded. Then I turned to Hanna and told her that I had bought three different kinds of rice. And I added: ,,The rice is right there, in front of you on the sink."

Jordan and I continued watching TV, expecting Hanna to start cooking any time now, but out of the blue she announced: ,,Well, actually, I am not in the mood for cooking rice. I'm going to eat some bread." Jordan and I looked at each other. We were probably thinking the same.

Like mad dogs and Englishmen, I had ventured out in the midday sun to no avail. A few lines by my favourite singer-songwriter, Loudon Wainwright III, came to my mind: *Oh God, I hate women, they mess up your life.*

The main problem with Hanna was that she became really stressed when the time came to write our Weekly Reports. We knew that, since we would not have any STOs, the WRs would be very important for our personal evaluations at the end of the mission. But Hanna took it a bit too serious, in my opinion.

She would sit all through the night working on our laptop. She typed with only two fingers and on top of that, she had to check many English words one by one, since her written English was not extremely good. Several times, I offered that I would do the typing while she dictated, but for some reason she didn't want to work that way.

On E-Day, we got up at 5 o'clock. Our first Polling Station offered us a surprise. It was not open! Instead, the police was busy keeping a small crowd away from it. We ordered our driver to park the car at a safe distance, so that we could make a hasty retreat, if need be.

As it turned out, this would be the weirdest thing that happened during any of my missions: apparently, the provincial Election Commission had instructed all polling stations to cross out the name of one candidate from the list of candidates for the presidency.

This instruction had been received only one day before E-Day, and on this particular polling station the polling staff had worked all through the night, crossing out his name on each and every ballot paper.

The funny thing was, as we found out later during E-Day, than most other polling stations had ignored the instruction, since—according to the electoral law—a ballot paper was only valid if it had not been tempered with. In the end, this candidate's name remained on most of the ballot papers, but not all. Chaos all over.

When you work in Africa, you must accept the fact that not everything is organized to perfection. Upon our discovery of the name-crossing, Hanna and I immediately sent a message to our Core Team. It would earn us a positive evaluation at the end of the mission.

The rest of E-Day went on quite uneventful. We visited a polling station that was situated just a few hundred meters from the border with Cameroun. Hundreds of Nigerians who lived in Cameroun crossed the border to vote there.

On the way back to Yola, we noticed an uproar in Fufore. All of a sudden, our escorts, Ezekiel and Ayuba, ran towards it. For a moment they had forgotten that they were supposed to work for us and that we were not allowed to interfere.

They relieved a colleague policeman, who had arrested a voter who had threatened to burn a ballot box. An angry crowd tried to prevent the policeman from taking the voter to the police station. The arrival of our two armed Mopols was enough to calm the situation.

We observed the closing and counting of several polling stations at a large school in Yola. Since there was no electricity, the polling staff had to do their work by the light of torches, candles and mobile phones.

We spent most of the evening and night observing the counting at the provincial level in the Shagari Dispensary. It was extremely hot in the room. A generator made a lot of noise outside, but the energy was used for lighting, not for cooling. After midnight, I managed to sneak back to the coolness of our guesthouse, to fill in our E-Day forms on the laptop.

When I returned to the provincial counting office, Hanna told me that some people had invaded a polling station in a village and burned all the ballot boxes. That turned out to be the major incident in our province, apart from the crossing out at several polling stations of one candidate.

At the national level, president Obasanjo's PDP had won the presidential elections with 70 per cent of the vote. According to the constitution, he was not allowed a third term, though. His successor was Yar'Adua. The governorships, House of Representatives seats and senatorial seats were divided over the different parties.

We spent most of the next days at the judicial premises, where people could file complaints. Not much to report there. Michael and Elspeth Smith, the American couple that lead the American University, had asked us to host a debate with their students, to explain what we did as election observers. We were so grateful for the guesthouse, that we accepted without hesitation.

The students were interested in our work, but they did not understand what the EU was doing in Nigeria, when the EU was not allowed to intervene or correct matters. ,,So the EU is completely powerless, even when fraud is observed?" Hanna and I explained that the EU conclusions and recommendations would be broadcast on CNN and the BBC and that the whole world would be watching it.

We had requested our Core Team if we were allowed to return to Abuja in one day. The security expert agreed, upon the condition that we would leave at first light, to make sure that we would arrive in the capital before dark. So at 06.00 hours we put all our stuff in the car.

While I sat in the car, Hanna had entered the guesthouse one last time. I waited for half an hour. I was about to go back inside and tell her that she was wasting precious time, when at last she entered the car. She explained that she really needed to clean up the kitchen. Women!

The road winded uphill and after one hour we entered the neighbouring province. Then our car broke down. Our two drivers could not detect the problem. Our car would not start again. After the extreme heat of Yola, it was only about 30 degrees of Celsius up there. Pleasantly chilly.

I explained to the two drivers and the two police escorts that according to our mission's security regulations, we were obliged to leave the car and the driver behind, while Hanna and I would travel on in the car of the police escort.

Our driver panicked. He did not want to stay behind, in the middle of nowhere. The police escorts offered to drive to the next town, about twelve kilometres away, to try to find a mechanic. Hanna and I agreed, but on the condition that they would return immediately.

I was sceptical, but the guys returned within 45 minutes, with a mechanic! It took the guy less than five minutes to find the problem: a blown fuse. It was replaced and our car worked fine again.

On we went. We had lunch at the Mr. Biggs in Bauchi, the Nigerian version of Kentucky Fried Chicken. Hanna and I paid for the two drivers and the two police escorts. After all, they had served us well.

On we went. We were nicely on time and heading west, towards the falling sun. There was only one problem: I could not find any of the towns we passed on our map. For some reason, they were not mentioned there.

At about 17.00 hours our escort vehicle signalled us to stop. The two police escorts walked up to our car and talked to Musa, our driver, in Hausa/Fulani. They seemed agitated. I demanded that they should speak English, so that Hanna and I could listen in on the conversation. But they ignored me. ,,Let them speak their native tongue", Hanna told me briskly.

An hour later, I received a call from Matt, our security expert. ,,Are you close to Abuja? Otherwise, you have to look for a hotel, to spend the night." I looked outside and noticed that we were just passing a huge stadium, so I answered: ,, We are entering the outskirts of Abuja. I can see the stadium from here."

Our car needed refuelling, so our driver drove to a petrol station. While he was busy refuelling, I walked up to a sign, which seemed to indicate that this petrol station was situated in Kaduna. I asked one of the guys of the petrol station if we were in Abuja. He replied: ,,No. This is Kaduna. One hundred kilometres north of Abuja."

I walked back to our car and told Hanna the stunning news. She was flabbergasted. It was getting dark and our security expert gave us the name of the ASAA Pyramid Hotel in Kaduna, which turned out to be a big city. He told us that another LTO team would also spend the night there.

An hour later, Hanna and I had dinner with two elderly male LTOs: Conny from Denmark and Josef, a Dutch speaking Belgian. They had been based in Katsina State, in the far north of Nigeria. I did not know then that Josef would be my much appreciated roommate on my next mission in Pakistan.

While we were still fuming at our driver, the two experienced LTOs were quietly enjoying their meal and beers. I learned something from them: go with the flow and don't get excited about little things that go wrong.

The next day we took the four-lane highway from Kaduna to Abuja. It had become obvious that Musa, who came from Yola, was totally lost in the rest of Nigeria. Since Hazeem, the driver of our escort vehicle, lived in Abuja, I told him to lead the way. Thanks to him, we reached the Hilton Hotel in Abuja before midday.

Wlodek was there, at the main entrance. He took a quick look at me and said: 'You have lost weight'. Only then I realized that I had pulled my waist belt to the very limit: I had indeed lost at least five kilos, without even noticing it. If you want to lose weight: all you have to do is work in the tropics for six weeks.

Hanna and I paid our police escorts their well-deserved bonuses. Ezekiel and Ayuba apologized for the fact that they had refused to speak English to us the previous day, when they realized that our driver had taken the wrong road westwards. We replied that on the whole, we had been very happy with them.

They also told us that they had to hand fifty per cent of their bonuses to their superiors. Well, what could I do? Corruption is rife in Africa. I cannot change an entire continent in just six weeks.

In The Netherlands, Queens Day was officially celebrated on 30 April, but for some reason the Dutch embassy was already celebrating it on 29 April. Monique, Kees and I were invited. I drank too much beer. All in all it had been a good mission for me, but it had been very intense.

I had to be social all the time and it had been extremely hot in Yola. It had drained my energy levels. On the way back, during the stop-over at Heathrow airport in London, I did not want to have to listen to any other observer any more. I found a secluded spot, where I waited it out until my flight to Amsterdam left.

Later, when we met on the airplane, Kees told me angrily that he had been looking for me at Heathrow. But this would not be the last mission to drain my energies. It's a demanding job, especially since I am not a social person at all. It's tough for me, but it's addictive at the same time. After all: each mission is an adventure.

Did I find a Goofy for my wife's collection? Yes, I did. In a most unexpected place. One day, while travelling to outlying villages, we passed a huge market at a crossroads, in the middle of nowhere. I spotted earrings with Goofy's. I purchased two sets of them.

My wife was happy with them, for her collection, but she declined to put them in her ears. She had heard too many stories of people whose ears had become infected, due to rusty African earrings. She appreciated my efforts to find the Goofy's, though. She still wanted me back.

Chapter 7

PAKISTAN - 2008

'Benazir Bhutto has just been assassinated'

I was not really keen on going back to Pakistan. My wife and I had lived in Islamabad for a year, in 1989-90, when I worked for the anti-drugs organization of the UN and she worked for a UN-demining project, training Afghans to detect landmines.

During that one year in Pakistan, both of us had suffered food poisoning. Three times, in fact. We had lived in Africa for six years and in Latin America for four years, without any stomach problems. Pakistan turned out to be something else.

On top of that, the men in Pakistan were staring at my wife all the time. She did not care about it, but I did. I found it very uncomfortable. But, as my wife pointed out, a Pakistan mission would look good on my CV. It is considered to be one of the toughest missions, nearly in the same category as Afghanistan and Palestine.

And it would be a short mission, only four weeks. So I applied. I was first selected by the Dutch Ministry of Foreign Affairs and then also by the EU. Or at least, that's what I thought. I received a long email from the EU that I was selected and that they immediately needed my health certificate as well as my electro cardiogram.

Two days later, to my surprise, I received another email from the EU. There had been a mistake. I was not selected. Instead, I had been added to the reserve list. I was furious. As an election observer, I am used to do as I'm being told, but this was something different.

They had made a mistake. Not me. And I had already visited my doctor. My electrocardiogram was already being processed. All this I sent in a reply to the EU. One day later, they kindly apologized and said that I was duly selected after all.

The EU informed me that apart from the regular vaccinations, all observers would need to be vaccinated against Japanese encephalitis.

So I took a train to Amsterdam, to visit the tropical disease section of the University Hospital. The doctors there have all worked in tropical countries, which means that they know what they are talking about.

They could not believe that I needed this vaccination against Japanese encephalitis, because it is only prevalent in rice fields in Southern Asia and only during the rainy season. Of the 48 LTOs, only 6 would be based in the southern part of Pakistan, where the rice fields are. On top of that, the rainy season had already passed and—obviously—we observe elections, not rice fields.

The doctors said that it was crazy to be vaccinated when there was no risk at all. The chief doctor even wanted to call the EU, to ask why in the name of Jesus they had ordered this vaccination, which in itself is extremely dangerous, since one per cent of all recipients get a serious allergic reaction. Because of this, the vaccination against Japanese encephalitis is totally forbidden in Germany.

I had brought a copy of the EU-email with me, so I could show the doctors that I really needed this vaccination: no vaccination would mean no mission. The doctors said that they did not want to jeopardize my mission, therefore they would give me the vaccination, which had to be given three times at specific intervals.

Each time I had to travel to Amsterdam and each time I was the only person required to remain at the hospital for at least half an hour, so the doctors could observe if I developed any allergic reactions. Luckily, I was fine. My German colleagues were furious, since they had to be vaccinated by the mission's Pakistani doctor. They demanded an explanation.

It was not until four weeks later that the explanation was provided to us: it appeared that the EU had asked a trainee to find out which vaccinations would be needed for Pakistan. This trainee had looked at the WHO site, where about two hundred possible diseases were listed. The trainee had just picked out Japanese encephalitis from that list. At random.

It was to be a short mission, but to a high-risk country. Therefore, prior to our departure, all observers would receive a one week security training in Tirrenia, the port of Pisa in Italy. The Continental Hotel, at the seaside of Tuscany, was fully paid by the EU. They planned to put me in a room with another LTO, Martin from Austria. But I had learned my lesson.

I went to the reception, paid a few extra euros and the hotel gave me a room of my own. I could sleep my siestas without being disturbed. I did not know it at the time, but later, during our mid-term briefing in Islamabad and also during my Kyrgyzstan mission of 2010, Martin would turn out to be a total asshole.

The training was useful. Michael Gahler from Germany, our Chief Observer, was not there. The Chief Observer, habitually a member of the European Parliament, joins the mission only in the beginning, for a few days, and then later, around Election Day.

Therefore, for the observers, the most important member of the CT is the Deputy Chief Observer. He/she is the day to day boss of the mission. In this case, the Deputy CO was an elderly Danish man called Jörgen, who frequently fell asleep during the briefing sessions. Not a good omen, I thought. He was not a bad guy, though. He had been a journalist as well as a diplomat. Just like me.

To brief us on the security situation in Pakistan, an Austrian guy of Indian origin who worked for IOM in Manila (I'm not making this up), was flown in especially for us. He knew a lot about Pakistan. Too much, in fact, for at one point he stated that female observers should not be deployed in the North-West Frontier Province. This caused an uproar: he was nearly lynched by the female observers.

It became even funnier when he started to instruct us as to how observers should behave during political rallies. Mat, our security expert, grabbed the microphone and said briskly: ,,For security reasons, our observers are not allowed to observe any rallies."

To end on a high note, the Austrian of Indian origin explained to us how we should observe polling stations. This was too much. ,,We are observers", someone shouted. ,,We know how to observe polling stations. That's our job."

Apart from security instructions, we were briefed on Pakistani history and politics. I usually sat next to Alberto, from Barcelona. He had been my STO in Venezuela. Now he was my colleague LTO. And—I did not know it at the time—just a few years later he would be my boss, when he worked at the EU Elections Unit in Brussels.

Which taught me an important lesson: always be nice to your STOs. One day they might become your superior. In my hometown I never met a Spanish speaker, so I took the opportunity to practice my Spanish with Alberto.

In the evenings I had a few beers with the other Dutch LTOs. There were five of us: three men and two women. I also had a beer or two with Josef and Robert, two elderly Belgian LTOs. Pleasant chaps. Josef was Flemish and Robert came from the French-speaking Wallonia. Both spoke fluent Dutch as well as French.

Apart from the theoretical sessions, we received two days of practical security training at the training grounds of the Italian special forces, in the middle of a Tuscan forest. For the young, tall and healthy looking Italian male and female soldiers in their neatly ironed camouflage outfits it must have been quite a sight when we stumbled out of the buses: a bunch of elderly, casually dressed men and women, strolling slowly towards the instruction room.

But, just like during my LTO training course in Pisa in 2005, the look on the faces of the Italian soldiers changed, when their commanding officer explained that all of us, observers, had been deployed to the most difficult regions of the most difficult countries in the world. And we, observers, stayed there for many weeks all by ourselves, with only our partner as company.

The Italian special forces told us later that they had been deployed to Irak and Afghanistan, but that they were always based in large military compounds with their own Italian television and their own Italian cooks, without any contact with the local population. They developed a lot of respect for us, observers, since we lived amongst the local people.

We received the same security training as the special forces. We were put in a car that drove up to a road block manned by masked men with Kalashnikovs. They shot the driver and pulled us out of the car. They searched us, while we had to stand against the car, with our arms and our legs spread out. The aim was to teach us to comply with the requests of the bad guys, in order to stay alive and wait for help.

Other instructors took us to a house that was booby trapped from top to bottom. They showed us landmines and tripwire mines in the forest. With gas masks on, we had to wait in a makeshift prison, to be liberated by the special forces. Since I was sweating, my gas mask became fogged. I couldn't see a bloody thing, but I did not dare to take off my gas mask.

It was quite frightening, when they threw smoke bombs and flash bombs into the rooms. As hostages, all we had to do was lay down flat on the floor and wait for instructions. But the worst was yet to come: we were driven to yet another location in the forest, when all of a sudden our bus was attacked by masked men with AK-47s.

The bus driver was shot dead and one by one they put hoods over our heads. The most scary part is when they lead you down the bus steps, since you are effectively blindfolded. I was afraid I would break an ankle. They took us to a tent, where they 'tortured' us for about one and a half hours.

Even though it was November, the Italian sun was heating the tent and I was sweating profusely under my hood. They told us that anyone could drop out of the exercise at any time. I heard Olly, an English LTO, say that he had had enough. He took off his cap. But I was determined to hold out until the bitter end.

I come from a family of small farmers: we don't give up easily. When the Italian soldiers finally removed my cap they congratulated me. I had earned their respect. They told me that this part of the training was usually given to military personnel, not civilians.

After the security training in Pisa, we had to wait a full month before being deployed. Because of the state of emergency in Pakistan and the house arrest of Benazir Bhutto, the departure date was postponed a few times. Then Benazir's house arrest was lifted and our mission got the green light.

Officially, our mission was labelled as an 'EU LEOM', the L meaning Limited: limited in duration, as it would be less than four weeks, and limited in numbers: only 9 CT, 48 LTOs, 3 SLOs and around 20 STOs.

When I finally arrived at Schiphol airport to board a plane to Islamabad, it was 25 December 2007. A peculiar day. For Dutch people, Christmas Day is not as important as it is for many other nationalities, since we give presents to our children on Santa Claus Day, the 5th of December.

But also for the Dutch it remains a special day, during which you normally visit your family. So on 25 December, nobody wants to be in an airplane: neither the crew nor the passengers. That means that on Christmas Day, the airport is practically deserted. But the few people that were there were all in a good mood. The cabin crew did their best to offer the passengers a special Christmas flight, with Christmas treats.

In Islamabad we were taken to the Holiday Inn, only a stone throw away from the Red Mosque, where disturbances took place on a regular basis. This was strange, since just one month earlier, in Pisa, we had been instructed to avoid potential hot spots. In addition they put us in rooms on the first floor, at the street side. A potential terrorist could easily throw a rock through the window, followed by a hand grenade.

I shared a room with Josef from Belgium. In this case voluntarily, since we had to pay a lot of money for our rooms. This way, we shared the cost. Josef was great company, as I remembered from the hotel in Kaduna, Nigeria. And he spoke Dutch. He was born in Flanders.

Most of the Dutch speaking Flemish are not fond of the French-speaking Belgians from Wallonia, to put it mildly. But Josef was an exception: he insisted on being addressed as a 'Belgian'. He was probably the only Belgian who wanted to be addressed as a Belgian.

Usually, Dutch speaking Belgians marry Dutch speaking Belgians and French speaking Belgians marry French speaking Belgians. Mixed marriages are an exception. But Josef's wife was born in Wallonia. At home, apparently, he spoke French.

In Pakistan it's four hours later than in western Europe, so by the time we arrived in Islamabad is was already mid-morning. Even though it had been a night flight, I had not slept on the plane. Martin, the irritating guy from Austria, was sitting next to me and kept talking to me incessantly during the entire flight.

Luckily, and contrary to normal practice, we were allowed a few hours of free time, before the briefings would start. I told Josef that we could take a nap. He agreed, but to my horror he also said that he had called the reception, since our toilet was leaking.

,,Are you mad?" I ranted. ,,Do you know will happen now? This is Pakistan. They will send repair men, who will make a lot of noise for hours. Now I can forget about my nap." It happened exactly like this. Three men came to our room. As is the custom in Pakistan, they discussed the problem loudly, but did not repair it.

I could not sleep. And I did not sleep much during the following night either, since it was very warm in the room. I did not dare to open a window, for fear of someone throwing something through it.

The next day, 27 December, buses took us to the Serena hotel, the most expensive and most secure hotel in Pakistan, owned by the wealthy Agha Khan. For some reason, the Core Team was based in the safe Serena hotel, while the LTOs were based in the Holiday Inn, perilously close to the Red Mosque.

In a spacious conference room we were briefed all day. Fortunately, the room was air conditioned, since I could hardly keep my eyes open after two sleepless nights. In the afternoon, I had to go to the toilet. I passed an adjacent conference room, heavily guarded by security staff.

Through the windows I saw Benazir Bhutto, sitting next to president Karzai of Afghanistan, with a bunch of people in front of them. When I lived in Pakistan, in 1989-90, Benazir had served as Pakistan's first female prime minister. I had seen her a few times at close range. And now yet again.

Towards the end of the afternoon, we were led to a smaller meeting room adjacent to a garden, where people could venture out to smoke. There were snacks and alcoholic drinks. In Pakistan, only five-star hotels are allowed to offer alcoholic drinks to their guests.

Ordinary Pakistanis are obliged to live without alcohol, but the rich and powerful can drink as much as they want. Rich Pakistanis book rooms in expensive hotels, not only to drink, but also to observe western women in swimming dresses at the swimming pool. Pakistani women were allowed to swim, but only fully clothed and behind curtains.

After a long day filled with briefings, the mood was elated. Our Chief Observer, Michael Gahler, addressed us. He would turn out to be one of the best Chief Observers of all my missions.

They handed each of us a sheet of paper with security instructions. We were not allowed to visit western restaurants like McDonalds, Burger King and Kentucky Fried Chicken, since these were prime targets for militants. We were only permitted to travel in taxis owned by two renowned taxi firms. We were not allowed to go out alone and female observers always needed to be accompanied by at least one male observer.

All of this appeared a bit paranoid to us, but then the microphone was handed to a security official of UNDSS. His name was James and he was an African American. He provided us with security advice that was geared specifically at the current situation in Pakistan. He confirmed all that was written in the security instructions sheet.

At some point during his speech his phone rang. I thought it strange, since someone who was holding a speech would normally switch off his phone. Was it part of an act? He put his phone to his ear, dropped the microphone and then his eyes grew big. I was now convinced that it was an act, aimed at keeping our attention.

The American talked to some other persons for a few minutes and then picked up the microphone. ,,We just received news that in Rawalpindi a bomb exploded near Benazir Bhutto's vehicle. Apparently, she has been taken to hospital."

We were all shocked. Some LTOs, who were in Pakistan for the first time, did not know where Rawalpindi was situated. ,,It's just five kilometres from here", I explained.

That was the end of the briefings. We strolled through the garden in small groups. Some LTOs listened to CNN or the BBC. The news was not good. We were told that for the time being, we would not be transported back to the Holiday Inn.

If something happens to an important Pakistani politician, his or her supporters will immediately block the streets in protest. These crowds can be very dangerous, especially for westerners. So for several hours, we all remained there.

The good news was that it gave me time, for the first time in my life, to get familiar with mobile phones. At home I had never possessed a mobile phone, but on these missions it was the most important means of communication. One of the youngest LTOs, a 28-year old Dutch-speaking Belgian called Dominiek, taught me how to open it and replace the sim card.

I became so skilled at it, that by 23.00 hours I could do it with my eyes closed. As our greatest footballer, Johan Cruijff, used to say: 'Every disadvantage has its advantage'. What he meant was that he didn't care if his opponents would field extra defenders against him, since 'more defenders means less attackers'.

Then we received the sad news that Benazir had passed away. We were told that we could not go back to the Holiday Inn. Supporters of her party, PPP, had blocked major roads in Islamabad. We had to stay in the five star Serena hotel, while our suitcases were still in the Holiday Inn.

Luckily, the Serena hotel provided us with toothpaste, shampoo and shaving cream. Once again, I shared a room with Josef from Belgium. By now, he was my best observer friend. Since everything had to be done in a hurry for a large number of people, the hotel gave us a room with only one bed.

A huge, king-size bed, but still it's a bit awkward to sleep in one bed with another man, especially when you're not gay. But as an observer you get used to anything. This was an emergency. And as they always tell us on these missions: 'Thank you for being flexible'.

The next day, it was confirmed that the road between the Serena hotel and the Holiday Inn was secure. Under police protection, we were taken to the Holiday Inn to pick up our suitcases. For a few more days we were confined to the Serena hotel, where all of us celebrated New Year's Eve in a conference room, with lots of beer.

Believe it or not, Pakistan produces its own beer: Murree Beer. The Murree Beer Brewery was started by the British near the cool, elevated town of Murree, at the foothills of the Himilaya, just a few hours north from Islamabad. Nowadays, the brewery's headquarters is situated in Rawalpindi.

The company produces not only the renowned Murree beer, but also whiskey and other alcoholic and non-alcoholic beverages. In Pakistan, by the way, it is not illegal to drink alcohol, as long as you are a foreigner and a non-Muslim. It is forbidden to drink it in public places, though.

On 30 December 2007, the five Dutch observers were invited to the Dutch embassy. We were picked up by two armoured vehicles. Finally, I saw a bit of Islamabad. It looked very much the same as in 1989-90.

Apparently, the embassy was led by two Willems, Willem I and Willem II, like the Dutch kings of the good old days. Willem I was not in town, so we were received by Willem II. He had also invited several representatives of local observer organizations. Quite interesting for them as well as for us.

On the 1st of January 2008, most of the streets were safe to travel again. Since many observers, especially those from Eastern European countries, don't want to spend their money on expensive hotels, it was decided that we could move to a cheaper hotel: Best Western.

They gave Josef and me a room at street level at the back side of the hotel, where local people passed by on a footpath, just a few meters from our window! So far for all these elaborate security rules and regulations.

After we had stayed there for two nights, Marianne and Hillie, the two Dutch female LTOs, asked me if I could accompany them to a local tailor at Jinnah Market. They wanted to order tailor made Pakistani dresses.

While their measurements were taken at the tiny tailor shop, we received a strange phone call from our security people: our hotel was on fire! They instructed us to stay put where we were and not return to the Best Western.

After an hour or so, we decided to return anyway. When we arrived at the hotel's car park, we saw smoke coming out of the hotel entrance. Hillie, who made documentaries, told me that her very expensive camera was still in her room. I advised her not to go into the hotel, but before I could restrict her, she ran straight into the smoke.

I wanted to follow her, but one of the Pakistani security assistants of our mission literally grabbed my shirt from behind. I watched in horror, as Hillie disappeared into the smoke. Luckily, about ten minutes later, she reappeared. She was coughing, but she held her precious camera in her hand.

It turned out that the fire had started in the sauna, downstairs. Not an act of terror, but an overheated fuse. The leadership of our mission decided that we had suffered enough. When the smoke had cleared a bit, they instructed us to collect our belongings and once again return to the Serena hotel.

„*Habemus Serena*", said Michael Gahler, our CO. A German with a sense of humour! This time, we would stay in the Serena hotel until the day of our deployment. And this time they gave Josef and me a room with two separate beds. The EU compensated us for the extra costs.

On top of our LTO salary, hazard payment and per diem, they paid us 83 euros extra per day. Since Josef and I shared a room, I only had to pay half of the room rate of 250 dollars per day. Some eastern European observers even shared a room with three persons, so each of them only had to pay one third of 250 dollars.

All in all, I earned a net 187 euros per day in our 'Golden Cage'. Seven days per week. And we had a good time in the Serena hotel. Every morning, Josef and I enjoyed the fantastic buffet breakfast, which was included in the room rate. Every evening we had dinner with Robert, *le professeur* from Wallonia, and several other observers.

The good news was that I got to know lots of other observers. Normally, I only meet my fellow LTOs during the briefings and debriefings in the capital city, but then everybody is so busy that there's little time to have a chat. Now, we had all the time in the world.

Every day, at 11.00 hours, we were briefed in a meeting room. On most occasions, there was hardly any news for us. But we used our time to get acquainted with our rather complicated communications equipment, like the BGANs and sat-phones. On a few occasions, we were taken on sightseeing trips in minibuses, always accompanied by the police.

While we lived in a golden cage, on TV we watched our colleague-observers in Kenya being evacuated in military helicopters. Disturbances had broken out after E-Day and at least a thousand Kenyans lost their lives, while hundreds of thousands were displaced.

One of the sightseeing trips took us to Jinnah Market, close to where my wife and I had lived in 1989-90. We also visited the modern Faisal Mosque and the rooftop restaurant with a great view of Islamabad. It looked exactly as I remembered it.

A few days later, Roger, my English partner on this mission, asked me to accompany him to the rooftop restaurant. I thought he wanted to discuss our upcoming mission, but it turned out that he had forgotten his glasses there. We took a taxi up to the restaurant, which was closed to the public, but to my surprise the rather corpulent owner went straight to a drawer and took out Roger's glasses.

Roger asked if we could get a cup of coffee. Of course we could. The owner then told us that he had visited England as well as Holland. He did not allow us to pay for the coffee. That's the other side of Pakistan: the people are unbelievably hospitable.

For two weeks, there was uncertainty as to a new date for the elections, but then the news came that a new date had been set: the elections would now be held on 18 February, instead of the original 8 January. All LTOs were free to decide whether to return to Europe on 18 January, the date in our contracts, or on 28 February.

Half of the LTOs had to go back home, because they had other obligations. The other half, including myself, decided to stay on. So instead of a very short mission it became a very long mission. I was going to make a lot of money.

On 11 January, we finally left for our duty stations. We travelled to the city of Lahore over the newly constructed highway in a convoy of six vehicles, under the command of my partner, Roger. He was 67 years old and retired, but had spent his entire working life in the Royal Navy, so he was used to convoys.

He had even served on a hospital ship during the Falklands (or Malvinas) war of 1982. He did not want to talk about that period of his life, not even after I told him: 'Roger, man, you're a Falklands veteran. That means that you're part of history'.

Rudy, the Belgian security liaison officer, who would become a good friend of mine during the Sudan mission of 2011, had reserved the most horrible guesthouse I had ever seen: the Rest Inn, in Gulberg III, Lahore. Nearby was a much better place, the Sunfort Hotel, but most LTOs thought that it was too expensive, even after the Sunfort had lowered its rates considerably.

Luckily, Sandra, an English LTO affectionately known as Sandy, went out to look for a decent place to stay. She found a much better guesthouse: Regent's Villa Guesthouse in New Garden Town. We stayed there with three LTO teams, but one team would leave within a week. One of the departing LTOs was a Dutchman, with a not so Dutch name: Michiel Irish Stephenson.

His family had moved from Scotland to Holland eight generations ago. Interestingly, his son, with exactly the same name, was also an observer. On his last evening in Lahore, Michiel invited us to the famous rooftop restaurant Coco's Den in the old centre of the city, but he refused to invite Sandy.

Later that evening he told me: 'We've been here a week now and she has not spoken one word with me. She totally ignored me'. I thought this was strange, since I had not noticed any problem with her. But soon after, it appeared that something was indeed wrong with her. Terribly wrong.

During day time, the two remaining LTO teams travelled to their assigned districts, but in the evenings, the four of us would walk to Purkat Market, a nearby shopping area, with several restaurants. After a few weeks, my partner Roger announced that he would go out with Sandy, so the two of them could talk about typical English things, like cricket.

This came as quite a relief to me, since it meant that I could go out with Sandy's partner, Robert, *le professeur*. From then on, Robert and I would visit a different restaurant every evening. Lahore is a big city and there are lots of restaurants.

Robert was a very interesting guy: he had been a professor of Middle Eastern affairs. He spoke Turkish, Arabic, Urdu and a few more languages. More importantly, even though he was originally a French-speaking Belgian, he was fluent in Dutch.

This made life easier for me and also for him, since his Dutch was better than his English. As an extra bonus, no one could understand a word we were saying. Robert was an intellectual, but he was not very practical. One evening he told me something remarkable.

He told me that every time when Sandy and he interviewed local Pakistani's, Sandy would start the conversation by saying that she hoped that the PPP, the late Benazir Bhutto's party, would win the elections. On top of that, she said that in her opinion George W. Bush, the American president, was the biggest terrorist in the world. The Pakistani's really loved to hear this.

The problem was that both of these remarks were totally out of bounds with the Code of Conduct that we had signed as EU-observers. We are supposed to be neutral and impartial at all times. I was flabbergasted when Robert told me about her remarks. I couldn't believe it.

I advised him to inform our Core Team immediately, because if he waited any longer, he himself would be accused of complicity and probably be kicked out of the mission. Sooner or later, one of the Pakistanis would talk to our Core Team, and then Robert would also be in deep trouble.

At first Robert said that he did not want to betray his partner, but Robert and Sandy were arguing continuously. Apart from all this, Sandy had insulted Mubashir, the owner of our guesthouse. Mubashir was a Pashtun, originally from the North-West Territories, near Peshawar.

The Pashtun are a proud people and don't take insults lightly. Mubashir told her to leave his guesthouse or else he would talk to our Core Team, organize a press conference and even call the EU in Brussels.

Roger and I thought that he was bluffing, but the next day, when we returned from our districts, Roger received a phone call from Brussels: Mubashir, the owner had not been bluffing at all. Roger considered Sandy to be his friend and therefore he offered to mediate between her and Mubashir.

That same evening Roger tried to convince the owner to give Sandy a second chance. Since my door was open, I could hear every word. Mubashir explained that Sandy had insulted him. Roger tried to calm the man, but just then Sandy stormed out of her room. ,,He's lying", she shouted at the top of her voice. ,,And he keeps his wife locked in her room all the time."

This last thing was true. I had once or twice seen a glimpse of his wife in her room, but she never came out of it when we were there. Even so, Mubashir was a likable guy. And he liked me. Several times, he invited me to join him for a meal.

The two of us would then be eating a very tasty chicken curry with our hands and chat about the history of the Pashtuns and football. Mubashir knew all the players of the Dutch national team by name, which was extraordinary, since Pakistan is a country of cricket, polo and hockey lovers.

Obviously, the EU in Brussels had informed our EU Core Team in Islamabad. A few days later, all of us had to travel to Islamabad for a mid-term briefing that would last several days. The Core Team asked Roger and Robert what really had happened. This time, Robert informed the Core Team that Sandy broke the Code of Conduct during every meeting they had with local Pakistanis.

This was the end of the line for Sandy. She was allowed to continue working with Robert until the STOs arrived. She had to move to another guesthouse, though, and she would have to return to Europe together with the STOs. She would receive a 'not recommended' evaluation, which meant that she would be blacklisted for at least five years.

No more missions for Sandy in the near future. For the EU, at least. To my surprise I saw her again in early 2012, when she and I were LTOs for the OSCE EOM in Russia. Roger was also there. He was still very fond of Sandy.

I never had any problems with her, but still: I found it a bit strange that she was blacklisted by the EU, but not by the OSCE. Apparently, there was no communication between those two organizations.

In total, four LTOs would be kicked out of the mission: Nasrin, the elderly lady from Hungary who had developed a psychosis after Benazir had been assassinated, was the first. Next came two young LTOs from Spain and Portugal.

They worked in one team and apparently had purchased marihuana by the roadside, which had been reported by their driver, who didn't realize that his LTOs were doing something illicit. The drivers are regularly contacted by the CT, to ask if the cars are still OK. The driver just mentioned the marihuana, as a matter of fact.

This incident made me realize one important thing for all my future missions: our drivers were called several times a week by the Core Team and the Service Provider, not only to check if the vehicle was still OK, but also to ask how the team was doing. Big brother was watching us.

On top of that, all the drivers were working for the same company, so they all knew one another. And all of them have mobile phones. Drivers spend most of their time waiting in their cars, so they have plenty of time to chat with one another. I realized that I should always be careful with the drivers and treat them well.

On later missions, I found out that our drivers knew much more about other LTO teams than my partner and I did. And even when the drivers don't really mean to harm us, they might provide negative information to others, in some countries even to the secret service.

Amjad, our 30-something driver, was a pleasant chap. He didn't know anyone in Lahore and he didn't find a decent place to sleep, so he slept in the attic of our guesthouse, together with several other drivers. They slept on matrasses in a large room, without privacy and without a secure place to store their personal belongings.

All in all, Amjad, was not happy in Lahore. He was married to an American woman and was fluent in English. He lived in Abbottabad, a non-descript town, just one hour north of Islamabad. His brother owned a car company there. Little did I know that Osama bin Laden also lived there. Just a few years later, Abbottabad would become world news.

After about a week, Amjad had had enough. He returned to Abbottabad. He was replaced by Major Imtaz, who turned out to be quite a character. He was a retired army major. In Pakistan, the army is held in high esteem, since the army protects the Pakistanis from their arch-enemy: India. Army officers form a class of their own. They stand above the law, in fact. And they act accordingly.

Major Imtaz drove like mad, ignoring red traffic lights and ignoring all other traffic rules as well. When we approached a police road block, he simply drove to the front of the line, opened his window and shouted something at the policemen. They were mostly young and so intimidated by Major Imtaz' display of authority, that they let him pass without further ado.

But we, EU observers, are always instructed to play by the rules. So Roger and I had a few words with our driver, via Moazzam, our interpreter, since Major Imtaz' English was very basic. His knowledge of vehicles was also limited: the very first time we drove along the highway, I noted that he didn't drive faster than 70 kilometers per hour.

Through Moazzam, I asked the Major why he didn't drive 100 kilometers per hour. His reply was that the car wouldn't go faster. This was incorrect, since Amjad drove 120 kilometres per hour sometimes.

Then I noticed that he was driving in third gear all the time. I instructed Moazzam to explain to the Major that there was also a fourth gear and even a fifth gear in this car. Major Imtaz obliged and yes: after that, we drove 100 kilometres per hour. It was a miracle!

I glanced at Roger. He looked back at me with a glint of horror in his eyes. If a driver doesn't know how to use the gear, what else does he not know? Anyway, we were glad that, about a week later, Amjad returned and became our driver once again.

Every day we visited our three districts: Sheikhupura, Nankana Sahib and Hafizabad. It took us about two hours to get there, so I had to get up at 06.00 hours. At 16.00 hours, we had to return to Lahore, since we had to be back before dark. We always took the newly constructed highway, which had very little traffic, because car drivers had to pay toll.

One afternoon my phone rang. It was Wlodek, our security assistant. ,,Jos, tell your driver to slow down. He's driving at 120 kilometres per hour." I then remembered that our vehicle had been equipped with a tracking device.

During the midterm briefing in Islamabad, our security expert had in fact showed it to me on his computer. I saw our own car on the screen. It was parked next to the Serena hotel. Yet again, Big Brother was watching us. All the time.

There was not much sightseeing in our districts, but one Friday afternoon (in Pakistan, Friday is what Sunday is in the West) we visited the Sikh temple in Nankana Sahib. It was the second most important Sikh temple in the world, after the one at Amritsar, just across the border in India.

We had to take off our shoes and socks and we had to wear a little scarf on top of our heads, but we were allowed into the inner temple. ,,Can we take photographs?" The man in charge of the temple looked surprised. ,,Of course you can take photographs. Why not?"

We also visited the imposing Hiran Minar artificial lake, built by the Mogul emperor Jahangir. One morning, I received a call from 'Ellen' from the Dutch embassy. If I was all right. ,,I am fine", I replied. The next day, she called again, just when Roger and I were in a meeting with fifteen judges in Sheikhupura.

I walked out of the room and asked Ellen why she was calling me day after day, since it was interfering with my work. She explained that the Dutch ultra-rightist parliamentarian Geert Wilders had announced that he would publish an anti-Islam movie.

I told her that on my visibility jacket was written 'EU Observer', so nobody could possibly know that I was Dutch. But Ellen, obviously, had been constructed to stay in contact with all the Dutch in Pakistan. In January, she called me every day. Then, in February, it was all over. Without explanation.

All educated Pakistani's speak English, so usually we could interview them without our interpreter. But many ordinary Pakistani's don't speak English. This was the case with most of our police escorts. In Pakistan, the police are used to escorting VIPs. They have developed a rather peculiar system for this: each police district provides its own escorts for traveling dignitaries.

This meant that at each boundary of each police district, a new escort vehicle would be waiting for us. It was a complicated system. We had to file our traveling plans 48 hours in advance to the Security Expert of our mission, who would then forward it to the police.

There was a little problem: most ordinary policemen do not speak English. In addition, it would be very complicated to exchange telephone numbers with literally hundreds of policemen. But we were observers and observers are resourceful. We found a simple solution.

We had been provided with two VHF radios, which are usable at a range of less than 25 kilometres. We would hand one of them to the police escort and the other one to Moazzam, our interpreter. We talked to Moazzam in English and he translated it into his VHF radio. This worked very well.

Sometimes, we were accompanied by two police cars. A funny thing happened at a crossroads in a rural area. Pakistan is a hierarchical society, which means that poor people always must make way for dignitaries.

A donkey cart was blocking the crossroads. Our police escort vehicle used its honk, but the cart remained where it was. All of a sudden, a policeman jumped out and ran towards the donkey cart. He hit the driver several times on his back, with a two meter long, thin stick.

I had lived in Pakistan for a year and visited the North-Western Frontier province many times, so I was quite used to this. But Roger looked on in horror. He told Moazzam to accompany him to the chief of our police escort. In our car, Amjad and I were laughing. I heard Roger explain that the EU logo was visible on our car and that the EU could not be associated with barbaric practices.

A few days later, the same thing happened with a motorcycle driver, who was blocking the road. Again a policeman hit him on the back. Again Roger explained that this was unacceptable for an official EU mission. But the problem was: our police escorts were never the same ones.

In Pakistan, labour is cheap, so there are hundreds of thousands of policemen. When Roger returned to our car, I told him that we could not change the habits of 160 million Pakistanis during our short stay in the country. Roger just grunted.

EU EOMs are obsessed with our own security, so in the beginning our vehicle had also been equipped with an HF radio, usable for very long distances. There were two problems with these HF radio's: firstly, I can't remember any time they worked properly, so we never used them.

Secondly, the HF radio required an antenna of nearly two meters high, that was fitted on the front bumper of our vehicle. One day, when we drove into a village, the antenna hit a plastic pipe, that was used to transport natural gas to the houses. Extremely dangerous. We reported this to the Core Team and we were allowed to dismantle the antenna. We deposited it in the back of the car and never used it again.

During the mid-term briefing in Islamabad we met the LTOs that had arrived to replace the ones that had left our mission. It was nice to meet Kees again, the Dutch LTO of my Nigeria mission. Just one month earlier, he had been evacuated by helicopter in Kenya.

He told me that Hanna, who had been my partner in Nigeria, had also been evacuated in Kenya. I remembered that we had watched all this while we were confined to our comfortable Serena hotel in Islamabad. Compared to Kees and Hanna, we were having a boring time in Pakistan!

A funny thing happened when in the evening we were transported to a club house that belonged to the French embassy. None of us had had alcoholic drinks for weeks on end, so when we spotted a bar with Heineken beer, all of us started drinking like mad.

It is very difficult to obtain alcoholic drinks in Pakistan. When I worked for the UN organization against drugs in Pakistan, the UN had found a solution for this: the UN owned its own alcoholic shop, based in Rawalpindi, where only UN staff were allowed inside.

To this day I still remember the monthly quota: every month a UN staff member could purchase four crates of beer, four bottles of whiskey, four bottles of other liquors and fifteen bottles of wine.

So on the very first day of every month I drove over to Rawalpindi to buy my entire quota for the month, which did not cost much anyway, since for UN diplomats it was tax-free. The only problem was that I never drink whiskey and I don't like the taste of wine in a hot climate.

But four crates of beer is not much when after playing volleyball at 36 degrees Celsius several friends and colleagues would join my wife and me for cold beers. So my beers were gone after just a few days. I tried to exchange my bottles of whiskey and liquor for crates of beer with other UN staff. With limited success.

All over the world, Muslims have a love-hate relationship with alcohol. In 1989-90 I travelled twice a month to the Swat and Dir districts, north from Peshawar and close to the border with Afghanistan. I got to know the police quite well. One day, a police commandant invited me to his house. He had told me earlier that if any Pakistani was caught with alcoholic drinks, a hefty fine would have to be paid.

They might even have to go to jail, but in any case: the alcoholic beverages were confiscated. After my visit to the police commandant's house, I knew what happened to the confiscated drinks, because at one point he asked me what my favourite whiskey was. Apparently, he was convinced that all westerners drink whiskey.

I said that I could not name any brand. He invited me to his kitchen, opened his fridge and there I saw the largest collection of whiskey's I had ever seen in my life. Black label, red label and every other label: it was all there. A Dutch ambassador, I forgot which one, once told me that the Islamic world was slowly but steadily losing its credibility because of these hypocritical attitudes.

Many Muslims say one thing, but practice the opposite. Saudi princes travel to London or Paris to party for weeks on end with lots of alcohol and women. When they return to their native Saudi Arabia, they put on their traditional cloths and act the pious Muslims once again.

Anyway: after our return to Lahore, Sandy moved to another guesthouse. A few days later, the STOs arrived. For the very first time, the EU decided to combine LTO and STO teams. My STO team mate for the next ten days would be Ana Paula from Portugal, a very experienced observer.

Ana Paula was credited for many of the photographs in the EU Observer Handbook. In 2009, she would be my colleague LTO in Bolivia. And in 2011 she would be my Observer Coordinator in Nicaragua. Which goes to show—once again—that you should always be nice to your STOs, because one day they might become your superior.

So Roger went with the other STO, Larry from Canada. A funny thing happened, when we had to decide which car to take: ours, or the one in which the STOs had arrived. I told Roger: ,,Either you take our car and driver, in which case I want our interpreter, or you take our interpreter, in which case I want our car and driver. I need either our driver or our interpreter, because they are familiar with our three districts and the new arrivals are not."

This caused quite a stir, since both our interpreter and our driver wanted to continue working with me and not with Roger. Roger was not a bad guy, but he was extremely set in his ways. For Roger, the most important thing in the world was to be always on time.

When we were a little bit late for a meeting, he visibly started shaking. This was a bit weird, since Pakistanis arrive always one hour late at meetings. I have to say, though, that when it came to the writing of our Weekly Reports, Roger was much more relaxed than Hanna had been in Nigeria.

Roger would dictate, I did the typing. He checked it one last time and then we transmitted the WR to the Core Team. No stress there. In the end, Roger got our car and driver Amjad and I got our interpreter Moazzam. Amjad took me apart and said that he really preferred to work with me, but I told him that I could not reverse my deal with Roger.

Ana Paula and I had a good mission in the remote Sangla Hill ('Single Hill'). There were no hotels in the entire district, but Rudy, our Belgian liaison security expert, had visited the area and had talked to the bosses of the Huda Sugar Mill factory. They owned a guesthouse, which they used for visiting consultants and technicians. We were welcome to stay there.

While we were still in our guesthouse in Lahore, Ana Paula asked me how much we would have to pay for the sugar mill guesthouse. Since I did not want Roger to listen in on this, I told her in Portuguese that I believed it would be free of charge, since most probably they never charged their own consultants for staying in their guesthouse.

This turned out to be entirely true. Not only did we stay there one week without having to pay a penny, we also got all our meals free of charge. The guesthouse came with a cook. He prepared very nice meals for us and the two consultants who were also staying there.

They also showed us around the sugar mill, where small farmers arrived around the clock with their carts laden with sugarcane. They were mesmerized by Ana Paula, who—with her scarf and dark-rimmed glassed—looked like a twin sister of Benazir Bhutto.

I am not particularly fond of Pakistan, but I have to admit that Pakistani's are always hospitable. Wherever Roger, Ana Paula and I went, they offered us at least coffee or tea, but usually also soft drinks and something to eat: sweet cookies or even pieces of tasty chickens and enormous club sandwiches. My favourite country in the world is Bolivia. This is a bit strange, since Bolivians never offer anything to their guests, not even a glass of water.

When E-Day approached, all Pakistan's leading politicians left the country. It is the custom that the winner of the elections puts his opponents in jail, on corruption charges. It may take a year or longer to sort out these allegations, so it's wiser to await the election results in London or Dubai.

Ana Paula and I worked well together and E-Day went by without major incidents. As always, we spent a long night at the District Electoral Centre. The Huda Sugar Mills factory allowed us to use their fax machine, to transmit our E-Day forms to the Core Team.

A few days later, Roger and I ventured out yet again with our old team. Just like during the old days, a donkey cart was blocking the road and a policeman hit him with a long stick. „Roger: you should do something", I urged my partner. Amjad and Moazzam were grinning, but Roger didn't move and didn't say a word.

By now, apparently he had learned that indeed it is impossible to change the habits of 160 million Pakistanis. Since Sandy had travelled back home with the STOs, Robert had a new partner: Anne from the UK. She was of our age and very relaxed.

From Islamabad, Sandy called Roger and told him that she had received a 'Not Recommended' evaluation. This meant she would indeed be blacklisted by the EU for five years. „She probably deserved it", Roger confided to me. Then, as an afterthought, he added: „But still it's a pity. I really liked that girl."

A few days earlier, Ana Paula had told me that during her East Timor mission, Sandy had screamed at her partner. I never had problems with Sandy, but during the debriefings of our mission in Islamabad, one of the LTOs told me that Sandy and himself had been LTOs on the Lebanon mission, not long before our Pakistan mission.

During that Lebanon mission, she fell in love with a Lebanese security guard. She took this guy with her to the UK and married him. Shortly after the marriage, her Lebanese lover told her briskly that he never wanted to see her again. All he wanted was a UK passport. No wonder she was a bit screwed up, when she arrived in Pakistan.

We paid Amjad and Moazzam their last bonus and salary and debriefed them. What were their opinions about Roger and me? I expected both of them to be quite evasive, or diplomatic, but Moazzam said that he had found Roger a bit too strict at times. About me, he said that I was 'always cool'. A nice compliment. Amjad was even more critical of Roger.

Amjad said that Roger had reigned 'like a military commander' and that Roger didn't understand anything about the ways Pakistanis drove their cars. As I had done many times during this mission, I tried to break the tension by cracking a joke. I told Amjad that compared to the other LTOs, Roger would certainly be among the better ones. Which was actually true.

All of us travelled back to Islamabad in a convoy, but Robert sat with me in the back of our car, while Roger travelled with Anne. Out of the blue, Robert received a phone call from Brussels: why had he pushed the 'panic button'? Robert answered that he had not pushed anything, but then we realized that he was not in his own car.

We called Roger, who told us that the driver in Robert's car had accidentally pushed the panic button. Which proved, in any case, that the security measures were really working. In Islamabad, we stayed at the Crown Plaza hotel, with a clear view of the Faisal Mosque.

I received a good evaluation. The Core Team was very satisfied with Roger and me. Other teams had given them quite some problems. In fact, they gave me three 'very good' and the rest 'good'. In Venezuela, I obtained one 'very good' and in Nigeria two 'very good'. So I was improving, even though I vowed that I would never be an over-achiever.

When I handed my neatly numbered receipts of our petty cash over to the Finance Officer, Roger looked on with satisfaction. Out of the original 250,000 rupees, only 2,790 were left. Next, we handed all our mission stuff over to Olivier, the Logistics Officer. I handed him my bulletproof vest, together with the heavy tiles that—supposedly—defended the front and the back against AK-47 bullets. ,,I never used it", I told Olivier. ,,Thank God", he replied.

Two days before our departure from Pakistan, we were told that half of the LTOs had to stay on for another day. All of a sudden, the insurance company realized that it was a bit of risk to put all 48 of us in the same airplane. As EU-observers in Pakistan we were insured for nearly the same amount of money as war correspondents. Which is a lot of money.

The insurance company would go broke, if all of us would perish at the same time. The EU offered 300 euros plus a free night in the hotel for any LTO who was willing to stay one more day in Islamabad. I refused. After ten weeks, I had had enough of Pakistan. I just wanted to go home.

But Robert accepted the deal. He had a good reason for this. When we handed our remaining petty cash back to the mission's Finance Officer, the receipts showed that Robert had paid his interpreter twice for the same week. It was only a few hundred euros, but Robert was furious. He felt betrayed. Azam, his interpreter, was the twin-brother of Moazzam, our interpreter.

They seemed such nice, bright chaps. Of course, Azam knew that he had received too much money, but when Robert called him he denied any knowledge. Robert even wanted to travel back to Lahore, but I managed to talk him out of it. Eventually, Robert decided to take his loss and pay the amount out of his own pocket. As an observer, sometimes you have to swallow your pride.

The very last evening of the mission I received a call from Kees: 'Let's have a beer at the Marriott hotel'. With two other LTOs we took a taxi. Inside the Marriott hotel, one of the LTOs knew the way. He opened an unmarked door and led us down a series of stairs to the 'Rumours Cellar Bar'. There, hidden in the basement, you could order as much cold beer, gin or whiskey as you wanted.

Little did we know that half a year later a suicide terrorist would blow up a truck loaded with explosives near the entrance of that same Marriott hotel. The entire front of the hotel was blown away. An important lesson: the strict security rules that we hate so much are there for good reasons!

Apparently, the target had been president Asif Ali Zardari, who was supposed to have been at the Marriott at the time of the explosion. But he wasn't harmed. After the assassination of his wife, Benazir's party PPP won the sympathy vote. The Pakistani voters did not want to perpetuate president Musharraf's military rule. PPP and Nawaz Sharif's party PML-N agreed that Zardari would become president, since his son, Bilawal Bhutto Zardari, was too young.

It had been quite a mission. It was supposed to be a short mission, but turned out to be one of the longest. Security was always an issue. But in the end, it had been a good mission for me: good partner, good driver, good interpreter, good STO, good CT, good SP, good guesthouse, good Area of Operation.

I had earned a lot of money as well. But it had been a challenging mission. In fact, it would turn out to be the only mission after which I had a kind of burn-out: after I got back home, I picked up my work as a regional journalist, but I really had to force myself to do so.

Did I find a Goofy? Yes, I did. In the small supermarket in Lahore, near our guesthouse, where I bought my bread, cheese and orange juice. I noticed a green banner of nearly two by two meters. Goofy appeared on it, along with several other Disney figures. I was sure it was not for sale, but I asked anyway. Yes, I could buy it and at a very reasonable price as well.

Apart from that, a few weeks earlier, we passed a children's playground near the cricket stadium in Sheikhupura. A Goofy was painted on a sort of obelisk, about two meters high. I handed my small digital camera to our interpreter and asked him to make at least ten photographs with me next to this Goofy. They turned out quite nicely. I mailed one to my wife. She liked it. She allowed me to return home.

Chapter 8

BOLIVIA - COCHABAMBA - 2009

'The president grows coca leaves for the American cocaine market'

I was delighted to be able to go Bolivia as an LTO for the EU. My wife and I had lived in La Paz in 1986/87. I worked for the anti-drugs organization of the UN, while she ran the Dutch consulate. Bolivia is my favourite country in South America. In the whole world, in fact.

I played football with the boys of our UN office. We also made Andean folk music. Not because I was talented. The boys and their girl friends allowed me to play the third guitar and sing the fourth voice. Not too loudly. But who cares: I simply love the Bolivians.

As a twist of fate, Evo Morales, the president of Bolivia, had been chairman of the coca growers in the Chapare region of Cochabamba province. The first thing he did, after having been elected president, was to kick the American anti-drug agency DEA and also USAID out of the country.

Evo Morales wanted to be re-elected as president, but in order to achieve this, he had to change the Constitution. So he called for a referendum, a trick he had learned from his good friend and benefactor Hugo Chávez, president-for-live of Venezuela. Another clever trick he had learned from Chávez was to buy the votes of the poor people.

Chávez used his oil money not only for 'social projects', but also for direct payments to the poor in the form of *bonos*, welfare pay. In return, he expected the poor to vote for him. And since the poor people are the vast majority in Venezuela, this guaranteed that Chávez would always win the elections.

Evo Morales would love to do the same in Bolivia, but he had a little problem: Venezuela was the fifth biggest exporter of oil in the world, so Chávez had plenty of money to hand out as if he was Santa

Claus. Bolivia, on the other hand, is the poorest country in South America.

Bolivia possesses natural gas, but since it is a landlocked country, it has no means to ship it out. And it has no money to develop its own gas-based industry. It's two giant neighbours, Brazil and Argentina, are not keen to invest in Bolivia, with its volatile political scene.

Before you know it, the Bolivians might decide to nationalize your property. It has happened in the past. So the gas remains deep down in the earth and Morales had no money to hand out to the poor voters.

But there was his good friend Hugo Chávez yet again. Chávez felt himself rather isolated in Latin America, so he needed to appease his socialist friends. Chávez transfered hundreds of millions of dollars to not only Evo Morales, but also to Daniel Ortega in Nicaragua and Rafael Correa in Ecuador.

In return, Chávez expected his leftist friends to support him internationally, especially against the US. Ordinary Bolivians were well aware of the special relationship between the presidents of Venezuela and Bolivia. They called Chávez the 'big monkey' and Morales the 'small monkey'.

In spite of all of this, the EU decided to send an observation mission to Bolivia and I was happy that I could return to the country I loved so well. Before my departure from Holland I already knew that I was going to be deployed in Cochabamba, the third biggest city of Bolivia, that sits at a very pleasant altitude of 2.700 meters.

In Cochabamba, the temperature is about 27 degrees daytime and about 18 degrees nighttime. All year round. It doesn't get better than this: you don't need a heater and you don't need airconditioning.

In fact, Bolivia is a country with extreme climates: on the *altiplano*, the plateau at 4.000 meters altitude, it is freezing cold at night. The three lowlying Amazonian provinces are hot and humid. I was lucky to be based in Cochabamba, with its moderate temperatures.

And my partner was to be a 63-year old woman from Denmark: Susanne. She had been in doubt about her departure to Bolivia, since only three weeks previously her mother had passed away.

The airport of La Paz sits at 4.000 meters altitude, therefore airplanes cannot take off when they are fully loaded with passengers and fuel. This means that there are no direct flights between La Paz and Europe. I flew first with KLM to Lima in Peru, where I met several other LTOs, among them was Ana Paula from Portugal, who had been my STO in Pakistan.

We had to spend half a day at Lima airport. Luckily, the best *ceviche* in the world is served in Peru and there are several restaurants at the airport. Finally, around midnight, we departed for La Paz. We arrived at 02.00 hours and I immediately realized that now we were at 4.000 meters altitude: I felt a bit dizzy. My legs seemed to be weak.

To make matters worse, I was selected by the customs people for a thorough inspection of my suitcase. By the time I arrived in hotel Europa (an appropriate name to house an EU mission) it was 04.00 hours. It was warm in my room and I had a jetlag. I could not sleep any more.

We had to wait for other observers, so the next day the Core Team organized a touristic trip to the Valley of the Moon. It's a spectaculair natural formation, but I had been there several times already, so I informed them that I preferred to take a nap instead. I also went for a walk in the city center. Nothing had changed since 1986: just like then, the main street was blocked by a demonstration.

To demonstrate is the national sport in Bolivia. This time, the taxi drivers were on strike for higher payments. Next week it could be the miners. Or school teachers. Or nurses. There is always some group on strike and they always block the main street in La Paz. When you live there, you get used to it.

The briefings went on for two full days. Mostly in Spanish, so it was quite tyring for me. On top of that, I was affected by the altitude and still suffering from a jetlag. As always, I realized that I had to persevere, to get through the bloody briefings.

On the second day I went out with some observers to have lunch. When I returned to hotel Europa, I was approached on the pavewalk by the political expert of the Core Team. His name was Par and he was Swedish.

I had a feeling that I had seen him before, but I could not remember where that had been. He told me that he had the same feeling. I asked him if he had been on a mission in Venezuela, Nigeria or Pakistan, but he said 'No'. Then he asked: ,,Were you an observer in Guatemala, in 1995? And did your father grow flowers?"

It dawned on me that Par had been my partner in Guatemala, thirteen years previously. I remembered that we had been quarreling a few times, but he assured me that he had fond memories of that mission.

The best moment of every mission is when I step in the back of a Toyota Land Cruiser and we take off for our duty station. La Paz sits in a valley at 3.600 meters and it takes at least half an hour to wind up to the altiplano, at 4.000 meters.

We travelled with three other teams. We soon lost track of the Oruro and Potosí teams, so we continued with the other Cochabamba team, comprised of my ex-STO, Ana Paula from Portugal, and Francesco from Italy.

It took us six hours to get there. Once in Cochabamba, a problem became apparent: our vehicles had been rented from a company in La Paz and therefore our drivers also came from La Paz. They had never visited Cochabamba. In fact, I knew Cochabamba better than they did, because I had been there a few days in 1986. And I had a map.

Rafael, our driver, was a typical mountain driver. As we would find out, he was very good on mountainous roads, but quite bad in a strange city. Our car was not equipped with a GPS and Bolivians are not used to reading maps. So for the next four weeks I sat down on the other front seat, with a map of the city on my lap. That worked quite well.

A nice little guesthouse called Hotel Anteus had been booked for our two teams. Usually, the Core Team decides where each team is supposed to work, and usually they assign one team to the city and the other team to the rest of the province, but in this case they had told us that we could decide it amongst ourselves.

So Susanne and I sat down in the garden with Ana Paula and Francesco. We decided that each team would cover half of the province and half of the city. Ana Paula was really keen on covering the low-lying

Chapare region, since it was expected that Evo Morales would vote there. This would attract the attention of the Core Team.

Ana Paula wanted desperately to become a member of a Core Team, so she worked hard, in order to obtain a good evaluation. Apart from being the president of Bolivia, Evo Morales was also still the chairman of the coca growers in Chapare. I took Susanne apart and told her that I knew that it was really hot in the Chapare region, with lots of mosquitoes, and that I preferred the cooler mountainous regions. Luckily, Susanne agreed.

We made regular trips to outlying areas, where Rafael, our driver, felt at home. He was an established driver on the small, curving and sometimes slippery dirt roads. One day we had been driving for about four hours, when we found ourselves blocked by a fastflowing river. We were only a few hundred meters from the town of Tapacarí at the other side. We could clearly see the town, but we could not get there.

Or maybe we could, for we saw another car traverse the stream ahead of us. We decided not to take the risk: if the waters would rise just a little bit more, there was a real possibility that the we could not return. Then we would be stuck in that little town, for God knows how long. We decided to return to the city of Cochabamba. We lost an entire day. As an observer, sometimes, you just have to swallow your pride and accept your loss.

Since in the countryside many indigenous people hardly speak Spanish, we decided to employ an interpreter. Someone recommended Elizabeth, a school teacher. She was a young indigenous woman who lived in the outskirts of the city, but spoke fluent Quechua.

Her father worked part of the year in the coca fields of the Chapare region. We soon realized that we did not really need her, since there were always young boys and girls around, who were willing to translate for us and did a better job than Elizabeth.

We also found out that our interpreter had never visited the city center: she sat in the front seat of our car, to direct Rafael through the city center, but she only knew one road: the road that led straight through the central market.

After we got stuck for the third time in the busy market area, I decided to take matters into my own hands. I sat down in the front seat and directed Rafael to the major roads around the city, where there were no traffic jams.

One morning we drove to her house to pick her up, but instead of her an unknown man attempted to step into our car. He said that he took her place. We couldn't believe it. Who was this guy?

We sent him away, of course. After all this, we had enough of our useless interpreter. The day after E-Day, Susanne and I decided to pay her, but not give her a recommendation.

Susanne and I interviewed people every day. We interviewed archbishop Salari, even though it was not very useful for our reports. Not only did he not want to talk about politics; we found out that he was not even a Bolivian. He was an Italian, who had spent 35 of his 70 years in Bolivia. A nice guy, but not of any use for our mission.

One day we visited a remote mountainous village called Apilla Pampa, where we simply asked a young boy to translate for us. After having lived in a big city like Cochabamba, we had to get used to the quietness and slow pace of the countryside. Interestingly, the village had been electrified very recently. Several taps for drinking water as well as wash basins had been constructed.

Presents from Evo. No wonder they were all going to vote 'Yes'. They had been told that if they voted 'No', they risked losing everything yet again. Union leaders would check that indeed everyone had voted 'Yes'. Evo used the same persuasive 'carrot and stick' tactics that Hugo Chávez used in Venezuela. Some people call it 'Controlled Democracy'.

We stopped over at a small community called Sipe-Sipe. The community leader explained that, just a few days earlier, there had been a community meeting, where it was decided that everybody would vote 'Yes'. This didn't sound very democratic to me, but he explained that it was a long-standing tradition.

It was called *voto comunitario:* community vote. According to the man, all the villagers had agreed to this. I asked him how they could control if the people really voted 'Yes', since each individual voter would vote in the secrecy of the polling booth. „They always comply", he answered simply.

One trip took us to the town of Capinota, about two hours from Cochabamba. After having interviewed the caretaker mayor, the police chief and several party representatives, we had a little time left. Since we always wear our visibility jackets, we are very visible. At the central square, a man approached us.

He looked around him, to make sure no one was listening in. Then he told us that all the people in the surrounding villages were forced to vote 'Yes' by their unions. Anyone who voted 'No' would be punished: either they had to pay a fine, or they would lose the land they rented. ,,The *campesinos* are not allowed to think for themselves," the man added.

Before we returned to our car, I told Susanne that I had something to do. The best Andean music is made by a group called the Kjarkas. They are the Beatles of the Andean music. They tour all over the world. Most of the Kjarkas belonged to one family: the Hermosas. Originally, the Hermosa family came from Oruro province. They spoke Quechua as well as Spanish.

They moved to Capinota after the father got a job there, as a school teacher. I noted that the little theater in the center of Capinota was named after Ulysses Hermosa, one of the founding members of the Kjarkas, who had died from cancer at the tender age of only 39.

He wrote the song *Llorando se fue*, which a few years later became a world-wide hit under a different name: *Lambada*. Some Brazilians had translated the Spanish into Portuguese and added some musical instruments.

The Kjarkas took the Brazilians to court, after which a judge ruled that a fair portion of the money of *Lambada* should be paid to the Kjarkas. The amount was never made public, but apparently it ran into the millions of dollars.

I asked around in Capinota and of course everybody knew the house of the Hermosa family. It stood sadly abandoned, just half a block from the central square. The family members now lived in expensive houses in Cochabamba city.

When I returned to the car, Susanne asked me where I had been. I told her that I had been on a pilgrimmage to the house of the Kjarkas. She replied that she had never heard of them.

Than Rafael also returned to the car. Susanne asked him where he had been. ,,I went to see the house of the Kjarkas", he told her. On the way back, the Kjarkas song 'Munasquechai' was played on the radio. I told Rafael to turn up the volume and he and I sang along with the Kjarkas, partly in Quechua and partly in Spanish. Susanne was astounded.

When I lived in Bolivia in 1986/87, there were no supermarkets, only small shops. Now, there were several supermarkets in Cochabamba, which made shopping a lot easier for us, since we were always short on time. Our guesthouse was situated near quite a number of restaurants, so we could go there on foot.

Most evenings we went out eating with three observers: Susanne, Francesco and myself. Francesco preferred the 'O Sole Mío' restaurant, owned by Italians and serving great pizzas, but Susanne and I wanted to explore other restaurants as well.

For some reason, Ana Paula hardly ever joined us. She worked very hard, in order to obtain a 'highly recommended' evaluation, which comes in handy when you aspire a position in a Core Team.

It came as a surprise to me that she was so ambitious. Just one year earlier, in Pakistan, as my STO, she had been very relaxed. Apparently, she was not very enthusiastic about her partner, Francesco. I thought he was a nice guy.

One day, the ruling party held a political rally in the city center. On our way to the rally, Susanne and I noted that life went on as usual in the streets of the city. All the shops were open, traffic was normal. But at the major crossroads a huge crowd had gathered. Much to our surprise, they were all *indigenas* from the countryside.

It's odd to see 50.000 traditionally dressed countryside people in the heart of a modern city. They looked out of place. A bit further down the road we spotted the dozens of buses and trucks, that had been used to transport them to town. We later learned that they had been forced to join the rally by their union leaders. If a *campesino* did not show up, he had to pay a fine of 200 bolivianos.

A huge stage had been erected on top of a flyover. The local and national dignitaries of the ruling party were all sitting there. Since Susanne and I were wearing our observer jackets and our accreditations, we were allowed to stand just a few meters from where Evo Morales held his speech.

He was a good speecher. He knew exactly what his followers wanted to hear. Two hours later, we observed a rally by the opposition parties in the centre of Cochabamba. Only about 1.500 people were there, mostly young or elderly middle class ladies from the city.

One day we got a flat tyre. Luckily, we were in the town of Mizque, where we found a local garage. They fixed it, but still: we had lost a few hours. Since observers are not allowed to drive in the dark, we had to call our security expert to take a decision: either stay here, in a horrible hotel, or risk returning to Cochabamba.

It would only be an hour or so in the dark and we promised to stay in touch with our security expert. Of course it took longer than one hour. In the mountains, even when you can clearly see the lights of a city, it still takes a long time to reach it because of the curved roads. But we made it back.

Susanne and I usually had lunch in *La Villa,* just one hundred meters from our hotel across the road. It had a very pleasant inner courtyard. The owner was half Bolivian, half American. He had lived in the States for many years. He was always happy to see us. He usually came over to our table for a chat. Once he was closed, but he allowed us to enter anyway, as his only customers. He served a great *ceviche.*

I have to say that the writing of our Weekly Reports went smooth. Susanne dictated, while she went through her notes. I did all the typing. She would check everything one last time, before mailing it to the Core Team. No friction there, apart from the fact that Susanne was a bit chaotic at times.

Interestingly, Francesco handed us a copy of his WR, which was probably written mostly by Ana Paula. It was a good WR, more detailed than ours, but ours contained more analyses. I wonder which WR the Core Team would like best.

One morning, all four LTOs were invited to participate in the Breakfast TV Show of the regional Canal 11. A very basic, but effective studio. The show was broadcast live. Even the commercials were live: the camera simply switched to a lady standing a few meters away from us, next to a washing machine, that she heralded as the best washing machine in the world.

When I answered one question a bit too enthusiastic, Ana Paula kicked my leg. Most LTOs get nervous when dealing with the media. Another morning, Susanne and I were interviewed at length by the weekly magazine Opinión. The article would be published on E-Day. We visited Opinión and they allowed us to review the text.

It was better than I had gotten used to in developing countries. We suggested just a few corrections to them. When the magazine was on sale, our article looked great. Three pages with several photographs of Susanne and me! I bought five copies of the magazine, for my family and friends back home.

We were informed that Par, the Core Team's political expert who had been my partner in Guatemala, would visit Cochabamba. We had to prepare a programme of visits for him. Both Cochabamba teams would accompany him, in two cars. For some reason, Susanne insisted that Rafael, our driver, should take the lead.

,,We have been driving through Cochabamba for several weeks", she said. ,,He should know his way around, by now." As I feared, this was a disastrous decision. Rafael got lost completely in the small one-way streets. I braved Susanne's wrath and retook my place on the front seat. With the city map on my lap, I directed Rafael in the right direction.

For some reason, probably lack of funds, the EU had decided not to recruit STOs for our mission. But some teams would be reinforced by locally recruited STOs: Europeans who work at European embassies. Cochabamba is a popular destination for Europeans who live in La Paz, since it has a very pleasant climate.

We were informed that two employees of the French embassy would join us in Cochabamba, for only three days. They would arrive on Saturday and depart on Monday. Their only full day in Cochabamba would be E-day. I picked up Sebastién and Mathilde at the airport.

They were young and friendly. Maybe I should revise my opinion of the French: not all of them are horrible. 33-year old Sebastién had been living in La Paz for quite some time, but 21-year old Mathilde had just arrived in the country. For both of them, it would be their very first observation mission.

LTOs like to work with embassy people, because they live in the country, they speak the language, they are well aware of the culture and they volunteered to do observation work. Therefore, they are motivated. We only have to brief them on our work methodology, the E-Day communications and how to fill in the forms that we use on E-Day.

On the other hand, LTOs don't like to work with Europarlementarians. They do not know the culture, they do not speak the language and, since they are elected, they cannot be controlled by our observation mission. Quite often, some of them appear on national television even before voting has finished, to declare that they did not observe any problems.

Europarlementarians are totally independent from our mission, but still, we are supposed to assist them in any way they require. It has to be explained here that the head of our mission, the Chief Observer, is also a member of the European Parliament, but the Chief Observer is usually duly committed to our mission.

Anyway, at a rather late stage Susanne and I were informed that we would be blessed with an observation team from the European Parliament. The other Cochabamba LTO team, Ana Paula and Francesco, were spared the ordeal, since they would spend two nights at the rather distant Chapare region.

So on the evening before E-Day, Susanne and I set out for the restaurant where we would brief the Europarlementarians. While walking on the pavement, Susanne instructed me not get into an argument with them.

,,How do you know beforehand that I am going to have an argument?" I asked her. ,,Because I know you", she replied simply. I was amazed, because we had been working together for just a few weeks. I had never met her before our mission. How did she get to know me so intimately in such a short period of time?

Unfortunately, she proved to be right. I couldn't stop myself. The two Europarlementarians were men in their late forties or early fifties. Both were accompanied by assistant-secretaries. The Rumanian guy also had an interpreter with him, since he did not speak one word of Spanish.

The Italian guy turned out to be a communist. I wondered what a communist was doing in Bolivia as an election observer, since communism, by definition, is anti-democratic. Communism is dictatorship, as I had experienced first-hand during my three years in Mozambique.

They were not too bad, actually, but at some point during the conversation, the Italian guy mentioned that the coca produced in the Chapare region was for domestic use in Bolivia.

I explained to him that the coca from the Yungas region, near La Paz, was for domestic use and that all the coca from the Chapare region was used for producing cocaine, to be exported to the US. The Italian said that Evo Morales had told him personally that the coca from Chapare was for domestic use.

I explained to him that I had worked in Bolivia for the anti-drugs organisation of the UN and that I knew for a fact that the coca from Chapare was not suitable for chewing, due to the fact that Chapare was situated at a much lower altitude than Yungas.

Because of this, it is considerably warmer in the Chapare and the leaves are thicker and much more bitter, making them unsuitable for chewing. ,,So you call the president of Bolivia a liar?" the Italian asked me. Next to me, Susanne stiffened on her chair.

,,I am just explaining the situation to you", I replied diplomatically. And I added: ,,On top of all this, the leaves from Chapare contain six times more cocaine than the leaves from Yungas. Which makes the Chapare leaves more profitable, when turned into cocaine." When we walked back to our hotel, Susanne did not utter a word.

We thought that everything would be fine on E-Day, but we soon found out that there was a little problem. Susanne and I got up at 04.30 hours and drove yet again to Apilla Pampa, the remote town in the mountains, where it was cold and there was no signal for our mobile phones.

We had our satphone, of course, but it is very expensive to use. I always carry it with me, but I consider it to be our back-up system, in case of an emergency. Up on that mountain, for the first and only time, tensions between Susanne and me erupted.

During our time in Cochabamba, it had irritated me quite a few times that Susanne was always telling everyone what they did wrong. Now she asked me if I had charged my mobile phone. I said: ,,Yes, of course. I'm a professional."

Moments later, Susanne handed her own mobile phone to Elizabeth in the front of the car and asked her to charge her phone! Elizabeth searched for a cable. Finally, she found one, but it didn't fit, since it turned out te be the charging cable for our BGAN. This was my chance to get back at Susanne. I told her: ,,I have the right cable."

,,Here in the car?" she asked me.

,,Yes, in my mission bag. I'm a professional."

,,Then give it to me," she said.

,,But you just told me that you had charged your phone."

She gave me a nasty look and said: ,,My phone is charged."

,,Then you don't need my cable", I concluded.

,,It's charged, but it will soon turn into the red", she replied. Angrily, she added: ,,You just want to show your power, by keeping that cable to yourself." That was too much for me. I decided to tell her the truth.

,,You are always telling people what they do wrong. You tell Francesco where to keep his hands when he's eating. You tell Rafael how his own dashboard works. You tell the owner of *La Villa* how to cook his own rice. You tell me not to chew on my inner cheeks. But as it now turns out, you're not so perfect yourself."

This was the only fight we had during our mission. After having observed the opening of a polling station in Apilla Pampa, we drove back to the main road, where we had a signal. I immediately received a call from our Core Team: ,,Jos, call your LSTOs. They don't know how to fill in the forms."

It has to be said that some questions on those forms are a bit ambiguous, but experienced observers have filled in so many forms over the years that they don't notice it anymore. Anyway: after a brief discussion, our two young, enthousiastic French embassy employees promised to fill in the forms the way we wanted it and not the way they wanted it.

For the rest, E-Day went fine. Traffic is prohibited in Bolivia on E-Day, but as observers we had received a special permit. This had the advantage that the roads were empty. We moved fast. And we did not hear anything anymore from our two Europarlementarians.

The only problem was that we, as LTOs, had to copy the E-Day forms of our LSTO team and we had to transmit their and our forms to the Core Team by phone. Since Susanne was a bit chaotic, I volunteered to do it. But there was a problem: when the windows of our car were open, I couldn't understand a word of what Ximena, at the Core Team, was saying on the phone, since people and traffic were making noise all the time.

There was no shade in sight, but I decided to close the windows anyway. I was sweating profusely and my throat went raw, after reading 9 forms with 68 questions each to Ximena. Later that evening I dictated 7 more forms to her, but this time from the coolness and quietness of my room at Hotel Anteus. That went smoothly.

Susanne and I observed the closing in a school with dozens of polling stations. No problems there. It was not a complicated election, as people could only vote 'Yes' or 'No'. As expected, the 'Yes' vote won and the new constitution was accepted with 61,43 percent of the vote, thus allowing Evo Morales to be re-elected as president later that same year.

The last couple of days in Cochabamba, Susanne and I took turns in observing the counting at the provincial level. It went smooth. It took a few days, before all the results had come in, but luckily it was decided to close the provincial office for the night, since everybody really needed a rest.

The provincial electoral office turned out to be one of the best organized I had ever encountered. I didn't know it then, but ten months later I would encounter the worst provincial electoral office in the province of Oruro. It's very simple: when you have good people, you have a good organization. When you have horrible people, you have a horrible organization.

When the two teams finally returned to La Paz, we asked the other team to take the lead, since after more than four weeks our driver Rafael was still not familiar with the city of Cochabamba. It turned out that the other driver was not much better: instead of taking us straight onto the main road to La Paz, he drove across the bridge into the city center.

We thought that the other team wanted to say goodbye to some people there, but the car never stopped. Yet again we lost half an hour because of a driver's incapability to familiarize himself with a new situation.

During a coffee break along the road, I suggested to pay a short visit to Tihuanacu, which I had visited several times in 1986/87. Some observers are totally not interested in archeological sites, but in this case all four of us agreed.

Tihuanacu is situated near Lake Titicaca, at about one hour drive from the main road to La Paz. There is not much to see there, but it's a magical site, predating the Inca empire.

Back in hotel Europa in La Paz, Susanne was hit by altitude sickness, which was a bit strange, since we had been living in Cochabamba at 2.700 meters, only 900 meters lower than La Paz. Anyway, she lay down flat on top of my bed, with a terrible headache, but still provided her input to our Final Report while I did the typing.

She wanted me to look for some medicine in our medical kit, which I really hate to do, because these kits are packed so full that once you open them, you can't close them anymore. So it happened.

I cannot remember having used anything of any medical kit on any mission, but apparently some observers use all kinds of medicines. The medical kits are donated to local hospitals at the end of each mission.

The next day, the debriefings took only a few hours. I am usually not in the mood anymore to discuss things that have passed anyway, but when the *voto comunitario* was discussed, I couldn't keep my mouth shut. I said that it didn't seem to be very democratic, when people are told what to vote.

Other LTOs argued that it was the indigenous, traditional system of Bolivia. ,,There was no democracy in the old days," I insisted. ,,It was a feudal system. Is that what we still want today? Or are we here to promote democracy?"

As always, my evaluation said 'recommended for future missions'. It is good enough for me. I'm not an overachiever. I like to do a good job, but I am not going to work my ass off to obtain a 'highly recommended'.

As a matter of fact, I did not want to be a member of a Core Team in any case. I was praised when I handed over the receipts of our petty cash. ,,He is well organized", Susanne told the Finance Officer.

We had some time to spare, so Susanne and I visited the tourist areas of La Paz, to buy souvenirs. It is always a good sign when my partner still wants my company. It means the relationship—and therefore the mission—had been good. We were also invited for lunch by Sebastién and Mathilde, our newly found French embassy friends.

They told us that they had really enjoyed their very first observation mission. Luckily, we could move around on foot through the center of La Paz. Yet again, traffic at the main street was completely blocked by demonstrators.

The return trip to Lima went smooth, but I had to wait ten hours at Lima airport for the direct flight with KLM back to Amsterdam. While eating a great *ceviche*, I listened to the stories of other observers. One team had been robbed of their petty cash in their own hotel. They had forgotten to close a suitcase.

Another team had fallen in love with one another. Tonje, the young Norwegian LTO, was visibly shaken by the separation from her Spanish lover Herminio. Now she had to go home, to face her sweetheart there. Life can be complicated, sometimes. That's why I always prefer not to become too intimate with my partner.

Tonje started crying when she told us about it. Her boy friend, back home, would not be happy when she told him the truth. It is always helpful to pay attention to the experiences of other observers. I decided there and then to buy a more expensive suitcase, in order to protect my valuables better. And I decided never to fall in love with my partner. Better to stay out of trouble.

Did I find a Goofy in Cochabamba? Yes, I did. Two in fact: a Goofy bag and a Goofy pant for children. I also spotted a painted

Goofy at the entrance of a kindergarten. I asked our driver to take a photograph of me, with my arms spread out, under the painted Goofy. I mailed it to my wife. She liked it. I was allowed to return home.

Chapter 9

BOLIVIA - ORURO - 2009

'Bolivia is a great country that lost all its wars'

I received an invitation from the Dutch Ministry of Foreign Affairs to go to Bolivia again, in the same year 2009. Presidential elections were scheduled to be held on 6 December, along with parliamentary elections and – rather surprisingly – elections for traditional leaders. This seemed a bit weird to me, since there was no democracy in the good old days. It was a feudal system.

I gratefully accepted the invitation to work in my beloved Bolivia yet again. This time, contrary to the first Bolivia mission, I also received an invitation for a briefing at the ministry in The Hague. I found out that I was not the only Dutch LTO.

The other one was Kees, a very experienced observer in his early sixties. Curiously, his wife Cynthia was with him. She was selected as the only Dutch STO for the mission. Kees hoped that she would be his STO.

The briefing went well. The ministry's country expert quickly realized that the three of us had lived in Bolivia and that, in fact, we knew more about the country than he did. When the three of us walked back to the train station, a strange thing happened: out of the blue, Cynthia asked me if I recognized her.

I looked at her in astonishment. I absolutely could not remember having seen her before, anywhere in the world. Then she said: ,,Did you not go to Guatemala as an observer, in 1995?" I said yes, but still I could not remember her. She calmly added: ,,Do you remember Liesbeth, who was always wearing colourful long dresses? And do you remember that young guy from the ministry?"

It dawned on me that indeed we had been in Guatemala with five Dutch observers and that Cynthia had been one of us. I tried to save face by explaining that I had done two missions to Guatemala, another one in 1996, and that I also could not remember my colleagues from that second mission. I have a bad memory for faces.

Kees, her husband, tried to smoothen the awkward situation by asking me which province I preferred in Bolivia. I replied: ,,Any province will be fine for me, except Oruro, since there is nothing of interest there." Just one day later, we received the deployment plan by email. Of course, they were sending me to Oruro.

When Kees and I boarded an airplane, it was not to Bolivia, but to Spain. The Service Provider had organized part of our briefings at the outskirts of Madrid, for efficiency reasons. At least, that is what they told us. In reality, we would be briefed double, since the briefings in La Paz, a few days later, were exactly the same as always.

The real reason why we had to spend two nights in Madrid was that we were all together to sign our contracts while we were still in Europe. Otherwise, a representative of the Service Provider would have had to travel all the way to La Paz, with the contracts.

In the airplane, Kees told me that he and his wife had laughed their heads off, when they read that I would be living in Oruro for seven weeks. ,,But you are lucky with your partner", he added. And he was right. My partner was called Pedro. He had been born in Colombia but was now married to a Scottish woman.

Pedro had lived in Glasgow for nine years and he possessed a UK passport. His English was still very basic, though. The first thing Pedro asked me was if I my English was good. I told him that my English was the best of all the LTOs. He looked relieved.

To my astonishment, he called his wife on his mobile phone, to tell her that my English was good. Later, I would learn the reason for Pedro's curious phone call. During the first mission of 2009, when I had been deployed in Cochabamba, he had been deployed in Oruro and his partner had been Sandor, an amiable but talkative elderly man from Hungary.

Sandor smoked three packets of cigarettes per day and had lived in Spanish speaking countries for many years as a diplomat. All of this was not the problem. The problem was that neither Pedro nor Sandor were able to write proper English.

A few weeks later Pedro showed me their first Weekly Report: indeed, it was badly written. In fact, it had been so bad, that the Core Team had told them to write all future reports in Spanish, in spite of the fact that English was the official reporting language. As a result, at the end of the mission, both of them received quite negative evaluations.

With me as his partner, Pedro did not have to worry about the reporting. I would do all the typing in English. Little did we know that at the end of the mission we would both receive a 'highly recommended' evaluation, because apart from his English he was a very good observer.

The briefings in Madrid were boring. Pedro fell asleep, several times. I had to hit him with my elbow, because the Core Team might make a note of it. To my dismay, I noticed a huge crack in my old suitcase. I should have purchased a new one.

When I called my wife, she suggested me to buy tape. Luckily, they gave us a few hours off and luckily I found a Carrefour supermarket, with lots of tape. To be on the safe side, I taped the inside as well as the outside of my suitcase.

The second evening all LTOs were transported to the nearby town of Alcalá de Henares. I had never heard of it, but I learned that it was the birthplace of Cervantes, author of Don Quichote, the first modern novel ever to be written. A statue of Don Quichote and Sancho Panza stands prominently in front of Cervantes' house.

More importantly for the history of the world, in my opinion, Columbus met Isabel and Ferdinand, *Los Reyes Católicos,* for the very first time in Alcalá de Henares, which is a very pleasant medieval town. Local volunteers re-enacted scenes of Don Quichote for us at various locations. Columbus was not re-enacted.

All LTOs boarded a plane the next morning. I spotted a machine that wrapped your entire suitcase in thick layers of plastic, for just 6 euros. That solved the problems with my torn suitcase. But then, Aerosur, the airline, had a surprise in store for me. On KLM flights, you are allowed to carry 23 kilos in your suitcase and 10 kilos in your hand luggage.

Aerosur did it differently: a maximum of 30 kilos in your suitcase, and only 6 kilos in your hand luggage. My hand luggage was 9 kilos, therefore I was not allowed to take my bag with me. I took out my laptop, my contract and all important items and put them in a plastic bag.

I sealed my hand luggage bag with two small locks and handed it over to the airline staff, expecting never to see it again. All around me, entire Bolivian families were carrying three or four bags each. They were not penalized. So much for equal rights.

After a delay of nearly half a day, the plane took us first to Tenerife on the Canary Islands and then to Santa Cruz de la Sierra, the second city of Bolivia, situated at sea level in the hot and humid Chaco plains.

We should have spent the night there, but because of the delay we had only a few hours left in the hotel. I decided not to fall asleep. I had left my alarm clock in my bag, which was still in the plane. I was afraid I would miss the bus to the airport. Instead of sleeping, I took a shower.

Early the next morning, while it was still dark, we boarded the plane to La Paz. For the second time that year I arrived at 4.000 meters altitude. And for the second time it hit me hard: my legs were wobbly yet again, also because of the sleepless night.

But my suitcase arrived. So did my bag! I couldn't be happier. I decided to buy a new suitcase once I was back in Holland. The most expensive and most secure suitcase I could lay my hands on. At the parking lot of the airport I was greeted by Rafael, who had been my driver in Cochabamba.

Rafael was happy to see me. ,,Is Susanne also coming?" he asked. I said 'No'. Then he asked if he would be working with me again. I replied that that was not in my hands. A few days later I learned that Rafael would be working in La Paz, as a driver for the Core Team.

The briefings at the Hotel Europa in La Paz were largely a repetition of the briefings in Madrid. When leaving an elevator, I bumped into Marta from Portugal, whom I had met during the course for Legal/Election Experts in Brussels, just a few months earlier.

Now she was the Election Expert of our EU EOM in Bolivia, a prestigious position. The Election Expert is widely regarded as being the number three of an EU EOM: after the Chief Observer and the Deputy Chief Observer.

So Marta was now a Core Team member, while I remained a plain and simple LTO. Was I jealous? You bet I was, even though I always said that I never wanted to be a member of a Core Team. Which is the truth. I am a field boy.

I don't want to be locked up in a hotel for eight weeks with a bunch of over-achievers, most of whom are not very likable. There's no escape to the relentless group pressure. Still, I was a bit jealous. Little did I know that Marta would be my much appreciated LTO partner in Mozambique in 2014.

During that mission, she confided to me that she had faced a hard time in the CT in Bolivia. Once, she had made a little mistake in her Spanish writings. She was scolded for it in front of the entire group. She confirmed what I already knew: being a member of a CT is prestigious and it pays better, but being an LTO is less stressful and much more fun.

During the briefings my wife informed me that, sadly, our dog Bep had been put to sleep by the veterinary. Bep was a crossbreed Labrador/Flat coated Retriever and she had been born in our house in 1997. She died of old age, but still it amazed me how the death of a dog could affect me so much. I decided not to tell anyone, for fear that I would start crying. I'm a softy, really.

After three days, I was happy that Pedro and I could step into our car and head off for Oruro. It takes only three hours to get there and since Pedro had been employed there in January, he guided Umberto, our driver, straight to the Hotel Gran Sucre in the centre of the city.

Pedro had already called them, to ask if he could stay in the same room as in January. They put me in a suite, at first, probably thinking that a rich European could easily afford it. Then they offered me an isolated room at the very back of the hotel, far away from the noisy elevator. Pedro negotiated the room rates down for both us: I had to pay only 24 dollars a day and the buffet breakfast was included.

We had the afternoon to ourselves, so we walked to the central square, just three blocks from our hotel. I noted that Oruro was not as ugly as I remembered it. In fact, it looked quite nice, with several interesting colonial buildings. And preparations were underway for the most important event of the year: carnival. Oruro is the carnival capital of Bolivia.

We joined the spectators and for four hours we admired dozens of music and dance groups parading through the streets. They had come from all over Bolivia, but the best groups came from Oruro. That evening, I Skyped with my wife for the first time.

I had finally decided to buy a private laptop. There was no Wi-Fi in the hotel, so I had to go down to the lobby, where I could plug my cable into the wall. A bit cumbersome, but it worked and it was free of charge!

The next days we were very busy interviewing all the usual suspects for our Weekly Reports: representatives of the Regional Election Commission, political parties, the media, human rights organizations. I was a bit worried about my Spanish, since Pedro was a native Spanish speaker, but it was not a problem.

Spanish people speak a rather sophisticated Spanish, with a real Spanish accent, but Pedro was a Colombian, thank God. Since I had lived in Bolivia for a year, sometimes I even used local phrases, which the locals found very amusing. In Bolivia, everybody says '*no mas*' at the end of nearly every sentence. I did the same.

And when I told them that in 1986 I had played Andean music with the Bolivian colleagues of my UN office, they liked me even better. Even so, I always remained a distant European, while Pedro was sometimes referred to as 'our South American brother'.

We visited La Patria newspaper. I have been working as a local journalist in my home region in The Netherlands, but I had actually graduated as an economist. Since every year about fifty journalists get killed in Third World countries, I never introduced myself as a journalist, but always as an economist.

At one point I was asking the editor of La Patria some rather journalistic questions, that somehow caught his attention. He was a bright fellow, for he asked me, only half in jest: ,,Are you sure that you're not a journalist?" A few days later Pedro and I featured in an article, with photograph, in La Patria. Luckily, the Core Team was happy with it.

Pedro was especially interested in traditional power structures, so we also visited a number of indigenous organizations, of which there were quite a lot in the countryside of Oruro province. We realized that the Core Team would be especially interested in this, since the role of traditional power structures had become more manifest after the new constitution had been approved.

Pedro was very good at this. We used an entire day to write our Weekly Report. Pedro typed his observations in Spanish in his room. Every half hour he would come to my room to hand me his printed notes. I translated it into English on my private laptop.

I also summarized everything, since Pedro not only talked too much, he also wrote too much. We worked together very well. After our WR1 Pedro told me: „We are going to work like this for the rest of the mission."

The city centre of Oruro is surprisingly small. We could get nearly anywhere on foot, so in the evenings we did not need our driver to go a restaurant. I knew that some observers were vegetarians, but I had never had a partner who was a vegetarian.

Pedro was not a vegetarian out of conviction, though. Before he met his Scottish wife, she had lived in India for a year. There, she had become a vegetarian. So he became a vegetarian too.

Now Pedro, his wife and their twin daughters, who were nine years old at the time, were all vegetarians. The problem was: Pedro knew of only one vegetarian restaurant in the entire city of Oruro. This was an Indian restaurant, called Govinda. The first week we went there every day for lunch.

I love Indian food and I don't need to eat meat every day, so that restaurant would have been fine for me, except for one problem: the Indian restaurant was always crowded and unbelievably noisy. Even when Pedro and I sat opposite one another, I could not understand a word he was saying.

Then, thank God, we found out that there was another vegetarian restaurant called *Vida Sana,* meaning 'Healthy Living'. It was situated even closer to our hotel, with great food and little noise.

The owners were a young, cheerful couple, who were vegetarians out of conviction. They served freshly cooked different meals every day. Very nice food and very cheap. I might become a vegetarian one day.

In fact, everything was very cheap for us, because of the favourable exchange rate. Since Bolivia's economy was going down the drain, the exchange rate was going down the drain as well. This was good news for foreigners. They received more and more bolivianos for their dollars or euros, but it was bad news for Bolivians.

For Bolivians it became more and more expensive to buy dollars or euros, so it became more and more difficult to travel abroad. In addition, imported items became more and more expensive.

All of this did not matter to the people who voted for Evo Morales, since they belonged to the 70 per cent poor people of Bolivia. Poor people don't travel abroad and cannot buy imported goods in any case.

So every day, at lunch time, we had a very nice three-course meal for less than 3 euros. Every evening at 19.30 hours, after we had read the Daily Brief from the Core Team, we went to a 'normal' restaurant, because I insisted on having a Huari beer with my evening meal. In general, vegetarian restaurants don't serve alcoholic beverages.

Pedro did not object. He simply ordered soup and salad with potatoes. And potatoes they have plenty in Bolivia. In fact, the potato originated in the Andes. In Bolivia and Peru, there are more potato varieties available than anywhere else in the world.

Pedro was very money conscious. He preferred the cheap restaurants, where a full meal would cost around 1 euro. The more expensive ones would charge 3 euros. In my view, there wasn't much difference between 1 and 3 euros.

I explained to Pedro that the EU paid us a salary of 66 euros, plus 104 euros for expenses every day. That's 170 euros per day and they pay us seven days a week, since we work seven days a week.

For our hotel rooms, we paid only 16 euros per day, thanks to Pedro's negotiating skills. And a decent breakfast buffet was included. We could easily afford a 3 euro meal! But Pedro remained unconvinced.

Anyway, in the very centre of town, just two blocks from the central square, we discovered a very nice pizzeria called *Bravo*. Since everything was cheap anyway, I ordered the most expensive one on the menu: the 'Pizza Bravo', for 3 euros.

One of the best pizzas I have ever had in my life. It was only during our last days in Oruro that I discovered that the thin, tasty slices of meat on my pizza were in fact llama meat. So much for my attempts at becoming a vegetarian.

We travelled quite extensively through Oruro province, which is very large, but sparsely populated. In fact, the province was so large, that another LTO team would cover the parts to the south of Lake Poopo: the great salt lake.

This team was defined as a mobile team, also covering parts of neighbouring provinces. One member of this team was Ivan, who would later be my Observer Coordinator in Honduras in 2013.

We travelled south, along the eastside of Lake Poopo. After two hours we reached the town of Challapata, where we met some traditional leaders. Further south we passed through Huari and finally we reached Santuario de Quicollo. The members of the town council were three women and two men, all in traditional dresses.

Because of the drought, they could not offer us tea, so they offered us coca leaves instead. I refused politely. A bit later, from the top of a hill, we had a good view of the waterless Lake Poopo, which actually looked like a ghost lake. All around us, the landscape look barren, with only a few dirt roads.

One day, we decided to visit Orinoca, the birthplace of president Evo Morales, at the west side of Lake Poopo. It was a long, long drive, through a desert like area, with only a few scrubs here and there. The asphalt road soon turned into a dirt road. For hours, we did not see any human beings, only a few alpacas and llama's.

Thank God I always have a thermos flask with hot coffee with me. When we approached the town, situated at the very edge of the great salt lake, the road became a very wide, high quality asphalt road. Only for about five kilometres, though. Inside the town, the roads became dirt roads again.

It appeared to be a rather poor little town at the end of the world, with an unobtrusive central square. Evo had not done much for his birthplace, in spite of being both president of the coca growers and of the country. But the locals remembered him fondly.

They told us that several times a year he visited his birthplace. By helicopter! And they told us that he had arranged the finances for a huge, new football stadium, called 'Coliseo'. Pedro estimated that there were three times more seats in the stadium than the total number of inhabitants of the town.

A few years later, Evo ordered the construction of a museum, that was entirely dedicated to himself. He probably thought: 'Ronald Reagan and Bill Clinton have their own museums, but I am a president as well'. The museum cost 7 million euros. The modern building towers over the surrounding houses of the poor.

On another extended daytrip we visited an area with lots of traditionally built houses, belonging to the Uru-Chipaya culture. It looked like a Dogon village in West-Africa. Pedro took hundreds of pictures.

We interviewed the mayor of Chipaya town and several traditional leaders. Around 2,500 before Christ, the Chipaya's were the first to move from the coastal areas to the *altiplano*. They arrived at the Andean plateau long before the Amaya's and Quechuas.

On yet another trip we took off in the direction of the border with Chile. All Bolivians hate the Chileans. After Bolivia had lost a war against Chile, Chile had taken control of the town of Iquique on the Pacific coast. From then on, Bolivia was a landlocked country.

Bolivia, my favourite country, lost all its wars. In the early years of the nineteenth century, the country lost territories to Brazil and Argentina. Then they lost their access to the pacific ocean to Chile, after which the Bolivian navy was confined to Lake Titicaca. Ultimately, Bolivia decided to take on Paraguay, but lost again. Paraguay took a large chunk of the Chaco region.

But even though the Bolivians hate the Chileans, they still need access to the Chilean ports, so at the border we noticed a long queue of trucks, waiting to be checked by the border control. There was a petrol station, where 'foreigners' (meaning Chileans) had to pay twice as much for car fuel.

This was intended to deter Chileans crossing the border, just to fill their tanks with cheap Bolivian petrol. Evo kept petrol prices low, since he needed the votes. But what happened was that Bolivians smuggled petrol to Peru and Chile, where they sold it for twice as much. As a result, there were continuous shortages in Bolivia. So much for Evo's brilliant solutions.

At the village Curahuara de Carangas we were invited to attend a meeting of 'originals', traditional leaders. On we went to Sajama National Park. The village of Sajama appeared to be completely deserted. We later learned that the inhabitants were either working in Chile or in the city of Oruro. The few that had stayed behind were herding alpacas or llamas in the fields during the day.

Finally, at Sajama Hostel, we encountered a human being. She sold us ten eggs and a little salt in a plastic bag. With this, we drove to the famous geysers. Umberto had never even heard of the word 'geyser', but Pedro had his mind set on boiling eggs in the natural hot springs.

He had forgotten that we were now at an altitude of 5,000 meters, where water boils at a lower temperature. We were shivering from the cold and it took half an hour before the eggs were finally boiled. But they tasted great and the mountain Sajama, at 6,542 meters the highest mountain of Bolivia, was turned fabulously red by the setting sun.

At the hostel, they served me llama meat with potatoes and a large bottle of Huari beer. I slept very well, under six blankets and with all my clothes on. The next morning, our engine didn't start. It occurred to me that it was simply because of the freezing cold. Luckily, the car was standing in the sun.

I instructed Umberto to open the hood, so that the engine—hopefully—would be warmed by the sun. Pedro and I, meanwhile, went for a walk through the village. The centuries old little church was totally deserted.

A beautiful, colonial, white plastered church. It looked as if it had been erected specifically for a Sergio Leone movie. When we returned to the hostel, Umberto had already managed to start the car.

Back in Oruro City, Pedro and I observed a rally by MAS, the ruling party, in the stadium. Like in Cochabamba, nearly all 15,000 spectators were *indigenas.* Yet again I marvelled at the sight of so many people from the traditional countryside in the middle of a modern city. Evo Morales, himself, would be the main speaker.

Thanks to our accreditations, we were allowed very close to the podium. The only problem was that, because of the 'Bolivian Hour', we had to wait in the cold rain for the arrival of the dignitaries. The grass was getting wetter and wetter. My feet were drenched. The next day I was suffering from a cold.

One evening, on our way to the cheap '333' restaurant, Pedro and I entered a small shop to buy some stationary. The owners were an elderly couple, dressed in traditional clothes. I decided to play a little trick on Pedro. I had learned a few lines of a Kjarkas song in Quechua by heart, so I greeted the couple in their own native language.

Pedro looked at me in utter surprise. He had been born in Colombia, but didn't speak a word of Quechua. I said 'Munaskechay', which means 'my dear love'. The old woman smiled and replied in Spanish: *'Gracias'*. Pedro was impressed.

One day, we were visited by Alessandro, the Observer Coordinator of our Core Team and Miguel, the coordinator of our Service Provider. Alessandro was a German with Italian/Spanish roots and Miguel was a Belgian with Venezuelan roots. Pedro, of course, was a British Scotsman with Colombian roots. I was a plain and simple Dutchman with Dutch roots.

Alessandro and Miguel would be with us for just a few hours, since they came straight from Potosí and would continue onto La Paz that same day. We took them to Oruro's best restaurant, Las Terranas, for lunch. Funnily, the waiter was a Spaniard from Jerez de la Frontera, who for some reason had ended up in Oruro and couldn't stop talking. It became annoying.

At the very end of our mission, when Alessandro handed us our 'highly recommended' evaluations, he remarked that he had enjoyed his few hours in Oruro, except for this Spanish waiter, who talked too much. I wanted to tell him that Pedro also talked too much, but I wisely decided that it was better to keep my mouth shut.

On Wednesday 2 December a funny thing happened. I did not tell Pedro that it was my birthday, because I did not want him to tell everybody, upon which they would all start singing for me. I hate to be the centre of attention. We had been interviewing people all day and at 19.00 hours the Daily Brief had come in, so at 20.00 hours we prepared ourselves to go to a restaurant.

Before leaving our hotel, I told Pedro that I invited him, since I had just turned 55. He looked at me in astonishment. ,,No, I invite you", he said. And he continued: ,,It's my birthday today." I was sure he was pulling my leg. It sounded like a bad joke. ,,I don't believe you", I said.

Pedro showed me his passport. He was right, of course. We were both born on the 2 of December: me in 1954 and he in 1957. We solved the problem by letting me pay this time and Pedro the next day. I took him to the second best restaurant of Oruro, called Nayjama. Apparently Evo Morales always ate there when he was in town, so it had to be a good restaurant.

The next day, our STOs arrived. Two teams. We had made reservations in our hotel, which was reasonably good and relatively cheap, but of course one of the eastern Europeans wanted a hotel that was even cheaper. Rytis, from one of the Baltic states, was a bit of an annoying idiot. Thank God, the other three were fine.

We deployed one team near the border with Chile, for a couple of days. The other team would observe along the eastern shores of Lake Poopo. But we made a mistake: while preparing the deployment, Pedro and I had mixed up the numbers of the STO teams.

As a result: Rytis and Luminita believed that they would be deployed to the interesting Sajama region, close to the border with Chile. In reality, we had intended Rubén and Olga to go there. Rytis and Luminita were disappointed. A stupid mistake from our side.

We solved the problem by allowing Rytis and Luminita to observe along the western shores of Lake Poopo, up to the very interesting Chipaya region. Pedro and I would than observe along the boring eastern shores of Lake Poopo. Everybody happy. That's the work of an LTO: solving problems and making people happy.

E-Day went fine. No major problems. The STO teams had to call Pedro and me on the phone and read all their observation forms to us. We filled them out by hand and then entered the forms on an Excell sheet on our laptop.

Several times during the day we went back to our hotel Gran Sucre, to transmit the Excel forms to our Core Team. We also had to call our STO teams to fill in the qualitative forms. Plenty of work, but it went smoothly.

The next day, Rubén and Olga arrived just before dark in our hotel. No sign at all from the other team. At 22.00 hours, I drank can of Paceño beer and went to sleep. The next morning at breakfast Pedro told me angrily what had happened: Rytis and Luminita had arrived at 23.00 hours, which is against all safety regulations.

On top of that, they had just left their car on the street in front of our hotel. Their driver had already left in a taxi, so Pedro had to drive their car into the hotel's garage. On top of that, they had completely ruined one of the tires. It needed replacement, before they could return to La Paz.

But all four STOs were ecstatic about their mission. Which was good news for us, since they would talk favourably about us to the Core Team. The next couple of days, the six of us took turns in observing the counting at the provincial level.

We met other observers there. The OAS had fielded a few observers, all of them very young. The Carter Centre was also represented. It was quite boring. The *actas* that were brought in were scanned and processed. Sometimes nothing happened for hours.

We decided to take a little time off, for some cultural visits. We took the STOs to the regional anthropological museum and into a former silver mine. Quite surprisingly, the entrance to this mine was hidden inside a church, that stood only two blocks from the central square.

It was now open for tourists. There were electrical lamps everywhere in the mine shafts, but still I was glad that I had brought a torch, just in case the electricity would fail. I'm an experienced LTO.

In the end, all four STOs were delighted about the mission. Pedro and I discussed the evaluations that we would give them. Pedro believed that Rubén had done the best job and therefore should receive a 'Highly Recommended'.

I agreed that Rubén had done the best job, but I was hesitant, since I remembered the fuss Milan and I had encountered in Venezuela in

2006. We had given a 'Highly' to one STO, after which the other three STOs had been angry. So I told Pedro: „Let's give them all a simple 'Recommended', since all of them have done a decent job."

Pedro grudgingly agreed, but later I realized that I had made a mistake yet again: Rubén had really been better than the other three. Rubén was disappointed and rightly so. He came to my room for a private conversation. He explained that his Spanish government required two 'Highly Recommended' evaluations from a Spanish STO, before this STO could be promoted to the ranks of LTOs.

I had never heard of such a rule, but I promised to take it up with Pedro once again, but Pedro and I decided to leave it as it was: if we gave Rubén a 'Highly', the other three would be envious and they might reveal negative things about Pedro and me to the Core Team, so it was in our interest to make all four STOs as happy as could be.

Even so, I felt sorry for Rubén. Rubén's good job became even more impressive when he told me that he had faced real troubles with the altitude of 4,000 meters. After his arrival from Spain at the airport of La Paz, he had been breathing through an oxygen mask for three hours!

As expected, Evo Morales won the elections in the first round with 64 per cent of the votes. His party, MAS, obtained a two-thirds majority in parliament.

After having served three terms as Bolivia's president, Evo Morales was Latin America's longest serving president. Yet, he wished to stay in power for a fourth term. In order to change the constitution, he called for yet another referendum.

To his surprise, this time the Bolivians voted against another term for him. Evo had neglected the economy and many Bolivians were poorer than ever before. But Evo had another trick up his sleeves: he instructed the Constitutional Court to allow him to run for a fourth term, regardless of the outcome of the referendum.

On 20 October 2019 he won the presidential elections, initially with less than 50 percent, which meant a second round would be held. Counting was halted and when it resumed, Evo had obtained more than 50 per cent of the vote. International observers considered this to be illegal.

Thousands of Bolivians took to the streets, to protest against this obvious electoral fraud. After two weeks of increasing protest, the Bolivian police and army sided with the protesters. The 60-year old Evo was forced to resign. He fled to Mexico, where he was granted political asylum by the leftist Mexican government.

He later moved to Argentina, also with a recently elected leftist government. After his party won the elections in Bolivia in late 2020, Morales was finally allowed to return to Bolivia.

Pedro and I travelled back to La Paz, where we were the last LTO team to be handed their evaluations by Alessandro, the Observer Co-ordinator and Peter, his deputy. While we were waiting outside their office, Kees, the Dutch LTO, greeted us. ,,I think you're going to be very happy", Kees told us. What did he mean? Did he know something that we did not know?

A few minutes later, Alessandro and Peter handed us our 'Highly Recommended' evaluations. I was a bit surprised. Pedro and I had formed a good team, but I had been a member of other good teams. In my view, at least.

Anyway: I was very happy with the 'Highly'. We found out later that, out of 34 LTOs, only six LTOs had obtained a 'Highly'. When Pedro and I talked enthusiastically about it in the presence of other LTOs, I noticed that several of them gave us nasty looks. They envied us, which gave me a good feeling.

Many observers are overachievers. A 'Highly' looks good on your CV. Little did we all know that the 'Highly Recommended' would be abolished just a few years later. It was deemed much fairer to evaluate all observers who did a decent job as plain and simply 'Recommended for Future Missions'.

Pedro and I were lucky that we were among the last observers to obtain a 'Highly'. We were a good team, actually. Pedro was a very good observer, especially analytically, and he had specialized in traditional Latino democratic structures. He was a bit chaotic, though. His written texts in Spanish were too long and his English was horrible.

I am much more organized and I was able to summarize his Spanish epistles into clear and concise English. It was very funny that one day when we had an argument about something, he told me to become a bit more Latino, meaning less rational and less structured. I replied that he should become a bit more European, meaning better organized and less panicky when there was a little problem.

Did I find a Goofy for my wife? Yes, I did. One day I was strolling around the market, not too far from our hotel, when I spotted an orange children's pyjama with a Goofy painted on it. „What age?" the lady asked me. I thought she wanted to know my age, but another customer told me that she wanted to know the age of my child.

I laughed and I told the lady that I only wanted the shirt because of the Goofy, so she could keep the pyjama pants. As usual in Third World countries, she believed that I was trying to negotiate the price down. I convinced her that I would pay the full price, which wasn't much in any case, and that she could keep the orange pants.

After that, something happened that usually doesn't happen to me: I lost my bearings. I was sure that I was walking back to our hotel, but after about half an hour I realized that I was walking in the wrong direction.

I panicked, but I was too proud to ask for directions. After all: I was not a stupid tourist. To the contrary: I lived and worked in Oruro. It took a considerable amount of time to find my way back. My wife will never know how much it had cost me to obtain the bloody Goofy pyjama.

Chapter 10

KYRGYZSTAN - 2010

'So this is what ethnic cleansing looks like'

My most memorable mission would be to a country that I had never even heard of. And to a region that I thought was absolutely out of bounds for me, since I did not speak one word of Russian. As it turned out, I was selected for the mission after a sequence of accidental events.

Normally, I would leave my mobile phone at home, but on 19 May 2010 I decided to take it with me, while I took the dogs for their afternoon walk. I remember the date, since it was my father's birthday. And the reason for taking my mobile phone with me was that Els, an old female friend of my wife, had come to visit us.

The two of them decided to visit some interesting parts of the medieval town center of Enkhuizen. I expected them to call me, since I know our hometown much better than my wife does. Just a few kilometres outside Enkhuizen there is a forest, called Streekbos.

The forest has been man-made, like all nature in The Netherlands. Until 1978, it was agricultural land, where cauliflower was grown. It was decided to plant trees, to create a forest. I was walking the dogs in an open space of the forest, when my phone rang.

The sun was shining brightly, so I could not see who was calling. I expected my wife to call, but it was clearly not her voice. My first thought was that it was her friend and that they were trying to pull my leg.

But it turned out to be somebody else entirely. I did not recognize the voice. The caller explained that her name was Connie and that she had worked at the Dutch Ministry of Foreign Affairs for thirty years in various capacities, but never in the department that handled election observation missions.

She had been called upon to temporarily replace my focal point, Nathalie, who had taken four months of maternity leave. Connie asked me if I was willing to observe the constitutional referendum in Kyrgyzstan, as an LTO for OSCE.

I said: ,,Kyrgyzstan, where is that?"

She replied: ,,I don't know."

I said: ,,Could you look it up, please, since I am in the middle of a forest, right now."

,,OK. Just a minute", she said.

Within minutes she came back on the phone: ,,Kyrgyzstan borders Kazakhstan, Uzbekistan and Tadzhikistan."

I knew enough. It was an ex-Soviet republic. I said: ,,OK. Listen, I would like to go there, but I don't speak Russian."

,,They don't ask for Russian", she said. ,,They only ask for English."

I had always assumed that at least a basic knowledge of Russian was obligatory for observers in the ex-Soviet republics. I was wrong. I then realized that my focal point had never asked me for these parts of the world, since—obviously—I appeared on the lists for English, Spanish and Portuguese speaking missions.

If there were not enough Russian speaking observers, it made more sense to recruit an observer who spoke only English and therefore could not be recruited for Spanish or Portuguese speaking missions.

Through a stroke of luck, I was contacted by a replacement at the ministry. I thought it would be interesting to go to another part of the world for a change. Also, it would be a good experience for me and it would look good on my CV. I told her that I was available.

Immediately after that, there was another surprise. I was accustomed to EU missions. After having been selected by the Dutch government, I needed to be selected by the EU. This entire process would take several weeks. The EU required a 'Fit To Work' certificate and so on. In this case it was different.

She told me that I would be leaving for Kyrgyzstan within just eight days. Could I come to the ministry tomorrow? I was a bit overwhelmed at the speed of things, but I agreed. Luckily, when I visited the ministry the next day, I had brought my passport with me. They needed my passport details for the contract.

I thus learned about another important difference between the EU and the OSCE. The EU has plenty of money, so each EU observer obtains a contract from the EU and gets paid by the EU. All contracts and all remunerations are the same.

The OSCE, to the contrary, does not have money. So each observer signs a contract with his/her government, which means that some observers are more equal than others. In fact, some governments pay their observers very well, while others receive so little money that they can hardly afford the cheapest hotel.

Some of the governments that pay very well are Norway, Germany, Switzerland and, lucky for me, The Netherlands. The countries that pay very badly are, of course, the eastern European and Asian countries.

This was a problem, because in some teams one observer was paid very well and the other very badly. Since the two partners in a team must communicate with each other continually, it is advisable to stay in the same hotel.

This usually meant that an observer from a western European country would have to stay in the same cheap hotel, or even cheap apartment, as the partner from let's say Rumania or the Czech Republic. And cheap hotels are cheap for a reason: they are a lot less comfortable and a lot less safe than more expensive hotels.

After I got home with the dogs, I sat in the back garden with my wife and her friend, while I tried to locate the country Kyrgyzstan in our forty-five year old Bos Atlas. Unfortunately, the Bos Atlas was so old that the country was not mentioned there at all: it was still a part of the good old Soviet Union.

And I could not find the capital Bishkek either. I later found out that the city had changed names several times: originally it was called Pishpek. In the good old Soviet days it was called Frunze.

The next day, I signed my Dutch contract at the ministry, after which, temporarily, I became a ministry employee. A few weeks later I even received the ministry's staff magazine! The money was good. Even slightly better than on my EU missions. And no 'Fit to Work' certificate was required. Apparently, neither the ministry nor the OSCE cared about my health situation. Which was fine with me.

One week later I found myself in a Turkish Airways plane, bound for Istanbul. The ministry had sent me my flight ticket. Since it was an intercontinental flight and since I was now a ministry employee, they had provided me with a business class ticket. Such luxury!

I changed planes at Istanbul. A pleasant airport. I liked it. While I was waiting at the gate to Bishkek, I observed my fellow passengers. There were about one hundred of them. Since this was to be my first mission in the Russian speaking world, I was quite sure that I had never met any of my fellow observers.

I was observing the other passengers, to see if I could spot an observer. In my mind, observers are not like ordinary people. Observers go to horrible places, to support democracy. They are used to all kinds of hardships. Like modern knights.

As it turned out: observers do not stand out in the crowd at all. They look the same as everybody else. Like serial killers. Many people believe that serial killers are nasty looking individuals, but they look exactly like you and me.

I noted that one passenger was a young women, finely dressed and on high heels. Observers usually wear shabby clothes and outdoor shoes, so I was absolutely certain that she would never be an observer. How wrong could I be!

Just one day later, I was introduced to her: she would be my new partner in the southern city of Osh. Her name was Florence. I had never heard of her, but—as I would find out later—she had a fearsome reputation amongst the Russian speaking observers.

She was French, from Lyon, but her grandparents had been immigrants from Armenia. On later missions, when I mentioned that Florence had been my partner, other observers would look at me with pity in their eyes. They would invariably ask the same question: 'Did you get along with her?'

I would always answer: 'Yes, she was one of my best partners. She was a bit of a character, though.' I soon found out why she had a such a reputation. At least once a day, she would burst out in anger. It didn't bother me. To the contrary: I thought it was very funny.

Invariably, when she burst out, people would freeze and then look at me without daring to utter a word. I soon fell into the habit of waiting a few precious seconds and then explaining: 'She's from Armenia'. After this had happened a few times, Florence told me angrily: 'Don't say that again; I'm from France'.

But the next day she had another burst, people again looked at me for a way out and I said exactly the same thing: 'She's from Armenia'. I expected her to direct her anger at me this time, but no such thing happened.

In fact, we had a very fruitful relationship after that. She tried to control her anger. I tried to be nice to her. She was a good observer. She spoke decent Russian and she had been an observer in Kyrgyzstan previously.

All of this happened in the city of Osh, a few days after our arrival in the country. Before that, I had to endure the mission's briefings in Bishkek. The first night of the mission was horrible. We arrived in the middle of the night at hotel Asia Mountains 2 in a sprawled-out suburb of Bishkek.

My room, on the second floor, was extremely hot. I could not manage to get the airco to work. I went down to the reception, but the poor girl said that all she could do was to send a mechanic the next morning. I could not open the windows, because of the mosquitoes and the noise of the traffic. I did not sleep at all, that first night.

Bishkek is a widespread city, with a number of typical Soviet buildings in the center, including the White House, the seat of the government. The streets are lined with trees, but the pavements are of poor quality. Not much better than Africa. The side streets were even worse.

A major problem for me was that everything was written in Cyrillic script, either in Russian or in Kyrgyz. I could not read a word of either. It turned out to be quite an effort to change some money and to buy a few beers in a small shop near the hotel.

The briefings were held in the Core Team's office building. I was used to EU missions, with lots of LTOs and relatively few STOs, but OSCE missions prefer the opposite: they use lots of STOs and very few LTOs. In fact, there were only 7 LTO teams and they were expecting a staggering 300 STOs.

On EU missions, the Chief Observer is always a member of the European Parliament, but on OSCE missions the Chief Observer is an ambassador of a member state. In this case, it was the Slovenian ambassador.

For some reason, the general atmosphere within the Core Team was not very pleasant. There seemed to be a lot of tension between CT members. I cannot remember anyone ever laughing. Not a good sign.

On a positive note, I must say that the general atmosphere was a lot more relaxed than on EU missions. The OSCE is not as obsessed with our security as the EU. And the OSCE and the EU use practically the same work methodology, including the reporting. That made life easier for me.

I did not know any of the LTOs and of the CT I only knew the Observer Coordinator: Dimitra from Greece. I met her in Nigeria, where she had been a colleague LTO. She was quite a character, but she was OK. She was very experienced. The LTOs were also OK. The 14 LTOs were staying in two rather small hotels: Asia Mountains 1 and 2.

After the briefings had finished, the LTOs from our hotel ate sushi and drank beer on the roof terrace of restaurant 'Veranda', at the corner of Gorki Street and Sovetskaja. The name Sovetskaja has been changed recently, but the old name still appeared on city maps. We partied on the roof of 'Veranda' until 02.00 hours.

The next morning, at 07.00 hours, Florence and I were transported to the airport. We boarded a very small and very old Russian plane. On EU missions, this would never have been allowed, but this was an OSCE mission.

Luckily, ever since I obtained my flying license in 1986 in South Africa, I had never been afraid of flying. Even when the engines fail, any plane can simply glide back to earth.

I was not really panicking this time, but when we flew over snow-capped mountains with just a few meters to spare, I got the jibbers. I could almost touch the rocks. Florence got really nervous. After we landed at the airport of Osh, I took a closer look at the planes' tires: they were totally worn down!

But we arrived safely. It was very hot in Osh, the second city of Kyrgyzstan with 250.000 inhabitants. The sun was burning on our heads. I started sweating. Luckily, our Russian driver, Anton, and our Russian interpreter, Svetlana, were waiting for us.

We were off to a bad start though: our car wouldn't start. Anton managed to find some men who were willing to push the car. Finally, it kicked on. First we drove around the city to check out apartments, since these were cheaper than hotel rooms. The apartments, however, were not the best I had ever seen.

They were very cheap, though. They cost only 200 dollars per person per month. We visited a small guesthouse at Tashkentskaya street at the other side of the river, with just four bedrooms, and this appeared to be a much better deal. It was called Zhukov's Guest House and the owners were ethnic Russians. They would even provide us with meals, at a little extra cost.

The next day, we intended to interview anyone who had anything to do with the upcoming elections, but to our surprise everyone talked about the tensions between the two ethnic groups in the city. No one was interested in the upcoming referendum.

I have to explain a thing here: the city of Osh was historically inhabited by urbanized Uzbeks. The Kyrgyz were a nomadic people, of Turkish-Mongol origins. The Kyrgyz lived in the countryside in their Yurts. They herded camels and horses, much like the Mongols.

The Kyrgyz were also good warriors and fought bravely in the Soviet army during the Second World War. Because of this, Stalin had ordained that the city of Osh should not be a part of Uzbekistan, but of Kyrgyzstan, even though the vast majority of the inhabitants of Osh were Uzbeks and the Uzbek border was just a few kilometres away.

By any standards, Osh should have been part of Uzbekistan, but Stalin in all his wisdom decided otherwise. It felt a bit like the partition of Africa. Gradually, over the years, the Kyrgyz gave up their nomadic existence and took residence in the city of Osh.

So the numbers of Kyrgyz rose steadily, but the better educated Uzbeks still owned most of the businesses. This caused a lot of tension between the two ethnic groups. As a result, the Uzbeks and the Kyrgyz hated each other, even though all of them were Muslims.

The Kyrgyz are moderate Muslims, while the Uzbeks are much more strict in their religion. This was obvious to anyone, since in an Uzbek shop one would never find any alcoholic drinks. In Kyrgyz shops, on the contrary, you can choose from at least twenty different beers and even more different vodka's.

We worked hard, every day. We interviewed the Uzbek owners of Osh and Mansion TV stations. They had broadcast several ethnic outbursts and both had been reprimanded for it by government officials, who feared that these broadcasts would add fuel to the already smouldering ethnic tensions. The owners of the TV stations felt intimidated by the not-so democratic Kyrgyz who were in power.

Florence and I worked well together. I accepted her daily burst of anger and she accepted my 'She's from Armenia'. One evening, we had dinner at a restaurant with Martin from Austria. He worked at the OSCE office in Osh. Curiously, Florence, our interpreter Svetlana and myself had worked with him previously. I did not like him.

When I went to Pisa at the end of 2007, for a five-day security training in preparation of our Pakistan mission, I was supposed to share a room with Martin. Instead, I paid a little extra money and obtained a room for my own.

About a month later, when we flew to Pakistan, Martin was sitting next to me in the plane. During the flight, he kept on talking to me incessantly all through the night. I didn't get one minute of sleep, because of that idiot.

During the midterm briefing of our Pakistan mission, in 2008, Martin had been a member of our working group. My partner at that mission, Roger from the UK, had been chairman of our working group. Martin annoyed him so much, that even good old Roger lost his temper.

I later told Roger, rather sarcastically: 'Now you realize, Roger, that I am not the worst partner in the world'. Later, during the Egypt mission of 2014, Christa, the elderly German observer, told me that she also thought that Martin was a horrible guy. Anyway: the dinner at the restaurant in Osh ended in total disaster. At one point, Florence walked out of the door and said that she never wanted to see Martin again.

A few days later we were visited by another LTO team: Jonathan form the UK and Hilde from Norway. They were based in Batken, which was such a backward place that they had to travel to Osh to purchase necessary office supplies and hire an interpreter. They stayed in our guesthouse.

The four of us went out for a meal and a few drinks at the Czar restaurant. The evening started very pleasant, but ended in disaster after Jonathan ordered more and more beer. I like to drink a few beers in the evening, after the work has been done, but compared to Jonathan I am a moderate drinker.

He ordered four half-litre pints, but Florence and Hilde refused, so he placed two in front of me and two in front of himself. Then he started drinking. He drank and drank, until he became so drunk that he started having arguments with Florence.

Not a good idea, as anyone who knows Florence will confirm. They had a nasty fight, albeit only with words. In the end, poor Hilde was crying. I sided with Florence. A wise decision that she greatly appreciated.

One evening, new visitors arrived at the guesthouse. I heard them talking about the beer in the fridge and if they could just drink it. I popped in the kitchen and said: 'Yes, you can drink it, as long as you replenish it, since it is my beer.'

One man turned out to be the UN Resident Coordinator in the country. He was an American. I asked him if he had known Erick de Mul, who had been my best Dutch friend within the UN system. He said yes, of course he knew him. After that, we spent a pleasant evening together.

I spent another evening drinking beer with the ex-UNICEF representative to the country. The next evening I invited Florence to join me for a beer at the outside table. She accepted the invitation, but after she sat down, she said: ,,You never invited me when these other people were here. I am just a stand-in." I felt a bit ashamed. I realized that it was quite true. I'm a horrible guy.

We visited the town of Kara Suu, close to the border with Uzbekistan, at about thirty minutes from Osh. Here, for the first time, I noticed that many Kyrgyz men have golden teeth. Lots of golden teeth. The first time someone smiles at you with a row of golden teeth in his upper as well as lower jaw, it looks frightening. Like the bad guy in a James Bond movie.

But in the end you get used to anything. At the post office, two ladies complained that observers did not do anything about the fact that all the time the wrong persons were elected. We explained that we, as observers, were not allowed to vote. The Kyrgyz people elect their own representatives.

Since everyone in Osh was talking about the ethnic tensions, Florence and I mentioned this in our first Weekly Report. I did the typing and Florence was dictating from the couch. We worked continuously the entire day, until 22.00 hours. By that time, thankfully, Ana, the political expert of the Core Team, arrived from Jalalabad.

We were a bit apprehensive about her, since Les, the amiable elderly American LTO who was based in Jalalabad, texted us that Ana had overruled all his preparations for her meetings with local officials. But Ana was not bad at all.

In fact, both Florence and I liked her. Ana was Russian, but she lived in London. She confirmed that the general atmosphere within the Core Team was not very positive. As it turned out, Ana was the only one within the Core Team who was not afraid to tell the truth, now and then. Because of this, all other members of the CT avoided her. Ana was the black sheep.

We received two comments on our WR: firstly, we should have concentrated on the upcoming referendum, instead of on the ethnic tensions. Secondly, the Core Team had decided to give ratings to the quality of the WR's. Of the seven LTO teams, we had ended up in second place: not bad at all.

The first place, the best WR, had been written by Peter, who was based in Naryn, up in the cold mountains near the border with China. Little did I know that ten days later he would be my next partner.

The next day we took Ana to meetings with the governor of Osh province and other dignitaries. Ana was fine. I was not. The continuous typing of the previous day had exhausted me. I had developed a terrible cold. But we had a nice evening chat with Ana on the patio of our guesthouse. Ana smoked cigarettes and drank vodka. That's my kind of girl.

One day later, after Ana had departed, all hell broke loose. Florence and I had dinner with Mark Gregorian, a BBC journalist with Armenian roots, who was in Osh to train local journalists. We were with him at a Korean restaurant in the centre of Osh. At about 23.00 hours Florence and I took a taxi home.

An hour later, the BBC journalist called Florence. From his Crystal Hotel in the centre he observed two groups of youths fighting each other viciously. He saw fires and he could even hear gunshots.

Half an hour later, he called again. A huge group of youths, armed with sticks, were marching towards his hotel. He was afraid they might storm the hotel. He would be stuck there. We called Svetlana, our Russian interpreter. She told us that her Uzbek neighbours were knocking on each other's doors.

That night, we didn't sleep much. There was only one other guest in our guesthouse: a Danish journalist called Henrik. He had no hair, even though he was hardly 40 years of age. He was extremely anxious about the situation. He did not sleep at all. This was a bit strange, since he had specialized in covering conflict areas.

The next morning, as usual we had a delicious breakfast in the garden. Our BBC source called again. His hotel had not been stormed, but he could hear groups of youngsters fighting nearby. We heard it too, by now: screams of anguish and pain, in the far distance. Then, all of a sudden, four army helicopters scooped down on the city centre, at the other side of the river.

Vitaly, the very friendly Russian owner of our guesthouse, told us that a road block had been erected just a few hundred meters away. Vitaly and I walked towards the small shops nearby. The Uzbek shops were closed. Only one Kyrgyz shop was still open. I decided to buy enough beers for the next couple of days. We didn't know how long we would be stuck in our guesthouse.

Just around the corner, Vitaly and I observed a roadblock, consisting of small rocks and tires. Some Kyrgyz young men with long wooden sticks were hanging around. A few cars drove up to the roadblock. After a short conversation, the Kyrgyz youth move some tires to the side, to let the cars pass.

Vitaly was nervous. Even though he was an ethnic Russian, he looked a bit like an Uzbek. And these youngsters were quite unpredictable. Many of them lived in the countryside. They had been provided with transport by unscrupulous Kyrgyz leaders. The youngsters had not had much sleep and some of them might have used alcohol or drugs.

Because of the roadblocks, we decided to stay in the guesthouse. Better safe than sorry. Robin, our Core Team security expert from the UK, advised the same. We soon learned that Robin was quite useless. He first advised us to go to the UNICEF compound and then to the OSCE compound.

Robin said that security officials in Bishkek had told him that there were no roadblocks in Osh. We called Anton, our driver, who said that there were dozens of roadblocks all over the city, manned either by Kyrgyz of Uzbek youngsters. We also called Svetlana. She said that she had seen her 'very ordinary' Uzbek neighbours return to their houses with looted goods.

We were not sure what to do. Vitaly told us that there were army barracks just down the road. If matters got worse, we could make a dash for these barracks. All during the day, the frightening screams of desperate people seemed to get closer and closer to our guesthouse.

That second night, I slept only four hours, but it was a deep sleep. The next morning Florence asked me if I had not heard her banging on my door. I said 'No'. She said that a group of Kyrgyz youngsters had been outside the gate of the guesthouse, demanding entry, to check if any Uzbeks were hiding inside.

Vitaly, the Russian owner and his son denied them entrance and told them that they would use their guns and their German shepherd dog to defend themselves. All in all, it must have been very noisy, but I had been so tired that I slept soundly through it all.

During the morning of the third day it was relatively quiet, but in the distance we saw columns of smoke rising up into the air. Strangely enough, the electricity was still working and water was still coming out of the tap.

I checked the BBC and CNN websites. Their journalists reported that ethnic hostilities had broken out all through the south of Kyrgyzstan between the Kyrgyz and the Uzbeks.

Nearly two thousand people would die, most of them Uzbeks, and there would be around two hundred thousand displaced persons, also most of them Uzbeks. This tragedy would go largely unnoticed by the rest of the world, because it coincided with the Football World Cup in South Africa.

Football is more important than bloody clashes between Muslims in a far-away country. On top of that, no westerners and no ethnic Russians were harmed during the conflict.

The BBC was already comparing it to the war in Bosnia and calling it 'ethnic cleansing': 99 per cent of the army and the police were Kyrgyz. They sided, of course, with the thousands of Kyrgyz youth that roamed the streets of Osh and other cities in the south of Kyrgyzstan. The Uzbeks stood no chance. Kyrgyz people painted the word 'Kyrgyz' on their houses, to prevent arson.

It appeared that the Uzbek army was on full alert at the other side of the border, just a few kilometres from Osh. Uzbekistan is much larger and more developed than Kyrgyzstan, therefore the Uzbek army is much stronger than the Kyrgyz army. If the Uzbeks decided to intervene, than the Kyrgyz army would surely be crushed.

But the Uzbek army did not cross the border to protect Uzbek citizens in Osh. Uzbekistan decided to stay out of the conflict. They closed their border, even for their own kinsmen. As a result, tens of thousands of displaced Uzbeks were herded close to the border fences, under the burning sun.

Yet again we were served a delicious fresh meal in the summerhouse in the back garden by the Russian owners of our guesthouse. I decided to play a little trick on our Danish journalist: I ran into his room, shouting: 'You must come now; you must come now'. He looked bewildered and asked: 'Are we under attack?' I said: 'No, you have to come, because lunch is being served.'

I should not have done it, because while Florence and I were enjoying our meals, Henrik did not eat anything at all. His plate remained full on the table, while he talked incessantly in Danish on Skype. He seemed to be comforted a bit by his laptop and the familiar voices of family and friends, even though they were in far off—and safe—Denmark.

I talked a few times on Skype with my wife. I explained the situation to her. ,,You sound remarkably calm", she said. Well, maybe I sounded calm, but the truth was that I had checked out the back garden, to see how I could escape when a band of youngsters would storm the guesthouse.

There was no escape. There were high walls all around. At the back of the garden, though, there was a cellar that was probably used for storing food stuffs. I could hide in there, but I would also be trapped in there.

Early in the afternoon, a small car arrived at our guesthouse. The driver and the two bodyguards remained in the vehicle, but Martin stepped out of it and said the he would take us to the OSCE compound, on the other side of the river.

We introduced him to Henrik, our Danish friend. ,,He's a journalist. He's not with the OSCE, so we cannot take him", Martin said bluntly. Henrik went even paler than he was already. He literally begged us not to leave him behind. Without Florence and me, he would be all by himself in the guesthouse.

I discussed the situation with Florence and we decided that we simply could not leave Henrik behind. Apart from that, there was only one seat available for the two of us, so Florence would have to sit on my lap. And there was no space for even our hand luggage. We told Martin that we preferred to stay in the guesthouse.

,,Whatever you want", Martin said. He stepped into the car and drove off. Later, Robin, our mission's security expert told us that he had heard the entire conversation, since Martin kept his phone switched on. Robin confirmed that we had made the right decision, not to leave Henrik behind.

Meanwhile, Florence had established contact with the French embassy and Henrik managed to contact some Danish diplomats. I could not help them, since there was no Dutch embassy in Kyrgyzstan. By now, all three of us had packed our suitcases.

As it turned out, the French ambassador was on good terms with the American ambassador. And the Americans were using the international airport of Bishkek for their operations in Afghanistan, so they were a force to be reckoned with in Kyrgyzstan. And they possessed resources.

At about 16.00 hours, Florence received a phone call: the three of us would be picked up by a bus, under protection of the Kyrgyz army. We were allowed to take our hand luggage with us, but no big suitcases. Much to my surprise, the bus indeed arrived.

It was a civilian bus and our protection consisted of two elderly army men, with grey hair and big bellies. One was driving the bus, the other stood at the door. They were unarmed. But we had no choice. We hastily said goodbye to the Russian owners of our guesthouse and off we went.

We were the only passengers. The bus halted briefly at the first roadblock. Our Kyrgyz escorts talked to the Kyrgyz youth and within minutes they created an opening in the roadblock. More roadblocks would follow. All of them let us pass, after a brief conversation in Kyrgyz.

Just before we crossed the river, the bus halted at a compound. Several young Americans came on board. The same happened at the other side of the river. More young Americans entered the bus. They were very young indeed. They looked bewildered. They told us that they worked for the Peace Corps.

By the time there were about fifteen of us on board, the bus halted at one of the army compounds in the centre of Osh. By this time, we had passed several houses and shops that had been burned to the ground or were still smouldering. An aery sight. Obviously, the owners had been Uzbeks. 'So this is what ethnic cleansing looks like', one of the Peace Corps volunteers remarked.

To the surprise of all of us, our two escorts stepped out of the bus and disappeared into the army compound. This really frightened me. Even though they were unarmed, just a few stern words from them were enough to keep the Kyrgyz youths at length. I looked around and saw several small groups of Kyrgyz young men walking with long wooden sticks, some of which had a knife tied to the tip.

Several of them passed our bus at just a few meters distance. They probably had not slept for two nights and maybe they kept themselves going on drugs or alcohol. They looked menacing, but made no attempt to enter the bus, probably because we were parked in front of army barracks.

Then something happened that really stunned me: Florence was standing straight up, next to me, making photos of the Kyrgyz youngsters. ,,Put your camera away", I hissed at her. I normally do not lose my temper, but to put all of us in mortal danger for a few stupid photographs, was beyond me. Thank God, she lowered her camera.

After what seemed to be an eternity, our two unarmed and aging escorts returned. Several jeeps, belonging to the American consulate, arrived and positioned themselves behind our bus. They were carrying American and Kyrgyz embassy staff. We started moving again in a convoy, with the jeeps following us.

We saw more burned-out shops and houses and we saw looters walking with computers and TV-sets. Other than that, the situation seemed quiet. Then we pulled up behind an army tank, with about ten Kyrgyz soldiers sitting on top of it. I wondered what the tank was doing there. We soon found out.

The tank led the way to the army's helicopter base, just a few hundred meters away. Then we noticed a large group of Kyrgyz youngsters, blocking our road. Now the tank would come in handy, but the problem was that the soldiers manning the tank were Kyrgyz and the youngsters were also Kyrgyz.

The youngsters blocked the road and the tank crew stopped the tank, not wanting to drive over their own kinsmen. It was a standoff. The youngsters, about one hundred of them, had no weapons except for their sticks. They shouted at the soldiers to hand over their Kalashnikovs, so that the youngsters could kill more Uzbeks.

The soldiers, of course, were not willing to do this. The situation remained tense, for about ten minutes. All of a sudden, one of the youngsters stormed the tank, climbed on to it and wrestled a Kalashnikov from one of the soldiers. He ran away with it. As a result, several soldiers fired their Kalashnikovs into the air. Confusion all around.

I looked at the scene in shear surprise. I wondered why the soldiers did not just fire at the youngsters. Well, as it happened, one of them did. I saw the bullet smash into a shoulder. The boy fell to the ground.

Then I looked around me. All the passengers on the bus had dropped to the floor. I was the only one still standing. I instantly dropped to the ground too.

At that point, the tank started moving again. The youngsters blocking the road retreated. Our bus followed the tank and behind us the American jeeps did the same. We drove into the army compound, where we were taken to a helicopter platform. I thought we were safe, but then we were told to get onto the bus again, since these were not the right helicopters.

On we went, again. At the other side of the army compound, two more helicopters were parked. We stepped out of the bus and then we heard the staccato noise of a Kalashnikov. The bullets flew over our heads. Probably it was the Kalashnikov that had just been wrestled from the soldiers. Everyone lay flat on the grass, including myself.

Luckily, nobody got hit. We entered an old Russian army helicopter. To my surprise, the two huge fuel tanks that had been placed inside the passengers area, were totally unprotected. One bullet would be enough to let them explode.

When we flew over the city centre, we saw dozens of columns of smoke rising up into the air. Uzbek shops and homes, that had been put to the torch. I was afraid someone would shoot at us, but we made it safely to the airport, where everything was quiet. We had left the war zone behind us.

We waited on the tarmac for an hour or so. It was not dark yet. Then we were ushered into a chartered passengers plane. The plane was full, so I kept my little suitcase on my lap. I was so tired after two nights with little sleep, that I fell asleep even before the plane took off.

At Bishkek airport, a mission vehicle was waiting for us. It was dark by now. We urged the driver to take us to our hotel as quickly as possible. That was a mistake: we were stopped by the traffic police.

Henrik, our Danish friend, flipped completely and shouted at the policemen 'Do you know what we have been through?' Florence and I told him to quiet down and let our driver do the talking.

After checking in in our hotel Asia Mountains 2, we walked to the shopping center, where we enjoyed sushi and cold beer on the rooftop of restaurant Veranda. We were joined by two other teams that also had been evacuated: Johathan and Hilde from Batken and Les and Karina from Jalalabad.

The last two had travelled ten hours by car during the day. The mission had told them to wait for a Russian driver, since Russians were not targeted by neither Kyrgyz nor Uzbeks.

But all of a sudden, their Kyrgyz driver had told them to put their suitcases in the car, since there was a problem. There really was a problem: half an hour after they had left their hotel, they received a telephone call that the entire hotel had been put to the torch.

All of us were relieved that we had escaped the ethnic war. The OSCE Election Observation Mission allowed the six of us a full week to recover in Bishkek. The only problem was that my big suitcase was still in the guesthouse in Osh.

I had only two spare shirts with me and a total of five underpants. There were no shops in the vicinity of the hotel and washing a shirt would take two days, so that was not an option. But we had a great time in Bishkek.

Karina, from Denmark, had developed a very serious stomach problem in Jalalabad, so she was medically evacuated out of the country. The remaining five of us would, every day, have lunch in 'Istanbul', a nearby Lebanese restaurant that was owned by a Palestinian. And in the evenings we had a few beers on the hotel's balcony. During daytime we took taxis to visit the huge city centre.

I managed to buy a box with 20 Dutch cigars. They were thinner than the Dutch Wild Havana's I was accustomed to. They were expensive and they were old. They were so dry, that they almost fell apart. But they were the only cigars I could find in the entire city. My own box with Wild Havana's was in my suitcase in Osh.

I really enjoyed that week in Bishkek. No work, no stress. It was not sure if the mission would continue. Because of the ethnic clashes, all 300 STOs had been told to stay at home.

Then, much to our surprise, it was announced that the referendum would still be held as scheduled. The LTOs would remain in the country, but for security reasons OSCE decided not deploy STOs. The mission was therefore scaled down to a LROM, a Limited Referendum Observation Mission.

The five of us would be re-assigned to different duty stations, since we could not go back to the south. To my horror, I received a phone call from Dimitra, the Observer Coordinator. She told me that I had to join Peter in Naryn, up in the mountains close to the border with China.

His partner had been Lazet, a sympathetic elderly lady from neighbouring Kazakhstan. She had returned to her native country, after having been insulted by the Kyrgyz day after day. Apparently, the Kyrgyz not only hated their western neighbours, the Uzbeks, they also hated their northern neighbours, the Kazakhs.

A few years later, it became apparent that the Kyrgyz also hated their southern neighbors, the Tajiks. Several border wars would be fought between the Kyrgyz and Tajik armies. All this because Stalin had drawn new border lines on the map, without taking ethnic realities into consideration.

During the days of the Soviet Union these border lines existed only on paper, so there was no problem. After the fall of the communist empire, however, these border lines became physical realities. All of a sudden, farmers could not reach their fields at the other side of the border anymore. And people were separated from their relatives.

Now I was deployed close to the eastern border with China, where there were no hostilities. I was happy with the mountains, since it would be less hot there than in Osh, but I was not happy with Peter. During the 2007 mission in Nigeria, three teams were staying overnight in a hotel in Gombe. Dimitra was there, with her partner Wlodek.

The next day, they would travel to Maiduguri in the far north-east of Nigeria, where just a few years later Boko Haram would terrorize the population. Peter was also there, with his partner Analisa from Italy.

I reminded Dimitra that the next morning, Peter and Analisa were having breakfast at separate tables. Not a good sign. I was very much afraid that Peter was a horrible guy. I didn't want to spent two weeks with a horrible guy, after all that I had been trough in Osh, so I asked Dimitra to book me a flight back to Holland.

To my surprise, she said she couldn't do that. She explained that on OSCE missions the member states paid their observers and also booked their flights. So I had to contact my ministry in the Netherlands.

There was a problem, though: it was already late in the afternoon on Friday. The people of the ministry would have left their offices for sure, and they would only be back on Monday.

The other LTOs were trying to convince me to just go to Naryn. Les even offered to take my place, so that I could take his place in a Bishkek team. But Dimitra called me and said: ,,Jos, don't tell this to Les, but he is 73 and therefore really too old to go up into the mountains. We have had so many problems already on this mission; we don't want any more problems."

I skyped with my wife and she also advised me to just go to Naryn: ,,Maybe Peter is not so bad after all." Florence also was willing to change places with me, but Dimitra told her bluntly: ,,Listen, Jos knows the rules. He has to go."

I argued with Dimitra that my big suitcase was still in Osh, but she said simply that it would be sent to Naryn at a later stage. After all this, I decided to go to Naryn. So I found myself in a car for five hours, with a driver who spoke only Kyrgyz and Russian.

Vladimir was OK though. We were stopped at three checkpoints by the police, but everything went fine. When I arrived at the Celestial Mountains Guesthouse, Peter was extremely happy to see me. He had been without a partner for more than a week.

I moved into the best room of the hotel: the room where Lazet had stayed in. It was called a 'luxury suite', which meant that it had its own bath room. Adjacent to the hotel compound stood several Yurts. The Yurts were popular with tourists, but to me they looked rather uncomfortable.

My room was fine. It looked like a student room in the 1970s. There was no fridge, so I kept my bottles of beer cool in a bucket full of water. The hotel's breakfast, as I would find out, proved to be amongst the worst I had ever had. I sadly remembered the fantastic meals we were served in Vitaly's guesthouse in Osh. But that's the life of an observer: it's not all oranges and sunshine.

I soon found out that Peter was not a bad guy at all. In fact, he was very much OK. I realized that it must have been Analisa, his Italian partner, back in Nigeria, who was the difficult person. Peter turned out to be likable, intelligent, a good observer, and he had been married to a Russian woman for fifteen years, so he was fluent in Russian.

Peter had one great passion: photography. One day we drove in the direction of the Chinese border. Twice, Peter told the driver to stop the car. Then Peter would walk a few hundred meters up a mountainous slope, to photograph birds. Asel, our interpreter and I remained in the car. She surprised me, by confiding to me that Peter was only happy when he took photographs.

But Asel was young and had never travelled beyond the borders of Kyrgyzstan. Therefore, she never had a profound conversation with Peter. When Peter was alone with me, he became quite animated when we discussed topics like music, movies, history, archaeology and politics.

So Peter was OK. There was a problem, though. Peter's hands were shaking continuously. I wondered if he suffered from Parkinson's disease, but I was too chicken to ask him. Many people think that I'm a tough guy, but I'm really a softy at heart.

Close to our hotel stood an old T-34 tank in a park. Children were playing on it. With some difficulty, I managed to climb on top of the tank. I handed Peter my small digital camera and asked him to make some photographs. I later found out that all of them were shaky.

We had a good time, though. Asel, our interpreter, was a nice young woman. The climate was pleasantly cool and Naryn was a quiet little town, with only 40,000 inhabitants. Less than one hundred Uighurs and Uzbeks lived there; not enough to create ethnic problems.

And more good news: a few days later my suitcase arrived. It was still locked, so nothing was missing. My hair dryer was still there, as was the thermos for my coffee. And my Wild Havana cigars, made in a Dutch factory. I could finally put on a clean shirt, clean socks and clean underpants. Such luxury!

We undertook several trips to the surrounding districts, including one trip that took us close to the border with China. One late afternoon, Peter and I climbed a mountain on foot. I explained to him that there are no mountains in The Netherlands and that it was not a natural thing for me to do. Peter felt at ease on top of that mountain. I was happy when, finally, we walked back down.

I received a number of phone calls from Florence, my previous partner. She was now observing in Bishkek. She told me that I had to call Raul, our Deputy Chief Observer, because Martin was telling lies about Florence and me on social media. Apparently, he accused us of not wanting to be rescued by OSCE, since we didn't like OSCE.

I never consulted any social media, so I was not bothered by the fact that an idiot was spreading lies about us. But Florence kept calling me. Since it was important to her, I called Raul, who assured me that he would call the OSCE office in Osh. After that, Martin did not spread any more false gossip.

R-Day passed without incidents. There were no STOs, but in the hotel we were joined by several western diplomats from Bishkek. One of them explained to me that he had come to Naryn because he was afraid that the ethnic violence would spread to Bishkek because of R-Day. Things remained relatively calm though.

In order to cover a few rural polling stations, we travelled to the town of At Bashi, along the road to the border with China. No problems there. At 19.30 hours we arrived back in Osh at the green-red hospital in the city centre, to observe the closing and counting of a polling station.

I searched my mind where I had seen that hospital before. Than it dawned on me: it looked exactly like Albert Schweitzer's colonial hospital in Lambaréné, Gabon, that my wife and I had visited in 1982.

As expected, the 'Yes' vote had won. The new constitution was approved. What was the new constitution about? Well: about lot's of things, the most important being that interim president Ms. Roza Otunbaeva could remain in power, as well as the introduction of a semi-parliamentary system. A bit vague, actually.

A few days later, Peter and I returned to Bishkek. Asel, our interpreter, travelled with us. She liked Bishkek better than Naryn, which, I have to admit, was not the most exciting place for young people. On the way back we halted for an hour or so at the shores of Lake Izzy Kul (meaning 'warm waters').

The lake is 130 kilometres long and 70 kilometres wide. Quite impressive, but not as magical as Lake Titicaca in Peru/Bolivia. I have to say, though, that we were at the wrong side of the lake. We were at the south side, while the famed sanatoria were at the north side. We did not have time to visit them.

The debriefings in the OSCE offices went well. Our departure from Osh had been in such haste and chaos, that I had completely forgotten to pay for our guesthouse. Luckily, Svetlana, our Russian interpreter, met Florence and me in Bishkek, just before we left the country. I gave her the money in cash euros and an accompanying letter. The Russian owners had been really nice to us.

On the Turkish Airlines flight back I was the only observer travelling in Business Class. Back home in Holland, hardly anybody had noticed the ethnic violence in far off Kyrgyzstan. Everybody had been watching the Football World Cup that had been played in South Africa.

The Dutch national team made it all the way to the final, where they lost 1-0 to Spain. Football is important, I know that. Much more important than a few ethnic clashes in a small, little known country in far-away central Asia.

I just wondered how the Uzbeks and Kyrgyz would ever manage to live together again in Osh, after so much ethnic hatred and violence. Both ethnic groups possessed their houses and businesses there. Neither group could just simply move away.

In the end, the Uzbeks and Kyrgyz must have found a way to live in close proximity to one another, since, as far as I know, no major outbreaks of ethnic violence have happened since that fateful June 2010. Or maybe it simply did not make the headlines in far-away western Europe.

CHAPTER 11

SUDAN
First (Registration) Phase - 2010/2011

'You're obliged to stay at Khadaffi's hotel'

In November 2010, South Sudan was still a part of Sudan. After decades of war between the black, southern Christian peoples and northern Islamic Arabs, the southern Sudanese were finally allowed to hold a referendum with only one question: 'Do you want South Sudan to be an independent country?'

Since it was a very important referendum, the EU fielded an observation mission, not only for the referendum phase, but also for the preceding registration phase. In order to become an independent country, at least fifty percent of the registered voters would have to vote in favour of independence. That made the initial Registration Phase just as important as the final Referendum Phase.

South Sudan produces oil, but for decades the revenues went to North Sudan, leaving South Sudan one of the most miserable regions in Africa. The entire country has only 40 kilometers of paved roads. South Sudan has two more problems, though. Firstly, indeed it has oil, but it is a landlocked country and the only pipeline runs through North Sudan.

Secondly, during all those years of struggle against the Arabs of northern Sudan, the peoples in South Sudan were united because of a common cause. What would happen after independence, when there was no common enemy to fight?

One thing seemed sure: South Sudan was facing an uncertain future. About half a year after I had returned home, I read in a newspaper that a South Sudanese minister had been shot by his driver. This seemed weird.

It became even weirder, when I learned that his driver was a family member of the minister. A few days later, I learned that each minister in South Sudan appointed only members of his own tribe to his ministry. They simply don't trust any outsiders.

As we now know, just a few years after independence Southern Sudanese tribal leaders starterd fighting amongst themselves for the spoils of the country. Since they did not trust one another, none of them invested a penny in their own country. Instead, they purchased property in neighbouring countries, like Kenya and Uganda.

Nowadays, nobody has any faith in the future of South Sudan. But back in November 2010 we didn't know all this. At Schiphol Amsterdam Airport, the Dutch customs official asked me where I was going too. ,,First to Nairobi, then on to Juba", I replied. He looked a bit puzzled. ,,Juba: where is that?" he asked.

"Well, they told me it's the future capital of South Sudan. They're going to have a referendum there. I'm an election observer for the EU." He handed me back my passport and gave me a doubtful look. ,,Better be on your way, then. I wish you success."

The flight to Nairobi took a little more than eight hours. There were several other LTOs on the plane. It's always nice to gossip about our colleagues, even though that means that you hardly get any sleep. We had to wait another six hours at Nairobi Airport. Not the most exiting airport in the world.

There were twelve LTOs there. I did not have the local currency, but an Irish LTO offered me a cup of coffee for free. She was very nice. Her name was Sheena and she would be my partner for the next ten weeks.

It was only a short flight to Juba. The airport of Juba, the capital of South Sudan, is a pitiful sight. We were welcomed by a bald man, who did not introduce himself, but apparently worked for the Service Provider. He looked Italian to me.

We were driven to the airport hotel, consisting of several rows of containers turned into bed rooms. My room was OK. The airco worked, even though there is no electricity in South Sudan. The hotels and restaurants have generators, though. Very noisy machines.

Thank God for my ear plugs. As usual, after two flights and a lengthy stopover at Nairobi airport, we were promised that we could take the rest of the day off, but also as usual this was not to be.

We were allowed to take a quick shower, after which the briefings started.

I entered the conference room and looked for my name. There were eight LTO teams, but I could not find my name. Finally, on the table at the very front, I spotted my name. Hurray! But then I noted something very strange: they had made a mistake.

Below my name, in brackets, was written one word: Khartoum. This could not be correct, since we were here for the South Sudan referendum. I had accepted the mission to South Sudan specifically because I knew that South Sudan was Christian and Christian means beer.

EU missions are usually deployed in tropical countries, where it is very hot and you sweat your butt off all day. Therefore, after a long day's work, I really like to sit down in the cool evening air and have a nice cold beer, to get some liquid inside my body.

Now they were sending me to Khartoum, the capital of North Sudan, where there was no beer at all, because North Sudan had introduced Sharia law. I could not believe they were sending me there. But they explained that half a million South Sudanese lived in Khartoum and that all of them were allowed to vote in the referendum.

There was also good news: my partner would be Sheena, the nice 62-year old Irish woman who had offered me a cup of coffee at Nairobi airport. As it would turn out, Sheena would become one of my best partners. We worked very well together.

The next day, during lunch break, I took a stroll along the little shops that lined the airport road. All of them sold beer: Heineken, Budweiser, Amstel, Carlsberg. Stacks and stacks of beer. Sadly, I realized that these would be the last beers I would see for the next ten weeks. In Khartoum, there would be no beer.

I did not see anything of Juba. Two full days we were involved in briefings. The last evening they took us to restaurant Paradiso, with a large open courtyard. Very nice Ethiopian food, that we ate with our hands. The local beer also tasted fine.

Since it was pitchdark, I did not see anything of the city. It was only on the third day, when we flew away with Ethiopian Airways, that I saw the great river Nile below me. There are direct flights between

Juba and Khartoum, but we were not allowed to take them, since the EU was obliged to follow the very strict UN MOSS safety rules and regulations.

This was because EU observers fell under the UN security system, in case there were security problems in the country. This was fine with me. After my evacuation by military helicopter in Kyrgyzstan I appreciated any help by the UN System. The EU paid a lot of money for this to the UN, and it was a good thing, since the UN would take care of us when the shit would really hit the fan.

The only problem was that the UN had blacklisted the vast majority of Sudanese national airlines, which meant that we would have to fly from Juba to Khartoum with either Kenyan Airways or Ethiopian Airways, in other words via either Nairobi or Addis Ababa.

Of the eight LTO teams, two were deployed to North Sudan. Sheena would later tell me that Mariusz, the observer coordinator, had asked her if she was happy with me. She told him: 'Yes, very much so'. She suspected that one of the other LTOs had wanted to take my place, since South Sudan is not the most inviting region on the planet.

I knew who this LTO was, since I had talked to Wlodek from Poland a few times. I knew Wlodek from previous missions. He's not a bad guy. He told me that I had been very lucky, since I would stay at the most luxurious hotel of Khartoum, while he would be staying in the middle of nowhere under horrible conditions.

I heard him talk to Mariusz in Polish, several times, but in the end Mariusz decided not risk being accused of giving preference to one of his countrymen, so he did not change the LTO teams.

A few weeks later the Core Team would accidently forward an email exchange to all LTO teams. It was actually a private exchange between Wlodek and the Core Team. It was very funny. The LTO teams in the South had been equipped with BGANs: an apparatus that must be connected to your laptop and then pointed at a satellite, in order to be able to connect to the internet.

Now Wlodek had already been disappointed that he was deployed in the poor South and not in the luxury hotel in Khartoum, which of course had electricity and WiFi 24/7. He was obliged to use te BGAN every day, but the BGAN is very expensive: every minute of satellite time would cost around twelve dollars. So the BGAN was only to be used for the most necessary communications, like email exchanges with the Core Team.

But Wlodek was addicted to the internet. During the briefings, he was always reading Polish newspapers on his private laptop. And he habitually checked the weather in Warsaw. In South Sudan he did the same. He used the BGAN several hours per day, to the dismay of the Core Team, who asked him to restrict himself a bit.

Wlodek's reply was hilarious: 'You sent me here, in the middle of nowhere. Nothing works here. There's nothing to do here, except to use the BGAN. And now you're telling me to use it less. I can't believe it'.

So twelve LTOs were deployed to different parts of South Sudan. Two of them would later be medically evacuatied to Nairobi: one caught malaria and the other one was bitten by some insect, after which his arm got all swollen up. Sheena and I had no such problems in Khartoum.

Another LTO team would be deployed to North Sudan, but they would be mobile and travel to different areas. They were a rather odd couple: an elderly, rather bossy English woman called Stella and an elderly Finnish man called Jorma, who was a bit withdrawn. Jorma was 67, Stella was 64 and Sheena was 62, leaving me, at the tender age of only 55, to be by far the youngest.

The four of us arrived at Addis Ababa airport, which looked a lot better than Juba airport. It looked even better than Nairobi airport. We had to stay there for a little more than eight hours. Somehow, Sheena found out that Ethiopian Airways would take us to a hotel in the centre of Addis, free of charge, when our stopover would be more than eight hours.

That sounded good. We went to the manager's office, but he explained that there was a problem: our plane had had a delay of one hour, which meant that we would spend only seven and a half hours at Addis Ababa's airport.

We told him that it was not our fault, that the plane was delayed. But he remained adamant: seven and a half hours is less than eight hours, therefore we could forget about our bus trip to the center of Addis. There is a kind of logic to this: African logic.

The four of us arrived at Khartoum airport at 02.00 hours. Mario was waiting for us there. He was the Khartoum chief of IOM, our Service Provider. A nice Italian guy. I liked him. He asked if we had any booze in our luggage, since during the previous elections an EU-observer had been detained at the airport for several hours, because he carried a bottle of whiskey in his suitcase.

We did not carry any alcohol, so there was no problem. The airport was deserted, apart from the twenty or so arrivals from our plane. We were taken to our hotel. For security reasons, we had to stay at the most expensive hotel of the entire country.

It was a very modern hotel, in the shape of a huge egg, covered all around with blue glass and white stripes. It was known as the Burj el Fateh, or simply as the Burj. Or the Egg. In order to build the hotel, a little obstacle had to be removed first: Khartoum's zoo. A minor problem. Who cares about zoo's anyway?

A few days later, I found out that the owner of the hotel was Colonel Khadaffi, the Libyan dictator. The locals called the hotel: 'Khadaffi's Egg'. For a few days, Khadaffi even stayed with us in his own hotel. The romantic story that he slept in a tent in the desert was made up, for publicity reasons.

We never saw Khadaffi, since he possessed his own luxury suites somewhere between the 13th and the 17th floors, only accessible via a hidden elevator. After Khadaffi's death the hotel became a Corinthia hotel.

Khadaffi visited Sudan at the same time as Hosni Mubarak, Egypt's long-term ruler. They were there to discuss the future of Sudan and South Sudan, together with Sudan's president Bashir and South Sudan's leader Kiir. The region of Darfur was also on the agenda.

I have nothing against luxury. To the contrary. There was a problem, though. Since Sudan had introduced Sharia law, our western credit cards were not accepted anywhere. So we could not pay our hotel. The EU EOM found a very agreeable solution: the EU would pay for the hotels. For all observers on this mission.

Normally, they would then deduct 30 percent of our salaries, but in this case, since it was a rather complicated country in any case, especially for our colleagues in South Sudan, the EU decided that there would be no deduction.

So I would be paid the full amount and the very expensive hotel was free of charge. Of course, breakfast was included. The breakfast was the largest buffet I had ever seen in my life. It kept me going all day.

I loved Khartoum. Sheena and I only spent a few euros on evening meals. During those ten weeks I saved so much money that I purchased a new car for my wife.

The first six weeks in Khartoum were fantastic: most members of the Core Team were based in Juba. The only Core Team member in Khartoum was Richard, the very likable Irish legal expert. Mario was the only international expert of the Service Provider and Sheena and I were the only LTOs based in Khartoum.

We had a great time. Every day, Sheena and I and our interpreter and driver would go around visiting Polling Stations, where South Sudanes voters were being registered. In the evenings, Sheena and I visited a restaurant, usually accompanied by Richard.

Richard was particularly fond of the famous Acropole hotel, that was owned by a Greek family, who had been born in Sudan. During the Ethiopian famine, many journalists had stayed there. It was cheap and it was a nice place with friendly people, but the food was quite basic. I preferred the open-air Assaha Lebanese Village restaurant, that was a bit more expensive. It looked like a medieval castle.

A funny thing occured during nearly every evening meal: Sheena would explain to the waiter that she was allergic to gluten and therefore could not eat bread. To a Sudanese, this was incomprehensible. All meals are served with bread. So every evening, Sheena would be served a meal with bread, no matter what she told the waiters.

I would simply have given up and just ignored the bread, but Sheena was Irish: she explained evening after evening to different waiters that it would be a waist to serve her bread. They kept serving her anyway. What I found a little bit annoying was that we could never eat in a pizzeria, since pizza bottoms also contain gluten.

Normally, as Long Term Observers, we would go around everyday interviewing people, to collect information for our Weekly Reports. In this case, however, the Core Team had explained to us that, during the Registration Phase, our job would largely be to visit as many Polling Stations as possible. Like an extended E-Day.

This became a bit boring, but the good news was that Khartoum is a very big city: lots of different urban districts to explore. One evening, just before dark, Richard, Sheena and I walked over to Tuti Island, where the White and Blue Nile converge.

I knew Tuti Island from the books by Wilbur Smith, but it was a disappointment. There's not much on it: just a poor, sandy neighbourhood with a few small mosques, some vegetable gardens and a stone factory.

Our interpreter, Mohammed, was a young student of medicine. At least: he told us that he studied medicine. We hardly needed an interpreter, since most polling staff were educated and spoke English. The polling staff were a mix of northern and southern Sudanese.

We did not observe serious problems between northerners and southerners, but a few times, when we managed to talk to southerners in private, they confided to us that they were discriminated by the northerners. All the voters were southern Sudanese, of course. Many spoke a little English.

All educated northern Sudanese spoke decent English. In hindsight, this is remarkable. Three years later I would be working as an observer in central Egypt, where hardly anyone speaks English. How is this possible? Egypt receives millions of tourists every year, while only a handful of tourists ever visit Sudan.

We needed our interpreter to communicate with our driver, though. Omar, our driver was OK, but spoke only Arabic. Our driver and our interpreter had one thing in common: bot of them could not read maps and could not orientate themselves in any way. Luckily, we had been equipped with a GPS.

I became an expert with the GPS. In the central parts of Khartoum, streets have names, but in the poor suburbs, where half a million South Sudanese live, the streets have no names and the houses have no numbers. These are huge areas and they all look the same.

On my GPS, I marked all the schools where we encountered polling stations, so that we could find them back easily. The first weeks we were driving around trying to find schools. We had a list with all the polling stations and once we reached an outlying district, our interpreter and our driver would open their windows and ask for directions in Arabic.

The good news is that Khartoum is one of the safest cities on the planet. A woman can walk the streets at night all by her own, without being bothered. That's the advantage of Sharia law: any thief or assaulter will be punished so severely, that people think twice before committing a crime. It's also a laidback city. Most people are relaxed and friendly towards westerners.

Even though Khartoum was very safe, Sheena and I received instructions from our Core Team that we should attend a two-day safety training course at the UNMIS compound at the international airport. I prepared Sheena for the 'kidnapping', that would surely occur. It did.

Afterwards, the Malinese UN soldiers apologized to us that they had been a bit rude, when they forced us down onto the sand with hoods over our heads. I had, in fact, experienced worse 'kidnappings' for training purposes. We also had to escape from a burning car in the middle of a mine field.

The good news was that we met several UN staff, one of whome was a Canadian women called Michele, who said she could arrange a bottle of whisky for us. In due time.

When we were in the car, Sheena was always reading a book. I, on the other hand, was always looking outside. One day, Sheena asked our interpreter if women were allowed to drive under Sharia law, since in Saudi Arabia they were not. I already knew the answer: I had seen hundreds of women drive cars.

Mohammed was genuinely surprised that she asked that question. ,,Of course women are allowed to drive", he replied sternly. Then Sheena asked him if male and female students went to college together. Again, Mohammed was surprised. ,,Of course", he said. ,,Why not?"

Obviously, Sheena was comparing Sudan to Saudi Arabia. They are totally different societies, though. The Sudanese leadership was in favour of Sharia law, but most ordinary people were not. Most Sudanese are moderate muslims. As was confirmed when, one day, Mohammed invited us to his house.

We noted an enormous flatscreen TV in the living room. He switched it on and to my surprise we were watching MTV. Very loud western music. It's comforting to know that ordinary youth in Sudan want the same things as ordinary youth in the rest of the world: to watch MTV and to be able to go to a cinema or a discotheque, in order to meet the opposite sex.

Then it was 2 December: my birthday. I did not tell Sheena anything, except that I wanted to have dinner with her in the best place we had encountered: Assaha Lebanese Village restaurant. When we sat down in the inner courtyard, I told her that dinner would be on me, since it was my birthday. She told me that she had expected something like this. Thank God she didn't sing for me.

When we got back to our hotel, a huge cake stood prominently on a small table in my room. On it was written: 'Happy Birthday'. I immediately called Sheena and told her that I was grateful for her cake, but she said that she did not know anything about it. I realized that the hotel had scanned our passports, so the hotel staff knew our birthdays.

By now, we learned that the Registration Phase had been extended with one week. So one more week we visited RCs. Unfortunately, Mohammed, our interpreter, had already booked a flight to Saudi Arabia, to visit his father.

We recruited another interpreter, also named Mohammed. Mohammed II was not much different from Mohammed I: both could not find their way around Khartoum. Yet again, we ended up 'happy hunting' for RCs. One afternoon, Sheena had a fight with Mohammed II.

Sheena wanted to visit RCs in a far-off shantytown, but Mohammed II advised not to go there. ,,That area is really unsafe. Lot's of drunkards", he protested. We went there anyway. We didn't see any drunkards, but it was a very poor neighborhood. I had a feeling that much more than half a million southerners were living in Khartoum. And that, referendum or no referendum, they would not return to poor South Sudan.

We were instructed by our Core Team to take Rosalind Marsden, the EU Special Representative for Sudan and her secretary, Luca Zampetti, to a few RCs. Rosalind had been UK Ambassador in Sudan for three years, so she knew much more about the country than Sheena and me.

But the visits went well. We selected an RC in Omdurman with an elderly Nubian as its chair. We knew that he liked to talk to us, westerners, and that his English was good. Rosalind was happy.

The plan was still that Sheena and I would fly back to Juba via Addis Ababa for debriefings and then fly back to Europe via Nairobi, but Richard advised us to send an email to the Core Team, asking them if we could fly straight from Khartoum to Amsterdam with KLM. Thus, we could spend a few more days in our beloved Khartoum. What was the use of those debriefings anyway?

To my pleasant surprise, the Core Team agreed. My wife was not happy, because it meant that I would come home a few days later than originally foreseen. But Sheena and I were elated that the horrible trip Khartoum-Addis-Juba-Nairobi-Amsterdam had been cancelled. We'd rather stay one more week in our luxurious Khadaffi hotel, with permanent electricity, permanent WiFi and the biggest buffet-breakfast in the world.

The mobile phones that we received from our mission had been programmed in such a way that international communications were impossible. Therefore, I had purchased, with the help of our interpreter and driver, a local Sim-Card. My wife and I skyped everyday with eachother, but the problem was that I never knew when I would have time to skype, so every day I had to warn her to switch on her computer.

I had to change the Sim-Card every day, but after a week or so I found out that my new Sudanese Sim-Card functioned just as well on my private, rather old-fashioned mobile phone. So no more changing Sim-Cards: I left it permanently in my private Dutch phone. It was very cheap to send an SMS to Holland from my Sudanese Sim-Card.

The day before we would travel back to Europe, we met our replacement LTO team: Cyril from France and Rosemary from Canada.

I wondered what they were going to do, since the Registration Centres had all closed by now.

They appeared to be over-achievers, since their first question was: 'What are the bullet points in your Weekly Reports?' Cyril would later become Observer Coordinator on French speaking missions. The ultimate proof that he really was an over-achiever.

Chapter 12

SUDAN
Second (Registration) Phase - 2010/2011

'When they have no common enemy, they'll fight each other'

On 8 December, we were allowed to return to our home countries for ten days. Before I knew it, it was 18 December and I was supposed to board the direct KLM flight between Holland and Sudan, but there was a problem. Schiphol Airport near Amsterdam was covered under a thick layer of snow.

In Holland, we only have snow on average for one week per year. We are not used to snow. We don't know what to do about it. Planes were delayed or even cancelled. Some passengers had been waiting at the airport for more than 24 hours, since other airports in Europe were also covered with snow.

My plane was scheduled to leave on time, but there was a problem: the departure hall was completely filled with stranded travellers. I couldn't get through. So there I was: I had arrived at the airport on time, but I simply could not get to the KLM counter to deliver my suitcase.

Normally, the Dutch are good at organizing things, but in this case no one took charge: not the airport authorities, not the security staff, not the airlines. So there was no movement and I could not get through. I nearly panicked. Finally, I explained to people that my plane would be leaving within one hour.

Reluctantly, they let me through. I handed over my suitcase and received my boarding pass. I had to run to the security checkpoint, but the security staff don't care about passengers being late. They only care about security. All the time, the minutes were ticking away.

In the end, there was no need to be worried, since my plane was delayed a few hours. I reached Khartoum airport rather late that evening. So did my suitcase, thank God. In Holland it was ten degrees below zero, in Khartoum it was thirty degrees above zero. The mission had sent a driver to pick me up. At 23.25 hours I arrived at the Burj el Fateh, also known as Kaddafi's Egg.

It felt like coming home. I knew all the men and women at the reception. Yes, women also worked at the reception. And no, they were not veiled. The Sudanese government had imposed Sharia law on the country, but most Sudanese were not really in favour of it.

Yet again, the hotel had reserved a room close to the elevators and yet again I managed to get a much quieter room at the very end of the hallway, but I had to wait until the next day. This was not a problem, since I had arrived ahead of everybody else. Many observers were delayed because of the snowfall in Europe.

Before I left for Holland, Mario had asked me to bring back some smoked fish for him. It took an effort to find good old Mario, since the IOM offices had moved to another floor in our hotel. Finally, I found him. I also managed to find Richard.

There was a problem: I had left a lot of my stuff behind in his office, but by now his office was occupied by Veronique de Keyser, our Chief Observer, who was a member of the European Parliament for Belgium. Luckily, Richard still possessed the key to the drawer in his old room. He handed me Sheena's stuff as well.

Sheena arrived two days later. While I was enjoying the best breakfast buffet in the world, she joined me at the table, just like before. The first thing we found out was that Omar, our driver, had been sacked. Apparently, while we were back home in Europe, the drivers had gone on strike and Omar had been their ringleader.

The drivers had a point, though. Like in many Third World countries, they were paid very poorly by their company, even by local standards. Sometimes, they even have to wait for months before receiving any of their pitiful salaries.

Quite often, the EU EOM therefore decides to pay a bonus to the drivers. But in this case, maybe cordoned by the host country, it was initially decided not to pay them a bonus. Later on, we received instructions to pay the drivers for 'overtime'.

This resulted in the funny situation that the drivers daily salary was only 10 SDG, while 'overtime' was 15 SDG. I am always in favour of paying bonuses to our drivers, not only since their salaries are ridiculously low, but also to enhance their commitment towards our mission. Or am I selfish here?

In any case, we now had a new driver, Ahmed, who turned out to be quite a grumpy guy and didn't know where to find any of the spread-out polling stations. But Ahmed spoke a bit of English. That was an improvement, even though we would have preferred our old driver.

Before Sheena arrived, I had been walking around the hotel, since there was nothing to do. Now Sheena and I were both walking around the hotel without anything to do. We still had to wait for the Core Team and the other LTOs. This time, the mission would be much bigger and half the Core Team would be based in Juba, the other half in our hotel in Khartoum, since the Sudanese government sat in Khartoum.

Sheena and I walked to the National Museum, just a few hundred meters from our hotel. Mohammed, our interpreter, joined us. He had never visited a museum before. It's definitely not the best museum in the world, but they do have a statue of the only pharaoh mentioned by name in the bible: Taharqa, also spelled Taharka of Taharqo.

In the bible he's called Tirhaka. He ruled in the early seventh century B.C. when most of the Old Testament was put to paper. Taharqa belonged to the so-called Numibian dynasty: black pharaohs from the northern part of present-day Sudan.

Why do I mention this? Because the most important pharaohs are not mentioned in the bible: Ramses II, Hatshepsut, Tutmoses III, Amenhotep IV, also known as Akhnaton, who was the first human being on earth to worship only one god instead of many gods.

A few lines in Psalm 104 in the bible were apparently copied from writings on Akhnaton's walls at Tell el Amarna. Why then, is he not mentioned in the bible? His wife, Nefertiti, is also not mentioned. Nor is his son, by another wife, Tutankhamon.

While we were in the museum, I rather unexpectedly received an SMS in Spanish from Alberto, who had been my STO in Venezuela and my colleague LTO in Pakistan. I liked him very much.

He had been living in Frankfurt for twelve years with his German girlfriend, but he now lived in Brussels, where he worked fulltime as an observer. He formed an LTO team with Alessandro from Italy, who would later be my press officer in Honduras.

They would be based in Khartoum, like us, and we would share the responsibility over two STO teams. We decided that Sheena and I would cover Omdurman, the huge part of Khartoum on the westbank of the Nile. They would cover the rest of the city. And they would be responsible for assisting the MEP's who were scheduled to observe in central Khartoum. Thank God for that.

The other LTOs had also arrived. They would cover other areas in North Sudan. Sheena and I assisted in the briefings of the new arrivals. By now, we were old Sudan hands. The staff of the Service Provider also had their offices in our hotel.

I especially liked Edmundo, the American Security Expert, and Rudy, his Belgian deputy, who had been my security liaison officer in Pakistan. ,,Sudan is easier than Pakistan", was the first thing Rudy told me.

I would spend quite a few hours in Rudy's office. Edmundo was always complaining that he could not understand a word of what we were saying. ,,The working language of the mission is English", Edmundo told us several times. We told him that he should learn Dutch instead.

A weird thing happened. One evening, Edmundo took me apart and told me that I was not allowed to leave the hotel the next day. I asked him why, but he said that he wanted to talk to the Dutch embassy first. I said that I could go with him to the embassy, but he said no.

The next day, after he had returned from the Dutch embassy, he finally explained what the problem was. Apparently, 'a certain group of Sudanese' were planning to abduct Swiss or Dutch nationals, since this group believed that only the Swiss and the Dutch governments would pay ransom money.

I was flabbergasted. I told Edmundo that the official policy of the Dutch government had always been never to pay any ransom money, since paying would only inspire more criminals to abduct Dutch nationals.

Edmundo said that I was right, but the problem was that this 'Sudanese group' believed otherwise. His visit to the Dutch embassy had made one thing clear though: the threat was limited to the Darfur region, more than one thousand kilometres from Khartoum, so there was no direct threat for me.

On Christmas day, we travelled in two cars to the northern part of Sudan, to visit the famous Numibian pyramids. Apart from Sheena and me, legal expert Richard and his assistant Sami were with us, as was press officer Eberhard from Germany and the Sudanese security assistant of our mission.

Alberto and Alessandro did not join us. They had already visited the pyramids in April, when they had been LTOs in Khartoum. Our Observer Coordinator, Roman from Slovakia, had also been an LTO then, so the three of them knew one another very well.

The trip took about four hours. By then, Sheena and I had lived in Khartoum for five weeks, but we had never left the city limits. Now, for the first time, we drove through the desert. I like deserts. Where there is no water, there are no mosquitoes.

My wife and I had hitchhiked all through the Sahara desert back in 1982, after we finished our studies. In Sudan there is very little vegetation, but we saw lots of camels, goats and donkeys.

Luckily, it was mid-winter, so it was only 30 degrees Celsius. The pyramids were fantastic. They are smaller and steeper than the pyramids in Egypt, but there are more pyramids in Sudan than in all of Egypt. Furthermore, there are no tourists in Sudan. We were the only visitors.

I felt like the 19th century explorers, who were the first to discover these now world famous archaeological sites. We also visited an area that looked a bit like the Valley of the Kings near Luxor. Many Sudanese pharaohs had been buried there, but all the graves had been looted.

The guard allowed us to enter the graves. Luckily, we had brought our torches. The paintings on the walls were very much like Egyptian wall paintings, including the same kind of hieroglyphs.

A few years later, on Dutch television, I saw actress Joanne Lumley enter the same graves, with probably the same guard. She must have been there at the same time that we were there.

On the way back, close to a bend in the river Nile, we passed a graveyard. ,,My nephew is buried here", our Sudanese security assistant said. ,,He was eleven years old when he went for a swim in the Nile. He was grabbed by a crocodile."

We all enjoyed the day. In fact, we enjoyed it so much that no one was in a hurry to return to Khartoum. I received several calls from Edmundo. He became more and more pissed off, when he learned that we would not be back before dark. In the end, it was almost 22.00 hours when we finally arrived back at the hotel.

I explained to him that I thought we'd better travel slowly in the dark, to avoid accidents. He reluctantly agreed. Anyway, his own security assistant had been with us, so we were quite safe. But there are good reasons not to travel in the dark, as we found out.

Not only were camels, goats and donkeys walking on the road, but the few cars that we passed had either hardly any light at all, or their lights were so bright that they blinded us. The security rules of our missions really make sense.

During the Registration Phase, Sheena and I had visited all polling stations in Omdurman over and over again. We had neglected our Weekly Reports, though. We were reprimanded by Roman, the Deputy Observer Coordinator. He said that the reports made by our replacement team, Cyril and Rosemary, had been much better.

We explained to him that, during the registration phase, we had received specific instructions from the Core Team that visiting registration centres was to be our absolute priority. Every day, we had to transmit the forms. After Cyril and Rosemary took over from Sheena and me, the RC's had been closed, so they could not visit them.

But I had to admit that Roman was quite right, so we started interviewing more and more representatives of political parties, the media and aid agencies who worked closely with the South Sudanese living in Khartoum. In short: we started working as LTOs instead of STOs.

There was a problem, though. Our new driver, Ahmed, told us that his mobile phone had been stolen from his home. His wife's phone had also been stolen. We explained to him that we could not solve all his personal problems for him, but that we needed to be able to contact our driver at all times. So we gave him two days to buy or borrow another phone. Otherwise, we would ask for another driver. Two days later he had another phone.

We observed the training of domestic observers and party agents in Hotel Rotana. At one point, I was talking to some people when I received a call from Sheena. I had to come to her immediately, because she was speaking to a Dutch woman. It took me a few minutes to finish my conversation.

In the meantime, Eberhard, the Press Officer of our mission, had joined Sheena and the Dutch woman. I overheard the Dutch woman say, rather annoyed: 'This man is not Dutch'. That's right. Eberhard was German. Later he told me that one of his grandparents had been Dutch, so he understood our language quite well.

On Friday 31 December 2010 Sheena and I had lunch with a Canadian couple in restaurant Solitaire II. We had met Michele during our security training at the UNMIS compound. Her husband, Howard, provided us with a short explanation on corruption in Africa in general and in South-Sudan in particular. It was a bit of a blow to Sheena's beautiful ideals.

Howard handed us each a bottle of Jack Daniels Red Label under the table. We gave him 180 US dollars in return, also under the table. A bit expensive, 90 dollars for a bottle of whisky. I don't even like whisky, but hey: what do you do in a situation of scarcity?

It is not illegal, by the way, for westerners to drink alcohol in Sudan. In fact, they have exactly the same rules as Pakistan: westerners are allowed to drink alcohol, but not in public places. And westerners are not allowed to import alcohol or to buy it from Muslims.

So our deal with the Canadians was absolutely legal. I locked the bottle of whiskey in a drawer in my room, so the hotel staff would not notice it. And I purchased dozens of cans of alcohol-free beer, to which I then added a little whisky, before going to sleep. Scarcity makes people inventive. Ask anyone in Cuba.

One day, just before dusk, we visited the world famous swirling dervishes at the huge cemetery in Omdurman where the Mahdi is buried. There were about twenty European spectators and hundreds of Sudanese. The Mahdi led the historic uprising against general Gordon in the late 19th century.

The new year started with a bit of a deception: we were not allowed to leave our hotel. Edmundo explained that the first of January was celebrated as Independence Day in Sudan. Huge crowds are always tricky business: you never know if tensions will rise. As westerners, we are at risk. In the end, nothing happened, but I agreed with Edmundo: it's better to be safe than sorry.

A few days later, the STOs arrived. We briefed them, together with Alberto and Alessandro. They were a good bunch: Mar from Spain and Roberts from Lithuania formed STO1 and Christer from Sweden and Marcia from Cyprus formed STO2.

Christer, a retired policeman from Sweden, had been my colleague LTO in Pakistan and Nigeria. I would meet Roberts on quite a few future missions. And I had met Marcia during my NEEDS course for Legal/Election experts in Brussels in 2009, even though I did not recognize her. It really annoys me that I have a bad memory for faces.

A funny thing happened when Sheena and I were quarrelling very publicly on the thirteenth flour of the hotel, near the elevators. The other LTOs and STOs were sitting just around a corner and overheard how Sheena was raging at me.

She was angry, because it had taken her weeks to get an invitation from a Sudanese judge from Nubian origin, to go over to his house and meet his wife and other educated Sudanese women. She wanted me to join her.

There was a problem though, because at the same time we were supposed to go out for dinner with our four STOs and the other LTO team. I calmly explained to Sheena that our STOs were far more important than a local judge, who was hardly involved in elections anyway, but she remained adamant.

Sheena yelled at me that I was a traitor. I calmly replied to her: „Listen, you go to your judge and I will go with the STOs." After this, the other observers greatly admired me for my ability to work with Sheena. Alberto and Alessandro later told me: 'They should name Tuti Island after you'.

But the truth was: Sheena turned out to be one of my best partners ever. We got along very well, apart from one or two quarrels over a period of ten weeks. Every morning, at the buffet breakfast, she made absolutely certain that there would be a chair for me at her table. She watched over me like a mother lion.

The day after the STOs had arrived, the LTO teams were ordered to join the STOs for an extended lunch in a meeting room at our hotel. Sheena was supposed to sit next to me, but a young French STO rather unexpectedly sat down on her chair. I didn't dare to send him away.

Minutes later, Sheena arrived. She bluntly told the French STO that it was not his seat, but hers. The STO hurriedly stood up and moved as far away from her as he could. ,,Now they all think that I'm a bully", Sheena concluded. It didn't seem to bother her very much.

So without Sheena I had dinner with our two STO teams and the other LTO team at the Assaha Lebanese Village restaurant. On the way back, I received a call from Alberto. Their car had a flat tire.

I instructed our driver to turn back. The streets of Khartoum are quite dark, so we placed our car behind Alberto's. Our car's headlights aided the two drivers, who replaced the flat tire with a spare one.

We also helped them with the lights from our torches. It strengthened the friendship between Alberto and me, which became particularly profitable for me, since Alberto would soon join the EU unit in Brussels that directed all EU EOMs. It's always handy to have a friend in a commanding place.

On Sunday 9 January Sheena and I had to get up very early. It was to be the first of seven Election Days. Apparently, in South Sudan, voters turned up in great numbers. In Khartoum, on the other hand, we were happy when one voter appeared in a polling station. For some reason, many waited until the very last day of voting: 15 January.

Yet again we transmitted our E-Day forms directly from our laptop in our car to the EU EOM's central computer. Thank God for external modems. I called our STO teams for their narrative reports, that we as LTO's had to transmit to the Core Team. No problems there.

On Tuesday 11 January a funny thing happened. The day before, Sheena had eaten something wrong. Her stomach was upset. And

Roberts had caught a cold. We decided that I would observe with Mar.

It was nice to work with another observer, for a change. Mar taught law at two universities in Spain, but she was also an artist. She carried her painting materials with her.

Since we spent most of our time waiting in polling stations, she made a beautiful aquarelle of an old Arab on a donkey cart loaded with potable water. I made up the balloon text: 'Where is the polling station?' the Arab asked his donkey. Our interpreter translated the text into Arabic. Wherever we showed it, it was u huge success.

It instantly broke the ice. I advised Mar to forget about her law career and focus on her drawings instead. ,,Anyone can teach law, but very few people have artistic talents", I added. Mar just laughed.

A day later Sheena and I visited a gigantic new prison at the very outskirts of Khartoum. In Sudan, prisoners are allowed to vote, but they are not allowed to leave the prison, so polling stations were established inside the prisons.

It was a huge, walled prison, but the great front gate stood open. We were allowed to enter without any problems, after which we had to cross several hundreds of meters of the inner courtyard on foot. In the burning sun. If this was the coldest period of the year, I wondered how hot it would get in the summer.

We found the polling station in a small building at the far side. But we were too late: all voters had already voted. In fact, 98 prisoners had been entered on the Voters List, of which 80 had voted.

The remaining 18 prisoners on the Voters List had all been released before they could cast their vote. They were not allowed to re-enter the prison in order to vote, even if they wanted too. In any case, as everyone knows: in Africa, it's best to stay away from prisons.

But since my wife has worked in the Dutch prison system for 25 years, I've gotten quite used to prisons. Sheena and I decided to observe the 'Closing and Counting' in RC1433 'Women's Prison'. We had learned, during a previous visit, that the main gate of the Women's Prison would be closed at 17.00 hours.

Because of this, the RC also had to close at 17.00 hours. Usually, observers remain until long after midnight in their final polling station, but in this case: we were the first to arrive at the Omdurman High Committee, where the results of all RCs of Omdurman would be processed.

We were joined later by STOs Christer and Marcia. At 22.00 hours we returned to Khadaffi's Egg to transmit our forms to our CT. Sheena was so happy that she gave me two cans of Becks from her little fridge. Not the alcohol-free variety, but real beer. I was surprised. „Who gave you these beers?" I asked her. She just laughed.

Quite a few famous people stayed in our hotel. Among them the ex-president of South Africa, Thabo Mbeki, and an ex-president of the US, Jimmy Carter. Carter headed the Carter Centre, who's observers I met on nearly all of my missions. They work with the same methodology as the EU and OSCE Observation Missions: with a Core Team, LTOs and STOs.

One of our STOs, Christer, met Jimmy Carter in an elevator. He managed to shake Carter's hand, even though Carter was surrounded by several American security guards. American ex-presidents are called 'Mr President' for the rest of their lives and they also retain their security guards for the rest of their lives.

What was the outcome of the referendum? Well, as could be expected, the turnout threshold was met without any doubt. Turnout proved to be 98 per cent, of which 99 per cent voted in favour of secession of South Sudan from Sudan.

A new country had been born, albeit the poorest of all of Africa and therefore of the whole world. And soon, warring factions would fight one another for the few spoils of the country, to the detriment of the poor South Sudanese people.

But all of this we did not know yet on the 15th of January, when it was Sheena's birthday. She had been waiting anxiously for the hotel to send her a birthday cake, as they had done for me, but nothing arrived. The next morning she asked the receptionist why I had received a birthday cake, while she had not.

It turned out the hotel staff had entered a wrong date on her hotel sheet: 3 September 1946, instead of 15 January 1946. A typing error. Sheena was infuriated. She reminded the hotel staff that I had received a very nice cake for my birthday. She demanded at least the same. Or did men have more privileges than women in Sudan? The hotel staff immediately ordered a birthday cake to be sent to her room.

To celebrate her birthday, Sheena invited the other LTO team, Richard and a few others of the Core Team and Service Provider and—of course—me, to join her on a short trip on the Nile. She did not invite Roman, the Observer Coordinator. She did not like him.

I had to carry her birthday cake to the boat. It was only a hundred meters from the hotel, but I was terrified that I would stumble and ruin the bloody birthday cake, for which she had fought so hard. The boat took us to where the Blue Nile meets the White Nile. There, we ate her birthday cake and drank a soft drink. It was interesting to see Khartoum from the riverside for a change.

On our last day in Khartoum, Sheena and I would receive our evaluations from Roman. Sheena went first into his office. Twenty minutes later she came out all red and excited. She took me apart.

While Roman called me from the open door of his office, Sheena told me that Roman had scolded her for our Christmas day trip to the pyramids. It was good that she told me this before I entered Roman's office.

I was not sure if Roman would give me a 'recommended' evaluation. The good news was that we, as LTOs, had to write an evaluation for our Observer Coordinator as well. To be on the safe side, I had written two evaluations about Roman: one positive and one negative.

If Roman would me give a negative evaluation, in return he would receive a negative evaluation from me. He indeed started about our trip to the pyramids, but I immediately cut him short. I told him that two members of the Core Team, Richard and Eberhard, had been with us, as was the Sudanese assistant of our Security Expert.

On top of that, our trip had been approved by the Deputy Chief Observer himself, who, by the way, was Irish, like Sheena and Richard. I told Roman that if he uttered one more word about our trip, I would immediately call our Deputy Chief Observer on the phone.

My bluff worked. Roman was nice to me. On top of that, he gave me a good evaluation. I therefore handed him my positive evaluation of him. Everybody happy. I rushed back to Sheena to tell her the good news. She was still fuming at Roman.

There was more good news. Originally, I was supposed to fly back to Holland via Nairobi. This was weird, since Nairobi was to the south, while Holland was to the north. On top of that, I had only one and a half hours at Nairobi airport to switch planes, meaning that the slightest delay would mean that my suitcase would not make it onto the other flight.

I received permission to fly directly from Khartoum to Amsterdam with KLM, but I had to leave one day earlier. My last evening in Khartoum I spent with Sheena, Richard, Eberhard and a few more CT members. We had diner in a small garden, belonging to a local restaurant. Eberhard and I smoked cigars.

,,Why is Jos in such a good mood?" he asked Sheena. ,,Because he's leaving tonight, straight back to Holland", she replied. Did I find a Goofy for my wife? No, I did not. Instead, I found a camel. I bought a necklace with a rather large golden camel. Gold is quite cheap in Sudan. My wife liked the camel. And the gold. I was allowed to return home.

Chapter 13

NICARAGUA - 2011

'The Sandinistas copied the not so democratic tactics of Hugo Chávez'

My wife and I had spent a week in Nicaragua in 1988, during the communist reign of the Sandinistas. At the time, it was like being back in communist Mozambique: the shops were empty and the people were lethargic. The restaurants had no food and the petrol stations had no petrol.

Leftist intellectuals back home in Holland supported the Sandinistas, but these leftists had never set foot in Nicaragua. They lived in Holland, in the comfort of democracy and capitalism.

In 2011, the Sandinistas were back in power. Aapparently, they had shredded their communist ideology. They were now democrats and capitalists, or at least that is what they were supposed to be. I really wanted to go back to Nicaragua to see if things had changed for the better, so when I received an invitation to go there as an LTO, I gratefully accepted.

I left home in the early morning of Wednesday 19 October 2011. It was still dark. Three neighbours just went to work. They frowned, when they noticed my big and small suitcases. Gerda and her son Jordi said nothing, but Dominique asked where I was going to. ,,Nicaragua", I replied. ,,Then you'd better be careful", she said. ,,I saw on television that some parts of the country have been flooded."

That sounded like an ominous start of my trip. But the train departed on time and at Schiphol Amsterdam Airport everything went reasonably well. I tried the self-service check-in, but the machine refused my suitcase. It was three kilos too heavy. I was obliged to go to a real KLM-madam, who told me that I had to pay a fine of ninety euros. The usual hassles.

In one of the airport's waiting areas I spotted a familiar face: Pedro, who two years previously had been my partner in Oruro, Bolivia. By now, he had lived in Glasgow for 11 years, with his Scottish wife and their young twins. In spite of this, his English was still poor, so we spoke Spanish.

He was disappointed that his partner was a Spanish woman. He was afraid that her English would also be rather poor. Pedro had not changed. He still talked too much. Just before I left home I had quickly checked my emails. My partner was going to be Alejandra from Belgium.

Alejandra sounded like a Spanish name, though. I hoped that she would be Latin American, because people from Spain speak very fast and use typical Spanish phrases. Our duty station was going to be Jinotega. That sounded good.

I had visited Estelí, also in the northern mountainous region and also at an altitude of about one thousand meters. That means that it's not so bloody hot over there, especially after dark. And a small town means no traffic jams.

The KLM flight to Panama departed on time, but when we flew over the south coast of England, the plane was hit by lightning. I was just dozing off and had a little cover over my eyes, when there was a loud bang. Even though my eyes were closed and in spite of the eye-cover, I clearly saw the flash of lightning.

Within minutes, the captain spoke quite frankly to the passengers. He said that we had three options: return to Schiphol, an emergency landing in southern England or continue our trip.

He said that, apparently, no vital parts of the plane had been damaged, so we would continue our trip. The only problem was that our individual little television screens in the front of our seats would not work for the remainder of the voyage. In spite of this, everyone on the plane was grateful for the captain's decision to carry on the flight as planned.

Well, things really had changed in Nicaragua. Hotel Barceló in the capital Managua was as western as could be. And after a visit to a huge shopping mall with lots of modern shops, I was thoroughly convinced that communism was definitely a thing of the past. McDonalds had finally arrived in Nicaragua. So had Burger King and Kentucky Fried Chicken. Civilization!

As on every mission, the most important thing for me was my partner. I met Alejandra in Hotel Barceló. The first thing I noted was that she was the smallest partner I had ever had. At 1.74 meters I am not the biggest guy in the world, but she was a full head shorter than me. The next thing I noted was that I could easily understand her Spanish. Judging to her accent, I guessed that she was born either in Argentina, Uruguay or Chile.

She told me that she came from Chile. She had fled the Pinochet regime in the seventies with a baby in her arms, when she was only 19 years old. She herself had not been politically active in Chile, but her husband had been. When they arrived in Belgium, neither of them spoke one word of French.

Now, Alejandra was reading French books. And she had divorced her husband. She was now living with her Danish partner in Guatemala. She asked me if I had been an LTO in Venezuela in 2006. I said yes. She replied that her Danish partner had been an LTO with me on that same mission.

I had totally forgotten about him, but when I looked it up, I noted that it was true. She knew about Paul, the Dutch LTO, who had had lots of fights with his Spanish partner during the Venezuela mission and had finally received a negative evaluation, after which Paul stirred up a few things at the EU in Brussels. It had, by now, become a well-known story among LTOs.

She would become one of my best partners. Alejandra's Spanish was much better than mine, of course. It would be easy for her to make appointments by telephone. I sometimes found it hard to understand what somebody else was saying in rapid Spanish through a creaking mobile phone, so if my partner makes the phone calls, I'm a happy man.

On top of that, Alejandra had worked for Oxfam and several other NGOs in Nicaragua for six years, so she knew the country much better than I did. My English was better than hers and I had a lot more experience as an observer. It was Alejandra's first mission as an LTO and she was a bit insecure about it. But together we looked like a promising team.

I quickly noted that both the Core Team and the Service Provider were amongst the best I had ever had. That was good news. The general atmosphere amongst the LTOs was also good. Ana Paula, the Observer Coordinator, had been my STO in Pakistan and my colleague LTO in Bolivia. She had a little surprise for us in store. She said that our Weekly Reports had to be typed in Spanish, instead of the usual English.

A few hours later she was corrected by José Antonio, the Deputy Chief Observer. He said that we were allowed to choose either English or Spanish. I told Alejandra that if she preferred to write in Spanish, she would have to do the typing, but if we wrote in English, I would do all the typing. ,,Let's do it in English", she replied.

Jinotega is a small, agricultural town, three hours to the north of Managua. Along the road we passed several areas that had been flooded after the incessant rainfall. Some houses were half buried in water. A strange sight for someone like me, living in Holland. About half of Holland is situated below sea level, but we never experience any flooding in Holland, since all the water levels are meticulously controlled.

Jinotega province borders Honduras, but we never came close to the border. There were hardly any people living in the remote mountainous regions between Nicaragua and Honduras. The roads were very bad over there. This was, in fact, the area where the infamous Contras had their bases in the 1980s. The Iran/Contra affair almost cost Ronald Reagan the presidency.

The good news was that, Luís, our driver, had been based in the area in those days, as an enlisted soldier in the army of the Sandinistas. He met his wife in a village there, so he knew the region very well, even though he came originally from Managua.

Usually, our drivers live in the capital city, where the car companies are based. And usually these drivers do not know the provinces they are assigned to. But in this case we were lucky: Luís knew our province better than anyone else. On top of that, he was a giant of a man. He was not afraid of anyone. He would protect us against the bad guys, if any.

With 60,000 inhabitants, Jinotega is a typical provincial town. No high rises, lots of little shops. The town looked a bit run-down. The pave walks were not in particularly good shape, but the people were very relaxed. The pace of life was slow, nobody was ever in a hurry. They don't see many tourists there, so everyone was nice to us.

The staff at the Hotel Café were very friendly. A strange name, though, for a hotel: Hotel Coffee. First they offered me a room that was close to the entrance. I asked if they had quieter rooms. They then offered me a small room on the second floor, at the very back of the hotel. I immediately liked it. So did Alejandra. She asked for a room close to mine.

They offered her the mini-suite, two doors away from my room. For the same price. This was good news for me, since we would have our little office in her mini-suite. This meant also that the mission laptop would be in her room, so I would not be bothered by it too much. More good news was to come, because as always I asked my partner to negotiate the room prices.

Alejandra turned out to be a very successful negotiator. At first, we were supposed to pay 45 dollars per day. Alejandra negotiated it down to 25 dollars per day. She told them that we were expecting four STOs, who would also stay in the hotel, but could be charged the full 45 dollars per day, since STOs stay short-term, while we stay long-term.

So it happened. I just hope the STOs will not read this book. The only problem was that there was no fridge in my room to keep my beers cool. My wife asked if there was an air conditioner. I said: ,,Yes". My wife advised me to place the cans of beer in front of the air conditioner. Which I duly did. It cooled the beers reasonably well. As an observer you have to be resourceful.

The next morning we had our first breakfast. Supposedly, breakfast was included in our room fare, but this applied exclusively to the continental breakfast: orange juice, bread, butter and coffee. I really love the '*plato typico*': fried banana, rice with beans, goats cheese and scrambled eggs. All this for just 4 dollars. Thankfully, I noted that Alejandra was neither a vegetarian, nor had she a gluten allergy.

Alejandra was a bit worried that our STO manual would not be finished on time. I reassured her. I had already written the part on the history of Jinotega. Most LTOs simply copy and paste some pages from Wikipedia, but in my experience STOs really appreciate a little extra personalized effort.

So I wrote about the Aztecs who had founded the town in the early sixteenth century. They called it Xinotecatl, in their own Nahuatl language. Xinotecatl means 'The valley where the corn grows high'. Interestingly, these early Aztec traders had travelled overland through Guatemala and Honduras.

Since there were no roads in those days, it took them many months to reach Jinotega. By the time they arrived there, they were informed of the arrival of the Spaniards, led by Hernán Cortez. Strange creatures had arrived by boat.

After Cortez had conquered Tenochtitlán, nowadays known as Mexico City, the Aztec traders realized that they could not return to their native land, so they remained in Jinotega and over the years their descendants mixed with local people. Their Aztec ancestry would be lost in time. Only the name Jinotega remained.

Alejandra thought that our STO manual was too lengthy, so I agreed to leave out this part on Jinotega's history, but on the evening before E-Day I had a few beers with some observers from the American embassy and some OAS observers, one of whom was a 25-year old Mexican woman.

I told her about the Aztec roots of Jinotega. She was flabbergasted: „So my ancestors traveled all the way here overland? In the early sixteenth century? That's really amazing."

Alejandro and I interviewed the electoral bodies, political parties, human rights organizations, local radio stations, and so on. We also visited several towns in the vicinity of Jinotega. Traveling went smooth, thanks to our driver Luís. In San Rafael del Norte we talked to several people who really hated and distrusted the Sandinistas.

Party affiliates of the Sandinistas went around, telling everybody that if they did not vote for the Sandinistas, they would lose their welfare benefits. But if they voted in favor of the Sandinistas, their region would receive more money for development projects.

The carrot and the stick: exactly the same tactics that Hugo Chávez had used so successfully in Venezuela. Not very democratic, but a sure guarantee to win the elections, since most voters were poor. When you're poor, you have little choice.

An unexpected thing happened when the two STO teams arrived. They immediately recognized the lobby of our hotel. ,,So this is where the interview took place", remarked Alfred from Austria. He told us that the Core Team had used our interview, which had been published in La Prensa, a national newspaper, to brief all the STOs on how to deal with the media.

We had been interviewed by Felix Rivera, the most respected journalist in Jinotega. His cameraman from TV-channel 48 was with him, so I thought we would appear on regional television, but Felix turned out to be correspondent for a national newspaper as well. Alejandra had been a bit nervous about the interview, but it went fine. His story was reasonably accurate.

It's a very sensitive subject during every mission. The EU wants the whole world to know about the Election Observation Missions, so observers are encouraged to give interviews, but there are a few things that we can never share with journalists: we cannot tell them what we have observed and we cannot give them our personal opinion on any election in the world.

This always poses a problem, since these are, of course, the things that journalists really want to know. So the journalists push us for the knowledge. And here is the problem: if an observer makes only the slightest personal remark, the EU reacts furiously and the observer can expect a negative evaluation at the end of the mission.

Because of this, many observers shy away from interviews: the rewards are small, but the risks are enormous. During the briefings of every mission we receive a media training, but even so, many observers remain insecure when it comes to dealing with the media. They are afraid of journalists. Except me. I am a journalist myself.

I know all the tricks in the book and I know exactly what I can and cannot say. I especially enjoy giving interviews to TV- and Radio-stations, because than I can control what I'm saying. Written stories in magazines and newspapers are beyond my control. You never know how they will write it down. But local journalists are a very important source of information for our Weekly Reports, and in any case: in a small town we cannot avoid them.

Anyway: our STOs were Alfred from Austria, Thomas from Luxemburg, Rebecca from Canada and Marie-Therèse from French-speaking Belgium, but living in Portugal. The last one introduced herself by saying: „My name is Marie-Therèse. I don't accept Marie and I don't accept Therèse."

The other STOs and also Alejandra all looked at me, without uttering a word. They were clearly wondering how I would respond to this challenge to my authority. My answer to Marie-Therèse was swift and intuitive. „OK", I said. „Then I'll call you Marie-Antoinette."

The others probably expected Marie-Therèse to burst out screaming at me, or worse: to try to tear out my eyes with her finger nails. But nothing happened. I had gained their respect. We took our STOs to a rally held by Hallesleeven, the candidate for the vice-presidency of the ruling Sandinista party.

The rally was held close to our hotel, so we went on foot. We were allowed to get close to the speaker. Many STOs do not have much observation experience, so it's always exciting for them to be so close to the real action, that would be broadcast on regional TV later that evening.

Next, we took the STOs to restaurant La Perrera, at the edge of town, for a late lunch. There were no big tables, so the three women sat at one table, while Alfred and Thomas joined me at another table. They were young men, eager to do a good job and they were pleasant company.

It was very noisy because the TV was blaring and the traffic was passing by very closely. Because of this, I did not notice any problems at the other table, but later that afternoon, when we were alone, Alejandra told me that Marie-Therèse had rather viciously insulted Rebecca during lunch.

I was shocked: this is absolutely not done among observers. In the early evening, Alejandra and Rebecca came to my room. Rebecca started crying when I asked her about it. One of the things Marie-Therèse had said was that Canada was not even a member of the EU.

This is true, but Norway, Switzerland and Canada do provide funds and observers to EU EOMs and these observers have exactly the same rights as the observers from the 27 EU member states. Later that evening, when I was having a beer on the balcony of my room, I thought I knew what had caused the problem.

Marie-Thérèse was 60 years of age and she was a general practitioner. She was a French-speaking Belgian, but she had worked in hospitals in Lisbon for many years. Between medical doctors and nurses there is a strict hierarchy: doctors on top, nurses below.

So probably Marie-Thérèse had come accustomed to a certain position. And Rebecca, at about 45 years of age, was an easy target. In any case, the very serious row between Marie-Thérèse and Rebecca prompted me to take decisive action. The next morning Alejandra and I briefed our STOs on Jinotega province.

I had rented the hotel's small Conference Room and wanted to pay for it from the petty cash, but received an email from Pedro that it was against the mission's rules. It was a small amount of money, so I paid it from my own pocket, instead of starting an endless fight with my arch-enemy Pedro. I profoundly disliked our Logistics Expert from Portugal.

I opened the meeting with a few remarks on how to behave vis-a-vis other observers. I told all four of them that it was a short mission and that we did not have time to babysit. I also explained to them that the two partners of a team are always jointly responsible for anything that happens to the team.

And I finished by saying that if any of them behaved irresponsibly, I would immediately call the Observer Coordinator of our Core Team, and request that the irresponsible observer would be sent back home to Europe and put on the black list.

As an afterthought, I added that Ana Paula, our Observer Coordinator, had been my STO in Pakistan and my colleague LTO in Cochabamba, Bolivia. I told them that Ana Paula knew me so well, that she would consider any request from my side very seriously.

To my own surprise, my little speech proved to be extremely effective. From then on, Marie-Thérèse was very cooperative. In fact, the six of us became good friends. A week later, when the time came to say goodbye to our STOs, Marie-Thérèse even shed a little tear.

I met Marie-Thérèse again in 2016, during our Peru mission, when both of us were LTOs. She was very happy to see me. I believe I was the closest to her of any of the 50 LTOs. Sometimes you start off with someone on a wrong footing, but you end up on the best possible footing. Or the other way round.

E-Day came and went without problems. As expected, the Sandinistas won the elections. Daniel Ortega won the elections again in 2016. Maybe it's more accurate to say that his running mate won the elections. Her name: Rosario Murillo. She's Ortega's wife.

Ever since the 2007 elections, she always appears with him on television. She always wears lots of make-up and she has lots of rings around her fingers. She's always wears dresses that are fiercely coloured.

To many Nicaraguans she's known as the wicked witch behind the thrown. Actually, since the 2016 elections, she's not behind the throne anymore. She's in front of the throne. Ortega officially made her his vice-president.

So Rosario Murillo became first lady and vice-president, all at the same time. In April 2018 demonstrations were held against the ruling party. The demonstrators were mostly students, who were fed up with all the mismanagement and repression.

Rosario dealt with the demonstrations by ordering the police and the army to use any force necessary. At least 65 persons were killed. It's obvious to anyone who has seen Daniel and Rosario together on television, that she is wearing the pants. Daniel appears to be docile, when she sits next to him.

And Rosario is the one who finds a solution whenever there's a problem. After the April 2018 demonstrations, she ordered an increase in pensions and social security benefits. Opposition leaders were imprisoned. The Hugo Chávez solution. It worked. But for how long?

But back in 2011 we did not know all this. For the next couple of days, the six of us would continually observe the counting at the provincial level by taking shifts with different partners. Alfred from Austria had been outstanding as an STO, and he volunteered to do the first night shift.

As it turned out, it all became a bit too much for him and he became very sick from exhaustion. The next two days, he did not leave his room. Funnily, Alejandra kept calling Alfred 'Albert', because her 32-year old son was called Alberto.

We had a pleasant time with the STOs. Thank God, the EU had by now abolished the infamous 'Highly Recommended' evaluation altogether, both for LTOs and for STOs. This made it easy for Alejandra and me: all four STOs had done a good job. All of them received a 'Recommended for Future Missions' evaluation.

After they had left, Alejandra and I finally had time for a bit of sight-seeing. Our hotel sold curious black potteries. We asked who had produced these and they gave us directions. It was not far from Jinotega, but we had to drive through the bush for several kilometres.

Luckily, it had not rained for several days. Otherwise, the dirt roads would not be passable even for our land cruiser. The black pottery was produced by several small producers. They lived in simple houses, but they were clearly accustomed to visitors: the different potteries had prices attached to them. We purchased a few of them.

On the way back we had to pass a cart pulled by oxen. This was my photo moment. I asked if I could sit on top of the cart. Of course I could. I handed my camera to Alejandra and she made some photographs of a Dutch country boy on top of a South American oxen cart.

On the way back to Managua, we stopped over at a German *finca* near Matagalpa, where Alejandra had spent quite a few pleasant weekends during the six years she had lived in Nicaragua. It was a nice park, with a lake at its centre. When we were back at the Hotel Barceló in Managua, Alejandra visited some old friends in the city.

Meanwhile, I handed the receipts of our petty cash to the Finance Officer of our mission. Pedro saw me and yelled that I did not have to pay the Conference Room in Jinotega from my own pocket, as long as I provided justification. I calmly told him to shut up.

A few hours later Alejandra called me. Did I want to visit the biggest mall of the city? Of course I did. Ever since communism had ruined Mozambique, I really love supermarkets and malls. So we did. It's always a good sign when your partner still wants to see you, during the debriefings in the capital city. Compared to Jinotega, Managua looked very big, very busy and very dirty. And the people looked less friendly.

At Managua airport we had to wait several hours, for our flight to Panama. Monique, the Dutch LTO who lived in Cuba with her Cuban husband, was also there. I noted that her bags were filled to the rim with tooth paste, shaving cream, deodorant and more of life's essentials.

It was clear that she was returning to a socialist paradise. I sympathized with her. ,,I have lived in a communist country for three years", I told her. ,,I know what scarcity does to you."

Did I find a Goofy for my wife? You bet I did. More than one, in fact. And, thanks to Alejandra, I found out that in Spanish speaking countries, Goofy is called Tribilín. This is a bit weird, since in Bolivia and Venezuela I had always asked for Goofy's and everybody understood immediately who Goofy was. No one ever told me that he had a different name in Spanish. Which goes to say: you're never too old to learn.

Chapter 14

RUSSIA - 2012

Phantom polling stations: they really do exist

On Friday 9 January 2012, at 13.00 hours, I woke up from my daily siesta. Still half asleep I went downstairs, where my wife told me that she had just received a call from the Ministry of Foreign Affairs. I was awake instantly. ,,They want to know if you want to go to Russia, as an LTO. But you must answer them within half an hour. Otherwise, they will call another observer."

I had not even been home for two months, but my mission to Nicaragua had been relatively short, only four weeks. And it had been a smooth mission, so I did not feel tired at all. I discussed it with my wife. She said: ,,Russia is a very important country. It will look good on your CV. It is also a very interesting mission and not in Africa or Latin America for a change. This is a chance in a lifetime. Go for it."

Apart from this, I wanted to experience the notoriously brutal Russian winter for once in my life. I have spent a large portion of my life in the tropics, but that was because my work was there. Not because I enjoy the scorching tropical sun and the sweating. In fact: I don't like hot climates at all. Thank God, the Netherlands enjoys a moderate climate.

So I dialled the number of the ministry. Just in time. My Focal Point told me that the other two Dutch LTOs were Russian speakers. There would be a briefing at the ministry within a week. I needed to hand over my passport, to obtain a visa.

When I entered the ministry, early in the morning, I was a bit nervous. We were briefed by one of the Russia experts of the ministry. My two colleague LTOs were real Russia old hands. I knew quite a bit about Africa and Latin America, but the Russian speaking world was alien to me.

But all of them were pleasant company. They put me at ease quickly, even though I could hardly follow the conversation. They were talking about political parties and candidates, past and present. It was dizzying. I made notes, in the hope to increase my knowledge in the coming days.

Our passports were collected and we were told that we would receive our visas later that same day. Ineke and Willem told me that they didn't have time to spend the entire day in The Hague. Could I collect their passports? I was so grateful for this mission, that I agreed.

As a result, I spent the next six hours visiting each and every department store in The Hague. I had to wait an additional two hours at the ministry: apparently, the Russian embassy staff had left their offices for an extended lunch. But finally, I received our passports, duly stamped with visas.

On Sunday afternoon, I met Ineke and Willem at Schiphol airport and handed them their passports. The flight to Moscow took only four hours. We arrived at the Grand Marriot hotel in the early evening. Two diplomats from the Dutch embassy were waiting for us in the lobby.

They briefed us on the political situation and the upcoming elections. They left at 22.00 hours. The three of us had not had diner, so we decided to go out and eat something in a nearby Subway restaurant. When we got outside the hotel, the Russian winter cold hit me like a sledge hammer.

Jesus Christ, this was really cold. In Holland, we are used to wind and rain, but not to freezing temperatures. The coldest temperature ever measured in Holland was -27 degrees Celsius, but this had been close to the eastern border with Germany.

In my province, in the western coastal part of North-Holland, it has never been that cold. So this was the infamous Russian winter, underestimated by both Napoleon and Hitler. With disastrous consequences. Thank God, I had bought myself a real thick winter coat. And ski socks.

The next day, the 40 LTOs were briefed at the hotel. I met my new partner, Megan, a 50 year old English woman. Our base would be Nizhny Novgorod, about 600 kilometres east of Moscow. During the communist days, the city was called Gorki. It became well-known in the west, after the dissident Sakharov had been put under house arrest there.

I was a bit surprised to see that Megan was not wearing any make-up nor jewellery, but she seemed cheerful enough. She had grown up on a farm, just like me. She had studied Russian and after that she had lived in Russia for fifteen years, teaching English.

I was quite convinced that she was a lesbian, but she never spoke about it. She knew, of course, that the large majority of Russians still disapprove of homosexuality. It may sound cowardly, but it's best to avoid the subject. Culturally, many Russians lag far behind the West. They think like Western Europeans were thinking during the 1950s.

To my surprise, during the briefings I ran into Roger, my old English partner from the Pakistan mission. He was happy enough to see me. The first thing he said was that Sandy was also there. It dawned on me that the electoral observation departments of the EU and the OSCE were not communicating with one another. The OSCE apparently did not know that Sandy had been blacklisted by the EU.

Personally, I had not had problems with Sandy during our shared time in the guesthouse in Lahore, but she had been kicked out of that EU-mission for good reasons. During later missions I learned from other English observers that Sandy had given them her own side of the story, which was, of course, favourable to her.

But Sandy knew very well that I knew the real story, since I had befriended Robert, her Belgian partner at the time. I was not going to be fooled. Sandy and I shook hands, but she avoided my gaze. For the rest of the Russia mission, we avoided each other.

The last evening in Moscow, Ineke and I walked over to the Bavaria restaurant, where a group of LTOs would gather. I am not a very social person and I generally do not like group sessions, but in this case I enjoyed it. While eating a German *bratwurst* with *sauerkraut*, we talked about our previous missions.

When the Dutch LTO Monique was mentioned, everyone paid attention. She's a bit of a legend among the observers. She wrote a large part of the Observer Handbook. Everyone paid even more attention when the French LTO Florence was named. When I said that she had been my partner in Kyrgyzstan, they all turned to me in horror.

„How did you hold out with her?" Someone asked me. „At least two of her partners ran away from her, as fast as they could." I gained their respect, when I told them that after each outburst from Florence, I told our interlocutors that she was from Armenia. When I added that Florence had been a good observer, some LTOs gave me a doubtful look.

The mission's working and reporting languages were English, which was fine with me. After three days, Megan and I were driven to one of Moscow's railway stations. The driver unceremoniously unloaded our suitcases and mission materials onto the pavement and then just left us there.

I asked Megan to go and find out which would be our train. Since everything was written in Cyrillic script and since most Russians don't speak English, German or French, it would be quite useless for me to venture out. So I remained there on the pavement, guarding our stuff, all the time shivering from the bitter cold.

Megan and I had an old-fashioned train compartment to ourselves. More than enough space for all our stuff. Coffee and basic food was included. In 1988, my wife and I had booked a trip on the Trans-Siberian Express, an eight day train trip from Moscow to Beijing, but we had to cancel it because of our jobs at the time.

Now I found myself on a real Russian train and on a part of the real itinerary of the Trans-Siberian Express. But I have to admit: after ten hours of looking at a snow covered forest, I had seen enough trees for the rest of my life. Just imagine eight days of this!

By the time the train arrived in Nizhny Novgorod, it was already dark. And it was cold. Even colder than in Moscow. I remained inside the railway station with our stuff, while Megan ventured out to find a taxi. It took us to the Marins Park Hotel that had been reserved for us.

It was a big hotel, close to the Oka river and adjacent to a large statue of Lenin, that had not been torn down. The hotel had a bar, so Megan and I drank a large pint of beer to celebrate the start of our mission.

The next day we invited several candidates for the position of interpreter and driver. The mission had prepared a list for us. We quickly agreed on signing on the 23 year old Jekaterina as our interpreter and 57 year old Alexei as our driver. They would turn out to be good choices. They had actually worked together for an STO team during the previous elections.

From the start, Megan shortened Jekaterina's name to Kate. Alexei was a very nice guy, but did not speak one word of English, French, German, Spanish or Portuguese, so I could only communicate with him through either Megan or Kate. Or by using hand signs.

The next day, I moved to a large corner room with a nice view of the Oka river, for a slightly higher room rate. No problem. On EU missions I would have to pay for the hotel myself, but on OSCE missions the Dutch Ministry of Foreign Affairs would reimburse me for the hotel. Regardless of the cost. Why stay in a shitty little room, when you can stay in a spacious semi-suite at no extra cost to yourself?

We decided to check out other hotels, guesthouses and even apartments. The apartments were very cheap, but also badly furnished. Some contained beds without matrasses, let alone sheets. Some hotels were OK and Megan even managed to lower the rates for us, since we would be staying long-term and our STOs would also be staying there.

Finally we found a guesthouse with only 11 rooms in the city centre, with a Spar supermarket at only 75 meters distance. They offered us two spacious rooms at the quiet top floor, with a view of the Kremlin of Nizhny Novgorod, situated at the confluence of the Wolga and Oka rivers.

There are lots of Kremlins in Russia. The word Kremlin simply means 'citadel': a fortified area, usually occupying the high ground near a river. The guesthouse was a nice place, called *U Domika Petra*: Peter's Residence. A simple but nourishing breakfast was included.

Every morning, breakfast was prepared by Ludmilla, an elderly lady, who simply could not believe that I did not speak one word of Russian, since I looked very much like a Russian. I probably looked more like a Russian than most Russians.

Because of that, she would talk incessantly to me in Russian. I just kept nodding, as if I had understood everything. Which seemed to be fine with her: she probably did not expect an answer anyway.

I speak seven languages, but no Russian. It's very difficult to learn. To start with: the Cyrillic script is difficult to decipher. Luckily, I could easily go shopping in the Spar supermarket, at only 75 slippery meters, through the snow, uphill from our guesthouse.

The Russians use the same numbers as the rest of the world, so I could read the prices on all the products. Thanks to our interpreter Jekaterina, I mean Kate, I had purchased a Spar members card, giving me a ten per cent discount.

Since the cashiers were computerized, I could read the total cost on the little screen. So I gave the cashier money and my Spar card. I knew what they were asking me next, since they were always short on coins. So I quickly handed over my coins. Everybody happy. They were absolutely convinced that I was a Russian.

Only once or twice it went wrong, when I handed the cashier my coins and she asked me an additional question. I answered in English that I did not speak one word of Russian. Then they usually got angry; they were so sure that I was a Russian, that they thought I was pulling their leg.

There was a TV in my room, but all channels were in Russian, except one: France24. It was a French channel, broadcasting in English and repeating itself every hour. But it was better than nothing. Their coverage of the international news was quite good.

The only problem was that I had to watch president Sarkozy every day. The good news was that Russians love sports, so there were quite a few Russian sports channels. I watched football matches and I became a staunch supporter of the local ice hockey team: Torpedo.

A rather unexpected problem was that it was very hot in my room. The old, centralized Soviet city heating system was still being used, which meant that you could not lower it. In fact, three separate pipes entered my room. To lower the temperature a little bit, I switched off one of them.

That proved to be disastrous, because—unknown to me—it heated also the room straight below me. This room had been vacant during the first week, but then a guest arrived. The hotel staff opened the room and immediately noticed that everything inside was frozen solid.

The owner of the guesthouse, a women in her fifties, was furious. She yelled at me, translated by our interpreter, never to switch off the heating system again. So I had a problem. I decided to do the same that all Russians do: to open a window at night, even though it was -22 degrees Celsius. Or even colder.

The only problem was that, for some reason, my two little windows were placed at two meters above the ground. But Russians are resourceful and, believe it or not, I was becoming more and more of a Russian.

Every evening I placed a chair under one of the windows, opened it just a fraction, placed a small broom between the window and the window sill and then tied the window to the window sill with a shoelace.

It worked. Several nights it had been snowing, which meant that the next morning I had to scrape a huge pile of snow from the inside of my window. Every morning, I carefully closed the window again, in order not to arouse suspicion. By now, I was terrified of the female owner of the guesthouse.

Megan and I started interviewing people. I decided not to slow her down, by insisting on perfect translations. So Megan took the lead, while Kate did her best to translate everything into my ear. It was not easy for Kate, since she hardly ever practiced talking English. She was used to translating written texts from English to Russian and vice-versa. Talking is something else.

We decided to visit the chairman of the SEC, the electoral body for Nizhny Novgorod province first. His office was inside the Kremlin. It's easy to enter the Kremlin on foot, but to enter by car is quite a different story. The old Stalinist bureaucracy is still firmly in place in some parts of Russian society.

But we managed to get in and then we had to walk along endless corridors in the enormous building. Everything in Russia is big. But the chair was friendly and so were his staff.

One thing you have to get used to in the Russian winter is that indoors—both inside private houses and offices—it's hot. Really hot. It's at least 27 degrees Celsius, wherever you go. So after entering a house or an office, you must take off your coat immediately. Outside it's -22 degrees Celsius, inside it's +27 degrees. I was usually sweating, while taking my notes.

Another remarkable thing is that whenever you enter a private house, you have to take off your shoes. I had experienced this in Kyrgyzstan, where ten per cent of the population are ethnic Russians, but that had been in midsummer, so I didn't understand why I had to take off my shoes. The harsh Russian winter explained everything.

The first day in my hotel room I placed my shoes in a corner. Within half an hour, I noticed a puddle of ugly, brownish liquid leaking from the soles of my shoes: in Russia, after every snowfall, the roads are treated with a mix of salt and sand.

No wonder you have to take off your shoes, when you enter a private house. In offices, you could keep your shoes on, usually. As a result, the same brownish puddles would appear under our shoes, rather embarrassingly.

The cold was not my main problem. My thick winter coat and ski socks protected me well enough, the only problem was that, outdoors, it was impossible to stand still. You could not stand still and wait for a taxi, because than you would freeze to death. As long as you are moving, you create friction. And friction means warmth.

I soon realized that my main problem was the snow. In Holland, we have snow only eight days per year, but Russians live permanently in snowy conditions for a full five months per year. After six weeks, I was really sick and tired of the bloody snow.

But the Russians are used to it. Kate told us that Russians like the winters better than the summers. In a land climate, the summers can be very hot. More elderly Russians die in summer from the heat than in winter from the cold. And in winter there are no mosquitoes.

Megan and I discovered a peculiar restaurant, called Terra Nostalgia, at the main shopping street, only 500 meters from our guesthouse. The food was not great, but it was cheap. And the ambiance was amazing, with communist paraphernalia everywhere.

We were not sure if the owners regretted that the communist days were a thing of the past or if they were making a mockery out of 70 years of communist dictatorship. Maybe it doesn't matter: history is history. You can't go back and do it all over again. In any case: huge black-and-white photographs showed Stalin, Molotov and Lenin.

Typical communist day-to-day tools were on display. The waiters spoke only Russian and the menu was written in Cyrillic script, but Megan translated a few things that really sounded funny. You could order a typical kolkhoz meal or a real Russian cocktail, called Molotov cocktail. Russians have a good sense of humour.

On Saturday 4 February, we observed an anti-government demonstration. There were about 500 demonstrators. We followed them all along the main shopping street: Bolsjaja Pokrovskaja street, for pedestrians only. A podium had been erected at the very end of the street against the wall of the Kremlin, where the Oka river met the Volga river.

In front of the podium everyone was standing motionless. Now I felt the cold. I had prepared myself: under my pants I was wearing pyjama pants. Kate was not prepared like that, even though she grew up in Nizhny Novgorod.

After about 45 minutes I noticed that Kate was shivering and turning white. I talked to Megan and we decided to send Kate to our warm car, since Alexei always kept the engine running. Later, back in our hotel, it took my legs two hours to warm up again.

One of our STO teams would be based in the city of Saransk, so we decided to check out the place for a few days. It was about four hours by car. Since Megan spoke Russian, she sat in the front passenger seat. I sat in the back, with Kate, with whom I could talk English.

It was quite funny that the heating system of the old Subaru was working at full capacity, but it only heated the central part of the car. The window on my side was soon frozen completely on both the outside and the inside. I could not look through it.

The worst problem was that my leg at the window side was freezing cold, while my leg on the inside of the car was pleasantly warmed by the heating system. I solved the problem by taking off my coat and placing it between my leg and the door of the car. A Russian solution. This worked nicely.

The four of us stayed two nights in a hotel in the very centre of Saransk. We interviewed a female interpreter for our STO team. She appeared to be OK. Construction had just started on a completely new stadium for the Football World Cup, to be held in 2018. By Russian standards, Saransk is a small town, with only 300,000 inhabitants.

Nizhny Novgorod has five times more inhabitants, but no World Cup matches would be played there, since the governor of Saransk was a friend of Putin and the ex-governor of Nizhny Novgorod, Boris Nemtsjov, had been an outspoken adversary of Putin. That's how things work in Russia.

Putin didn't like Nizhny, but as it turned out, in the end, a few matches were eventually played there. Not even Putin can have everything his way. When we returned to Nizhny Novgorod, we decided to have a team meeting with the four of us, to evaluate if all four of us were satisfied with the way things were going.

Since we would pass by Kate's parent's house, she invited us to hold the meeting there, but Megan refused. To bump unannounced into someone's house is simply unthinkable to any English. What if the people were not dressed formally? What if they would not be prepared to receive guests?

More importantly: we had not brought a present with us; no flowers, no bottle of wine. During my Honduras mission in 2013, I would find out that Norwegians are even more formal than the English, but I can assure you that in The Netherlands we are not that fussy: when someone invites you, you simply accept the invitation.

A few days later we did visit Kate's parental house, though, since her father would be one of the drivers for our STO teams. It was a cosy, spacious apartment in a typical Soviet building block. We ate a very nice dinner at the kitchen table.

One thing about the Russians is true: they love vodka. Kate's father offered me a glass. I accepted it, but since the evening was just beginning, I drank sparsely. Very nice people, though.

Back home, in Holland, I had never met a Russian. The only Russians I knew were the bad guys in Hollywood movies. In reality, Russians are hospitable and have a good sense of humour. And they don't hate western Europeans at all.

On another day, we set out to explore the nearby city of Dzerzhinsk, named after the first boss of the KGB, Felix Dzerzhinsky, who had actually been born in Poland. Dzherzhinsk is reputedly the most polluted city in the world. Poisonous gasses like Sarin had been produced there.

Now, several huge industrial sites stood abandoned, but apparently the pollution is still there: underground. Funnily, when a Dutch journalist called Jelle Brandt Corstius visited Dzerzhinsk for his TV program, he was offered a cucumber to eat. He asked if the cucumber had been grown in Dzherzinsk. The answer was: 'Yes'. He refused to eat it, because of the poisonous earth.

Actually, Dzherzinsk doesn't look too bad. The people living there appeared to be friendly. At least to us. Kate and Alexei informed us about a very nice hotel, at the outskirts of the city. Hotel Rancho mimicked the American cowboy scene. We decided that one of our STO teams could stay there comfortably.

During the previous elections, Kate and Alexei had stayed at the Hotel Rancho with their STO team, consisting of a Spaniard who did not speak Russian and a Kazak woman who did not speak English.

So Kate had to translate continuously between the two STOs. On top of that, the Spaniard was not interested in elections and the Kazak woman did not want to spend any money. After this experience, Kate was happy enough with Megan and me.

I had read about the legendary Shukov tower, of which only two remained in the entire world: one near Moscow and one near Dzerzhinsk. When I mentioned the word 'Zhukov', Alexei, our driver, started talking enthusiastically about Russia's greatest hero of the second world war: general Zhukov.

My Russian is extremely poor, but this I did understand. I asked Megan to tell him that this was another Zhukov. In fact, his name is usually spelled as Shukov. This Vladimir Shukov lived from 1853 till 1939 and had constructed a kind of Eiffel Tower, miraculously using four times less steel, while maintaining the structural strength of the construction.

He had achieved this by using an intricate pattern of thin steel bars. He wanted to construct a copy of the Eiffel Tower in Moscow, that would be 50 meters higher than the Eiffel tower in Paris, while still using less steel. But Lenin was against it. ,,Our army needs the steel more than you", Lenin told Shukov briskly. So Shukov could only construct pylons for electricity lines.

The only problem was how to find Shukov's tower. I knew that it stood close by the Oka river, but local people apparently had no knowledge about it. Finally, at the end of a winding dirt road, we reached the river and yes: there it stood. It really was an amazing structure.

There was no human being anywhere in sight, but a fence had been placed all around the base of the tower and two german shepherd dogs roamed freely inside the fence as guardians. I stepped out of the car and took fifty photographs.

My companions looked on in amazement, from the warmth of the car. A crazy Dutchman toiling through the snow around a steel tower, that had once served as a pylon for power lines across the river, but was now standing idle. It's twin pylon, at the other bank of the river, had been taken down in 2005, and it's iron had been used as scrap.

Originally, both pylons rose to a height of 128 meters. I was standing in front of the only remaining diagrid hyperboloid transmission tower in the entire world, but to my companions it looked just like a stupid pylon.

One afternoon we passed by the apartment building in Nizhny Novgorod where Sakharov, the Soviet Union's most famous dissident, had been held under house arrest, until he was released by Gorbatsov. The city was called Gorki at the time, after the Soviet poet Maxim Gorki.

The unobtrusive apartment where Sakharov and his wife Elena Bonner had lived was now a museum. A historic place, but we were the only visitors. Most Russians prefer to forget the Soviet past and move on with their lives. They do revere their heroes though: the main avenue in Nizhny Novgorod is called Gagarin Avenue, after Yuri Gagarin, the first human being in space.

On another occasion, we observed a meeting of opposition groups in the Red October Cinema. One of the speakers was Boris Nemtsov, a tall, handsome fellow and a charismatic speaker. He had been governor of Nizhny Novgorod oblast (province) and deputy prime minister of Russia under Boris Jeltsin.

He seemed destined to become Jeltsin's successor, but Jeltsin decided that his successor would be somebody else: an unobtrusive guy called Vladimir Putin. Jeltsin's ultimate mistake.

After having served two terms as president, the Russian constitution stipulated that Putin was not permitted to serve a third term. Putin found a simple solution to this problem: he would serve as Prime Minister from 2008 to 2012, while his former Prime Minister, Medvedev, would serve as president. The real power remained firmly in the hands of Putin. After 2012 the two of them would switch roles yet again.

Boris Nemtsov would be assassinated in 2014, on a bridge near the Kremlin in Moscow. In 2017, five Tsjetsjens were convicted for it, but to this day no one knows who actually ordered the assassination. One thing is clear though: politics in Russia is tricky business. No wonder most Russians stay clear of it.

We met Aleksej Navalny, the 37-year old opposition leader, several times. After the icy cold manifestation of several opposition groups on 4 February, he had been apprehended by secret service agents. They put him in a car, beat him up and released him at the outskirts of the city.

A few days later we met Navalny again in the office of the opposition: his face was badly bruised. Navalny told us that the secret police repeatedly had asked him what a guy from Moscow was doing in Nizhny Novgorod. Apparently, people from Nizhny did not like people from Moscow. This sounded familiar to me. In Holland, people from Rotterdam really hate people from Amsterdam.

In 2012, Navalny was still relatively unknown to the world. This would change in 2019, when he had been poisoned, allegedly by the Russian secret service. To us, in a small office in Nizhny Novgorod, Navalny did not appear to be a cheerful fellow. Most Russians are pleasant people, who like to socialize and crack jokes, but Navalny kept his distance. I never saw him laugh or even smile.

In 2017 Navalny was convicted on corruption charges. Because of this, he could not participate in any future elections. By Russian law, anyone who has been convicted of any crime is not allowed to stand for office. It's a useful tool for the people in power to get rid of potential opponents.

We visited Sergach, a large village at about 150 kilometers from Nizhny Novgorod. Until then, winter had been cold, but with little wind and snow. Now, we found ourselves in a blizzard. Quite frightening, especially since the road became slippery. But I realized, to my own astonishment, that I was becoming more and more Russian: don't complain, just go on.

On the way back, we saw three trucks that had slipped off the road. Alexei just laughed about it. Russians are tough cookies. In Holland, the TV channels would never show dead or dying people, but on Russian TV they have no such sensitivities. Every evening I saw men, women and children involved in car accidents.

On another occasion we visited the town Semenov, named after Simon, which accidentally is my middle name. Semenov is famous because of its brightly coloured wooden carvings. The local electoral official took us to the little museum, with lots of these carvings on display.

Megan did most of the talking. I tried to support her as much as I could. Fortunately, the STO Manual that we had to prepare for our STOs, had to be written in English. Since I love history, I could contribute quite a bit to it. But one of us had to travel to Moscow by train, to pick up the STOs. Obviously, this had to be Megan, since she spoke Russian and could read the Cyrillic signs.

While in Moscow, Megan had handed our STO manual to our Saransk STO team. They would travel directly to Saransk, so I would never meet them. I talked to them on the phone a few times, though. Aida from Kazakhstan and Ferenc from Hungary sounded professional and positive on the phone.

The next day Megan returned with the other six STOs. Kate and I were waiting for them at the little restaurant inside the railway station: each STO team had to sign contracts with their drivers and interpreters before they were allowed to enter their cars, because of the insurance.

They were a good bunch: Elena from Bulgaria and Heiko from Germany would observe in Nizhny Novgorod. Adeline from France and Stefan from Poland would observe from Hotel Camelot in Sergach.

Valerie from the UK and Yildirim from Turkey would observe from Hotel Rancho in Dzherzinsk. They were all quite young, except Valerie, who was 73 years of age. She was very energetic still and she had a lot of observation experience.

All three teams spent their first and last nights in our guesthouse, U Domika Petra. Elena and Heiko stayed in our guesthouse for the entire period. I particularly liked Heiko. The days that Dutch people hated German people belong definitely to the past. Ever since my wife and I worked for the UN as aid workers, we nearly always had German friends.

E-Day went quite well, without major issues. We had instructed our STO teams to fax their forms from their hotels and not from local authorities. At one point, we found out that the Sergach team, Adeline and Stefan, had not obliged: they had sent their faxes from the fax machine of the district authorities.

There was a reason for this: they were broke. It was so bad that, upon their return to Nizhny, Adeline asked if she could borrow 100 euros from me. The next day, I accompanied the STOs back to the railway station. After they had boarded the train for Moscow, Megan and I paid a visit to several human rights people, whom we had met before.

To our amazement, their mobile phones had been hacked by the security forces. The moment they switched on any of their mobile phones, they heard sheep blaring. It seemed like a scene from a cheap B-movie, but it was all too true: they allowed us to listen to it.

One day later, we were invited to a meeting of all the opposition parties. They said they had proof of major riggings of the elections by the electoral authorities. As an experienced observer, I get this kind of information during each and every election, so I always insist on evidence.

On my previous missions, no evidence was ever produced, but this time it would be different. Very different. Megan and Kate sat in front of our laptop, checking the online election results of hundreds of polling stations. They checked the ones that the opposition had mentioned to us as having been phantom polling stations and—surprise, surprise—all of these polling stations showed the same results: a turn-out of 99 per cent, of which 97 per cent had voted for Putin.

In real elections, a result like this is impossible. Turn-out is never higher than 80 per cent, because there are always voters who are sick or travelling. A 97 per cent result for one candidate is also impossible: even when every voter had wanted to vote for that one candidate, there are always people who make mistakes.

So it was clear that something was very wrong here. Putin and his advisors realized this too, so six years later, during the 2018 presidential election, they aimed for a more realistic 70/70: a 70 per cent turn-out, of which 70 per cent would vote for Putin.

Megan and Kate noted that the 16 polling stations were situated in three of the eight electoral districts within the city of Nizhny Novgorod. I proposed that Kate and I would visit the electoral authorities in these three districts. In the meantime, Megan would continue to check the websites.

Kate and I visited the director of one district who, during the previous election, had banned the OSCE observers from entering the district electoral premises. I feared he would do the same to us, but this time he received us in his office.

I asked about the phantom polling stations. He told us that he had nothing to do with it, but then, to my astonishment, he handed me a note, without saying another word. Kate took a quick look and told me that it was a list of 16 polling stations in three districts.

Exactly the ones that we had identified as phantom ones. Kate pointed at the bottom of the note: it was signed by the president of the Electoral Commission of Nizhny Novgorod oblast. The highest electoral official in the entire province!

This was shocking, incriminating evidence of electoral fraud by the highest authorities. I asked the district director if I could get a copy of the note, but he said: ,,You can have it. I don't want to see it anymore." Obviously, the man was disgusted at such flagrant fraud.

Kate and I returned to Megan with the note. We scanned it and sent it to our Core Team in Moscow. The CT was immediately aware of the importance of this. ,,Can you go to the president of the Electoral Commission of Nizhny Novgorod oblast and confront him with this note?" they asked us.

An idea struck me. In Russia it is perfectly legal to open a newly created polling station up to three days before E-Day. These new PSs could be based in, for example, a railway station, to accommodate travellers. We had to be absolutely one hundred per cent sure that the PSs on our list had not existed.

I discussed this with Megan. ,,Listen: I propose that you continue searching the websites and that I will visit several of these phantom PSs with Kate. I'm quite sure that they did not exist, but I want to be absolutely sure."

Megan agreed. Kate and I first visited a cemetery, that was mentioned on the list. There were five shops there. The owner of the flower shop and the owner of the coffins shop told us that they had been working on E-Day, but that they never saw nor had heard of a PS in their vicinity.

After that, we visited a market, consisting of a covered area and an open air area. We asked a number of marketers: none of them had either seen or heard of a PS over there on E-Day. Than we visited a building where several Spa's and beauty salons were housed.

,,One of our STO interpreters works here," Kate told me. She called her on the phone. The interpreter agreed to go around and ask discretely about a possible PS. Half an hour later, she called us back. ,,No one in the building knows of any PS on E-Day."

This was definitive proof, that the PSs on the list had never existed. Yet, their results were mentioned on the Election Commission's website. We drove to the Kremlin, to confront the EC president with this. After all, he had signed for it.

Funnily, the president was in a good mood when he received us. He thought that we had arrived to pay him a last farewell visit. He even handed us some presents, as is the custom in Russia.

Then Megan showed him a copy of the note. His face turned white. I was making notes, with Kate translating in my ear. My notebook lay on my lap, so I watched his hands under the table. His hands had been calm, but now he was rubbing them furiously. He took of his wedding ring and put it back on: again and again.

I'm not a psychologist, but this meant, undoubtedly, that the man was guilty as hell. He knew also that he would be punished by his chief in Moscow, not because of the phantom polling stations, but because he had been so stupid that he had been exposed by international observers.

Democracy, Russian style. Putin must have studied the wise words of one of his predecessors, Stalin, who used to say: 'People who vote don't matter. The only people that matter are the ones who count'.

When we walked back to our car, we were elated. How often do observers observe real fraud by the authorities and obtain clear evidence of it? Three days after E-Day I received a call from Ineke, the Dutch LTO.

I started talking enthusiastically about our discovery of the 16 phantom polling stations, but she interrupted me and told me that, sadly, a relative of hers had passed away and therefore she had to return to Holland immediately.

When Megan and I boarded the train back to Moscow, both Kate and Alexei were in tears. We were a good team. During the debriefings, we were told that after our discovery of phantom polling stations, the other observers had been instructed to also look out for them. The Saint Petersburg team discovered 72 phantom polling stations!

In between the debriefings, Willem and I ventured out to explore Moscow together. Actually: he showed me Moscow, since he had been there many times. In Moscow the snow had been cleaned up nicely, but it was still freezing cold.

While we walked the streets, Willem didn't stop talking, which was a problem for me, since first of all he was a head taller than me and secondly: I had pulled my cap over my head, to protect my ears from freezing. The cap blocked all sounds.

I really had to concentrate on what he was saying. But he was a nice chap. He had retired at a young age, after having spent his professional life as a military man in the Dutch army.

A few weeks later, all Dutch LTOs and STOs were debriefed at the Ministry of Foreign Affairs in The Hague. Most of the other observers were old Russia hands. They loved to discuss past, present and future Russian politics.

I am not a Russia expert, but I surprised everyone when I handed my note with 16 phantom polling stations to representatives of the ministry. I told the other observers, half in jest: „I don't know much about Russia, but I know how to observe elections."

In later years I read a lot about Russian politics. It confirmed what I had observed during those six weeks in Nizhny Novgorod. It's hard to understand for westerners, but Russians have a different idea about democracy.

The Russians have had bad experiences with revolutions, so for many of them the most important thing is stability. Without stability, there cannot be prosperity, nor can there be a respected Russian state. This is why many Russians support Putin's 'controlled democracy'.

As long as Putin provides them with stability and a sense of national pride, they don't care that all other parties in parliament are in fact controlled by Putin. And they don't care very much that someone who is a real threat to Putin, like Aleksej Navalny, is persecuted mercilessly by the secret service.

Most Russians can't be bothered by the fact that Navalny was convicted for corruption on false charges, after which he could not legally be a candidate for the presidency. That's the way powerful and ruthless people deal with their opponents. There is no independent judiciary in Russia. Any judge opposing the authorities risks being harassed for the rest of his life.

And there's something else. In the west, we distinguish between people who are either politicians, businessmen or criminals. In Russia, this distinction does not exist. A person can be a politician, a businessman and a criminal, all at the same time. Ordinary Russians don't care about this. All they want is prosperity, which can only be achieved through prolonged stability.

So Putin does not necessarily need to rig the elections. Even without fraud, he will obtain 50 per cent of the vote. But Putin is haunted by a sort of masculine Russian sense of pride: he absolutely wants to obtain 65 per cent of the vote, to show the world that he undoubtedly is the most popular leader in a 'democratic Russia'.

In the end, Putin and his United Russia party won with 63,60 per cent of the vote. Second came Zyuganov, of the Communist Party, with 17,18 per cent. Zhirinovsky, leader of the ultra-nationalist Liberal Democratic Party, obtained 6,22 per cent.

Zhirinovsky died in April 2022. Compared to Zhirinovsky, Putin was a moderate nationalist. Remarkably, Zhirinovsky was the only member of the Duma who was not afraid to tell Putin the truth. Zhirinovsky was tolerated by Putin, since many Russians considered Zhirinovsky as a kind of clown anyway. And Zhirinovsky supported all Putin's nationalist adventures.

Putin's curious sense of pride explains the state-sponsored doping program during the 2014 Sochi Olympic Winter Games: Putin wanted the world to recognize the greatness of Russian competitors, which would then make him look great in the eyes of the Russian people. It didn't matter if the successes were achieved by cheating.

It has to be said: the annexation of the Crimean peninsula in 2014 greatly increased Putin's popularity. Historically, the Crimean peninsula has always been a part of Russia and not of Ukraine. Besides, 90 per cent of the Crimean population are ethnic Russians, so the Russian claim has some credibility. The Donbas region is something else: it is largely inhabited by Ukrainians, who speak either Russian or Ukrainian.

Western correspondents who have lived in Russia for many years reported that the 2018 presidential elections looked very much like a reality show, whereby everything was carefully orchestrated and the outcome of the elections was already determined before they even took place: Putin was going to win with close to 70/70.

Navalny had called on his followers to boycott the elections. Apparently, he had had some success after all. But it is a fact that even when the elections would have been completely free and fair, at least 50 per cent of all Russians would have voted for Putin anyway.

In 2020 Navalny was poisoned with the nerve agent novitsjok. The secret service had put it in his underpants. The same poison had been used against ex-spy Sergej Skripal and his daughter Joelia in March 2018 in Salisbury, UK. The British police traced the novitsjok back to two Russian secret servicemen.

Upon his return to Russia, early 2021, Navalny was immediately arrested and put in a prison cell. Navalny had his revenge, though. He posted a video on the internet with 'Putin's Palace' near Sochi. It had been built at the expense of the taxpayers for exclusive use of Putin and his cronies.

More than 100 million Russians watched this video and Putin's popularity plummeted. But he has enough tricks in his sleeve to continue to rule. And Navalny will never be popular. Navalny is a born activist, not a born politician. To sum it all up: many Russians don't like Putin, but they like Navalny even less.

The real Putin showed himself after the Russian invasion of Ukraine in 2022. All independent media outlets were closed. International journalists were forced to leave Russia, since they risked prison terms of up to 15 years for spreading 'fake news'. What is 'fake news'? Well: that's up to the Kremlin, to decide.

It was forbidden to use the words 'invasion' or 'war', since Putin had decided that it was to be called 'a special operation'. With the invasion of Ukraine, Putin shot himself in the foot. He managed to unite all Ukrainians and he managed to unite all EU members states and the entire western world against Russia.

Chapter 15

KENYA - 2013

'The slums are no go areas for our observers'

A few days before my departure to Kenya, I received the deployment plan for the LTOs. My partner would be Nevenka, a 45-year old woman from Slovenia and our duty station would be Nairobi, the capital.

I wasn't very happy about Nairobi. I had stayed there for a few days in 1985. I remembered the endless traffic jams. But worst of all, we would be close to the Core Team. While still in Holland, I received an email from my future partner.

Her passport name was Nevenka, but everyone, including herself, called her Nena. She wanted to exchange LinkedIn pages, in order to get to know each other a bit better. I replied that I was not active on social media. I'm old school. She would have to wait, to meet me in the real world.

As it turned out, Nena would be one of my best partners. She told me that she was not from Slovenia, even though she had been born there. She grew up in Croatia and because of that she possessed two passports. Since Croatia was not a member of the EU as yet, her only option to work as an EU observer was through her Slovenian passport.

Funnily, after we had been in Nairobi for several weeks, I showed her a message on the Dutch teletext service: Croatia had finally been admitted to the EU. Nena was delighted. In the future she could be an observer on behalf of either Slovenia or Croatia.

Our Chief Observer was, as usual, a MEP. His name was Alojz Peterle and, believe it or not, he was a Slovenian! Since we would be based in Nairobi, we would surely bump into him. Nena asked me right away to shield her from him, because if she would talk to him, he would immediately notice that her Slovenian was poor.

But first I had to get to Kenya. At Schiphol Amsterdam airport I ran into Hanna from Poland, who had been my partner in Nigeria. I remembered our relationship as having been rather strained, but she greeted me as a dear old friend. ,,Jos, what a great time we had in Nigeria. Do you remember that fantastic guesthouse that belonged to the American University?"

She introduced me to Agnes from Hungary. It's always nice to talk to other observers. In my home region in Holland I am the only observer, so I can never talk to colleagues. In fact, I hardly ever talk about my observation missions, since the people back home don't have a clue as to what an observer is doing.

To them, it's like listening to someone talking about that great holiday on a tropical island. When you've never been to that island, it doesn't mean anything to you. It's just boring. Most people believe that observers are a kind of well-paid tourists, no matter what you explain to them.

The KLM flight took us straight to Nairobi. There were several other observers on board. After a number of missions it feels like meeting old friends again. It was already late in the evening when we finally arrived at the Windsor Golf and Country Club Hotel, at the outskirts of Nairobi.

I had a few beers with other observers beside the swimming pool. It's nice to be able to sit outdoors, when you've just arrived out of the European winter. The next morning, I took my seat in the meeting room for the briefings.

The seat next to me was still empty, but just before the briefings were about to start, a women with reddish hair arrived. She shook my hand. ,,Hi, I'm Nena." First impressions are important and my first impression was good.

The next day, Nena told me that Berenger, her best friend, was living in Nairobi. Berenger came from Grenoble in France and she worked for the UN. She lived in a big house in Nairobi now, with Erwin, her Croatian husband, and their little son. As I understood, she and Nena had worked together for the UN in Zagreb.

More importantly, Berenger and Erwin had lived half a year in a small guesthouse at the outskirts of Nairobi. It was a curious guesthouse, since it did not advertise at all. Yet, it was always fully booked and several people had stayed there for a year or even longer.

You could only stay there if the owner liked you. The owner was Nenella Tozzi, an Italian woman who had lived in Africa for 70 years and would soon turn 90 years of age. Berenger agreed to introduce us to her.

But the mission had also reserved a hotel for us. Several hotels in the city center had been cleared by our security expert, so Nena and I decided to check out those hotels first. They were not too bad, but rather expensive. Next, we visited Nenella Tozzi's guesthouse, situated towards the end of Muthaiga Road.

We immediately liked it. It was a large compound with lots of trees. The grass was kept neat. It was surrounded by high fences and two large, castrated dogs roamed freely around the compound. All the neighbouring compounds also had dogs, so an intruder could never penetrate without alarming dozens of dogs.

I was afraid our Australian security expert would not allow us to stay there, but to my surprise Mark told us straight away: ,,My own house is in the same area. I know Nenella's house very well. It's as safe as can be. You can stay there. No problem."

The guesthouse was in fact an old colonial mansion, with only six rooms. We were welcome, thanks to Nena's friend Berenger. Nena even managed to negotiate a lower rate than I ever expected. Instead of 6,000 KES, we only had to pay 5,000 KES per day (1 euro = 110 KES). Included were both breakfast and dinner. Much cheaper than the hotels.

There was one condition, though: we could stay for a maximum of ten weeks, since Nenella's 90th birthday was imminent and lots of family members were expected to arrive from Italy. They needed all the rooms for them. That was fine for us: our mission was scheduled to last eight weeks.

Looking back, it was the best place I ever stayed in. Nena got a great room inside the main house, with a fridge and access to a roofed terrace. We would do all our typing at the round wooden table on that terrace, adjacent to the living room of the main house.

I myself slept in a little red-tiled house, at about twenty meters from the main house. There was no television in my little Hans and

Gretchen house, but I did not miss it at all. In the evenings I sat contentedly just outside my little house in the pitch-dark, with a cigar and a beer.

After a few weeks, the family adopted a third, medium sized dog called Nouschka. Like most dogs in Africa, it was a cross-breed. Her previous owners couldn't take care of her anymore. This dog would become my favourite.

I liked Nouschka and she liked me. Occasionally, she would even enter my little house. One evening she was lying fast asleep next to my bed. I locked the door and went asleep as well. A few hours later she woke me up: she preferred to sleep outdoors in the cool evening air, so I let her out.

Nenella told us that after the extreme violence of the elections of 2007, all shops had been closed. Nobody had expected this, so food supplies ran out quickly. ,,After a few days all our dog food was gone", she remembered.

I asked her if this time they were prepared for any disturbances. Nenella called one of the servants and asked him to show me the storage room. It was a large room, packed with sacks of rice, maize meal and pasta. And lots of cans of meat and beans.

What really caught my eye was the enormous amount of dog food. Later I told Nenella that dogs will eat anything, if they are hungry, from boiled rice to boiled potatoes. But she would not hear about it. ,,This time we are prepared. We will not go hungry and the dogs will not go hungry. I learned my lesson."

Scarcity really affects you, as I remembered from my years in communist Mozambique. But in the end, the Kenyan elections of 2013 turned out as peaceful as could be. There had been an attack in Mombasa, where 19 people were killed, but this had little or nothing to do with the elections.

Nena and I were, in fact, fully accepted as members of Nenella's extended family. At about 20.00 hours, every evening, a servant would inform us that diner was about to be served in the kitchen. Like a real Italian family, all the guests sat down around a large table.

Nenella, obviously the 'mama' of the family, always at the head of the table. Mario, her nephew of about thirty years of age, was usually there, as was Nicole, his Italian girlfriend. It was like the movie Novecento by Bernardo Bertolucci.

Occasionally, one or two friends of the family were also seated around the table. The servants had been trained by Nenella to cook Italian food, so every meal started with pasta: a different pasta every day. Nenella explained to me how to eat spaghetti: ,,No spoon, no knife. Just turn your fork from the outside to the inside."

Unfortunately, I'm a Dutch barbarian. After eight weeks, I was still unable to do it like an Italian. Once, we were even served chocolate pasta. After the pasta came the main course, usually with meat or chicken and vegetables, and finally dessert was served.

There was wine and soft drinks on the table, but I always brought a can of beer from my own fridge. I have fond memories of those evening meals, but I have to confess that, after this mission, I stopped eating pasta. There is a limit as to how much pasta a Dutchman can endure.

Conversation was mostly in English, but also in Italian. Nena had studied Italian, so she was fluent in it. Since I spoke Spanish and Portuguese, I could follow around fifty per cent of the Italian. Nenella and her nephew spoke Swahili with the servants, but the servants were fluent in English too.

I had written down a few simple phrases, like 'Good Morning' and 'How is your Family?' and asked our interpreter, Lucy, to translate these phrases into Swahili. I wrote it down phonetically, and kept the little paper readily at hand. Before going to the kitchen for breakfast, I would take a quick look at these phrases.

To Nena's astonishment, I greeted the servants in Swahili. To her even more astonishment, after my second phrase 'How is your Family', the servants would reply extensively. Of course, I didn't understand a word they were saying, but after they had finished, I just said 'OK' in English.

I just hoped they had not been telling me that the cow had foot and mouth disease or that grandmother had stumbled and broken her leg, but my reply apparently satisfied the servants. From then on, they would always greet me cheerfully in Swahili.

The servants were part of the family. One evening, the very first presidential debate in the history of Kenya would be broadcast. Normally, in Kenya, the candidates would hold rallies and they would send their supporters from door to door, handing out money or bags of rice or maize meal. To buy votes, in fact.

This time, Kenya would do it the modern way: all seven presidential candidates participated, one of them was a woman. Since Nena and I did not have TVs in our rooms, we watched it in Nenella's living room. All the servants were there too.

The debate was a novelty, even though everybody understood that only two candidates made a real chance: Uhuru Kenyatta and Raila Odinga. It was, in fact, a dynastic struggle, since their fathers had been the first president and vice-president of Kenya, after it became independent in 1963.

'Political Familism' this is called: the power over a political party remains forever in the hands of one family. It happens in many countries: Pakistan (Bhutto and Sharif families), India (Nehroe-Ghandi family), Syria (Assad family), Canada (Trudeau family). Not to mention dynasties in communist countries like North-Korea (Kim family) and Cuba (Castro family).

Everybody also understood that in Kenya tribal interests are the most important factor in politics. Uhuru (his name means 'Freedom' in Swahili) was the leader of the biggest tribe, the Kikuyus, who live in central Kenya. He found an ally in William Ruto, of the Kalenjin tribe, who live in the north of the country, near the Rift Valley.

Raila Odinga represented the Luo tribe from western Kenya, near Lake Victoria. Odinga was supported by several smaller tribes. Western intellectuals don't use the word 'tribe' anymore. They prefer the word 'people', but Africans have no such sophisticated feelings. To an African, a tribe is a tribe.

Tribalism is still predominant in most African elections. A Kikuyu would never vote for a Luo candidate. A Luo would never vote for a Kikuyu candidate. It is simply inconceivable. Your family and friends would never forgive you, if you voted for someone from another tribe. The voters wanted something in return for their vote, though. They expected to be rewarded with government jobs and government contracts.

When a Kikuyu won the elections, it would actually be wise to offer lots of jobs and contracts to Luo's, in order to keep the Luo's happy. But the Kikuyus would never accept this. A Kikuyu president simply had to offer everything to Kikuyus, otherwise he would be cast out of his own tribe.

In Africa, elections are not about ideologies, but about interests. African countries are not wealthy, so the little wealth that is available simply cannot be shared with everyone. African tribesmen don't care about the nation they live in; they care about their tribe.

Western ambassadors had publicly expressed their hope that Odinga would win. This made it a bit awkward for our EU EOM to be seen as neutral and impartial. For me personally, there was another problem: Uhuru Kenyatta and William Ruto were officially requested to appear at the International Court of Criminal Justice.

They would be under investigation because of their supposed role during the violence that followed the 2007 elections, during which 1,200 people lost their lives and more than 400,000 lost their homes. The ICC resided in The Hague. I was afraid many Kenyans would hold this against me, but luckily most people didn't know that The Hague was in The Netherlands. No one ever mentioned it to me.

That our EU EOM was not seen as independent became obvious when Nena and I interviewed Kenyan journalists. Several of them asked us: 'What is your interest?' In the end, the ICC-case was dropped, after several key witnesses had died under suspicious circumstances.

Nenella's life story was remarkable. Her husband had died thirty years earlier, at the age of 76. She was only sixteen years of age when she married him. He was sixteen years older than her. Before the second world war, they moved from Italy to Somalia. Since Italy sided with Nazi Germany during the war, Nenella and her husband were transported back home by boat.

By then, they had a baby daughter. It took months to round the Cape of Good Hope and then to travel north on the Atlantic Ocean, always at risk of being attacked by either U-boats or allied warships. Finally, the boat reached the safety of Gibraltar.

After the war, the couple and their daughter settled in Nairobi, where the husband became the representative of Alitalia, the airline.

He also started the very first travel agency in Africa. They constructed the mansion where I was now staying. After her husband's death, her children convinced her to convert the mansion into a guesthouse, not only because of the money, but also to have some company.

And great company she was. Many evenings, when Nena and I sat down at the wooden terrace table to do our typing, Nenella would join us. She told us great stories. And sad stories. Her oldest daughter had recently died from a brain tumour at the age of 71.

Pharaoh Ramses II lived well into his nineties, as a result of which ten of his sons died before him. Mentally, Nenella was still a hundred per cent, but her body was failing her. After each evening meal one of her trusted servants would lift her up from her chair. After that, she walked unaided, with the help of a stick.

In between Italian meals, Nena and I had to do a bit of work now and then. Our driver, David, was a pastor of about forty years of age. When he first told us that he was a pastor, I thought he meant that he was herding animals, but he explained that he was herding humans for one of the many protestant churches in Africa. He worked as a driver, because he needed the money.

David reminded us that we should be very careful in Nairobi, because he had been carjacked twice. At gunpoint, the bandits forced him to climb into the booth of the car. They then drove to the huge garbage dump at the outskirts of the city and released him there. They kept the car. He had to walk back all the way.

Our interpreter, Lucy, was a young mother, whose husband worked for The Star newspaper as photographer. Both our driver and our interpreter were Kikuyu. We soon found out that the we did not really need an interpreter, since all educated Kenyans speak English.

But Lucy was very nice, so we did not fire her. Instead, we just let her stay in her house on several occasions. There was also a logistical reason for this: Nairobi is a large and congested city. Nena and I lived in the far north of the city, our driver in the far east and our interpreter in the far west. To get everybody together in one car was a logistical nightmare.

According to the rules of every mission, the vehicle had to be parked at our guesthouse every night, while I kept the car keys. David, our driver, therefore had to travel nearly two hours by minibus to get to his house. The next morning, he had to travel two hours to get back to the guesthouse. But rules are rules.

Then it took us at least a full hour to reach the city centre, where we would pick up Lucy. In a small town, we would have driven over to her house, but in Nairobi this would have taken far too much time.

Nena and I had our own office within the premises of the Core Team. We shared this office with the 'mobile' LTO team, but they were hardly ever there, since they covered the areas around Nairobi. I told Nena that we would use our office no more than twice a week, since Core Team offices are usually quite depressive.

Core Team members are usually in their thirties or forties and extremely ambitious: they all want to be a member of a Core Team on future missions, so they all need the best evaluations they can possibly get. Many Core Team members work so hard, seven days a week for eight weeks on end, that the stress levels reach critical points.

It was quite funny: whenever we visited the Core Team premises, the members of the Core Team would come out of their offices one by one, to ask us about life outside their offices. Most of them were so engrossed in their office work that they hardly ever left their offices. We were their eyes and ears to the outside world.

The Core Team was not too bad, though. In fact, it was one of the best Core Teams and Service Providers I have ever had. I knew Richard quite well. He had also been the legal expert on my Sudan mission.

And our Deputy Chief Observer, Gillian from Scotland (I once made a terrible mistake by saying that she was from England; she almost kicked me out of the mission) had been my NEEDS trainer in 2009 in Brussels.

Gillian had given me a good evaluation at the time, so I liked her. But Nena and I spent more time with the staff of the Service Provider, especially with Mark, the security expert, and Conor, the finance expert. Both of them actually lived in Nairobi, so they informed us about local issues.

On several occasions, Nena and were obliged to invite Core Team experts to accompany us for interviews. Monika, the human rights expert of the mission, was a young and insecure woman from Poland. She rather hysterically accused us of interfering within her area of expertise.

Monika was jealous, since we managed to arrange interviews with interesting people, thanks to our driver and our interpreter, who had many local contacts. The other experts were more easy going.

Marek, the Media Expert, and Peter, the Press Officer, had been trying in vain to get an appointment with the editor of The Citizen, the biggest TV-station of the country and also the owner of 16 radio stations.

But David, our driver, was a pastor and the secretary of The Citizen was a member of the board of David's church. So it was a piece of cake for us to make an appointment. Marek and Peter accompanied us. The meeting went very well.

David had many connections. In Africa, that comes in handy. One afternoon, we dropped Lucy off at the entrance to a petrol station. A police officer signalled David to open his window. As it turned out, it was forbidden to park your car there, even for one minute.

We were fined 10,000 KES. I immediately called Mark on the phone. At the same time I advised Nena: ,,Open your window, so they can see that there are white people in the car."

A few minutes later, David informed us that the problem had been solved. ,,The senior police officer who is in charge here was my friend. We served together in the army." Later, in Mark's office, I pleaded with him not to punish David for his parking offence. ,,Don't worry," Mark said. ,,You did everything right by immediately calling me."

As EU LTOs we always contact the LTOs from other organizations. We visit the same venues, so we meet them automatically. On this mission, the African Union had fielded an LTO team in Nairobi. One morning, we were invited by the Carter Center, to meet their LTO team at the Hillpark Hotel, where the Carter Core Team was based.

While we waited for Jon from Sweden and Alba from Albania, I was approached by a bolding man. ,,Hi Johannes, how are you doing." I had learned by now to answer equally enthusiastically albeit neutrally, so I said: ,,I'm fine, how are you?" I desperately tried to remember who this guy was.

He noticed my inner struggles. ,,I'm Mariusz. I was the EU LTO Coordinator in Juba in 2010/2011." Of course I remembered him. The problem was that my partner Sheena and I had only been in Juba for three days of briefings. The next ten weeks we were based in Khartoum, so I never saw Mariusz again. We talked on the phone a few times. He was a nice guy. Most Polish observers are OK.

One day, Gillian, the Deputy Chief Observer, called us into her office. She explained that the mission needed more visibility and since we were the Nairobi LTO team, we should take a small group of national and international journalists around the city the next day, to show them what kind of useful work EU observers do every day.

Next, to our surprise, Gillian told us that we should dress neatly, since we would appear on national TV. She looked disapprovingly at my baggy pants with side sacks. To be honest, I had to admit that she was right. I looked more like a tourist than a serious semi-diplomatic EU election observer.

There was one problem, though: this was the only decent pants I had brought with me. Nena also needed new pants. We decided to go to the nearest Woolworths, but the problem was: it was already 19.30 hours and most shops would close at 20.00 hours.

We rushed to the mall. Thank God, the clothes shop was still open and the staff was helpful. We both found new pants. At reasonable prices. Two days later, Gillian gave us a compliment. She said that our TV appearance had been a success.

Funnily, during the mid-term briefings halfway the mission, several LTOs told us that they had seen us on TV, while they were out in the provinces. Nena and I cherished our few minutes of fame.

Observers are expected to work seven days a week and also every evening. In addition, observers are not allowed to leave their province, which in our case was the city of Nairobi. Luckily, one game park is situated within the boundaries of the city of Nairobi, so we were actually allowed to go there.

We could always say that we wanted to know the opinions of the game wardens as to the upcoming elections. And the Bomas, the cultural centre where all election results of the entire country would come in, were situated close to the game park.

There was another problem: our vehicle was equipped with a tracking device. We decided to leave the vehicle at our guesthouse. It would also be good for David, our driver, to enjoy a day off. After all, it was a Sunday and he was a pastor. He had to tend to his flock.

Nena had called a travel agency. They would send us a minibus that would be allowed to enter the game park. The minibus arrived at 06.00 hours on Sunday. There were no traffic jams yet, so we arrived at the game park within one hour. There, we had to wait at the entrance.

There were about twenty minibuses with tourists and there was only one ticket office. All the drivers were elbowing their way to the front of the line, African style. Since our driver was not the smartest person on the planet, it took him 45 minutes to obtain an entrance permit.

But the game park was worth it. I had visited it before, in 1985. It is not a very big game park and there is not much vegetation, so you get to see lots of animals within a short period of time. All Africa's big game are there, except elephants, and you can observe them at close range.

Our minibus halted only twenty meters from a group of lions feasting on a zebra. Nena took, literally, thousands of photographs. The funniest thing of this game park, I thought, was that all the time you noted the tall buildings of Nairobi in the background. It was wilderness, but never far from civilization.

On another Sunday, we took a taxi to the Karen Blixen museum. We were joined by Andrea, an Italian working at the Italian embassy, who was staying with us at Nenella's place. He was a cheerful guy, always the life and soul at Nenella's dinners.

It's a small but very interesting museum. It used to be Karen Blixen's house. Several scenes of the famous Out of Africa movie had been filmed on location. In fact, both Robert Redford's and Meryl Streep's costumes are on display there.

As is the red/green lamp that Karen used to let Dennis know if she was in a bad or good mood. One of the guides told us that Karen had caught syphilis and for the rest of her life had been treated with arsenic.

One Saturday evening, we invited Richard and Rosa, the legal experts of the Core Team, to join us for an evening meal in Nenella's kitchen. They loved it. They both said that they would love to stay at Nenella's guesthouse, if rooms were available. Sadly, that was not the case.

Nena and I were invited quite a few times by Berenger and her husband Erwin in their enormous, fortified house in Runda, at the outskirts of Nairobi. I have fond memories of these encounters. Erwin was a professional cook, but salaries for cooks are extremely low in Kenya, so he looked after their little son instead. One evening he cooked for us. It was delicious.

As usual, we sat around the large, round table in the garden. They had invited a few more people. One of them was Berenger's direct UN boss, an American woman of around fifty years of age, who had come down from New York. After she had left the table, I exclaimed loudly that I really hated lawyers.

A bit later, she came back. I asked her what her profession was. ,,I am a lawyer", she said. Everyone fell silent. All eyes turned to me. I waited a few seconds. Then I said: ,,I really love lawyers." She will never know why all the others were doubling over with laughter.

Erwin was looking for something useful to do, so I told him: ,,Why don't you take flying lessons? I obtained my flying license in South Africa, when I was living in Maputo, Mozambique." A few weeks later, it was Erwin's 39 birthday.

They invited us to join them in a Japanese restaurant inside Westgate Mall. I asked Berenger what she had given Erwin for his birthday. ,,Well, actually it's your fault," she replied. ,,I've given him his first flying lesson at Wilson Airport."

A friend of theirs was also there. His name was Tiresh, 39 years old, who lived in Nairobi. He was obviously gay. After I told him that I was from The Netherlands, he kept talking about extreme gay bars in Amsterdam. I had never even heard of these places. Tiresh also told us that he had known Nenella for twenty years. He and Nenella used to visit casinos together.

It was forbidden for us to visit the biggest slums. For good reasons. They are overcrowded, the roads are very small and as white and therefore rich people in an expensive car, we would obviously be targets for criminals. We were allowed to drive around Mathare slum, though, as long as we had a police escort.

We only did it once, since we had to plan our trip two days in advance and the locals are not fond of the police. We noted the 'flying toilets', though. Since there are very few toilets, people collect their excrements in plastic bags and toss them onto the rooftops.

We interviewed several district electoral staff. At one point, they told us that we'd better leave, since the food truck would arrive shortly. We drove away to a crossroads on a hill top. From a distance of about 500 meters we saw the food truck arrive. Instantly, a crowd formed around the truck.

Within minutes, people stormed the truck. A guy with a long stick beat the assailants, to no avail. Boys grabbed sacks of maize meal and ran away with it. It was a sorry sight, but what could we do? We were there for the elections, not to solve all the problems of the country.

Nena wanted desperately to take photographs inside the slums, so several weeks later, just before the end of our mission, Mark, our security expert, took us in his UN vehicle inside Mathare and Kibera slums. Since Mark lived in Nairobi, he knew exactly what he could or could not do.

I realized that Mark had been quite right: it is a rather uncomfortable feeling, being inside a slum, with so many poor people staring at our expensive vehicle, with white people inside. White people are rich, by definition.

The dirt roads were barely wide enough for one vehicle. They could easily block a road. Then we would have been at their mercy. I was relieved when Mark drove us back to the Core Team.

We were allowed to visit the camp of the Internally Displaced Persons (IDPs) though. Without police escort. It was a small slum in Ruai, Embakasi South. The IDP camp stood isolated, close to where Nairobi's sewers streamed into a lake. The IDPs had lived there since 2007, when they had to flee their home regions after the election-related violence.

To get to the camp, Nena had contacted a woman from the ministry that dealt with IDPs. We picked her up in the centre of Nairobi. As usual, she was not alone. She was accompanied by a man.

Nena started to explain that we only had room for one extra person in our car, but I stopped her short. I told her that I would sit in the very back of the car, next to our trauma kit.

The mission provided a trauma kit for each vehicle. The trauma kit contained specialist medical equipment, that ordinary observers could not operate, but it was explained to us that there are many doctors and nurses in Kenya. The only thing they lack is medical equipment. The trauma kit would come in handy in case of an accident. In the end, I don't think any observer ever used it.

Anyway, in spite of Nena's objections, I climbed into the back of our car. There were two little seats there. It was cramped. I sat down, with my knees close to my chin. Lucy couldn't stop laughing.

I had threatened Lucy many times that I would lock her into the back of our car with the trauma kit. And now I was sitting there. Nena turned her head to me every ten minutes, to ask if I was still all right.

When we were quite close to the IDP camp, the woman from the ministry said that we would have to pick up a third person to give us directions. Obviously, the woman had never visited the IDP camp, even though she was responsible for it. By now, I really wanted to visit this IDP camp, let Nena make her photographs and get it over with.

To make room for our new guide, Lucy had to sit in the back of the car with me. Now we were both cramped in the back. But we reached the camp. It was a sorry sight. It was the poorest place I had ever seen in Africa.

We had brought a plastic bag full of bread, but the IDPs had expected more, when they noticed our expensive car. Especially since there were whites in the car. Nena made her photographs. We talked to the IDPs.

To my surprise, all of them were going to vote in spite of having been driven out of their ancestral lands because of the 2007 elections. Apparently, they didn't mind that they would have to walk five kilometres to the nearest polling stations.

I did most of the typing for our STO Briefing Pack. Nena felt a bit guilty, but I told her that she arranged most of our appointments, something I really hate to do. I like typing, especially the historic and political parts. I always use samples of my own STO Briefing Packs of previous missions, so it's mostly routine.

Nena was much handier with the laptop than me. She managed to squeeze in lots of photographs, including historic ones, like a photograph of Dennis, the pilot and lover of Karen Blixen.

We usually arrived at our guesthouse just before dark. Then we sat down at the round wooden table at the terrace adjacent to Nena's room, to work on our reports. Every other evening, Nena was on the phone with her good friend Mafalda from Portugal. Mafalda was based as an LTO in Mombasa, the coastal city.

Her LTO partner, apparently, was a horrible guy, who treated Mafalda like shit. He came from Malta. Quite a few times, Nena was silently crying while talking to Mafalda. The tears dropped down Nena's face. I realized that, thus far, I had been lucky with my partners. Most observers are OK, but there are one or two rotten apples out there.

Since we were the Nairobi LTOs, Nena and I had to be present in our visibility jackets during the briefings of the STOs at the Windsor Golf Club. The EU in Brussels had deployed a hotshot to our mission.

It was my good friend Alberto from Barcelona, who had been my STO in Venezuela and my colleague LTO in Pakistan and Sudan. Gillian must have found it a bit weird that Alberto and I were chatting amicably in Spanish all through the briefing sessions.

Meanwhile, Nena had a long conversation with Alojsz Peterle, our Chief Observer. It was no problem that her Slovenian was not entirely up to standards: Alojsz turned out to be a nice guy.

Nenella's 90th birthday was approaching and all the rooms would be needed for guests from Italy, but we were able to book rooms for our STO team, since they would be staying for just one week. Our STO team had been staying in a downtown hotel for one night and they were delighted that they could move in with us in Nenella's little paradise.

It was an all-female STO team: Christina from Greece, who had no observation experience but had written her thesis about Kenya, so she was well-informed about the host country. Kathy from Luxemburg had been on the Core Team during my Venezuela mission as the mission's Press Officer.

Kathy had done several more missions. Both Christina and Kathy were very nice and positive and both had Italian surnames, which was strange since they came from Luxemburg and Greece. We worked together very well.

Since Nena and I were the Nairobi LTO team, we were supposed to brief the MEPs, who were expected to arrive from Brussels just before E-Day. Some of them are OK, but others are quite arrogant. As usual, they arrived with their secretaries and assistants. We handed them our STO Briefing Pack and answered their questions.

Not all 7 MEPs were present. One MEP wanted to observe exclusively in the Karen district. Obviously to visit the Karen Blixen museum. We later learned that several MEPs had been invited by local dignitaries to enjoy an extended lunch in the Muthaiga Club, so they hardly visited any polling stations at all.

We also had to brief three staff of European embassies, who had been invited to join our observation mission as 'Locally Recruited STOs'. They were Mariaana from Finland, Marie from Denmark and Jean-Michel from France. We briefed them in the Finnish embassy, just a short walk from the CT offices.

As always, the embassy staff were pleasant people to work with and very motivated. Since they lived there, we didn't have to explain the local situation to them. We only had to explain to them how we work on E-Day and how to fill in—and transmit—the forms. The three of them would go around in one car.

The closer we came to E-Day, the higher the stress levels. We took our STOs to a view point on top of a hill, from where we could safely observe a huge rally at the central Uhuru Park.

Christina contacted a Greek woman who lived in Nairobi. She picked us up and drove first to the Art Café in Village Market and then, later that evening, to three different discotheques downtown. To my surprise, we met half the Core Team there, including Monika, who by now was much friendlier towards us.

To everyone's relief, there were no major incidents on E-Day, except for the breakdown of the digital IT-systems. This meant that the votes had to be counted manually. It took several days before the final results came in.

In the end, to everyone's surprise, Kenyatta won the presidency in the first round, with 50,07 per cent. So there would not be a second round. We would go home!

E-Day went well for us. No major problems except that at the beginning of the evening, Nena and I had a terrible row over our laptop. Our STOs did not possess a car charger, so I had handed our car charger to them. I believed I could charge our laptop at the schools, where the polling stations were.

This turned out to be problematic. Some schools had no electricity. In other schools, the plugs were already used for other laptops or for fans. To make matters worse, the school where Nena and I would observe the closing and counting had no electricity at all.

Since we would be staying most of the evening at that school, I proposed that I would go back to Nenella's place, to charge our laptop. It was only ten minutes by car. But behind my back Nena had talked to the IT boys of our mission. They would send another car charger to us.

I was furious. I told Nena: ,,Within a team there should be communication and trust. If you do things behind my back, than I will do things behind your back." I was really angry, but when the IT messenger handed us the new car charger, my spirits were lifted instantly: the bloody thing didn't fit.

Nena had noted my anger and did her best to cheer me up. ,,You were right," she said. So I went back to Nenella's place and charged the laptop. I also made fresh coffee, to help me through the night.

After E-Day, Nena and I interviewed several Lio's from western Kenya. They were totally devastated. ,,Now our region won't get any funding for the next five years", they lamented. Interestingly, the father of Barack Obama, the first black American president, was a Lio. The Lio's talk proudly about him.

Malik Obama, a half-brother of Barack Obama, actually ran for governor of the western Siaya county, but lost the elections. Obviously, you need more than a famous surname to win local elections. Money, for example.

Shortly after E-Day, a rather curious incident occurred. An internal memorandum from the Core Team, intended for Brussels only, had been leaked to The Star newspaper.

The news dominated the front page. Our interpreter, Lucy, later confided that she had been afraid that she would be blamed for the leak, since her husband worked as a photographer for The Star. But Lucy did not have access to classified information like this. Nor did Nena and I.

Obviously, the memorandum had been leaked by a national staff member of the Core Team. And obviously, this had been a Kikuyu, since the memorandum had been rather critical of Uhuru Kenyatta's victory. To my knowledge, the perpetrator was never revealed.

On one of our last days in Nairobi we visited the Museum of Natural History. Lucy had never visited any museum. I showed Lucy another Lucy: a copy of the three million year old skeleton of Lucy. The original remained in Ethiopia. Our Lucy had never even heard of the other Lucy.

I desperately searched for the world-famous Coelacanth, that I knew was on display in the museum. Finally, I found its vitrine, but to my disappointed it was empty. No one at the museum could tell me if the Coelacanth had been taken out for maintenance purposes or if it had been sent on a world tour or whatever.

Most Kenyans have never heard of the Coelacanth, which became known all over the world as a living fossil. It was thought that this ancient fish had died out 65 million years ago, at the same time as the dinosaurs.

But in 1938, a South African caught one in his fishing net. At first, scientists believed it was a hoax until, a number of years later, several more Coelacanths appeared. The first ones near the Comoros Islands, but later also near the coasts of Madagascar, Mozambique, Tanzania and Kenya.

This fish, with its pre-historic appearance, lives in underwater caves that are sometimes 200 meters deep. More recently, Coelacanths were discovered near the Indonesian island of Celebes.

During our last working day in Nairobi, Lucy invited Nena and me to her house at the western outskirts of Nairobi. A nice apartment. Her photographer husband, her little son and her father-in-law were also there. The friendly old man spoke only Kikuyu and Swahili.

During the two days of debriefings, as usual at the very end of a mission, all LTOs would be lodged again at the Windsor Golf Country Club in Nairobi. I asked Gillian if Nena and I could stay at Nenella's place, since it was only a few kilometres from the Country Club, but the answer was no.

As was to be expected. Even though I would rather have stayed at Nenella's, I understand that no exceptions can be made to the rules. When you make one exception, everybody will ask for exceptions.

Half a year after I had returned home, Westgate Mall was attacked by Somali gunmen belonging to Al Shabaab. A total of 68 visitors, workers and guards were killed and 175 were wounded. It took the Kenyan army and police four days to eliminate the five attackers. Many shops were looted, reportedly not only by the bad guys, but also by the good guys.

Nena and I had visited this mall nearly every day, either for lunch or to interview party affiliates who lived in the nearby slums. Since our security team did not allow us to go into the slums, we invited these persons to meat us in a coffee shop in the mall. It's easy to contact people. Even in Africa, nowadays everyone has a mobile phone.

I liked that mall, even though it was a bit posh. Behind the mall there had been a Masai tourist market. At least, the salesmen looked like Masai, but one day our driver and our interpreter explained to us that most of the salesmen were in reality Kikuyu, dressed like Masai. ,,It doesn't matter", they explained to us. ,,Western tourists don't see the difference anyway."

Before I returned home, I told the other LTOs that my wife had changed the lock on our front door. ,,She doesn't want to see you anymore?" they asked me. ,,The old lock got a bit rusty", I explained. They looked at me with doubtful eyes, but it was the truth. I was welcomed home, once more.

Chapter 16

HONDURAS - 2013

'Thank you, observer, for being here'

After my long mission in Kenya, I did not fancy to go on yet another mission in 2013, but as it happens in the real world: things don't always work out the way you expect. I received an invitation to go to Honduras as an LTO.

I told my wife that I didn't want to go, but she said: „You've never been there. This is your chance. You always wanted to visit the Maya ruins of Copán." I explained that my chances of being deployed to the province of Copán would be less than 10 per cent and that for security reasons we were not allowed to visit other provinces.

But, as always, she was right: this was a chance in a lifetime to visit one of the five countries in Latin America that I had not yet visited. And in any case: another Spanish speaking mission would look good on my CV.

Luck was on my side, this time. At the very last moment I received the employment plan: yes, I was going to Copán! My partner was to be Jon from Norway, whom I remembered from one of my Bolivia missions. He was a gentle giant, at least a head taller than me. And he was of my age, so there would not be a generation gap.

So at 04.00 hours on a dark, cold Sunday morning in October 2013 my wife dropped me off at Schiphol Amsterdam airport once again. There I made a mistake. I checked my suitcase in through the automatic system of KLM.

I should have gone to one of the few remaining check-in counters where a real human being was in charge, because my suitcase should be forwarded to Tegucigalpa.

Now, because I had a separate KLM ticket to Spain, the automatic system decided that my suitcase would go to Madrid, where I would have to pick it up and check it in again. Little did I know what horror lay in store for me at Madrid Barajas airport.

As far as I could tell, I was the only observer on the KLM flight. It arrived nicely on time. My suitcase took a bit more time to arrive. The problem was: I arrived at terminal 2, but my flight to Costa Rica would depart from terminal 4S. There was a free shuttle bus to the other terminal, but I had very little time. So I decided to take a taxi and just pay for it from my own pocket.

The taxi driver explained that Barajas airport was in fact a human-made labyrinth, even for people who used the airport regularly. What had happened, according to him, was that a completely new airport building had been planned for all arrivals and departures, but then the money ran out. So the new building was smaller than originally planned and the old building was still in use.

I asked the taxi driver what the 'S' meant. He explained that the planes to Latin America would depart from terminal 4, but that I needed to check-in at terminal 4S. The 'S' stood for 'Satellite'. After check-in in terminal 4S I would then need to take the metro to terminal 4, because that was the only way to get there.

He dropped me off at 4S and I walked straight to the check-in counters. Several counters were open and there were very few people waiting in line. That looked good. It was only after about fifteen minutes that I had the feeling that something was wrong. Above each counter was written 'business class' in Spanish. And I had an economy class ticket.

Where the hell were the counters for economy class? I took a stroll along the huge hall and then I spotted an enormous queue, in front of a battery of economy class counters. I joined the queue, at the very end. What else could I do? I was running late. And I was still in S4, so I still had to take the metro to terminal 4.

Some twenty counters were open and the line was moving steadily, but there were hundreds of Latinos with their children, suitcases and boxes full of stuff. All flights to Latin America checked in here. Some had plenty of time left, but for others, like me, the clock was ticking.

I was close to panicking. What if I missed my flight? It was complicated enough, since I had to change planes at San José, Costa Rica.

Finally, it was my turn to check in my suitcase. It went fine. Then I had to figure out where to go next. First I had to pass through security.

Again I stood in an enormous queue. It took ages. I panicked. I told one of the security guys that I was already late for my plane. I was allowed to go to the front of the line. Then I realized that I had forgotten to take my laptop out of my little suitcase. More time lost. By now, I was sweating profusely.

Next, I had to board a metro to terminal 4. That went fine, but when I arrived there, I had to follow the signs to my gate number. I had to walk endlessly, passing lots of gates, but where the hell was my gate? Finally, I reached it. There were only two other passengers waiting, all the others had already boarded the plane. But I made it in the nick of time.

Ten hours later I found myself at the international airport of San José, Costa Rica. Compared to Madrid, this was a nice, small and well-organized airport. I met some other observers there. I shook hands with my new partner Jon.

Since we had to wait quite a few hours, we decided to head into town. With Concha, a Spanish observer, I waited fifteen minutes at the airport's exit gate, but the other observers didn't show up.

Concha told me that she had actually worked in San José as a journalist, so she was familiar with the city. We took a taxi and walked around the city center. It looked a bit like Santa Cruz, the second city of Bolivia. Not a particular pleasant place for tourists, but it was OK for a few hours. At least I saw a little bit of Costa Rica.

We boarded a small plane to Tegucigalpa. In fact, the plane was so small that there was no room for my little suitcase in the passengers area. I took out my laptop and my little suitcase was stored in the luggage area of the plane. After the ordeal at Madrid airport, this seemed like a minor headache to me.

We were taken to the Intercontinental hotel in Tegucigalpa, where we were told that we were not allowed to leave the hotel, since Tegucigalpa was the most dangerous city in the world. In fact, the second city of Honduras, San Pedro Sula, was the second most dangerous city in the world. Welcome to friendly Honduras!

We were allowed, though, to visit the huge shopping mall right across the street. Each time I crossed the street, I expected to hear gunshots, but nothing happened. Because of all the drive-by shootings, in Honduras it is forbidden for two men to be on a motorbike at the same time, but even so: I got nervous every time I saw a motorbike.

After two days of briefings, Jon and I set out for Santa Rosa de Copán in our land cruiser. Jon turned out to be one of my best partners and our driver, Erick, was a likeable guy. He was 25 years old, with a huge belly and he had served in the army for four years. This seemed to be a bit of a trend, lately, to recruit drivers with either a police or a military background, so they could double up as our security guards.

This was going to be an easy-going mission, provided we would survive the highway between Tegucigalpa and San Pedro Sula, the two most dangerous cities in the world. I expected to see shotguns sticking out of cars, but nothing happened. Just before San Pedro Sula we turned left to Santa Rosa de Copán.

The first night in hotel Casa Real was horrible: my room was tiny and the hallway had a tiled floor. This meant that the wheels of suitcases made terrible, screeching noises. The next day Jon and I went to see the daughters of the owner, to negotiate a better deal. I asked them to show me some other rooms.

At the very back of the hotel they showed me a suite, containing of a large living room including a fully equipped kitchen. Behind it were two separate bedrooms, each with its own bath room. The largest bedroom even contained a Jacuzzi. The price was lowered quite considerably. Since Jon and I were staying long term, they agreed that we should pay only 3,000 lempiras per day.

Jon said that the cost was still a bit above his budget, so I proposed that I would pay 1,700 per day, leaving 1,300 for him, but then I would get the big bedroom with the Jacuzzi. He agreed. It was great, especially since the living room absorbed all the noise from the hallway.

We received an email from the Core Team, stating that one of the LTOs had been robbed in his hotel room. This prompted me to ask the owners of our hotel if I could pay one month in advance. This way, I got rid of most of the cash advance that I had been paid in Tegucigalpa. When you don't have money, nobody can steal it. Jon would pay me his share of the suite rent every week in cash. Which he duly did.

I even had a balcony, where I could smoke my cigars in peace. Santa Rosa de Copán sits at an altitude of 1.200 meters, so it is not very hot there. The evenings are pleasantly cool. The only problem was that the Jacuzzi did not work. It took me three days to discover the cleverly hidden button: I filled it with water and pushed the button: a miracle! It worked. I asked Jon to take a photo of me in my fantastic Jacuzzi.

There was a coffee machine in our kitchen, but it was only suitable for coffee pads. I hated these modern coffee pads and since we were staying long-term, I bought a traditional coffee machine in the supermarket for only 23 euros. I had brought plenty of paper filters from Holland and the supermarket sold good quality coffee. At the end of the mission, I would give the coffee machine to our driver.

The first day, Jon asked if he could have a cup of coffee from my machine. I told him: ,,Listen, you can have as much coffee as you want, anytime you want and you don't have to ask me anymore." Unfortunately, the Norwegians are even more formal than the English, so the next day Jon asked again if he could have a cup of coffee.

I told him sternly: ,,What did I tell you yesterday? You don't have to ask me. You can take as much coffee as you want. We can buy as much coffee as we want in the supermarket, at a very reasonable price. If you worry about me paying for the coffee, just buy me a six-pack of beer next week."

But Jon was a true Norwegian. He never asked me again and he never took a cup of coffee again from my machine. Are all Norwegians like this? As an observer you learn a lot about other nationalities. One day Jon explained to me that the Norwegians hate the Swedes. This came as a surprise to me, since in Holland we cannot even tell the difference between a Norwegian and a Swede.

When we went out to interview election-related people in the centre of town, we always went on foot. It was no use to go by car there. Because of the cobblestoned streets, cars could only drive at walking speed. And since the small streets were one-directional, you had to go around and around to reach your destination. On top of that, our driver had never been there, so he could not find his way around.

Close to our hotel we noted a small coffee shop that was called Ten Napel. I explained to Jon that a famous football commentator in Holland was called Evert ten Napel. We went inside. The young woman served us an excellent fresh papaya juice and an even better cappuccino. I asked her what Ten Napel meant. „The owner is Dutch", she said.

I replied that I was also Dutch. She immediately talked to someone on the phone. Ten minutes later, another woman arrived who told us that her husband was from Holland and that he very much would like to see us, but that he was working for a German aid agency right now.

Could we come back towards the evening? Of course we could. Erik Velzing turned out to be a pleasant fellow. Ten Napel was his mother's surname. Evert ten Napel was his uncle.

Erik was a member of the Copán business community. He had lived there for fifteen years. He provided us with several useful contacts, one of which was another Dutch guy called Udo van de Waag, who owned a hotel in the only other town of the province: Copán Ruínas. Erik invited us to his birthday party, a few days later.

When we prepared to go to Erik's party, Jon started putting on a tie. I told him: „For Christ's sake: don't put on a tie. In Holland, no one ever wears a tie when going to a birthday party. You look ridiculous." Jon remained hesitant. Apparently, in Norway all men put on ties when going to a social occasion. The party was very relaxed. And nobody wore a tie.

To change the subject: EU missions are obsessed with security. There is a reason for this. Should an observer be abducted or killed by terrorists, than it might be the end of all observation missions. The Chief Observer of each mission is a member of the European Parliament, which means that Parliament is very much aware of the missions.

And why should any European lose his or her life as an election observer in countries like Honduras, Nicaragua, East Timor and Nepal? The EU does not need these countries. So inevitably, year after year, security measures are getting tighter and more advanced.

This time, the security experts had yet another little gadget in store for us. Each LTO team had to fix the satellite telephone with tape on top of the dashboard of the Toyota land-cruiser. The satphones had been equipped with a GPS tracking device. The vehicles themselves were also equipped with a tracking device, so it was in fact a double tracking system.

Every time we left the car, we had to take the satphone with us, so that we could also be tracked when we were not in the car. Jon and I found out the hard way that the system really worked when we decided to visit Copán Ruínas.

Just a few kilometres before the town, we passed the famous Maya ruins of Copán. Of course we decided to pay a visit to this legendary Maya site. It was much hotter there than in Santa Rosa de Copán, since the ruins sit at sea level. Then we found out that the tracking device on our satphone really worked.

The Maya's dug out several tunnels under their city. Jon and I lost sight of one another inside the tunnels, but after half an hour we both surfaced at the same exit. Immediately our mobile phones started ringing.

„Are you OK? What happened to you?" Clearly, underground the GPS of the satphone did not work. An alarm must have gone off on the computers of our security experts. They were afraid that we had been abducted. Big brother was watching us.

The ruins are fabulous. The Copán ruins are amongst the five most important Maya ruins, with Chichén Itza, Palenque and Tulum in Mexico and Tikal in Guatemala. Apparently, Copán was regarded by the Mayas as a spiritual centre, like Abydos for the ancient Egyptians and Mekka for present day Muslims.

Until the first half of the twentieth century, it was widely believed that the ancient Mayas had lived a peaceful existence. One of the early explorers, J. Eric S. Thompson, was responsible for this. He noticed that the present day Mayas are a gentle and peaceful folk, so he concluded that their ancestors must have been the same.

He could not have been more wrong! When experts started deciphering the Maya hieroglyphs, it became clear that Maya history consisted of continuous warfare and brutality between city states.

After each war, the defeated enemies were ceremoniously sacrificed to the Maya gods, by ripping out their still beating hearts. It reminded me of the observations of the 'peace loving' inhabitants of Samoa, as described by Margaret Meade in her 'Coming of Age in Samoa'. Years later, the Samoans confided that they only told Meade what she wanted to hear.

A week or so later we were visited by Ivan, our Observer Coordinator from Slovakia, and Alessandro, our mission's Press Officer from Italy. They only stayed with us for a few hours. We took them to the regional TV-station, who had interviewed us a few days earlier.

We asked for a copy of the broadcast. As always, I knew exactly what I could and could not tell the media. Alessandro was so pleased with my interview, that he posted it on our mission's website.

Ivan asked if we had had any problems. I said: „Yes. I had a terrible problem." I fell silent for a few seconds, to add some suspense. Then I continued: „The first three days, my Jacuzzi didn't work." After lunch, the two of them moved on to the neighbouring LTO team in the adjacent Lempira province.

This was an all-female team: Nadine from Luxemburg and Katerina from the Czech Republic. Three years later I met them again in Peru. Each of them asked me: „Weren't you the guy with the broken-down Jacuzzi in Honduras?" The observer world is a small world and stories go around and around.

The big cities in Honduras are dangerous, but a small town like Copán proved to be as safe as could be. Only 20.000 people lived in the colonial town. We were also visited by Martím, our Portuguese security expert, whom I knew from several previous missions.

Some LTOs think he's a bit weird, but I like him. In the evening, we walked with him to the central square, to show him that our town was a safe place. After that, we had a meal and a few beers at the open patio inside hotel Elvir, where turtles splattered around in a water basin.

It was there, that Martím received a phone call from an English LTO, who apparently felt lonely and was a bit sick also. They talked for half an hour. It went on and on. Martím remained polite and told him which medicines to get from the medical kit.

I asked him if this happened often, that observers called him at odd times, just to make small talk and that Martím would act as the mission's medical doctor. Martím said ,,Yes". And he added: ,,This is why we, in the Core Team, get paid more money than LTOs."

Martím had visited Ocotepeque, the neighbouring province, to check out a hotel for us. Since we were also responsible for Ocotepeque and since we planned to send an STO team there, Jon and I decided to go there for a four day visit.

Ocotepeque is something else. It's the most remote province of Honduras, bordering El Salvador and Guatemala. Not the most peaceful places on the planet. But the people in Ocotepeque were very nice to us, probably because they saw few westerners over there.

Our Mitsubishi land cruiser had a mechanical problem, so the car company sent a mobile mechanic to help our driver. Jon and I decided to go on foot, since it was not a very big town. It was a typical agricultural centre: lots of small shops with agricultural provisions for the farmers of the region.

Once in a while, a truck passed by, on its way to the border. Other than that, there was nothing there. While walking the streets of Ocotepeque town, we were approached several times by total strangers who had noted our visibility jackets. They shook our hands and told us that they were happy that we were there.

During my ten years as an aid worker for the UN, nobody ever thanked me for being there. As an election observer, it happened quite a lot, in different countries, that people thanked me for being there. My very presence was proof that the rest of the world had not totally forgotten about them.

We stayed there for three nights. In the evenings, there was nothing to do, so we just sat down with Erick, our driver, in the concrete patio of our hotel Maya Chortis. It turned out that Erick maintained regular contact with many other drivers, since they all worked for the same company.

This was an important lesson for me: drivers are a great source of gossip. He told us several LTO teams were not on a good footing with one another. Apparently, Erlend from the UK was constantly quarrelling with his partner Christina from Cyprus.

In another team, Cornelia from Austria was not on a good footing with her partner Lukasz from Poland. And one team had already fired their driver. To my surprise, this was our neighbouring Santa Barbara team: Monique from the Netherlands and Steven from Belgium. I know it's wrong, but I love gossip.

We visited San Marcos, the only other town in the province of Ocotepeque. The road was bad and San Marcos was a dusty little town. We also visited Antigua Ocotepeque, a short distance from 'modern' Ocotepeque. At the tiny central square stood a small and very old colonial church and an equally old huge Ceiba tree.

It was strictly forbidden for us to get near a foreign border, but to my horror I noticed a sign that said: 'Welcome to the border'. I had made a mistake. I believed that we were on the road to Guatemala, which was quite a distance, but we were actually on the road to El Salvador, which was only a short distance.

When we approached a checkpoint, I realized to my horror that this was actually the border crossing. I hastily instructed Erick to turn around. I hoped our security experts were tracking another team's vehicle and not ours. Anyway: we were not called on the phone and it was never mentioned by anyone. We had a lucky escape.

Jon's stomach had been giving him troubles. I wondered why, because I didn't have any stomach problems. Then he said: ,,Do you think it's because of the malaria pills?" I looked at him in astonishment. ,,There is no malaria in these parts of Honduras", I told him. ,,I was thinking the same", he said. ,,That's why I've decided to stop taking the pills."

A week later, Jon told me that he had another problem. The Service Provider had not paid him his money. It took him several days to figure out what the problem was: apparently his money had been transferred to a bank account in Hungary, instead of Norway!

He tried to solve the problem with the Service Provider, but for some reason this proved to be impossible. They could not get their money back from Hungary. Every morning at 08.00 hours Jon skyped with the manager of his bank in Norway, where it was already 15.00 hours because of the time difference.

Every morning the manager told Jon that no money had been transferred into his account. Jon was consumed with anxiety, since he had to pay bills back home and he really needed the money. Apparently, our Core Team was not convinced of the urgency of the matter. They didn't take action.

Finally, Jon decided that he had had enough. On Wednesday, he told me that he would return to Tegucigalpa and hence to Norway on Friday. Within two days! I had the impression that the Core Team believed it was an idle threat, since most observers fear for their future missions.

When you breach your contract for no good reason, you will be blacklisted for the next five years. Jon, who by nature is a very nice guy, had informed Ivan of his intentions, but he had done this in his characteristic low and monotonous voice.

The problem is that members of the Core Team and the Service Provider are quite used to LTOs shouting and screaming at them over the phone, so when someone talks very calmly, they assume that nothing is wrong and that those were idle threats. But Jon was dead serious and I was the only one who knew this.

For me, personally, his departure would be problematic, first of all because I would be alone for some time and then maybe get a horrible new partner. Secondly, I had paid the full amount for our suite up front and Jon was paying me his share by the week. If he left me, he would not pay me anymore. I desperately wanted to keep him as my partner.

So I took action. I sent an urgent email to our Deputy Chief Observer and the Chief of our Service Provider, to make them aware of the seriousness of the situation. I simply asked if I would be allowed to go out on my own or if I would have to remain in the hotel until Jon's replacement would arrive.

This worked! Within the hour, both Jon and I received phone calls from our Core Team and our Service Provider. They promised that the matter would be solved within one day. So it happened. Success at last: Jon stayed with me, thank God.

Aside from Jon's financial troubles we kept on working. We were contacted by a candidate for the National Party, who lived in the hamlet of La Entrada. What followed was like a spy movie. The guy met us at a petrol station. We followed his car to his house.

When we reached his house, he asked us to park our car inside his compound, since he did not want anyone to know that he had contacted us. Our car was very visible, since it had written 'EU Observation Mission' on both sides.

I told Jon that I did not want to park our car inside this guy's compound, for safety reasons. If the guy refused to open the gate for us, our car would be stuck there. It was against our safety rules and regulations. But the guy was very nervous, so we decided to simply sent Erick to a nearby petrol station with the car and wait for our phone call there.

Inside the house, the guy remained extremely nervous. He asked us three times if we could guarantee his anonymity, otherwise he and/or his family would be assassinated. We assured him that no one would ever learn his name.

Then he showed us the results of primaries in two districts: El Paraíso and La Jigua. All the results showed that one hundred per cent of all the votes were for one candidate: a member of his own National Party!

The guy was really disgusted by this obvious fraud. He explained that drug traffickers had taken over control of these two districts. The drug traffickers even deployed their own private little army there, dressed in their own uniforms. Jon and I typed a special report on this for our Core Team.

A few days later, our two STO teams arrived. It was already getting dark. Observers are not supposed to travel in the dark, so understandably our security expert got nervous. Martím called me: ,,Jos, go to the outskirts of town and wait for them there. They started their journey too late. You can guide them straight to your hotel."

But they arrived all in one piece. One team consisted of two youngsters, Rita from Portugal and Vajk from Hungary. Jon and I had already decided to send them to Ocotepeque for a few days.

The other team were a little less young: Markella, from Greece and Gencho from Bulgaria. Gencho seemed to be really quiet at first, but he turned out to be a very funny guy. They would spent one night in Copán Ruínas.

We took both STO teams to the famous Maya ruins and after that all of us visited hotel Don Udo's in Copán Ruínas, owned by Udo van de Waag from Holland. Udo had been an observer himself, during the previous elections, so he briefed us on the regional electoral situation.

Interesting stuff. And he served typical Dutch snacks, like croquets, bitter balls, lumpias and saté. The latter two are seen as typically Dutch in Holland, but in reality they originate from our former colony Indonesia. Udo told us that he had actually been born in Bandung, in central Java.

At the very end of the mission, I had an argument with Ivan, the Observer Coordinator. Ivan was young and ambitious, but a bit insecure. It was his first time as Observer Coordinator.

In Ivan's opinion, we should not have visited the Maya ruins, since we were not supposed to behave like tourists. I explained that very few people ever got the opportunity to visit the world famous ruins at Copán and that they were situated in our province.

Furthermore, I added, an archaeological site is not tourism. It is archaeology, culture and history. As observers, we are always encouraged to learn more about the history and the culture of the places we visit. In my opinion, visiting a discotheque or lying on a beach is tourism, but visiting an archaeological site is not. Ivan did not agree with me.

Just two days before E-Day, Jon told me that he had talked to Erick, our driver. Apparently, the drivers had not been paid their per diems yet, by their company. It happens quite often in Third World countries that workers are ruthlessly exploited by their companies.

The problem was that this had nothing to do with our mission: it was between the company and its drivers. But it became our problem, since the drivers threatened to go on strike. Just two days before E-Day! And apparently, our Erick was their ring-leader.

Obviously, Erick realized that we, LTOs would put pressure on our mission and that our mission, in turn, would put pressure on his company, since all the cars were needed during E-Day. E-Day is always the most important day of our missions.

Jon didn't realize how serious this was, but I realized that I had to inform our Core Team right away. Otherwise, they would blame Jon and me later, for not informing the CT of the impending strike. I sent an email and I knew that within half an hour my telephone would start to ring. So it did.

Of course, I was called by my arch-enemy Pedro, our Portuguese logistics expert. My worst nightmare. Pedro loves me, but I hate him. Pedro did not call me once, but four times. The horror, the horror.

Pedro promised to solve the problem, but I was so pissed off that for the remainder of our mission I didn't speak another word to our driver Erick. A bit childish maybe, but I am not only an observer. I am also a human being, with human weaknesses, like everybody else.

The day before E-Day, Jon and I were in the car, when I received a call from Ivan, the Observer Coordinator: ,,Jos, can you send me the E-Day routes of your STOs?" I replied that he could find this information, in detail, in our STO Manual.

But Ivan insisted: ,,No, no, you must send it to me." I explained that I was in the car and that our laptop was in our hotel. ,,Why do you insist that we send you our STO Manual, when apparently you don't read it?" I asked him. Ivan just hang up the phone.

Other than that, all went well before, during and after E-Day. The STOs caused us no problems. Jon and I observed in the villages of Cucuyagua and La Unión, along the road to Ocotepeque.

We soon fell into a routine: since I am not a very social person, I remained in the car, while Jon entered the Polling Stations. He filled in the paper forms. I transferred it into the electronic forms on our laptop and transmitted them straight to our CT, with the help of 3G. A great system.

We had to call our STO teams several times for our Qualitative Reports. Since Jon could not live without his daily croissant and cappuccino, we decided to transmit them from Ten Napel. It was closed. On we went to Jireth: also closed. Even Las Velas was closed. Apparently, all businesses were expecting some kind of unrest or even plunder during E-Day, but in the end nothing happened.

We observed the closing and counting at the school adjoining our hotel. At about 21.30 hours, Jon told me that he felt a bit dizzy. We decided to return to the hotel and transmit our remaining forms from our laptop to the mission's computer. Thanks to these computer to computer transmissions, there is no need for us to talk on the phone to a hired student anymore. Thank God for technology.

The next day, we debriefed the STOs. All four of them were very happy with their mission. They ventured some critical remarks about the fact that they had to transmit their E-Day forms by phone to the students that had been hired for the occasion by the Core Team.

It was a bit strange, since during my previous mission, in Kenya, all STO teams had been handed laptops, so they could transmit their forms electronically. To be fair: it would be one of the last times that the forms were transmitted by phone.

From then on, STO teams were handed tablets, with which they could transmit their forms electronically, from computer to computer. Some students were still hired, but only as a back-up system, in case of a computer breakdown. A few years later, all observers could also transmit directly from their smartphones.

In the evening, all six of us walked to Weekends Pizza, that served the best pizzas I had ever tasted. Unfortunately, it was closed. So we went to Las Brasas. When the bill arrived I surprised everyone by saying that I was going to pay for all six of us. ,,I have something to celebrate", I told them.

They thought that it was my birthday, but I explained that my parents celebrated their 60th wedding anniversary that very same day. It was worth the money, anyway, since all of them had been good and positive STOs. The total bill for the six of us was only 70 euros. For that amount of money, my wife and I could barely enjoy an average meal in a restaurant in Holland.

On their last morning, Jon took the STOs to Flor de Copán, the cigar factory, just behind our hotel. Thank God, the Core Team never found out about this, for they would have considered it to be tourism. It was an interesting visit though, including a lecture on local politics by the ex-mayor, who was now the owner of the factory.

The cigar factory employs 650 workers, mostly women. The factory produces everything itself, including the wooden boxes. It's not a very healthy environment, with chemicals being sprayed onto the tobacco leaves, to prevent them from drying out.

The end product are very expensive, handmade cigars, that originated partly in Cuba. Cuba cannot export tobacco to the U.S., but export to Honduras is not prohibited. So Americans are smoking Cuban cigars after all.

Two days after our STOs had left us, Jon and I were interviewing John Donaghy, an Irish/American missionary from Iowa who worked for Caritas in Copán. During the interview, Jon received a rather mysterious telephone call from a nervous Ivan.

,,Do not speak to the media", Ivan said. ,,Why not?" Jon asked him. ,,I don't have time to explain; it has to do with the STOs. Just don't speak to the media." A few hours later we got word from other LTOs about what had happened.

Apparently, one STO, an elderly man from Austria, had given a press conference at the airport of Tegucigalpa, just before he and the other STOs had left the country. He told the media that the elections had been rigged, because Xiomara Castro, candidate for the leftist party 'Libre', should have won.

This was very strange, since first of all as EU-observers we are always strictly neutral and impartial. Secondly, we always operate as an observation mission at the national level, which means that individual observers don't express their private opinions.

There is a good reason for this, because when all observers ventilate their own private opinions, it would be a cacophony of opinions: total chaos. Jon and I could hardly believe this STO had actually given this interview at the airport, but it was on the national news.

Jon did some research on this Austrian guy on the internet. What Jon found out was even more disturbing: this guy was very active in ultra-leftist circles, like the ones we used to have in Holland in the 1970s amongst students.

In fact, I thought that these Marxist ideas had become extinct since the late 1970s. Because, let's face it: who on earth still believes that Fidel Castro and Che Guevara are the biggest lights on the planet? Just visit Cuba and see with your own eyes what sixty years of communist dictatorship has done to the country and the people.

North Korea is even worse than Cuba. But of course, if you live in a comfortable, capitalist country like Austria, it's easy to support communist movements in other parts of the world. Lenin had a special term for western leftist intellectuals. He called them: 'Useful Idiots'.

We were allowed to travel back to Tegucigalpa via Lempira. It was 2 December 2013. To my chagrin, my wife had sent an email to our mission laptop, informing Jon that it was my birthday. Luckily, Jon had been so busy preparing for our departure, that he only read it one day later.

So, thank God, nobody bothered me on my birthday. Halfway, we caught up with Nadine and Katerina, the all-female LTO team that had been based in Lempira. They told us that the owner of their hotel had been a Dutch lady. It's a pity that we did not have time to visit that hotel.

After arriving safely back at the Intercontinental hotel in Tegucigalpa, Jon and I sat down in easy chairs next to the swimming pool, contentedly smoking cigars. I thought it was quite funny that we were approached several times by LTOs, who asked us how many years we had known each other.

As usual at the end of a mission, some LTOs were not on speaking terms with their partners any more, but Jon and I had our last meal of the mission together in the hotel restaurant.

On the last day of the mission I received my evaluation. As usual, I was recommended for future missions, but a rather nasty remark was written on it: I should work on my organizational skills. Very strange: I had never been criticized on the organization of my work.

I asked Ivan, the Observer Coordinator, who had been my colleague LTO in 2009 in Bolivia, what he meant. Ivan was young, ambitious and a bit nervous. He told me that when Jon threatened to leave I should have called him first, instead of the Deputy Observer and the Chief of the Service Provider. Apparently, Ivan had been reprimanded by the bosses.

I was taken aback. I explained to him that I had probably saved his career, because if Jon would really have left the mission, Ivan would have been blamed for it. Brussels does not take these things lightly. It would have been Ivan's last mission as a member of a Core Team. So I actually saved his ass!

Then, to my surprise, Ivan added: ,,And you should not have taken the STOs to the Copán ruins. We don't want people to regard us as tourists." I tried to remain calm. I answered him: ,,Listen: to visit an ancient Maya site is not tourism. It is history, culture, archaeology. Besides, Copán is the most remote of all the famous Maya sites. This is the chance in a lifetime to visit them. To not visit them would be totally crazy."

Ivan was not convinced. But the next day when we left—I was actually sitting in the bus already—he came to me and handed me a newly written evaluation, which was much more positive on my behalf.

He explained to me that Gabriel had instructed him to do so, since in front of all the LTOs I had spoken out against that crazy Austrian STO, who had given a press conference at the airport. Anyhow, Ivan and I were friends once again. To some extent.

Jon and I flew back to Madrid together, only to find out that our KLM flight to Amsterdam had been delayed because of a bad storm in Holland. I called my wife and told her not to go to the airport by car, because of the storm. The roads are dangerous, because of debris that's flying all over the place.

The few drivers that ventured out might unexpectedly hit the brakes or change lanes, to avoid a plastic bag of a tree branch that was suddenly flying over the road. So I told my wife that I would travel back home by train, which takes only one hour.

As usual, she did not listen to me. Her face was the first face I saw at the airport. Her car had been the only car on the road. All sensible people stayed at home. ,,What the hell are you doing here?" I asked.

She replied that because of the storm, most trains had been cancelled. ,,You should have stayed home", I said. ,,I'm perfectly fine here at the airport, with a nice cappuccino. I spent six weeks in Honduras. I can easily spent a few hours more at a well-catered airport."

For Jon it was even worse. His on-going flight to Oslo had already taken off, so he was obliged to sleep over in a hotel in Amsterdam. Back in Copán, we had discussed our home countries peculiarities: he told me that in Norway the socialist party had been in full control of the country for fifty years or so.

If you wanted a government job in Norway, it was obligatory that you became a member of the socialist party. I replied that this sounded like the Soviet Union to me. Thank God, things are different in Holland. Not that the Dutch are such nice people.

But Jon believed, rather naively, that in my country everybody was as nice as the people in Norway. I disappointed him by explaining that he believed this because he could not understand one word of the Dutch language. I told him that amongst ourselves, we are probably the rudest people on the planet.

Unfortunately, Jon soon found out that I was right: at midnight I received an SMS from Jon, stating that no taxi driver had been willing to take him to his hotel, since it was only a few kilometres from the airport and therefore the taxi fare would be minimal. The driver preferred to wait for another passenger.

He was furious. This would never have happened in his native Norway. Jon had learned the hard way: Dutch people are indeed horrible people. I can confirm that, because I'm Dutch myself.

A week or so later, I was debriefed at the Dutch Ministry of Foreign Affairs, together with the two Dutch STOs: Wim and Jan-Willem. Strangely enough, I met Wim during the briefings at the ministry before the mission, but Jan-Willem had not been there.

Apparently, Jan-Willem Bertens had been on the reserve list at first. Jan-Willem served as an STO in Lempira, adjacent to Copán. He was a special character. He was 81 years old and had served as the Dutch ambassador for Central America in the 1970s, when leftist activists were remorselessly persecuted by repressive regimes in the region.

He is still famous in The Netherlands, because he harboured dozens of labour leaders and leftist priests in the Dutch embassy. These people would otherwise have been killed or they would have disappeared from the face of the earth, as had happened to thousands of leftists all over Latin America.

Lempira is also the province where the winner of the elections, the right-wing Juan Orlando Hernández, came from. In April 2022 Hernández was extradited to the US on drug trafficking charges. According to the Americans, Hernández had turned Honduras into a 'narco state'.

This started already in 2009, when Hernández arranged 2 million dollars from drugs lord Alexander Ardon Soriano, to finance the campaign of his conservative National Party affiliate Porfirio Lobo. In 2013, when Hernández himself was candidate for the National Party, he managed to obtain one million dollars from Joaquín 'El Chapo' Guzmán, head of the Mexican Sinaloa cartel.

In 2017, Hernández was reelected, thanks to 1,5 million dollars from Ardon Soriano. But Hernández lost all protection, when in 2022 the leftist Xiomara Castro was installed as president. She was the wife of Manuel Zelaya, who had been deposed as president in 2009.

Interestingly, Hernández younger brother Tony has been detained in an American prison cell since 2018, on drugs charges. He was sentenced to life in prison. Also interestingly: Hernández managed to maintain good connections with the American presidents Obama and Trump, because of Hernández tough stance on immigration.

Did I manage to find a Goofy in Honduras? You bet I did. In fact, I discovered the biggest Goofy of them all. The problem was that this Goofy was on sale in a huge warehouse at the back of the mall just across the street from our Intercontinental hotel in Tegucigalpa.

I discovered it during the very first days of the mission, but I did not want to carry this huge Goofy all the way to Copán and back. Once I was in Copán, I worried that someone else could have bought my precious Goofy. Thank God, it was still there during the last days of the mission.

The Goofy was too big for my suitcase, so I tied it to my little suitcase. It looked quite funny. My colleagues probably suspected that I had gone Goofy myself. But my wife was very happy with the new addition to her Goofy collection. I was allowed back into my own house.

Chapter 17

EGYPT - 2014

'Is our interpreter a member of the Muslim Brotherhood?'

Dutch people don't like insecurity, so it was no surprise that a number of Dutch election observers called on their Ministry of Foreign Affairs to provide them with a list of upcoming elections, so that observers could plan their future missions well in advance. Not a bad idea, the only problem is that elections can hardly be planned.

Sometimes, an election is announced unexpectedly. It also happens quite a lot that planned elections are postponed to a later date. Or cancelled, all together. And you can never be certain if the EU or the OSCE will field a mission or not. Apart from budget restraints, there are political and electoral considerations.

So, for us, intrepid election observers, life remains insecure. We don't know where we'll be next month. For me, personally, that's fine. It's part of the adventure. But of course I adhered dutifully to the instructions of the Ministry. So, when they send me the list of upcoming elections for the year 2014, I duly filled in that Mozambique would be my first choice.

To my surprise, in March 2014, I received an invitation from the Ministry for the elections in Egypt, to be held at the end of May 2014. I discussed it with my wife. I really wanted to go back to Mozambique. We had a good time there in the 1980s. And it would be good for my Portuguese.

But Egypt was also appealing. We had been there in 1999, for a one week holiday in Cairo and Luxor. We both liked it. And I have a special interest in Egyptian archaeology.

Furthermore, right now I was formally invited for Egypt and there were no guarantees that I would be invited for Mozambique later in the year. We decided that I should apply. I was selected by the Ministry and then I was also selected by the EU. Little did I know that this would be a roller coaster mission.

The day before my departure I was invited to the Ministry for the customary briefings, by the Ministry's country experts. I met my fellow LTO there: Annemarieke. I had never met her before. There was also an STO: Pim. Just a few months later, Pim's life would end tragically in rebel-controlled eastern Ukraine: he was a passenger on Malaysian Airlines flight MH17, that was shot down on 17 July 2014.

The briefings went fine. The country experts are, of course, well-informed about the country that has been assigned to them. But they don't know anything about the methodology of our election observation missions. So they were just as interested in our missions, as we were in Egypt.

On my way back home, Annemarieke joined me in the train. She had lots of Third World and election experience and she had been born in a village near Alkmaar, just like me. That immediately created a bond between us. Contrary to me, she spoke Arabic. I would have to rely on an interpreter.

The next afternoon, I took the train to Brussels, where the LTOs would be briefed for two days. Annemarieke gave me a call: she was not going to travel by train, but by car. Her husband would drive her to Brussels. I had to change trains in Amsterdam. So there I sat at Amsterdam's Central Station, waiting for the Thalys.

A man walks up to me with a big suitcase. I immediately realize that I know him. But who is he? Then I remembered that I had seen his name in one of the most recent emails that I had received from the EU: Kees, my fellow LTO from our Nigeria and Pakistan missions.

He recognized me also. ,,Are you going to Egypt?" I asked him. ,,Yes", he replied. ,,Then we can travel together", I said. ,,Annemarieke is not traveling by train, so you can take her seat."

Within two hours we arrived at Brussels Midi station. A driver would be waiting for us there at Max's Café, next to the statue of a zebra. But there was no driver. That was our first disastrous experience with the service provider, GIZ. After 45 minutes we called the GIZ coordinator. She promised to send a taxi.

Indeed, a taxi driver appeared within twenty minutes. He took us to the Mercure Airport hotel, where we met the other 28 LTOs. At the reception, Kees introduced me to Melanie, who would be my partner in Egypt. I shook her hand and told her that I was happy that she was shorter than me, since my previous partner had been a head taller than me.

We spent two nights at the hotel. The day in between was filled with security briefings and first aid briefings. All of us had done lots of previous missions, so we did not learn anything new.

The real reason, of course, for which 30 LTOs had to travel to Brussels was to sign our contracts. And they wanted to put all of us on the same airplane, to make life easier for the Core Team and the Service Provider in Cairo.

Nobody ever thinks about making life easier for the LTOs, since we are considered to be the work horses of observation missions. Since most of the STOs are beginners, they are well taken care off. LTOs are supposed to be tough cookies and are therefore treated that way.

But still, we had to get up at 04.00 hours in the morning, to be taken to Brussels airport by bus. Apparently, Lufthansa was the cheapest carrier to Cairo, so from Brussels, we first flew to Frankfurt.

There, we had to wait four hours for our flight to Cairo. It turned out that the flight was overbooked. Lufthansa offered 400 euros to anyone who would accept a later flight. I didn't fancy missing part of the briefings in Egypt. In the end, we all made it to Cairo.

Normally, there would be drivers waiting for us there, to take us to our hotel. In this case, the hotel came to us. A bald headed man led the way. At first, I missed him completely, since he did not carry any identification, nor a list with the names of the LTOs.

He did not introduce himself to us either. But all LTOs assembled around him, so I did the same. I later learned that his name was Gilles from France and that he was our logistics expert. We followed him with our heavy suitcases.

I still expected to be taken to a bus, outside the terminal, but instead we moved up a rolling ramp. We walked along a glass-covered corridor, hundreds of meters long. After passing an X-Ray machine, we went down in an elevator. Then, all of sudden, we were in the lobby of a five-star hotel.

On my previous missions, everything at the hotel would have been prepared for us, so that we would only have to sign and receive our room key cards, but in this case each of us had to fill in a large form, with our passport details, even though those were already known to GIZ.

And each of us had to pay a deposit of 50 euros, or let them make a copy of a credit card, in case you were planning to consume anything from the minibar. It's not a good idea to allow people to make copies of your credit card, especially in countries like Egypt, so I deposited 50 euros in cash.

Finally, I entered room 363 on the third floor of Le Meridién hotel at Cairo airport. Little did I know that I would stay for nearly a month in that room. The mission started, as usual, with two full days of briefings and the handover of mission equipment and petty cash. Nothing new.

The only difference was that on a normal mission, immediately after the briefings, we would set out for our Area of Observation and start working. Not this time. We were told that there were a few problems: our satellite phone's, BGANs and car tracking systems were not cleared yet by customs.

In addition, the medical kits had not arrived from Europe and our accreditations had not yet been provided by the Egyptian Presidential Election Commission (PEC). On top of this, there had been a mistake in the Arabic text on our visibility clothing: it said that we were 'monitors', instead of 'observers'.

This was very sensitive to the Egyptians, since as observers we were not allowed to interfere, but monitors are generally regarded as people who are allowed to interfere. So the Arabic text had to be amended.

I had already noted that the Service Provider on this mission was not the best I had ever had. Both the chief of the SP and the Security Expert were French. Their English was poor, to put it nicely.

My English is good, but I couldn't understand a bloody word these Frenchmen were saying. This was worrying, since security is always the most important aspect of any mission. Why on earth did they hire Frenchmen on an English speaking mission?

As a result of all this, we were told that our deployment would be delayed by a few days. For twelve teams, this would not be such a problem, since they would travel by car to their Areas of Observation. But for three teams, including my own, it would be more complicated, since we would travel by air.

Mel and I found out that there were only three flights a week to the 'International Airport of Sohag', that had officially been opened by president Mubarak in 2010, just before he was ousted.

So we requested to be deployed by car. We did not receive an answer. Then we discovered that our base station was in Sohag, the southernmost governorate capital of our three governorates. This was strange, since the only road to New Valley, our third governorate in the western desert, passed through Assiut.

This meant that our STO team that would be based in the western desert, would first have to travel to Assiut and then to Al-Kharga Oasis in New Valley. It would make more sense that we would be based in Assiut, from where we could easily dispatch our STO teams to Sohag to the south and Al-Kharga Oasis to the west.

On top of that, Assiut was situated one hundred kilometres closer to Cairo, so we could travel from Cairo by car. We mentioned all these arguments in an email to the Core Team, but we never received an answer. But then, a few days later, we received the list with our six STOs.

At the top it read: LTO13; base station: Assiut. Out of the blue, our request had been granted. I explained to Mel that two thousand years ago Josef, Mary and baby Jesus had lived in a cave in Assiut. Also, the assassins who had killed president Sadat came from Assiut. It sounded like an interesting place.

So all 30 LTOs were locked up in Le Meridién hotel at Cairo airport. For security reasons, we were not allowed to leave the hotel. After three days, our Deputy Chief Observer and the head of the Service Provider, GIZ, came to our hotel to inform us on the situation.

It did not sound good. Apparently, the Egyptian security forces did not accept that the EU would use its own provider to make contact with the satellites. And the EU refused to use an Egyptian provider, since this would mean that the Egyptians could switch off our communications equipment any time they wanted. On top of this, Egyptian customs officials requested new forms and new stamps every day.

Later on, people from the Dutch embassy explained to me that all western companies paid bribes, to speed up the importation proceedings. But the EU could not pay bribes, of course. To make matters worse, the PEC did not seem in a hurry with our accreditations, without which it would be impossible to enter Polling Stations.

So we were confined to our luxury hotel. We fell into certain habits. The Core Team was not based in our hotel, but in the Sofitel hotel on Zamalek island in the centre of Cairo. I asked why the LTOs and the CT were based in different hotels. It took two hours to drive from one hotel to the other.

The answer made sense: ,,It's much easier to deploy the LTOs from the airport, at the outskirts of Cairo. We never expected that the LTOs would have to remain in Cairo for such a long period of time."

Every morning one or two members of the Core Team would travel to our hotel to brief us on the most recent developments. Usually, there was nothing to report. After the morning briefings we tried to master the Arab language.

Our teacher was a young, bright fellow from Syria. He tried his best, but it's a difficult language to learn. On top of that, the LTOs and the hotel staff spoke English all the time, so our Arabic remained basic.

Every day, a number of observers would lay in the sun at the swimming pool. Every morning we enjoyed the great buffet breakfast in the company of our fellow LTOs. Annemarieke and Rosa (Spain) eventually claimed their own tables, where they sat every morning.

Thank God it was a five-star hotel with lots of TV-Channels. I could watch CNN, BBC World, Al Jazeera English and ten sports channels, most of them broadcasting football matches. I wouldn't be bored. The first match I watched was Bayern Munich – Real Madrid (0-4). Every evening we would drink a few beers on the terrace, next to the swimming pool, of the Live Sports Bar with the older LTOs.

At the time I believed that the younger LTOs stayed in their rooms, surfing the internet or fiddling with their smart phones, but on later missions I met several of them again and they told me that nearly every evening they escaped via the gangway to the airport, where they took a taxi to a discotheque. Cheeky little bastards.

Kees called the Dutch embassy, to set up a meeting with the political expert. The Dutch ambassador was also keen to meet us. He invited us to come over to the embassy. We replied that we were not allowed to leave the hotel. ,,Then I will send an embassy car", the ambassador said. We replied that we would have to ask permission first, from our mission's security expert.

It took the security expert two days to reply. The answer was: 'No'. Weeks later we found out why it took so long to answer us: the security expert had forwarded our request to Brussels. We couldn't believe it. The Dutch ambassador then decided to invite Kees, Annemarieke and me for lunch in our own hotel.

The story took an even funnier twist: while we were waiting at the hotel lobby, Kees received a call from the ambassador: 'Where are you?' ; 'I am at the lobby' ; 'I am also at the lobby, but I don't see you'. We then found out that there were, in fact, two Le Meridién hotels in Cairo!

Egypt is a chaotic country: the traffic is chaotic, the football is chaotic and the five-star hotels are chaotic. Half an hour later, the ambassador showed up. He turned out to be a nice guy. He told us that there are always lots of conspiracy theories going around in Egypt, even at the highest levels.

One of these rumours was that the Muslim Brotherhood was financed by the US, in order to destabilize Egypt. Interestingly, several weeks later in Assiut, Mel and I were told exactly this rumour by some very serious people. I tried not to laugh.

After a few days in our golden cage it was announced that a bus had been rented, to take us to the Egyptian Museum and the pyramids of Giza. We were elated like school children on the annual school holiday. The bus took us to a 'real Egyptian restaurant' for lunch, where I was attacked by mosquitoes for the first time.

Our guide, Mohamed, looked at us and saw a bunch of pale-skinned European tourists. I tried to explain to him that all of us spend several months each year in the most difficult places on the planet in remote provinces in Afghanistan, Palestine, Pakistan, Nigeria, Sudan, Honduras and so on. To no avail. Mohamed saw what he saw: a group of pale looking, inexperienced tourists, fresh from the European winter.

My wife and I had visited the museum and the pyramids in 1999, but there is so much to be seen there, that you could easily spend three days without even seeing everything. All of us, LTOs, had a great day. A few days later, we were again loaded into the bus, with the same guide. This time we visited a popular bazaar and the famous Citadel built by Mohamed Ali, with a marvellous view of Cairo.

From our bus we saw the street life in Cairo. The traffic was not as bad as I expected. There were traffic jams, but people were not driving their cars as crazy as in Pakistan. And everywhere we saw women and children. So why were we confined to our hotel? What was the danger here?

It was especially bitter for Christa, the elderly German LTO with a lot of observation experience. Her house stood in Cairo. She had lived there for more than ten years and spoke fluent Arabic. But Christa, like the rest of us, had signed a contract with the EU and was therefore confined to Le Meridién Airport hotel.

I must explain at this point that I do understand that there is a reason for these tight security measures. All of us would like to continue doing observation missions, but most observers don't realize that we are walking a thin line. If one observer would be abducted or killed, this would probably be the end of all missions.

The reason for this is that our missions are high profile in the European Parliament, caused by the fact that the Chief Observer of an EU EOM is always a member of the European Parliament. Since there are some twelve missions per year, quite a number of Euro Parliamentarians have been Chief Observers.

And each parliamentarian knows lots of other parliamentarians. Therefore, the death of any of us would be in the headlines all over Europe. This had to be avoided at all cost. I watched Chelsea – Atlético Madrid (1-3).

As an EU EOM, we always explain to our interlocutors that we are impartial and neutral and that we are only interested in the electoral process, not in who wins the elections. We are always told that when we interview one candidate, we should also interview the other candidates, to avoid being labelled as biased.

Much to our chagrin, we found out that our highest boss, EU Foreign Policy Chief Catherine Ashton from the UK, had visited Cairo shortly before our arrival. During that visit she met the frontrunner for the presidential elections, El Sisi, but not the other candidate, Sabahi.

To make matters worse, she issued a statement that in her opinion El Sisi was the best candidate for the Egyptian people! After this, it was up to us to convince the Egyptians that EU EOMs are impartial and neutral …..

It was strange in itself that the EU deployed a mission to Egypt, since Egypt did not fulfill any of the requirements applied by the EU for observation missions. First of all, the winner was already known: El Sisi was going to win with a landslide.

Secondly, just before the mission started, hundreds of members of the Muslim Brotherhood were sentenced to death in the city of El Menya, after two mass trials that lasted just a few hours each.

Thirdly, the Muslim Brotherhood had been declared a terrorist organization and could not participate in the elections, even though its leader, Morsi, had been elected president of Egypt in 2011, winning 51 per cent of the vote.

Fourthly, the media were far from free. In fact, four Al Jazeera journalists had been in jail for more than four months, without trial. They allegedly wanted to interview members of the Muslim Brotherhood. A Dutch journalist had also been jailed for a few weeks, for the same reason. She was lucky: the Dutch embassy managed to get her out of the country.

Fifthly, the Egyptian interim rulers put a 'Protest Law' in place, which stated that demonstrations, political rallies and all gatherings of more than ten persons needed authorization by the authorities, three days in advance.

All of the above were flagrant violations of the 'International Standards for Democratic Elections'. It was clear that we were in Egypt for strategic reasons: Egypt is important for the EU, because of its strategic position in the Middle East and the Suez Canal.

Anyway: we were still locked in our golden cage. A few days after our last trip, we were taken to Sakkara, just to the south of Cairo, to visit Djoser's stepped pyramid, the first pyramid ever built. This was particularly interesting to me, since I had seen it on Discovery Channel, but I had never actually visited it.

After that, we made a few trips to the central island of Zamalek, where we were allowed to wander around freely for a few hours, but we were not allowed to leave the island. We never felt threatened there. Yet again: where was the danger? Why were we confined to our five-star hotel? Back in my room I watched Juventus – Benfica (0-0).

In between these touristic trips, Mel and I tried to keep ourselves busy by typing a large part of our STO Manual. Since we were responsible for three governorates, we could already describe some background and historical facts.

I wrote a short bit on Abydos, the first capital of Ancient Egypt. Abydos is situated to the south-west of Sohag. Mel wrote several pages on the situation of the Coptic Christians, a sizeable minority in our Area of Observation.

Every evening I skyped with my wife. Luckily, there is only one hour time difference between Egypt en Holland. One evening I received devastating news: my wife had had her routine biannual check-up for breast cancer.

Previous checks never revealed any worrying signs, but this time it was different: the doctors were not sure about the X-Ray. She would have to go to the hospital, for extra checks. She was close to panicking. At first, I wanted to keep this information all to myself, since it was nobody's business.

But then I realized that I had to inform my partner Mel, since there was a chance that I might have to fly back to Holland at short notice. Mel understood and wished me strength. I watched Everton – Manchester City (2-3).

By now, the LTOs were really getting bored. Even worse, we did not have a clue as to how long our ordeal would continue. We took bets, to guess on which day we would finally be deployed. The winner would receive 29 beers. Initially I put up 8 May, but that day had long since passed.

When Mel was asked what date she thought we would be deployed, I answered in her place: „The 16th of May, because that's her birthday." I was afraid Mel would react angrily, but she happily agreed. I watched Manchester City – West Ham United (2-0). Manchester City was now the champion of the English Premier League.

So, Friday 16 May arrived and we were still stuck at Le Meridièn Airport hotel. Anna, the other LTO from the UK, and me, had earlier agreed to jointly buy some presents for Mel. On the early morning of the 16th of May, Anna and I walked to the airport terminal together, through the glass covered corridor, and bought a few presents at the souvenir shop.

I had seen an inflatable King Tutankhamen there. Upon returning from the airport terminal, we spotted Mel sitting all by herself at the 'Helicopter Platform' of the hotel. Mel was very happy with the presents, especially with the inflatable King Tut, which I tried to inflate.

This, however, proved to be not as easy as I thought it would be. Thankfully, Anna read the instructions. I first had to fill the base with water, as a sort of anchor to keep the one meter high balloon in an upright position.

I tried to inflate it again. There were three valves. The head inflated easily, but the front and backside would not inflate at all. I tried for half an hour. The LTOs that came to felicitate Mel laughed their heads off. Then Paul from Austria set down next to me. „Let me do it, I have a five year old child", he said.

He pressed a valve with his fingers and after that it took him only five minutes to blow up the entire balloon. Mel lay down at the pool and I placed King Tut next to her on a small table in the shade, to prevent the balloon from exploding. There it stood all day, swaying gently in the warm wind. It was the success story of the day.

Mel's birthday would turn out to be a memorable one. Just a few days earlier, we had received the names of our six STOs, one of which was Mel's husband, John, an experienced observer. We had especially requested this and it had been approved by the Core Team.

At 19.00 hours, we were all assembled at the open air Live Sports Bar, for a surprise party for Mel, organized by Mafalda (Portugal) and Petra (Slovenia). There were flowers and there was a birthday cake.

Anna had been commissioned to take Mel to the terrace of the Live Sports Bar, under one or other pretext.

All of a sudden the entire Core Team and Service Provider arrived. Then I saw Mel arrive also, but without Anne. Something was wrong. Then Hanna (Poland) received an SMS from a Polish STO, who claimed that all STOs had been cancelled. Hanna asked Dainida, the sympathetic Observer Coordinator of the Core Team, if this was true. Dainida simply said: „Yes".

First we sang 'Happy Birthday' for Mel. Then we were told that all 60 STOs had indeed been cancelled. As to us, LTOs, we would hear within a few days if we would stay on until after E-Day of if we would be sent home earlier.

We would, in any case, stay in Le Meridién hotel and only observe in greater Cairo. The news was particularly disappointing for Mel, since her husband would not be coming to Egypt. The next day, we read the electronic versions of media outlets all over the world.

They mentioned that the EU EOM had been cancelled (which was not true; only the STOs had been cancelled) because administrative requirements had made it impossible to clear communications and medical equipment through the Egyptian customs, equipment that was necessary for the security and safety of the EU observers.

The question remains if all of this was due to non-willingness of the Egyptian authorities to allow the EU to observe their elections, or if this was simply a bureaucratic impediment by the customs people (did they expect bribes?). Or was all of this due to the incompetence of our own Service Provider?

Anyway, on Saturday evening Kees had arranged for all LTOs to go by bus to the Opera House, where the Egyptian Philharmonic would be performing. All LTOs went there, except me. I did not want to miss Barcelona – Atlético Madrid: an exciting match, after which Atlético was the new champion of Spain.

Just when all seemed lost, things started to move again. On Monday morning, 19 May 2014, my father's birthday, Annemarieke told me at breakfast that our communications equipment all of a sudden had been cleared from customs!

On top of that, our Chief Observer was coming to our hotel to meet with the LTOs (by now, Hanna from Poland, who had been my partner in Nigeria, had changed our title to LTTs: Long Term Tourists).

For the first two weeks of our mission we had no Chief Observer, due to the fact that elections for the European Parliament were scheduled to be held from 22-25 May. The parliamentarians were, understandably, preoccupied with their own election.

Finally, Brussels managed to find a parliamentarian who was willing to become Chief Observer: Mario David from Portugal. He had been in Egypt for only two days and on his way back to the airport, he had fifteen minutes for us. A charming man, but it was his very first observation mission.

Nevertheless, he had surprising news for us: since the communications equipment was now cleared by the Egyptian customs, the EU EOM would go on as planned. Even the STOs were called back. It would be a limited mission, since we did not have time to perform our long-term observation, but at least we would be deployed.

All 30 LTOs were elated. Questions remained as to why it had taken Brussels so long to put pressure on the Egyptians, because one thing was clear: after the international media mentioned that the EU EOM was cancelled because of some stupid administrative reasons, clearly some Egyptians at the very top had made a few telephone calls, after which all problems had been miraculously solved in an instant.

One of the LTOs who spoke Arabic explained to me that the real power in Egypt lay in the hands of a handful of army generals. El Sisi had been one of them, but since El Sisi was now running for president, he had effectively placed himself outside this small group of all-powerful military men.

All the more, one could ask why the EU had dispatched an observation mission to Egypt in the first place. Mel and I received new deployment instructions. On the new list, our duty station had been changed to Assiut, instead of Sohag.

And we would travel by car, thank God. On the early morning of Wednesday 21 May, we finally set out on the road with two other LTO teams. On the chaotic roads of Cairo, we soon lost track of the other cars.

We hoped that Mushin, our driver, would be able to find the exit to the 'military road', the newly constructed desert highway along the Nile, on the eastern bank. We could not communicate with him, because he did not speak English and we did not speak Arabic.

But he did fine. The military road is a toll road, so there was hardly any traffic on it. It runs straight through the desert and you are allowed to drive 120 kilometres per hour on it. It took us less than five hours to reach Assiut, much to the surprise of Wlodek, our Security Liaison Officer, who was based in Luxor.

Wlodek did not even know that the military road existed. For a good reason, since there is another desert highway on the western bank of the Nile. And there's the old, extremely slow road along the river, that runs through numerous towns and villages.

So we entered Assiut at 14.00 hours. Mushin crossed the bridge over the Nile. I told him we would be staying at the Watania Palace hotel, but Mushin had never heard of it. Later, we found out that he came from Menya, the city we had passed on our way to Assiut.

I gave him the telephone number of the hotel on a piece of paper. He called the hotel, but the directions he received were not very clear to him. Somehow he did realize that he had to cross another bridge, over the irrigation canal.

At the other side, we drove around in circles for some time. Finally, I noted the name of our hotel at the front of a building. In the days to come, we would find out that both our driver and our interpreter were absolutely hopeless in finding directions.

At the entrance to the hotel the police were waiting for us. It has to be noted here that in cities like Assiut and Sohag, the police are accustomed to 'protecting' visiting dignitaries. Even the few tourists that visit these cities are considered to be dignitaries and are therefore escorted by a police car.

After years of unrest, there were no tourists at all. But we were there: finally some westerners to protect. The leader of the policemen introduced himself as Mohammed. We entered the hotel where our interpreter would be waiting for us. He immediately came towards us and introduced himself as Mohammed.

We asked him where he had learned his English, but instead he started offering us deals for hotel rooms: we could each stay in a suite, for the price of a normal room. That sounded good. I just wondered how on earth our interpreter could offer us a good deal with the hotel.

Then another young man entered the lobby and introduced himself as Mohammed, our interpreter. It turned out that the first Mohammed was the hotel manager. We then realized that the chaos in Egypt was even worse than we had anticipated: the oldest son is customarily called Mohammed.

This means that there are millions of Mohammeds. On the bright side: it's easy to remember a name in Egypt. Just say Mohammed and you can't be wrong. One of the suites was not yet ready, so I offered to stay in an ordinary room for the first two nights. This had the added advantage that we set up our office in Mel's suite. I do admit that I'm a bit lazy.

We made plans with our interpreter for the next day, Thursday, which would in fact be the only day that we could do our regular work as LTOs: interviewing people. Just one day later, on Friday afternoon, our STOs would arrive, and we had to brief them. On Friday morning we had to finalize and print our STO manual for all six STOs.

On Thursday morning we planned to visit the Governor first. I could see the white Governorate building from the front steps of our hotel. Just a few hundred meters away. ,,Let's walk", I told Mohammed, our interpreter. ,,It's too far", he replied. ,,But It's just over there", I insisted. ,,No, no: it's too far. And it's too hot."

The last part was true. It was already 42 degrees Celsius in the shade. So we stepped in our car, but it takes the airco at least five minutes to produce cool air. On top of that, our car was approached on both sides by policemen. Both the driver and the interpreter opened their front windows and started arguing with the policemen. Arguing is the national sport in Egypt.

I wondered what they argued about, since the Governorate building was straight ahead of us. Hot air flowed into the car through the open windows. I told Mohammed that I had had enough and that I was getting out of the steaming hot vehicle and go on foot to the Governorate building.

That worked. Our car moved. Followed by a police car. Three minutes later we reached our destination. I was led to the office of Hussein. A chaotic office, with stacks of paper all over the place. I liked it. And I liked the man behind the desk, who smoked cigarettes incessantly.

Hussein had lived abroad for many years, spoke fluent English and introduced himself as the PR-man of the Governorate. The Governor himself was alas not available, but Hussein was. He even offered himself as interpreter for one of our STO teams.

He told us that he had already applied for an interpreter position, but that he had not received an answer yet. So we contracted him on the spot. Later that same day, GIZ sent us the name of another interpreter. When I studied the CV of the last one, it dawned on me that it was exactly the same CV as Hussein's.

I discussed it with Mel and we came to the conclusion that it was indeed one and the same person, even though the names were spelled differently. This was yet another problem in Egypt: names are often spelled differently in English, since they were translated from Arabic. For example: the town of Sohag was sometimes spelled as Suhaj. When spoken out aloud, it sounded the same.

Next, we interviewed the Chief Judge of the Court of First Instance, who acted as the president of the Presidential Electoral Commission in Assiut Governorate. And we introduced ourselves to the Chief of Police. Both received us cordially, even though we had not made formal appointments.

During the briefings, we had been told that in Egypt it is customary to make appointments, but I usually prefer not to do it, because it's cumbersome: they usually let you know that they are very busy and can only see you a few days later. Then, when you arrive at the appointed time, you have to wait for at least an hour. All these problems can be avoided by arriving unannounced.

The police headquarters was situated on the west bank of the Nile. Just opposite the Stephanie, a luxurious hotel boat. I asked our interpreter if we could have lunch there, but he did not know. In fact, we learned quickly that he did not know anything about Assiut, since he came from Sohag.

So we entered the hotel boat to find out for ourselves. It turned out to be fantastic! Much better than our own hotel. The receptionist showed us several great air-conditioned rooms on the river side. There were several restaurants, one of which on the open deck. The boat was also very safe, since it was moored close to the police headquarters and there was only one small entrance. Easy to defend.

We called Wlodek, our liaison officer, and asked him if we could stay on the boat. He said no, because he had not checked it out. He said it was forbidden for observers to stay on board of boats. A strange rule, but as an observer you get used to strange rules. Or was Wlodek talking bullshit? I never found out.

In the afternoon we managed to talk to representatives of the Sisi and Sabahi campaigns in the restaurant of our own hotel. The Sisi campaign was supported by lots of people. All over the city we noted huge Sisi banners, with also the names or photographs of local businessmen. These businessmen paid for the banners. The Sabahi campaign hardly received any support.

A funny thing happened when one of the two Sabahi campaigners lit a cigarette and blew the smoke straight in Mel's face. I wondered how long Mel would restrain herself. Well: not long. She politely told him that the smoke was bothering her. In western Europe, we are not used to smoking in public places anymore. And to blow smoke in someone else's face is absolutely not done.

On Friday morning we finalized and printed our STO manuals. At 15.00 hours, the two STO teams arrived, just two days later than us. Even so, as LTOs, we were supposed to brief the STOs on our Area of Observation. Back in Cairo, Mel had already written in the introduction of our STO manual that it was 'Hot, Hot, Hot' in Assiut. This turned out to be true. It was 42 degrees Celsius every day.

Mel introduced me to her husband, John. The six of us then headed for the Stephanie: we would brief the STOs on top of the open deck. It went well. One team, John from England and Guido from Belgium, had a lot of experience. We planned to send them to the desert oasis of El Kharga.

We had not checked this out yet, so hopefully they would return. The other team, Marc from Luxembourg and Sandra from Spain, would cover a part of Assiut and the surrounding country side.

On this mission, we were not obliged to have police escorts, but in Egypt the police are accustomed to escorting visiting dignitaries. They always do it, so there was no escape for us, even though we would probably have been safer without police escorts, since policemen were often targeted by militants.

But what could we do? Our mission's security experts had informed the police that we would be staying at the Watania Palace hotel. The ordinary policemen were ordered by their superiors to protect us at all times.

So all three teams had been assigned police escorts, who were waiting for us with their vehicles at the hotel entrance. After the briefings on the boat, we decided to walk back to our own hotel. The policemen were horrified. They had never experienced this.

Egyptian dignitaries never ever walk on foot. The policemen protested through our interpreters, but we insisted: we wanted to take the opportunity to stroll along the Nile boulevard. Grudgingly, the police followed us on foot.

They didn't understand anything about these crazy Europeans. On top of everything, we were dressed casually. Egyptian dignitaries are always dressed in suits and ties.

The next day, the STO teams travelled to their respective Areas of Observation. John and Guido's team did not have an interpreter yet, so we asked our own interpreter, Mohamed, if he was willing to travel with them to El Kharga. Mohamed, like most Egyptians, had never visited the western desert, but he agreed.

Mel and I travelled to Sohag, to brief our third STO team over there. They had arrived by plane from Cairo. Without interpreter we could not communicate with our driver, Mushin, but this was not really a problem. He was a cheerful fellow and a good driver.

Mushin did not know his way around Assiut, but all he had to do was follow our police escort, which had been instructed by Mohamed, our interpreter, before our departure. I was eager to take the desert highway, but our police escort had been instructed otherwise:

they headed straight for the old road along the western bank of the Nile.

The old road passes through lots of towns and villages, so it took us a full three hours to reach Sohag. By then, we had changed police escorts several times. Apparently, just like in Pakistan, each police district takes exclusive care of escorts within its own district boundaries.

At the Nile Hotel, adjacent to the old bridge of Sohag, Karoly from Hungary and Lloyd from Canada were waiting for us in the lobby. Nice, experienced chaps. 'The old foxes', they called themselves. Their interpreter would try to find an interpreter for our third STO team in Assiut. He would call on a number of his friends.

I asked him if he could also help me buy beer, since our own interpreter, Mohamed, did not know anything at all in Assiut. I didn't tell him that Mohamed was a devout Muslim and therefore refused to touch anything that contained alcohol. To my surprise, the interpreter asked me if I wanted ten per cent.

I didn't have a clue what that meant: ten per cent. Normally, beer has five per cent alcohol. Then it dawned on me that in some countries a different scale is used for measuring the percentage of alcohol. I suspected that in this case the Egyptian ten per cent could be the same as our five per cent. So I said: ,,Yes, please. Bring me ten per cent."

Then the interpreter asked me how many beers I wanted. I asked him how many beers he thought were available in the shop. He said nothing, just looked at me in surprise. I gave him the equivalent of 80 euros and asked him if 48 beers would be possible. With that, he left.

My hopes were not high, but a few hours later, when Mel and I prepared to return to Assiut, I asked the interpreter about the beer. ,,I put it in the back of your car", he replied simply and handed me my change. He also managed to get us an interpreter for John and Guido, who would travel from Sohag to Assiut the next day.

By 19.00 hours Mel and I were back at our Watania Palace hotel in Assiut. I immediately took my precious beers to my suite and stuffed a dozen or so in my two little fridges. I noted that they were half-litre cans.

Now I had plenty of beer for myself, my partner Mel and the four STOs, who were waiting for us at the rooftop terrace. Each team related their experiences of the day. John and Guido said that they had had a fantastic lunch in El Kharga oasis: a deliciously prepared fish. I said: 'That's impossible. There are no fish in the desert." To which Guido replied: "It was a sand fish."

It had been 42 degrees Celsius by the middle of the day and even after dark on the open rooftop it was still unbelievably hot. We were all sweating, so I went to my room to fetch six beers, that by now were lukewarm.

I was not sure if the hotel staff would appreciate people drinking beer in a place where no alcohol was served, so I carried the beers in an unobtrusive plastic bag. But the staff never made a fuzz about it. And the STOs were eternally grateful to me. They would report positively about me to the Core Team.

The beer turned out to be a dark beer. It tasted grate. And it was really ten per cent, I found out. After just one half-litre can of beer in the smouldering heat, we were all getting tipsy. Back in my suite I decided to smoke a cigar and drink one more beer on my hot, windless balcony.

A bad decision. I fell fast asleep. Nearly two hours later I woke up and swiped the ashtray to pieces on the tiled floor of the balcony. Boy, was that beer strong.

The two Election Days went well, thanks to the judges, who were in charge of all the Polling Stations. Only three institutions can provide order in the Egyptian chaos: the army, the secret service and the judges.

In most countries, polling staff comprises of teachers and civil servants. In Egypt, this would be impossible, since teachers and civil servants have no authority at all. The judges are a breed apart.

Like in Pakistan, Egyptian judges are always smartly dressed in a black suit and tie. Which made life easier for us: the moment we entered a Polling Station, we immediately recognized the judge.

Judges command authority, not only over the other staff at the PS, all of whom were civil servants, but also over the police and even the military, who were in charge of security, immediately outside the PS. A judge could even order a person to be detained on the spot.

The judges were not happy with the extra burden that was to be theirs. It's not their regular job, to be honest. To be in charge of a PS is a heavy responsibility, with just a little extra pay. On top of that, most PSs were situated in schools. That means no air conditioning and quite often not even a fan.

Judges are used to be sitting in air conditioned offices, with lots of servants to fulfil all their needs. It was quite funny when we noted that several judges had brought their servants with them, to pour their tea.

Some judges even brought a portable fan, since it gets bloody hot in these stifled class rooms. No wonder Egyptian children don't learn English at school: it's too hot in there to learn anything at all.

Mel and I agreed on a division of our work: she would fill in the paper forms and I would transmit the forms electronically to our Core Team in Cairo. This was a good system: from computer to computer. Unfortunately, our STO teams had not been provided with laptops, so they had to transmit their forms by telephone to a battery of students that had been recruited by our Core Team.

This created a lot frustration. During the debriefings I suggested to give laptops to each STO team, to make life easier for everybody. But I had suggested the same during previous missions, to no avail.

One thing was quite weird during this mission. We were only allowed to wear our visibility jackets during the election days. And there was to be no visibility on our car either. I received a call from Kees. He had had a lot of trouble with an Italian STO. He and his partner, Petra, had unsuccessfully tried for days to solve the problems.

The Italian STO was kicked out of the mission and his partner, Veronica from Slovakia, was called back to Cairo to join a Cairo team for the remainder of her STO mission. Thank God our STOs were fine!

I was just about to enter a polling station, when I received a call from my wife. She was in the hospital, with her sister Francine. Good news: she did not have breast cancer. She wanted to talk to me in length, but I told her bluntly that it was E-Day and that I was about to enter a polling station. ,,You have time for everyone, but not for me", my wife told me accusingly.

There were supposed to be two election days and the outcome was already clear to everyone: Sisi was going to win by a landslide. The problem was that turnout had been extremely low, at around 44 per cent. So the national PEC decided that a third E-Day would be held.

This was bad news for our STO teams, who had counted on one free day to visit several monasteries in the vicinity of Assiut. As expected, very few voters turned up during the third E-Day. The Muslim Brotherhood had called on its supporters to boycott the elections.

On top of that, some five million people did not possess an ID and many people with an ID lived in another part of Egypt than where they were registered. And many people simply did not bother to vote, since the outcome of the elections was already known to everybody.

The good news was that there were no major incidents during the three E-Days. And the counting, after 21.00 hours, went fast. In our PS, they simply counted the votes for Sabahi and the invalid votes. Since the number of total votes cast was known, the other votes were by definition for Sisi.

This system had the added advantage that there could not be any adding-up discrepancies. In our PS, Sisi obtained 93 per cent of the vote. Then the judge drove over to the Courts, duly followed by us. We were allowed to enter the room where the results of the polling stations of our district arrived.

All went well. Since the STOs had to travel back to Cairo the next morning, we decided to call it a day at 01.30 hours. The safe travel of observers is more important than the final results of the elections. Their drivers need a good night's sleep.

We went to the roof top terrace of our hotel, where I sat down with the STOs. They still had to transmit several of the E-Day forms. The lights were switched off, so we worked by the lights of our torches. As observers, we are used to unusual situations. By the time I finally went to bed, the sun was already rising.

The next morning, at 11.00 hours, I went to the lobby, to say goodbye to our STOs. Mel and I had told them not to leave later than 11.00 hours, to be on the safe side. You never know if there will be delays, due to an accident or mechanical problems. In countries like Egypt you don't want to travel in the dark.

But the STOs were not there. The receptionist, one of the very few people in Assiut who spoke English, told me that they had gone to visit the cave where Josef, Mary and baby Jesus had lived. I was not happy with that. But what can you do?

I went to see Mel in her suite. She told me that her husband John was getting fed up with his partner Guido, who kept on complaining about the third E-Day. Frictions between team partners happen all the time. It's normal.

You cannot choose your partner, but you are forced to work intensely with that person under quite a lot of stress and in a cultural environment that is totally different from what we are used to at home. Add to this that it was 42 degrees Celsius every day, and it would be a surprise if there was no friction between team partners.

The STOs finally left at 13.00 hours. Mel stayed in touch with John. We learned that they arrived before dark at Le Meridièn hotel in Cairo. No problem there. But now we had problems. And I have to be honest here: it was my fault. I lost my temper.

I never shout at people, because it's counterproductive and it's a sign of weakness. But this time several things went awry at the same time. Mel wanted to visit the Court building, to check out where the ballots were kept. I was against it, since it meant we would have to enter that chaotic building again. And they would not show us the ballots in any case.

The Court building was only 300 meters from our hotel, so I preferred to walk, instead of having long arguments with our police escorts again. But Mohamed, our interpreter, insisted that we should take the car. Mel sided with him, so we stepped in the car.

Surely, the arguments with the policemen started again. Both our driver and our interpreter joined in. I angrily told Mushin, our driver, to take off without police escort. After some persuasion, he did just that. We took the left turn from the hotel, as we had done at least fifteen times before, but those times we had a police escort.

This time, we did not have a police escort, and it turned out that it was a one-way road. We did not even know that, but we were driving the wrong way. With a police escort, that is no problem, but now we were stopped by some other police men.

Mushin, our driver, apparently had not been properly trained on security rules and regulations. He stopped the car and before I could react, he stepped out of the car, leaving the key in the ignition and the engine running. A potentially very dangerous situation. I mentioned this to Mel, but Mel was busy sending an SMS to someone.

Then things got even worse. All of a sudden, Mohamed also stepped out of the car. So there, Mel and I were still sitting in the back seats, with the engine running and all doors unlocked. I was furious. I also stepped out.

I joined the arguing with the two police men, one of whom was behind the wheel of a police truck. I instructed Mohamed to translate that we were going to their highest boss, the Chief of Police, right now. Mohamed was reluctant to translate. Obviously, he thought it better not to make matters worse.

Mohamed was probably right, but by now I was beyond reasoning. I shouted at him. I went back to the car and told Mel that I was going on foot to the Court building, just across the road. Mohamed protested. In Egypt, dignitaries never walk on foot. But I did it, anyway.

When Mel and Mohamed finally caught up with me, I told Mohamed that I was not in the mood to talk to the Supreme Judge. We took the elevator to the fifth floor, where all rooms were full with men drinking tea. We had to wait there, while someone was sent to yet another room.

The usual chaos in Egypt. Not even Mohamed knew what was going to happen next, but sure enough, within ten minutes we were led into the pleasantly air conditioned room of the Supreme Judge. He offered us coffee and answered all our questions. It calmed me.

Later, while we walked back to our car, Mohamed said that he had not been in a position to prevent the meeting with the Supreme Judge. I told him not to worry, but I did not apologize for my outburst one hour earlier. I should have. The next morning, at breakfast, Mel told me never again to shout at Mohamed. She was right, of course. I should not have lost my bloody temper.

So the STOs had left and we still had seven days in our duty station. By now, the Preliminary Statement had been released by our

Core Team. Normally, LTOs would then hand out copies of the Preliminary Statement to their interlocutors.

Not this time. It turned out that the Egyptians were offended by the tone of the Preliminary Statement. The Preliminary Statement reflected what Mel and I, and also our STOs, had observed. Inside the polling stations everything had been fine. Also, the counting and processing of results had been reasonably OK.

But the freedom of the press was not up to international democratic standards. Large gatherings of people were forbidden. A number of national and international journalists had been detained on dubious charges. On top of that, the police were battling with supporters of the Muslim Brotherhood nearly every day.

Several nights I would wake up at 03.00 hours and hear a rumbling in the distance. I have a little experience, so I can distinguish guns from mere fireworks. These were machine guns. We learned later that nearly every night the police and military battled with Islamic students at the Al Azhar University, at the far bank of the Nile canal.

At Assiut University, much closer to our hotel at the near bank of the canal, there were no disturbances. In the city of Menya, a judge had 'recommended' the death penalty for more than 700 supporters of the Muslim Brotherhood, after a mass trial that lasted just about two hours. Because all of this, people lived in fear. Not a good basis for democratic elections.

Our all-female LTO team in Cairo, Christa and Mafalda, had been insulted during a meeting with women's organizations. The speaker told the congregation that the EU Preliminary Statement was disrespectful towards Egypt.

Christa and Mafalda were forced to leave in a hurry, all the while being jeered at by a number of Egyptian women. It had been filmed and Mel managed to find the clip on YouTube. We looked at it in horror.

It must be mentioned here, that this was the very first EU EOM in Egypt. We were not used to Egypt and Egypt was not used to us. The Egyptians are used to communicating in the Arab way: using lots of vague semi-diplomatic phrases, but never using straightforward criticism.

That was considered to be disrespectful or worse: as interference in Egyptian culture. Add to this that Egyptians don't appreciate outsiders telling them how to run their things. In any case, the result of all this was that all LTOs were instructed by our Core Team not to hand out the Preliminary Statement to anyone.

On top of that, we were not allowed to leave our hotel after dark. So what were Mel and I going to do then, for the next week? We could not go to Luxor or the Red Sea, since observers are not allowed to leave their provinces.

Luckily, we were officially responsible for three provinces, or governorates, as they are called in Egypt. We had never visited El Kharga in the western desert. And we had only visited Sohag for a few hours. So we decided to stay three days in Sohag and to visit El Kharga for just one day, since no hotels had been approved for us over there.

This time we took the western desert highway to Sohag. Without police escort. Since our interpreter, Mohamed, came from Sohag, he would surely know his way around there. Alas, this was not the case. He told us that he grew up in a town in the province of Sohag, about 40 kilometres south of the city of Sohag.

Once again, neither our driver nor our interpreter knew their way around. Fortunately, we were spotted by the police. Immediately, they provided us with a police escort. They were local chaps and knew their way around. We followed them to what we believed was the Red Monastery.

Well: it was red and it was a monastery. It looked as if it was a thousand years old, but when the resident Coptic bishop invited us for a cup of coffee, he told us that this marvellously constructed building was only three years old. After that, the police guided us to two really ancient monasteries.

Since there had hardly been any tourists in Egypt since the fall of Mubarak, everyone was happy to show us around. The White Monastery is not really white and the Red Monastery is not really red, but both of them are very, very old. And they contain ancient Christian wall paintings.

In the Red Monastery we encountered a Polish student of archaeology. She was all alone in there, making drawings of the world famous wall paintings, that are in the process of being restored. A book, with photographs and explanations, was being prepared by her colleagues.

Mohamed, our 24 year old interpreter, whom we thought was from Sohag, admitted that he was surprised that the monasteries were there. He said that he thought that there was absolutely nothing of interest in Sohag. He had never been to a monastery in his entire life and now he had visited three monasteries in one day!

There was something about Mohamed, that both Mel and I had noticed. It takes time to gain a person's trust. He had already told us that he and his family had decided not to vote. Not because the Muslim Brotherhood had called for its members not to vote, he said, but because the candidate of their choice was in prison. A bit vague.

Bit by bit we found out that Mohamed was indeed most likely a supporter of the Muslim Brotherhood or maybe even a full member. He never asked us time off for prayers, but when he had to do some work for us in our office, which in fact was Mel's suite, he got very nervous when I left the room for a few minutes.

While he was alone with Mel, he insisted on keeping the door open. And when Mel and I told him about the Monty Python movie Life of Brian, he said that the movie was disrespectful towards religion.

At some point, he confided to us that several of his friends had been killed by the police in Cairo, during the student protests that followed the removal of Morsi by the army. This could only mean that his friends were supporters of the Muslim Brotherhood. Which put him close to the Muslim Brotherhood.

He was a reasonably good interpreter, he was clean shaven and dressed in western clothes, but he was very set in his ways. I told Mel that perhaps we were at risk. Mohammed knew about our whereabouts and our travel plans. He could easily have alerted some militants, eager to abduct or kill westerners.

In the end, nothing happened to us. That evening, after dark, Mel and I sat on her balcony on the fourth floor of the Nile Hotel in Sohag. The hotel itself was a bit rundown, but the balcony was great, with a cool breeze.

Just below us, several disco boats showed off their multi-coloured lights. I had brought a few beers with me from Assiut and Mel still had some wine left. That's the nice thing of being an observer: a view of the Nile, good company and a cold beer.

The next morning we wanted to visit the Chief of Police, the Governor and the Chief Justice. The police headquarters was just behind our hotel. In Assiut, we were instantly led into the office of the Chief of Police. Not so in Sohag.

They kept us waiting in a small room at the entrance. For twenty minutes, nothing happened. I asked Mel if she would agree that we'd just leave and visit the Governor instead, just across the road. After that, we could try the police again.

Mel agreed. So I shook the hand of the officer in charge, told him bluntly that we would be back later and left the room, followed by Mel. All of a sudden, the policemen panicked. As I expected, they all started arguing with Mohamed, since none of them spoke English.

I firmly took Mohamed's arm and walked with him to the Governorate building. There, things were even worse. Yet again, there was a little room at the entrance. The man insisted on seeing our passports.

Nobody had ever asked for our passports until then. Then the man guided us into a small room inside the building. While we sat down, the man walked out of the room with our passports. I jumped up and followed him. What if the man disappeared with our passports?

He walked up the stairs, into a room with several photocopying machines. He didn't mind that I was there with him. While he was busy copying, I took a look at Mel's passport. I had been curious about at her age, but I never had the courage to ask her. Now I noted that she was four months older than my wife.

After that, things went fine. The Governor was not there, but we were courteously received by a high-up official, who offered us coffee and gave us a briefing on Sohag Governorate. After that, we walked back to the police headquarters.

This time, we were immediately accompanied to the office of the Chief of Police. He was not there yet, but his deputy offered us coffee. We talked about football. Then the Chief himself arrived. We talked a bit more about football. By the time we left, everybody was happy.

It was not even 11.00 hours, so we decided to visit the famous statue of Merit-Amun in Akhmin, just a few kilometres down the road. Only foreigners are supposed to pay the entrance fee, so I paid for Mel and me. The old man did not have any change. It was clear that we were the first visitors in a long time.

The statue was fantastic, though. It is so big, that it was decided to leave it in its place and dug out the surrounding earth instead. Since there was no breeze, it was baking hot inside that pit. After that, we still had the entire afternoon. What to do?

I remembered that Mohamed's family lived in a town, some 40 kilometres to the south. They had not voted. It would be interesting to talk to them and ask them about their motives. After all: as observers, we are supposed to talk to the ordinary voters as well. I asked Mohamed if it would be all right with him. He said yes.

So off we went. Our police escort led the way. After about one hour, disaster struck. The escort vehicle was driving fast, as police cars usually do in Egypt. There was a gap of three hundred meters between us. All of a sudden, Mel screamed.

I instinctively grabbed the chair in front of me and ducked. Our driver, Mushin, violently swerved the car to the right and hit the brakes besides the road. A loud bang indicated that we had hit something. Then we stood still.

I had not seen a thing, but Mel explained that, in front of us, a white minibus had been overtaking a lorry. So the minibus was on our lane, coming towards us at great speed. Mushin had saved our lives, by reacting swiftly.

But it turned out that he had hit a man, who had been standing beside the road with his motorbike. The man was in shock, but otherwise unhurt. His bike had been severely damaged, though. So was the front of our car.

Mushin and Mohamed stepped out, to check on the man. Some villagers were there too. Luckily, our police escort came back immediately. Mel and I decided that I should call Wlodek, our liaison officer, to report the accident.

We stayed in the car, since you never know how local people will react when they spot westerners. There were some heated discussions, but the people who had witnessed the accident agreed that it had been the fault of the white minibus, which had sped away.

After about twenty minutes, we continued on our way. First, we made a brief halt at the nearest police station. On top of it, it read: 'Abydos Police'. We decided not to continue to Mohamed's family, but instead visit the nearby archaeological site of Abydos.

Yet again, when I paid the entrance fee, the man did not have change. Then a young man came up to me. He noticed our police escort. ,,Are you an ambassador?" he asked. ,,Not yet", I replied cheerfully. He was the site's resident archaeologist and he led us into the temple of Seti I, the father of Ramses II.

The wall paintings are amongst the best in Egypt. Mel was delighted. So was Mohamed. And also Muhsin. Our guide apologized for his bad English: ,,There have not been any tourists here, for many months", he told me. He took me to the small corridor with the names of nearly all pharaoh's who went before Seti I.

In Le Meridién hotel in Cairo I had read a couple of books on Egyptian history, so—to keep the conversation going—I told our guide that six pharaoh's were not mentioned there. One of them was the famous Hatshepsut, whose name had been omitted because she was a woman.

The others were all related to the heretic pharaoh Akhnaton, among them his son Tutankhamon. I told our guide that Horemheb was not mentioned on the wall, but he corrected me. He pointed at one of the cartouches at the very end. ,,You know a lot, but you make a little mistake. Here it reads: Horemheb, just before the name of Ramses I."

I asked him if we could visit the temple of Ramses II. ,,Follow me", he said simply. Behind Seti's temple we passed some unobtrusive ruins filled with water. ,,What is that?" I asked. ,,That is the Osirion", he replied. I had read about it, so I turned to Mel, Mohamed and Muhsin, to give them a little lecture.

,,This is the famous Osirion, where Isis assembled the body parts of her husband, Osiris, after which he came back to life and fathered their son Horus, through a ray from his eyes. This is why all ancient Egyptians had to make a pilgrimage at least once in their lives to Abydos. To ancient Egyptians, Abydos was the equivalent of what Mekka is to modern-day Muslims."

The remains of the temple of Ramses II were a bit of a disappointment, but our guide pointed out that the colourful wall paintings were of very high quality. We thanked him for taking so much time for us. He asked us to spread the word in Europe that Egypt was now safe again for tourists.

We were happy to be back in our air conditioned car, after having been exposed to the hot desert sun. But then disaster struck: we had hardly travelled five kilometres, when Mushin pointed out that the radiator was heating up. We stepped out of the car.

Water was leaking at the bottom, as a result of the accident earlier that morning. The car could go no further. According to our security instructions, Mel, Mohamed and I continued our voyage in the escort vehicle of the police. The police towed our car back to the Abydos police station, to try to repair it.

We were invited into the police station. After about half an hour, I asked them where the toilet was. To my surprise, a policeman led me out onto the open road. I followed him to a hotel down the road. Apparently, they thought that their own toilet inside the police station was not fit for western dignitaries.

The car could not be repaired, so it was agreed that the police would transport Mel, Mohamed and me back to the Nile hotel in Sohag. Mushin would stay with his car. His company, based about five hours away in Menya, would send technicians.

The police took us along the desert highway. They drove so fast, that I was afraid of getting involved in yet another accident. But we arrived safely at the Nile hotel, where we transmitted a written report of our accident to our Core Team.

The next morning, the car company provided us with a new car and a new driver named Béssim, who spoke a few words of English. Before returning to Assiut, we visited the High Court in Sohag.

The Chief Judge had travelled to Cairo, so we just left our business cards and our mission statement. Inside the deserted court room, we spotted the infamous cage where suspects are kept, like wild animals, behind bars during court hearings.

That evening, in our hotel in Assiut, we received instructions from our mission's security expert that all observers had to stay in their hotels the next day. Apparently, there had been another security alert.

We used this day to start writing our Final Report. With only two days to spare, we decided to pay a visit to El Kharga in the desert. Mohamed had already been there with the STO team.

For three hours we drove through the monotonous, greyish desert. When we arrived at the oasis, the thermometer in our car said that outside it was 49 degrees Celsius. The hottest temperature I have ever experienced.

We went to the police headquarters, to present ourselves. While we waited in a small room, Mohamed was taken away by police officers. No explanation was given. Without our interpreter, we were unable to talk to anyone. No one spoke English. After fifteen minutes, Mel got really angry.

She called Mohamed, but he did not pick up his phone. She got even angrier. When Mohamed finally re-emerged, she shouted at him that he worked for us, not for the police. A week earlier, I had shouted at Mohamed and Mel had criticized me for it. Now she was doing it herself. That's what Egypt does to you.

We visited the High Court, but no judges were present. Then Mohamed took us to the restaurant where John and Guido had consumed a deliciously prepared fish. Well: I have to admit: the fish was there and it was delicious. One of the best fishes I had ever had. In the middle of the desert, of all places.

Before leaving the oasis, we visited hotel Sol y Mar. A strange name, since we were in the desert and nobody spoke Spanish anyway. Lots of Sol there (meaning Sun), but definitely no Mar (meaning Sea).

It was a very nice resort, but there were no guests. The manager greeted us cheerfully. He said he hoped we would stay there, but we explained that we were just checking out the hotel for future missions.

It's a sad thing that for a number of years there were so few tourists in Egypt. It's not the fault of ordinary Egyptians. It remains a problem, though, that outside the tourist hubs hardly anyone speaks English. And they are very formal people. Other than that, they are hospitable, helpful and cheerful.

On the way back, Mel and I both noted that Mohammed and Béssim were engaged in a prolonged, heated discussion. On the one side, this was good, since Béssim was a Coptic Christian and at least the two religions were talking to each other. But later, when we talked to Béssim separately, he explained that Mohammed was very set in his Islamic ways.

At one point, Mohammed had accused Béssim of having been indoctrinated by government propaganda. Yet another indication that Mohammed was very close to the Muslim Brotherhood. Had we been lucky that we had not been abducted or even killed? We'll never know.

On our very last day in Assiut, we visited the cave where supposedly Josef, Mary and baby Jesus had lived. Yet again, Mohammed had never been there. It's a huge cave with a Coptic Church constructed inside it. Even though it's a bit touristic, it's still quite impressive.

At the beginning of the evening, we rented a disco-boat on the Nile. Mohammed and Béssim enjoyed the little boat trip. They even started dancing. Even on the Nile, our police escorts wouldn't give up: we were followed by a small police boat.

We said goodbye to Mohammed. On the way back to Cairo, we met Kees and Petra at a petrol station along the military road. We followed their car to Le Meridien Airport Hotel in Cairo.

During my last night in Le Meridien Airport Hotel my fixed hotel room telephone rang. I didn't pick it up. It must have been a mistake. But a few minutes later there was a loud knock on my door. I peeped through the looking glass. Two men in suits were standing there. I didn't dare to open my door. I did not want to be abducted.

I kept the door locked and asked what they wanted. ,,Are you alone in your room?" they asked. I said Yes. That was all. They left. The next day I learned that they had been looking for our Arabic teacher, who apparently had been an illegal immigrant from Syria and had stayed in the room of one of our LTOs for several days.

In the end, Al-Sisi was elected with a whopping 97 per cent of the vote. Turnout had been only 47 percent. Many Egyptians hoped that Al-Sisi would bring stability and prosperity back to Egypt. As it turned out, they got a bit more than they bargained for.

Al-Sisi not only persecuted the members of the Muslim Brotherhood, but anyone who opposed him. In the spring of 2018 he was a candidate for the presidency yet again. He was the only candidate, since nearly all his opponents were either put in jail or disqualified.

Since elections are supposed to be credible, one opponent was allowed to take part in the elections: Moussa Mustafa Moussa. Miraculously, this candidate managed to collect the obligatory 47.000 signatures of citizens and the support of at least 26 parliamentarians just seven minutes before the deadline.

While he did this, Moussa's Facebook page was still showing photographs of Al-Sisi. So the only opponent of Al-Sisi was a fan of Al-Sisi. To westerners, this may seem a bit odd, but to Egyptians it meant democracy: Egyptian style.

Once again, Egypt was governed by a strongman. It was as if Hosni Mubarak was back in full force. The EU and the USA looked the other way, since Al-Sisi was their ally in the war on terrorism. And the Arab Spring had brought nothing but chaos to countries like Libya and Syria.

At the end of each mission the LTOs are evaluated. Usually, some fifteen aspects of the mission are described at length. These include the language skills of the LTO, the ability to work in a different cultural setting, the ability to work together with colleagues, the quality of the Weekly Reports, the supervision of the STOs and so on.

This time, since the LTOs spent 28 days as tourists at Le Meridien Hotel in Cairo and only 17 days in the field, we received a simple evaluation, similar to the STOs evaluations. It simply said 'Recommended'. No more. Which was fine with me.

All in all, the observation mission to Egypt passed without major incidents. But then disaster struck. One week after our return to Holland, the three Dutch LTOs were invited to the Dutch Ministry of Foreign Affairs, for the customary debriefing. The only Dutch STO, Pim de Kuijer, was also present.

Pim had been deployed near Alexandria. While we strolled through the ministry's corridors, Pim was greeted by many people. It turned out that he had worked there. „Are you coming back?" someone asked. „I am too busy with other things", Pim replied.

Exactly one month later, I was shocked when I read his name on the front page of The Volkskrant national newspaper. Pim had been a passenger on flight MH17, that on 17 July 2014 had been shot out of the sky above eastern Ukraine.

As a representative of the Dutch Aids Fund, he was on his way to the World Aids Conference in Melbourne, Australia. At the tender age of only 32, he had become a victim in somebody else's war.

There was also good news: several Egyptians are living permanently in Enkhuizen, my hometown. They own restaurants and computer shops. Most of them are Coptic Christians. One evening I visited the snack bar 'Nooit Gedacht', whose owner is a sympathetic Egyptian lawyer, called Malak Mittias.

He is married to a Dutch woman and speaks reasonably good Dutch, but not good enough to practice law in The Netherlands. Instead, he owns a successful snack bar. I told him that I had just returned from Egypt.

,,Where were you based?" he asked. I replied: ,,Assiut, Sohag and El Kharga." Malak Mittias smiled. ,,I was born in Sohag", he told me. I replied that I must have been the only Enkhuizer who has ever worked in his hometown.

Chapter 18

MOZAMBIQUE - 2014

'I don't want to go to Tete and I don't want a Portuguese partner'

After Egypt, I was not particularly looking forward to doing yet another mission in 2014, but I knew that elections would be held in Mozambique in October. And I knew that the Dutch Ministry of Foreign Affairs might consider recruiting me, since very few Dutch LTOs speak Portuguese.

I shared my doubts with my wife. ,,It would be good for my Portuguese", I argued. ,,And a Portuguese speaking country will also look good on my CV." She was not looking forward to yet another period without me, especially since during my trip to Egypt she had been diagnosed with the possibility of breast cancer.

Thank God, it turned out to be benign, but even so, it had been emotionally tough on her. On top of that, our golden retriever, a trained guide dog for the blind, had died of pancreatitis. He was not yet six years old. To make matters even worse, my wife was at risk of losing her job at the Dutch prison system, due to cutbacks.

But the problem was that if I missed this opportunity, I would have to wait five years until the next presidential elections in Mozambique. And since we had lived there for three years in the 1980s, I really felt at home in Mozambique. I would rather do a mission in Mozambique than, a few months later, a mission in—let's say—Azerbeidzjan or Tajikistan. Or worse.

Sure enough, the invitation for Mozambique came in. I emailed the ministry that I was available as an LTO. They answered that if I had not heard anything by next Friday, I would not have been selected this time. The day came and went, and I did not receive any news from the ministry. Neither during the following days.

So, much to my chagrin, I had not been selected. The problem was that I had been totally convinced that I would be selected, so I had already told my family, friends, colleagues and neighbours that I was going to Mozambique. Now I had to tell everybody that I had not been selected.

On top of this, I had already started practicing my Portuguese for at least three hours per day, since by now my Spanish was much better than my Portuguese. But then, one week later, I looked at my emails and there was a message from the EU. I could not believe my eyes: the EU congratulated me with my selection as an LTO for Mozambique!

The next morning I received an email from the Dutch ministry, apologizing for the fact that they had forgotten to inform me about my selection. I gracefully accepted the apologies because, after all, let's be honest: all people who work make mistakes, including myself. No hard feelings. Only people who do not work do not make mistakes.

By now, my wife remained at home on sick leave. The general atmosphere at her work was at an all-time low, since half of her colleagues would lose their jobs, but nobody knew as yet who could stay and who would have to leave.

Not a pretty foresight. But I knew that she took good care of herself. I felt confident that I could travel to Mozambique. And we would skype every day. Another little problem was that I would miss my mother's birthday. I had already missed my parents 60 years marriage anniversary and my father's birthday.

I would also miss my wife's birthday this time. And the annual risk-weekend with two befriended couples, whom we have known since our student days, would have to be postponed.

One of our risk friends, Marie Lou, celebrated her 65th birthday on 20 September 2014, so in the afternoon my wife and I drove over to her hometown of Weesp. Some of the other guests asked me what I was doing. I told them I that I was a local journalist and also an election observer for the EU.

,,When is your next mission?" they asked. ,,Tonight", I answered. ,,I am flying to Mozambique tonight, for a six weeks mission." They looked at me in astonishment. ,,It's true", my wife came to my aid.

For ordinary Dutch people, a weekend in Belgium would already be a major adventure. But I am an observer. Observers are not ordinary people. That same evening I took the train to Schiphol Amsterdam Airport.

There are direct flights from Amsterdam to Johannesburg in South Africa every day and from Johannesburg there are flights every hour to Maputo, but as usual the Service Provider had a better idea: they sent me via Rome and Addis Ababa!

Three flights, with a very short stop in Rome and a very long stop in Addis. The stop in Rome would be only one hour and five minutes. I knew that I could make it, if I ran fast, but I feared that my suitcase would not make it.

It happened exactly like this. I arrived nicely on time at the brand new airport in Maputo, only to find out that my suitcase was nowhere to be seen. I was not the only one. Doloroza, an LTO from Sweden, had the same problem.

Claudio, the sympathetic Italian Logistics Officer of our mission, helped us with the paper work and told us that his own suitcase should have arrived three weeks ago, but had gone lost somewhere between Afghanistan and Mozambique. Welcome in Africa!

Luckily, ever since I had been evacuated by military helicopter from an ethnic conflict in Kyrgyzstan, I always keep emergency supplies in my 'run bag'. So I could live from my little suitcase for several days, without problems. Two days later my suitcase arrived. Still in one piece. Thank God. And still locked. In many countries they would have destroyed the locks to check the content of the suitcase.

The Core Team had their offices on the fifth floor of Hotel Rovuma in downtown Maputo. An old hotel, with an old elevator. I always advise people never to take an elevator in Africa, but in this case there was no choice: the entrance through the staircase had been hermetically locked.

Sure enough, on my very first day in Maputo I got stuck in the elevator, together with three other LTOs. The emergency button did not work. Neither did our mobile phones, because the elevator got stuck below ground level.

The good news was that, since I had lived in Maputo, I always carried a little flashlight with me, even during the day. So did Tommy, from Sweden. He had also lived in Maputo. After half an hour, all of a sudden, the elevator moved up a few meters.

We could see the first floor, through the crack between the doors. But the doors were still stuck. Then Tommy asked me to give him a light and he asked Slaveena for her shoe, which had a wooden sole. He smashed a big bolt with the shoe. To my amazement, it worked.

I was the first to clamber out of the elevator as fast as I could. I remembered the Dutch horror movie 'The Elevator', in which people get beheaded by an elevator with a mind of its own. Luckily, the four of us didn't lose our heads.

The LTOs were housed in the brand new Hotel Maputo, just two hundred meters from Hotel Rovuma. Hotel Maputo was so new, that the elevators had not been installed yet. The good news was that I did not have my big suitcase yet, so I did not have to carry it up the stairs to the third floor.

The bad news was that my key card did not work. I could not open my door. I had to go down to the reception, taking my little suitcase with, since in Africa you don't leave your stuff unattended at any time. The receptionist thought that I was incapable of opening the door, since I was—of course—an old idiot, having arrived freshly from Europe.

So he sent a hotel boy with me. Up we went. The boy could not open the door either, so down again we went. They gave me a new key card, for room 101 on the first floor. But room 101 would not open either.

Finally, I ended up in room 105. The key card worked, but in this room the airco was not working. In fact, none of the lights were working. Then I noticed the little key card holder, not next to the door where you would normally find it, but rather unobtrusively on the opposite wall.

I stuck my key card in it and yes: the lights came to life. Still no airco. I went down again and the receptionist gave me the remote control for the airco, with the ominous words: ,,This is the only remote control we have for the entire hotel. So you must bring it back immediately."

Now the airco worked, but I had to return the remote control to the receptionist. I could not take my key card out of the holder, because then the airco would stop again. So I went down and left my door open. This was not easy for me, as I am always very security conscious. I returned to my room as fast as I could. The airco worked!

There was no remote control for the flat screen TV either, but the next day the other LTOs told me that it didn't matter, since none of the TVs had been connected in any case. In my bathroom, I tried to hang my towel on the brand new aluminium holder, but the entire holder came loose from the wall.

On top of all this, I could not find any electrical sockets to charge my mobile phone. And both my window and my balcony door, only three meters above street level, could not be locked. This was Maputo as I remembered it: nothing works and everything is complicated. I felt at home right away. I love Africa!

That first evening we took a taxi to the Costa do Sol, the famed restaurant at the seashore, some ten kilometres from the city centre. It looked different, but the prawns were still excellent, as the other three LTOs agreed.

Slaveena and Doloroza had never been in Mozambique before, but Tommy and I had lived in Maputo, so we had fond memories of the Costa do Sol. In the old days, a legendary Greek woman had been the owner. She had ruled the place with an iron fist.

In those days, the beach had stretched for at least fifty meters in front of the restaurant, now it was only ten meters. Strange. Was it true then, that sea levels were rising? Anyway: the mixed fish platter, for four persons, was as great as I remembered it.

The briefings went well, but I noted that my Portuguese was still a bit lacking. However, this was mainly due to the fact that several members of the Core Team were Portuguese, who speak a much more complicated Portuguese than the Mozambicans. I realized this, when I visited the Dutch embassy.

I decided to walk to the embassy, to get a feel of the city that I had known so well thirty years previously. I did not have a map of the city, but since I had lived there for three years, I was confident that I could easily find my way around.

I was wrong. I believed the Avenida Lenin, still named after the communist dictator, ran east-west. It didn't. By the time I had reached the far end of the Av. Lenin, I realized that I had traversed the city diagonally.

I had to walk all along the Avenida Kenneth Kaunda, which I didn't mind, since it would bring me past my old office in the UN building. My office, at the corner of the second floor, was still there. But something had changed dramatically.

In the 1980s anyone could enter the building unobstructed. Quite often the receptionist was not even there. Now there were high fences all around the building. And there were guards. Times had changed.

Maputo looked different and yet it looked the same. In the 1980s, when it was communist and there was a civil war going on, there were hardly any cars on the four-lane roads. The shops were empty and the restaurants did not serve anything. Now there were lots of cars and lots of shops, even KFC had arrived in town.

But some things had not changed at all. The pavements were still dusty and riddled with potholes. In the evening the sparse lights of street lanterns was still blocked by the trees. You needed a flash light, even for a short walk.

I also noted that the Mozambicans were still moving slowly. I had always believed this had been because communism caused lethargy, but I was wrong: now that Mozambique had been capitalist for 25 years, they were still moving slowly.

The Dutch ambassador and the first secretary were having meetings, so I spoke one and a half hours with Felizberto, the Political Expert of the embassy. As a Mozambican he was very well informed on the political situation of the country. We spoke Portuguese all the time and I realized, to my relief, that I could still communicate quite easily with Mozambicans.

The second evening we decided to go to an Indian restaurant in two taxis. After only five minutes our taxi halted on one of Maputo's sparsely illuminated streets. The car had ran out of petrol. The driver stepped out with a plastic jerry can. ,,What are you going to do?" I asked him. ,,I am going to the petrol station over there. It's just a few hundred meters."

I was flabbergasted. It was against all our mission's security rules. ,,I have a better idea", I told him. I called the LTOs of the other taxi. They immediately sent their taxi back to pick us up. Our driver indicated by phone to the other driver where we were. He arrived within ten minutes.

The four of us stepped into the other taxi. I paid our first driver his 100 méticais, even though he had taken us just a few blocks from our hotel. I took pity on the old man and in any case: to me it's only 2,5 euros. Communism was a thing of the past, but now many Mozambicans were desperately short on money.

As to our deployment, the CT kept us in the lurch for three days. I secretly hoped that Marta from Portugal would become my partner. I knew her from the legal/election training in April 2009 in Brussels and from my Oruro/Bolivia mission in 2009, when she served on the CT as Election Expert. I liked her.

I knew for sure that my partner would be a woman, since there were 11 female and 9 male LTOs. Some of the other women appeared to be rather complicated characters, to put it nicely.

I decided to think positive, since Johan Cruijff used to say that a negative mind set attracted bad luck. A positive mind set, on the other hand, would attract good luck. As always, Cruijff had been right. To my relief, Marta indeed became my partner.

The bad news was that we were going to be deployed in Tete, the hottest of all Mozambican provincial capitals. Meanwhile, our Chief Observer had arrived. Judith Sargentini was a member of the European Parliament for the Dutch Green Leftist Party.

Judith was very nice. She had been a member of the Amsterdam city council for twelve years and I had been a member of the Enkhuizen town council for eight years, so we talked about Dutch local politics for a while. Unfortunately, Judith could not attend the briefings, since she did not speak Portuguese.

I introduced my new partner, Marta, to Judith in English: ,,Before I came to Mozambique I told everyone that I did not want to go to Tete province and that I did not want a Portuguese partner. But what do I get? Not only do they send me to Tete, but on top of that they give me a Portuguese partner as well." Judith turned to Marta and said: ,,Don't pay any attention to what he says. He's Dutch. Get used to it."

There are direct flights operated by Mozambican Air Lines (LAM) between Maputo and Tete every day, but there was a problem: one of LAM's airplanes had crashed a few months previously, so the UN had blacklisted LAM. Since our EU EOM had to abide by the UN security standards, we were not allowed to fly with LAM.

The only solution was to fly via Johannesburg, South Africa. That meant that we had to spend a night in Johannesburg. Just outside Joburg's airport are a number of reasonably good and reasonably priced hotels, but for security reasons we were obliged by our mission to spend the night at the airport hotel.

At 190 euros a night, this turned out to be one of the most expensive hotels I had ever stayed in. And the hotel did not even have a restaurant! On top of that, the rooms had no windows, since the hotel was based in an underground, bunker-like basement at the airport.

The good news was that the airport hotel had a direct access to the airport's transit area, with lots of shops and restaurants. I managed to buy a good DVD with 'The Gods Must Be Crazy'. The bad news of this nightly stop-over, apart from the expensive hotel, was that we could not retrieve our suitcases.

Unknown to us, our suitcases had been forwarded directly to our final destinations. My suitcase is locked with a figure-lock and also two key locks, so it is nearly impossible for any stranger to open it.

But Marta was not so lucky. At Joburg airport, her photo camera was stolen out of her suitcase. In the old days it was called Jan Smuts Airport, after the white supremacist leader. It was the safest airport in the world. In 2006, it was renamed Oliver Tambo Airport, to honour a leading ANC figure.

Since then, the airport has not been secure at all. Sadly, Marta lost all the photos that had been taken when her son was born, five months earlier. She had not yet transferred the photos to her computer.

All this because we were not allowed to fly with LAM. The story got a little twist, later on. Two embassy staff, an Englishman and a women from Norway, would join us during E-Day as locally recruited STOs.

The British embassy did not allow its staff to fly with LAM, but the Norwegian embassy did not have such a policy. As a result, the Englishman had to spend a night at Joburg airport, while the Norwegian woman travelled directly from Tete to Maputo, just two hours by plane!

In 1986 I had spent two nights in Tete. The only thing I remembered was that it had been unbelievably hot over there. With a UN colleague I slept in an air conditioned room at Tete hospital, where they had a generator that worked. In those days, Tete hardly had any electricity, in spite of the vicinity of the Cahora Bassa dam, the fourth largest dam in Africa.

When Marta and I stepped out of the cute little airport terminal, the brutal heat of Tete hit us like a brick wall. Thank God our driver, João Pedro, was waiting for us and the airco of the car was working. We headed for Masau Lodge, the hotel that had been reserved for us.

I immediately spotted a problem: our hotel was on the wrong bank of the Zambezi river, some five kilometres from the only bridge that was open to traffic. A new bridge was under construction several kilometres upstream, but had not yet been opened.

Masau Lodge was quite new and consisted of air-conditioned containers that had been converted into hotel rooms. It had a nice restaurant with a terrace overlooking the swimming pool and the majestic Zambezi river below. I just hoped the crocs would stay down there.

The owners were very nice too: he had been born on Mauritius and she was a white woman from Zimbabwe. They had a dog, that immediately took a liking to me. It was a great place for tourists, but not for us. We had a job to do and the problem was that we would be totally isolated there during the evenings, when our driver would not be with us.

On top of that, our driver would have a problem, since for security reasons the car would have to stay with us at the hotel overnight, meaning that the driver would have to find a way to get home, across the bridge which was five kilometres away. There were no buses or taxis there. It was the end of the world.

So the next day we told the owners that we regretted that we had to check out and find a place to stay on the other side of the bridge, near the town centre. Nelson, the owner of the car company, accompanied us on our quest to find suitable accommodation, that was not too expensive.

He was a nice guy and very helpful in checking out apartments. We knew, of course, that he would receive a commission from the owner. As usual, I told my partner to do the negotiations, since I am a terrible negotiator. We checked out three apartments.

One was a decent, quiet place, with functioning air-conditioners, but unfortunately it was a bit too far from the town centre. In the afternoon, Marta and I paid a visit to the Hotel Zambeze. It's location was ideal: in the centre of town. But the tourist guides were quite negative: guests had reported a very noisy place with unfriendly staff.

To be honest, the hotel was not too bad. The staff was quite helpful and showed us several rooms, including suites that were not noisy at all. We sat down with the Indian manager in his air conditioned office.

Marta explained that we would stay for at least one month and that we also expected several STOs to stay at the hotel for shorter periods. I asked if he could offer us a package deal: a two-room suite, that could be used as a room for Marta and also as our office, and a small separate hotel room for me.

,,No problem", he replied. He remained friendly while Marta negotiated the price down. And down it went. It turned out that it would be cheaper for us to stay at the Hotel Zambeze than in an apartment. In the end, I joked that if the price went down even further, the manager would have to pay us for staying at his hotel.

When we left, we told him that we would seriously consider his final offer. In the afternoon we visited the Paraíso Misterioso, owned by a Lebanese family. The hotel looked out on the Zambezi river and was situated less than two hundred meters from the bridge. Ismael, the young general manager showed us a few rooms, which looked quite OK.

Then he said that the hotel also owned an apartment, just across the street. We immediately liked it. Yet again, Marta negotiated the price down. There was only one problem: the place had not been used for many months and everything was covered under a thick layer of dust.

But Ismael assured us that he would set the cleaners to work immediately and that we could move in that same evening at 20.00 hours. In the meantime, we could stay in one of the vacant hotel rooms.

We used the time to start working on our first Weekly Report. In the end, it took the cleaners a little bit longer. At 22.30 hours we finally got the green light that we could move in. A very nice apartment with a kitchen, a huge refrigerator and air-conditioners that actually worked.

I allowed Marta to choose her bedroom first: she decided to stay in the one looking out at the main street. I took the one at the backside. I was lucky. Marta's room was set alight by passing cars all through the night and she could not sleep from the bloody noise. The next day I gave her some of my earplugs. But I did not offer her to swap rooms.

We installed the mission's laptop and the printer at the table in the central room. A huge flat screen TV set gave us lots of digital channels. The only problem was that there was no TV-guide and the channels were numbered at random. I had to scroll through hundreds of channels. It took me three days to find BBC World and CNN.

It was a very safe apartment, since there was only one key, as we found out the hard way. I usually kept the key, but one day Marta was in a hurry to leave our apartment. She grabbed the keys from the table and stuck them in the door. We went around interviewing people all day.

By the time we finally got back to our apartment, I realized to my horror that I could not find the keys. It struck me that the keys were probably still in the apartment. Our driver had already left. There we stood. Marta was angry at me, even though it was partly her fault.

I suggested to go the restaurant of Paraíso Misterioso, just across the street, since we had not eaten anything either. Luckily, we had brought the laptop with us, so we could do some work. Marta sat down in the restaurant and I went to the reception, to ask for a spare set of keys.

At the reception I had to wait fifteen minutes, before someone showed up. The girl called Ismael. Again fifteen minutes of waiting. When Ismael finally arrived, he told me that there were no spare keys. That was good news, since no one could enter without us knowing about it.

But it was also bad news: how were we going to get back inside our apartment? By now, it was already 22.00 hours. Most Africans are fast asleep at this hour. Luckily, in Africa people are creative: they usually find a solution. Ismael told me he would call a technician, who could probably figure out a way to open the door.

I gave him Marta's telephone number and told him that Marta and I were sitting in the restaurant. By the time I finally got back to the restaurant, Marta was eating a pizza and working on the laptop at the same time.

At that moment, an idea struck me: it was quite possible that our keys were stuck in the inside of the wooden door, where Marta had left them. If this was the case, than the wooden door was not locked completely, but just closed. The outer door, consisting of thick iron bars, was certainly locked, as I always simply closed the padlock.

But I could easily put my hands through the gaps in the outer door. Next, I could hopefully slide one of my credit cards through the side of the inner door, thus unlocking it. I went back to the apartment and, to my own amazement, it worked. The wooden door opened instantly. I carefully felt for the keys and yes: there they were!

I took them out, locked the door again and returned to the restaurant. Triumphantly I threw the keys in front of Marta on the table. She phoned the technician to explain that his services weren't needed anymore. Her anger had subsided. We were friends again.

I hate to admit it, but Marta was smarter than me and more energetic than me. She was also better with modern apparatuses. And, obviously, her Portuguese was infinitely better than mine. Luckily, even though she lived in Canberra with her Australian husband, my English was slightly better than hers, so I did most of the typing.

And I had my previous STO manuals on my laptop, that we could use as examples for our STO manual, so I could make myself useful, to some extent. There was one thing that I was better at than Marta:

I had more patience. This may sound funny, but if there's one thing you need in Africa, it's patience.

And you'd better not be a vegetarian in Africa. This was a bit of a problem, since Marta was in fact a vegetarian. Not because she was particularly fond of animals, but because she believed that she would live longer if she did not eat meat.

Apparently she had obtained this idea from her father, who had been a general practitioner on Madeira, the Portuguese island, where also the world's best footballer, Cristiano Ronaldo, came from. Since we shared an apartment, I had become a vegetarian too, to some extent.

Marta was a good cook. We ate lots of olives with feta cheese and vegetables. Every other day she would cook a mix of vegetables, after which she blended it all into a thick soup. I had never seen this way of cooking before, but it was very healthy and tasty, especially when I spiced it up with pepper or Tabasco.

After about a week, Marta told me that her family had lived in Mozambique for at least 40 years. In Nampula, central Mozambique. She was afraid to tell this to the Mozambicans, but I assured her that they would love to hear this. After all: when the Portuguese were in charge, everything had been much better than after 1975, when Mozambican communists took control of the country.

The first time Marta told Mozambicans about her family's history in Nampula, she was nervous. But as I predicted, the locals were delighted. „That means that you are one of us", they exclaimed. „We have a shared history."

After we had finished writing our reports for the day, I sat down on our balcony at the quiet backside of the house. Usually, this was after 22.00 hours. There, I enjoyed one of my Dutch cigars and a very nice Mozambican brown ale: Laurentina Preta. It tasted great, just like my favourite Newcastle Brown Ale.

Marta also liked this beer the best. I just wish we had a lovely beer like this in The Netherlands. We have Heineken, Amstel, Bavaria, Grolsch and lots of imported beers, but no Laurentina Preta.

There are two other things available in Mozambique, that are the best in the world: first there are the giant prawns, fresh from the sea and deliciously barbecued. No sauce needed. Secondly: the Mozambican samosas, filled with tasty minced meat. They have a particular taste, rather different from the original samosas from India.

By accident, I stumbled upon them in town, close to the bridge. We had seen the bakery there, when we drove by. We decided to buy fresh bread, but I entered the wrong door. I found myself inside a small restaurant, with a separate counter where they sold food items to take away.

I immediately spotted the samosas. ,,Give me five of them", I told the girl behind the counter. According to Marta, the samosas contained meat and because of that my life would be shortened by several years. I replied that I didn't care if I would drop dead instantly: I was going to eat my delicious samosas, and to hell with everything else.

In the evenings on the balcony, I was bitten by mosquitoes several times. I believed that there was hardly any malaria in Tete, but a few days later we had an appointment with a local government guy. His wife told us that the meeting had to be cancelled, because he lay in bed with malaria.

This prompted me to visit a pharmacy. The elderly Portuguese owner gave me pills that I had never heard of, but he assured me that they worked against malaria, especially in Tete. They were very small pills. Much smaller than the Malarone pills that I usually took. For some reason, I believe that bigger pills are better.

But I had no choice, so I bought the small pills. My wife and I had been stricken with malaria in 1982, when we hitchhiked from Holland to Zimbabwe. We stayed with a Dutch missionary at the time, in the jungle of Gabon, close to the border with Congo Brazzaville. Malaria is like the flu, but ten times worse, so from then on I did everything to prevent it. Successfully. I never had malaria again.

Even when you take pills against malaria, mosquito bites itch like hell. So I asked Marta if I could sit in the kitchen, which was open on three sides, but protected by mosquito nets. She had no objections. From then on I sat in the little kitchen with a beer and a cigar. I was never bitten again.

Our driver, Joâo Pedro, was a grumpy guy. On top of that, he arrived late, quite a few times. And he did not answer our phone calls. He told us that his mobile phone did not work, but in between his driving, he was always talking on his phone. After a week we had had enough.

Marta called Nelson, the owner of the car company, and asked for another driver. The next day Lucas was sitting in the driver's seat. He was not the smartest man I had ever seen, but at least he was cheerful. He always greeted us with a big smile. And he arrived usually on time. I liked him.

The three major parties had offices in the city of Tete. We visited all of them on a regular basis. Frelimo had a large, well-organized office, with air conditioned rooms. Renamo had a very small office, that was not air conditioned and rather smelly, since the toilet door could not be closed.

Renamo consisted mostly of elderly men, some of whom hardly spoke decent Portuguese. MDM had a small office at the other side of the bridge. MDM's staff were smart young men, but they lacked funds. Obviously, the ruling party, Frelimo, had the advantage here.

Of course, we also visited the electoral authorities on a regular basis. In Mozambique, CNE (*Commissão Nacional de Eleições*) is the leading electoral body, but the administrative and logistic work is carried out by STAE (*Secretariado* Técnico de *Administração Eleitoral*). Both organizations have offices at provincial and district levels.

In most cases, CNE and STAE communicate well with one another. Even though CNE is the leading organization, they lack resources, while STAE possesses plenty of staff, vehicles and computers. This creates frictions, sometimes. The STAE director at provincial or district level might consider him/herself as more efficient than the rather bureaucratic CNE.

We were not the only long term observers in Tete. Every now and then we would bump into Celestino from Angola and Antonetta from Zimbabwe. They were LTOs for the Electoral Institute for Southern Africa (EISA). They were a pleasant couple.

Celestino was a big, cheerful guy. Antonetta was always happy to meet me, since she didn't speak one word of Portuguese and most Mozambicans don't speak English. With me, she could communicate in English.

The funny thing was that they were election observers in a country that changed its president every eight years, while their own presidents had been in power for more than thirty years. Speaking of democracy!

With Marta I spoke English all the time, which made life easier for me. During meetings with local people, we spoke Portuguese of course. My Portuguese was certainly good enough for this mission, but it did cost me quite a bit of energy, even though the Mozambicans speak a sort of simplified Portuguese.

One evening, we received visitors in our apartment. A Brazilian couple. This meant that I really had to pay attention to every word that was said: one Portuguese and two Brazilians speaking fast Portuguese. On top of that, the air conditioner was quite noisy. Later, Marta told me that she thought I participated rather well in the conversations.

I believed I had missed half of what was said. One thing was quite funny though: I asked the couple where they lived in Brazil. ,,We live in a city that you have probably never heard of", they replied. ,,Try me", I told them. ,,My wife and I have travelled all around Brazil." They said that they lived in Salvador.

,,Salvador de Bahía?" I asked. They looked at me in astonishment. ,,Have you heard of it?" I laughed. ,,Much better. I have been there. I remember the colourful houses in the city centre, where the author Jorge Amado used to live. My wife and I even visited a *favela* at the outskirts of Salvador, since we believed that it was safer over there than the slums of Rio de Janeiro."

My wife and I noted that poor Brazilians did not have air conditioners, nor did they have fridges, but in every house stood an enormous TV-set. The two Brazilians explained to me that for Brazilians a TV-set is by far the most important thing in the world. ,,The men watch football and the women watch telenovelas. They can't live without it."

Back to work. One very hot day, it was 42 degrees Celsius, we were informed by MDM party that they would be campaigning in the Mateus Sansaô Muthembe suburb, where the poor people live. The MDM campaign consisted of one pick-up with about fifteen youngsters.

Normally, the local authorities tried to keep the three campaigns separate, to avoid tensions, but to our surprise, Frelimo was campaigning in the same suburb as MDM. Frelimo arrived with lots of vehicles and police cars. There was a good reason for this, since the future first lady, Madam Nyusi, was participating. I made lots of photos: you don't see a first lady every day in a poor suburb.

On Sunday 5 October we visited Cateme in Moatize. The new agricultural year would be officially opened by Guebuza, the president of Mozambique. As usual, the ordinary spectators had to wait for the dignitaries. Five hours, in this case.

I was quite prepared for this, but to Marta the long waiting was sheer torture. She is good at many things, but there's one thing that I do better: waiting patiently. Luckily, as always, I had brought my thermos flask with coffee with me.

We decided to pay a visit to Angonia the next day, where we would send an STO team. In preparation, we had filled the tank and Lucas parked our car, as always, at the protected parking lot of Paraíso Misterioso for the night. Then Lucas called us. He said that he could not close the electric windows of the car and that the engine wouldn't start anymore.

He had also been called by our Service Provider from Maputo, but he didn't understand what the phone call was about. Then it dawned on me: probably the SP had blocked our car. I remember that they had done the same during my Kenya mission.

I called our Security Expert, Jean-Michel, and yes: he confirmed that the SP had blocked our car, to check if the remote control worked. Well, it worked so well that the next morning our car battery was completely dead. I asked Jean-Michel never to do a funny thing like that again.

It was a good asphalt road to Angonia, that for several kilometres was constructed on Malawian soil. Angonia sits at an altitude, so it's much cooler there than in Tete City. We visited all the usual suspects. At CDE, not the male president did the talking, but the female vice-president. Later, in the car, Lucas told us out of the blue that she was his sister!

At STAE a multitude was blocking the entrance. We talked to several of them and they explained that they were all polling staff, that they had received two days of training and that now they were waiting for their 400 méticais remuneration.

It was chaotic: all of a sudden they had to hand over a 'Fit to Work' declaration as well as a declaration of 'Good Behaviour'. No one had ever told them about these requirements before.

We told them that we were observers and that we could not interfere on their behalf. We decided to visit the offices of Renamo and MDM first and after that return to STAE. Two hours later, the multitude was still there.

When they noticed us stepping out of our car, they applauded. It was a bit awkward, but it helped solve de deadlock. Disturbed by all the commotion, the Director of STAE came out of his office to explain to the multitude that all of them would receive their money.

There was one nasty incident. For Marta, that is. A few days later we were interviewed by Radio Mozambique in Tete City. At one point, Rigoberta, the cheerful interviewer, asked about our expectations for E-Day. ,,We hope that there will not be any violence", Marta replied.

I stiffened on my chair. We are not supposed to make such qualifications, since it could be interpreted that we were expecting violence. I hoped that it would be a simple local radio broadcast, but I was wrong.

The next day Marta was called by Sylvia, the Portuguese Press Officer of our EU EOM. Marta should not have made a remark about possible violence. Later that evening, when we arrived in our apartment, there was an email from Tony, our Deputy Chief Observer, who was also Portuguese.

He wrote that Marta had 'seriously breached the Code of Conduct'. I knew that Marta had made a mistake, but it was a small mistake, that could happen if you work long days in the bloody heat of Tete province. A few days later, Tony was a lot milder. The crisis was over.

I did most of the typing for our STO manual. Marta added our own photographs to the text. She was happy with the result. When Marta is happy, I am happy. We were going to have one STO and one LSTO team. The STO team lost a full day, since they had to sleep at Joburg Airport. We decided to send them straight to Angonia, where they would stay until after E-Day.

Since the five-star Park Inn/Radisson hotel was close to Tete's airport and close to the road to Angonia, we decided to brief them there. They were nice, they were young and they spoke decent Portuguese: Michal from Poland and Ivona. I have forgotten from which eastern European country she was. The briefing went well. They were eager to depart.

The only problem was that nobody had told their driver, Eugenio, that he was going away for three days. Just one day earlier, we found out that the STO driver would be João Pedro, our first driver that we had fired two weeks earlier. Marta called Nelson from the car company and explained that we could not accept this. He promised to send another driver.

Nelson had also forgotten to give the driver money for a hotel. Marta called Nelson, who arrived within an hour with a suitcase for Eugenio and some money. All problems solved. Well: most of the problems were solved. We found out that the backdoor of the land cruiser could not be locked.

Nelson assured us that this was not a big problem. Nothing would happen in Angonia. Africans are not as fussy as Europeans about these things. In the end, Nelson had been right: nothing happened in Angonia, except for a telephone call that we received from our mission's security expert.

In our STO vehicle, someone had pushed the panic button. I immediately called Michael. He confirmed that they had accidentally pushed the panic button. A beginners mistake, but at least he was honest. It could happen to anyone.

One day later, our LSTOs arrived. Gareth from the British embassy and Camilla from the Norwegian embassy, were staying at the Park

Inn/Radisson. We briefed them there and handed them our STO manuals.

They were cooperative and eager to do a good observation job. In the evening, we took them to Masau Lodge. We had a good time, together. After their return to Maputo, both of them were very positive about us during their debriefings with our Core Team.

Two days after our STOs had returned to Maputo, we received an email. Our STO Ivona had been assaulted at 16.00 hours on the Avenida Julius Nyerere, close to hotel Polana. I was astounded.

In the 1980s, this would have been unthinkable. Maputo was the safest capital in the world. Obviously, things had changed. Ivona had been threatened with a knife and ordered to hand over her valuables. Other than that, she escaped unhurt.

Very few tourists ever visit the Cahora Bassa dam. First of all, very few tourists ever visit Tete province. And second of all, if you want to visit the fourth largest dam in Africa, you are obliged to apply for a visitors permit at the office of the Dam Authority, situated in an unobtrusive back street in the town of Tete.

You don't have to pay an entrance fee, but the processing of the permit takes ten days. Tourists can't wait for ten days. But we could. And so we travelled to the dam. For some reason, Lucas took a road full of potholes.

Two weeks earlier, we had visited the town of Cahora Bassa with Joâo Pedro, and the road had been good. I was annoyed at Lucas. I asked him why he had taken this bad road. As is the custom in Africa, he mumbled something that I could not understand.

In spite of all this, we arrived at the dam. There, we had to wait half an hour for our escort. He was a nice Brazilian guy. We left Lucas behind and stepped over in the Brazilian's car.

The dam is an incredible sight. It's huge. And now I understood why the white Rhodesian pilots did not manage to bomb it: the dam had been constructed in a small, winding gorge, with mountain peaks on all sides.

We were obliged to wear protective head covers. We were allowed to take photographs of the outside, but not of the inside of the dam, which was even more impressive.

In a giant concrete hall, six enormous pipes rotated at great speed, powered by the gravity of the water. Inside, it looked like one of those giant German bunkers of WWII. That's one of the advantages of being an observer: you get to see things few people ever see.

The day before we were supposed to return to Maputo, Marta's mother got sick. Marta asked the Core Team if she would be permitted to fly straight back to Portugal from Johannesburg, without having to go back to Maputo.

Normally, all observers return to the Core Team for debriefings, to hand in the mission materials and to receive their individual evaluations. At first, the Core Team did not allow her to skip these obligations. It would set a precedence.

But Marta contacted an acquaintance of hers in Brussels. An hour later, she obtained the green light to fly back to Portugal from Johannesburg. This meant that I had to carry all our mission materials back to Maputo.

On top of that, while Marta boarded a plane to Europe straight away, I had to sleep another night at that expensive airport hotel. It was obligatory to sleep there. Michael, one of our STOs, had slept on a couch in the airport, to save money, but had been harshly reprimanded for it by the Core Team.

The next morning, I arrived at Maputo Airport, loaded with luggage, only to discover that my big suitcase had not arrived yet again. For the second time on this mission, I arrived at the Maputo Hotel without my big suitcase!

The good news was that most other LTOs would arrive later that night, so I had the rest of the day to myself. I decided to go to Hotel Polana, the fanciest hotel in Maputo, with a great view of the Indian ocean.

It was still a great place. In the communist days of the 1980s, there were hardly any tourists and very few businessmen. In fact, the only real business was development aid, so UN and embassy consultants were staying in Hotel Polana sometimes. But most of the time, the hotel had been practically deserted.

We, ordinary aid workers, had the swimming pool to ourselves. Now the hotel was reasonably occupied, as far as I could tell. I sat down at the terrace overlooking the swimming pool, with the ocean beyond it, and ordered a fabulous shrimp salad. Life is good in Africa, as long as you have money.

As always, Frelimo won the elections with 57 percent of the votes. Filipe Nyusi would be their president for the next eight years. My suitcase arrived and I obtained a good evaluation. Our STOs and LSTOs had been very positive about us. I travelled back with several other observers via Addis Ababa and Vienna to Amsterdam.

All in all, it had been a great mission. Marta had been one of my best partners and Tete was not so bad, after all. The only problem in Tete is that it's 42 degrees Celsius there, every day.

And there are no Goofy's. My wife understood this. She had lived with me in Mozambique for three years during the communist days. In our memory, Mozambique would forever be a country with empty shops.

Chapter 19

GUINEA - 2015

'Because of ebola, you're not allowed to visit hospitals or funerals'

After four long-term missions in 2013 and 2014, I needed a bit of a break. Physically, the missions are not demanding, but mentally they are quite stressful. Especially since I am required to be social at all times.

There's no escape: if I don't answer my phone, my colleagues are obliged to call our security expert. The security expert will then call my partner, our driver or even our hotel, to make sure that I'm OK.

So at the start of 2015, I was in a comfortable position: I could wait for an interesting mission. Little did I know that this year the ministry would only offer me French speaking missions. I had never been offered a French speaking mission before!

I speak seven languages, but French sits at the very bottom of that list. On top of that, there's only one people in the world that I really dislike: the French. And in a French speaking mission there are, by definition, lots of French from France.

To be honest, my wife and I met some nice French people in the countryside of Normandy and Bretagne. But Paris and the other big cities: that's something else. They are usually quite arrogant and they speak very fast French, without any consideration for basic French speakers, like me.

I also dislike the French language. At secondary school, I studied English, German and French for five years. It wasn't easy for me, since in those days the teachers concentrated on the grammar, instead of conversation.

Many years later I lived in a Mexican village for five months, for my university thesis on small-scale irrigation, and to my surprise I found out that I was conversing in Spanish with the villagers within just a few days. Without much of an effort. So I was able to master conversation in foreign languages. I was just hopeless at that stupid grammar.

To make matters worse, my French teacher at secondary school had a nasty streak. He was one hundred percent Dutch, but he looked French and he treated me French. He still gives me nightmares.

Even so, when my wife and I hitchhiked from Holland to Zimbabwe in 1982, just after we finished our studies, we spent a total of five months in Tunesia, Algeria, Niger, Cameroun, Gabon, Congo Brazzaville and Congo Kinshasa. And years later, when we lived in The Gambia, I spent several weeks in Senegal.

I knew therefore that my French was good enough to communicate with Africans. Africans speak simplified versons of French, English, Portuguese and Spanish, which suits me just fine.

The ministry offered me Burundi, Burkina Faso and Haiti. I had heard too many negative stories about Haiti, so I didn't want to go there. Burundi and Burkina Faso were not so bad, but I decided to wait for a non-French speaking mission.

For a good reason. Two of my partners on previous missions had received rather negative evaluations at the end of their ill-fated French speaking missions. Both Peter, from Austria, and Nena, from Slovenia, were coerced by their governments to go on a French speaking mission.

In Austria and Slovenia, like in The Netherlands, there are simply not enough observers who speak decent French. They did not want to go, but in the end they decided to be cooperative and do it.

As a result, both received a negative 'recommended-but' evaluation from their EU EOM, stating that their knowledge of the mission's working language needed improvement. Well folks: that was exactly the reason why they did not want to go on a French speaking mission in the first place!

Now I was in the same position as Peter and Nena: my own ministry offered me only French speaking missions, thus forcing me to accept one, but I knew that there was a good chance that I would receive a negative evaluation from the EU EOM at the end of the mission.

In the end, it was a good thing that I did not accept the Burundi mission, since the entire EU EOM was called back to Europe, after just a few weeks. Apparently, the president of Burundi had decided to run for an unlawful third period (the first period he had not been elected, but appointed, so he himself thought that he been elected only once and therefore could legally run one more time).

The Burundian opposition candidates pulled out of the elections. As a result of all this, the EU decided to cancel the entire mission. The EU only observes serious elections, and rightly so. But as an observer, it's terrible if you have to return home after just a few weeks and without having observed the elections.

In Burkina Faso the presidential guard, loyal to the ousted dictator Blaise Compaoré, staged a coupe d'état, just weeks before the elections. The army stepped in, after which the presidential guard retreated to their barracks. In this case, the EU decided to field an EU EOM, even though expectations for credible elections were rather limited.

Anyway, in July 2015 I received an urgent email from my ministry. They could not find a long term observer, nor a short term observer, for Guinea in West-Africa, also known as Guinée Conakry. This was not surprising, since on the website of the Dutch Ministry of Foreign Affairs the advice was given not to travel to Guinea, unless you absolutely had to.

The main reason was the risk of ebola, but it was also because Guinea is one of the least developed countries in Africa. The roads and railways, originally constructed by the French colonisers, have deteriorated to the lowest of the lowest levels after decades of neglect.

On top of that, your western bank card is quite useless in the country, so you need to carry large amounts of cash with you. Now the same ministry that was discouraging people to travel to Guinea was asking me to go to Guinea. To an ebola country!

Maybe I should not have mentioned on my CV that my French was 'reasonable'. Well, in truth, my French is quite reasonable, but would it be good enough for a positive EU EOM evaluation at the end of the mission? My wife encouraged me to just go for it. Since I am an obedient husband, I concurred.

I wrote an email to my Focal Point at the ministry, stating that I was willing to go to Guinea, but rather as a Short Term Observer than as a Long Term Observer, since my French was not good enough to write reports in flawless French.

Before I knew it, I was proposed to the EU as an STO for Guinea and just a few days later I received word from Brussels that I had been selected by the EU as well. So for the first time in nearly twenty years I was going to be an STO, instead of an LTO. A bit humiliating, but I had to swallow my pride.

I had not spoken French in 23 years, so I started practicing my French immediately. Three hours per day, for a period of two months, including weekends. I read Le Monde and Jeune Afrique on the internet, I did internet courses on the TV5Monde website, I read the teletext of Arte TV in French.

I listened to French music while reading the text at the same time. I rediscovered some French folk groups and singers, that I had not listened to since the 1970s, when I possessed a large collection of international folk music.

There was a little problem here, since most of my favourite musicians were from Bretagne. As a result, my Bretons became almost as good as my French (with special thanks to Tri Yann, Nolwen Leroy and Alan Stivell).

I really felt that my French was improving, but it was still a long way from being as good as my English, Spanish and Portuguese. Then I was invited to the Dutch ministry, for a pre-mission briefing, together with the only Dutch LTO, Alberto. He had been born in Italy, but grew up in Holland and possessed a Dutch passport. A likable lad.

The Guinea country expert at the ministry had set up a video link with the Dutch embassy, which was based in Dakar, Senegal. In Guinea, Holland only had a consulate. The acting ambassadrice and an embassy employee called Joost pointed out a number of things about Guinea to us.

Then it became clear that Joost would become a Locally Recruited Short Term Observer (LSTO), meaning that he would travel to Conakry and work with our mission as an STO, just like me.

We had to explain to him how EU EOMs operated and since it was Alberto's very first mission as an LTO, I had to do the explaining.

But Joost was a pleasant chap. No problems there. We would exchange emails for weeks to come.

On the way back home, Alberto joined me in the train to Amsterdam. I explained to him how things worked in the observer world. Many things he didn't know, like the fact that our cars were equipped with tracking systems, so that our security experts could follow us on their computer screens.

I also explained that they could switch off our engines from behind their computers. And that our drivers were called every other day, to ask not only if the vehicle was allright, but also if the team was allright. In other words: were there frictions within the team? ,,It sounds a bit like Big Brother to me", Alberto remarked.

With Burundi in mind, I feared for many weeks that our Guinea mission would be called off at the last minute, and that my hard work on mastering French would have been to little or no avail. But the Core Team arrived in Conakry and a week later the LTOs arrived in Conakry.

By now, I had received an email that I would be based in a small town called Télimélé, at the foothills of the Fouta Djalon mountains. And my partner would be Marie, a Belgian woman.

Then it was the turn of the STOs to travel to Conakry. Unfortunately, there was a problem. Only two European airlines operate regular flights to Conakry: Air France and Brussels Airways. Their flights, three times a week, were usually fully booked. On top of that, the Air France crews were threatening to go on strike!

In fact, the Air France crews had been on strike just six months previously, costing their company around half a billion euros. In Holland, we're not used to strikes, since everyone realizes that you should not put your own company at risk. When your company goes broke, everyone loses their jobs!

So in Holland, we're used to negotiating. Not so in France. They don't care about their companies. We were supposed to travel with Air France on Monday 5 October, but at first the tickets were changed to Sunday 4 October. A few days later, the tickets were changed to Tuesday 6 October. No reason was given.

For me, as a seasoned observer, this was completely normal EU behaviour, but some of my first-time colleague STOs found all of this quite disturbing. One STO, from Luxembourg, sent an email, copied to all of us, asking for an explanation, but—as usual--none was given.

So I had to fly to Brussels from Amsterdam, departing at 06.50 hours, which meant that I had to get up at 03.30 hours and my wife had to drive me to Schiphol airport, since the first train from my hometown of Enkhuizen would only depart at 06.00 hours.

The flight to Brussels takes only 45 minutes. At Brussels Airport, I had to wait three hours. I sat down near the departure gate of the flight to Conakry. I had studied the list of 26 STOs and I had concluded that I did not know any of them. But then a cheerful young fellow walked up to me and shouted my name: 'Hey, Jos'.

I did not recognize him. I have to admit: this has happened to me many times before. I have difficulty remembering faces, especially when I meet people in unfamiliar situations. The young guy shook my hand and sat down next to me.

I asked him who he was. He replied: 'I am Michal, from Poland. I was your STO, just one year ago in Tete, Mozambique'. He was right, of course. He had been a pleasant fellow and an enthusiastic STO, but I had hardly seen him, since we had sent him straight to a far-off district.

The flight to Conakry took six hours. I managed to sleep a bit, but then we made a stop at Dakar, Senegal. Most Africans left the plane there. I stood up and looked around, hoping to be able to identify some of the other STOs. But there is a problem: STOs look just like anybody else.

I spotted several young western women, who looked OK to me. One women looked quite domineering, she was a bit older than the others. I hoped that she would not be Marie. But of course, after landing at Conakry airport, I learned that she actually was Marie.

But Marie would turn out to be one of my best partners ever. She instinctively realized that I worried about my French, so Marie took on the role of protector: as a francophone Belgian from the town of Namur in Wallonie, French was her mothertongue.

Marie took the lead in all conversations that we had to undertake in French. And I would do my best to support her in any other way. In private, we talked English, so I could relax a bit.

It was her very first mission as an observer, but she had lived in Africa for a total of twelve years. Not only that: she had worked in the most difficult places: Somalia, Sierra Leone, Central African Republic, Congo, and so on. She was small in size, but she was a tough cooky.

Mary had worked on humanitarian missions and she had personally negotiated with rebel leaders. Several of her co-workers had been abducted and even raped. I had lived in Africa for nearly seven years, but I had never known anyone who had been abducted or raped.

The other good news was that she told me she was living together with a woman. I immediately sent an SMS to my wife with this good news. My wife is always afraid that, one day, I would elope with one of my female partners.

In truth, I keep intimate conversation with my partners to an absolute minimum, since I don't want to bothered by all kinds of personal problems. But in this case, Marie truly was a lesbian and therefore no threat to my wife.

Marie and I formed a great team. In Africa it is important that you treat your driver and your interpreter with respect, but you must also make sure that they know that they work for us and not the other way around.

The driver and the interpreter must understand that they must always be on time, since we cannot wait for them. But we should also maintain a good relationship, because if all hell breaks out in Africa, you really need your driver and your interpreter to be on your side. Both Marie and myself understood all of this perfectly.

After arriving at the Palm Camayenne Hotel in Conakry at about 19.00 hours, the STOs were not allowed to go to their rooms. Instead, we were ordered to pick up all our stuff first: one big metal box for each team, plus the satphone, tablet, medical kit, petty cash and visibility kit. I managed to ask for a trolley (*chariot* in my best French) and a hotel guy helped me to stash everything in my room.

Then we went to eat, since the hotel was all-included for us. There was only seat left free, when I arrived, so I found myself sitting between a number of quite young STOs, most of whom had little experience. They were surprised when Michal, my Polish STO from Mozambique, told them that I had done lots of missions as an LTO.

I was immediately bombarded with questions. We spoke English, since about half of the STOs were not really fluent in French. Like me. We were still talking animatedly, when I noted that at the other table everyone had retreated to their rooms, except Marie. I waved at her to come and join us, which she did. I knew there and then that she would be a good partner.

Since we had arrived one day later than originally planned, the Core Team had decided to concentrate two days of briefings into one day. They skipped the historical, political and cultural parts, and instead concentrated on the practical information that we needed to do our work properly. I had already done a lot of reading on Guinea, to practice my French, so I was well-prepared in any case.

We had been told that there were no shops in our Areo of Observation, so Marie and I visited a supermarket near the hotel. We purchased plenty of mineral water and canned food, just in case. In Africa you can buy bananas and other tropical fruits and vegetables at every street corner, but Marie and I decided better to be safe than sorry. You don't want to be hit by AWA: Africa Wins Again.

As usual, a reception was held for the STOs and EU embassy staff that evening, I briefly talked to Joost, from the Dutch embassy in Dakar, who joined our mission as an LSTO, together with nine other embassy staff from EU embassies in Conakry.

It was his first ever mission as an election observer and he was very excited. His partner would be a German embassy chap, based in Conakry, who had a car and knew Conakry very well.

The next morning, the STO teams would all depart from the hotel at 07.30 hours, with Guinean TV crews filming us. But two teams were ordered to leave earlier, since they had to drive nearly all day. One of those two teams was ours. I told Marie that this was good news, since we would avoid the Guinean journalists.

Our driver, Yaya, arrived at 06.15 hours, nearly on time, and within minutes we were on our way to Kindia, where our LTO team would give us their regional briefing. Since we were very early, the badly maintained roads of Conakry were not extremely congested, yet it took us nearly two hours to get out of the sprawled-out city.

At 10.00 we reached Kindia. Marie sat in the front seat and guided Yaya to the hotel, just outside the center of town. I was a little afraid that Claude, the French LTO, would speak very fast French. And since most French speak very bad English, I would be forced to speak French with him.

Anne was German. I was not afraid of her, even though I soon realized that her French was much better than mine. When we were alone for a few minutes, I talked German with her. She told me that she came from Eastern Germany, the region between Dresden and Leipzig.

All in all, the the regional briefing with Claude and Marie went well. I hid behind Marie, who instinctively took the lead. I could understand Claude quite well. The main problem was that he talked in a rather low, monotonous voice, while the TV set was very noisy. When I tried to turn down the volume, I accidently switched off the entire TV, provoking a nasty growl from the hotel manager.

Then we all drove into the center of Kindia, to change our euros into Guinean francs. For some reason, Marie had not wanted to change money in Conakry, so now the four of us, accompanied by the LTO driver, walked under the hot African sun towards the market.

I had to carry my bag with the satphone and everything, because I could not leave it in the car. Drivers sometimes leave the doors unlocked while they go out for a cup of tea. Better to be safe than sorry.

Inside a small and very hot shop, the owner was willing to change our money at the rate of 9.400 GF to one euro. In Conakry, the rate had been 9.300 GF to the euro, so I really did not understand why we were sweating and putting ourselves at risk for such a little difference.

And we were also losing about 45 minutes, that we should have spent on the road. Anyway: we both changed 300 euros, after which the LTO driver, to our amazement, started counting the 2.820.000 GF that we received in 5.000 billets (one 5.000 billet is worth approximately 50 eurocents). Talking about hyper inflation.

The next problem was that Yaya, our driver, had never been to Kindia and did not know where the exit to Télimélé might possibly be. But the LTO driver pointed it out and so, finally, we were on our way. Little did we know that we would not see any asphalt roads for the next eight days.

Nor would we see any other whites. In Télimélé, we occasionally saw one Chinese guy on a motorbike, though. We never talked to him, but someone told us that he was there to make preparations for a road construction project.

It would be another six hours on a winding dirt road with lots of potholes. I tried to read the STO manual, but it was impossible: the car was bumping up and down all the time. It was quite funny that Yaya, our driver, asked the way several times, while Marie and I knew from the rudimentary map that there was only one road to Télimélé.

You simply could not get it wrong! But Africans never read maps. Another funny thing was that, apparently, we were very popular with the villagers along the road. The children waved at us and shouted: 'Vote, Vote'. I waved back cheerfully at them, as though I was Prince Charles.

I had just learned that Polling Station in French is 'Bureau de Vote' and our vehicle had EU EOM visibility on the front and on the sides, so I thought that they were calling us 'Election Observer' in Fulani. But Yaya explained that 'Vote' means 'White Person' in Fulani. It is not a negative word, quite the contrary.

In The Gambia a westerner is called 'Tubab', which means the same as 'Vote'. It is in fact a positive denomination; a white person in Africa is authomatically regarded as belonging to the top one percent of society, with all the privileges that come with that position.

For example: I can walk straight into any Hilton Hotel in Africa, even when I am dressed casual. Nobody will ever try to stop me. But a black African, even when dressed in an expensive suit and tie, will be stopped and asked what business he has in that Hilton Hotel.

Marie sat in the front seat and asked if it was OK not to use the airco of the car. I said that I liked airco's, but that it was OK with me to open the windows. So when we finally arrived at the small hilltop town called Télimélé, just before dark, I was completely covered in red dust.

There was only one hotel: Petit Palais, meaning Small Palace. Well folks: it wasn't exactly a palace. Or maybe it was, in African eyes. In any case, the hotel rooms, with a balcony on the first floor overlooking the hotel car park, were OK. I took the big room, which was a bit more expensive.

Then we left Marie at the hotel. Yaya and I drove out in search of beer. He had never been in Télimélé, but he was a Peul/Fulani, like everybody else there, so he spoke the local language. It swiftly became dark, as Yaya asked directions to a bar that sold beer.

He did so seven times, and each time the locals gave him very clear directions, like 'Turn right, immediately after the cinema'. The problem was: there were only three buildings there, but all of them looked like a cinema.

After about half an hour driving around in circles, I was on the brink of giving up our quest, but then Yaya drove enthousiastically onto a small path, several kilometers out of town.

All of a sudden we stopped at a house surrounded by high walls. Two newly looking landcruisers were parked outside the closed gate. I knew that we had found our bar. Inside, there was a small, African discoteque. A funny place. And they sold beer. Lots of beer.

They advised me to buy '33', which I did. I bought 30 cans, since I was not certain if Yaya could ever find this bar again. Back in my hotel room there was a fridge, but there was only one socket in my room.

I pulled out the TV cable and tried the cable of the fridge. It worked! There are only two things I need in the tropics: coffee during the day and beer in the evening. Preferably cold beer, but in Africa I settle for warm beer.

Marie and I sat down at the little plastic table on our private balcony. It was pleasantly cool, since Télimélé sits on a hill top at 800 meters altitude. Marie even thought it was cold. She first put on one sweater, than another. We shared a can of white beans and sausages and we drank a couple of cold beers. Very pleasant.

When I was alone with Marie we spoke English, so I did not have to crack my brains on the bloody French all the time. I slept very well. My room had an airco that didn't cool. It just blew the air from outside into my room, which was fine, since the outside air was quite cool. And the monotonouse noise of the airco kept out all outside noises.

The next morning, a young man greeted us on our balcony. He introduced himself as our interpreter. I asked him to wait a few minutes. I quickly checked the STO manual that Claude and Anne had prepared for us, but there was no mention of an interpreter. Neither had our LTOs told us anything about an interpreter, during our regional briefing in Kindia.

But Mamadou said that he had talked to our LTOs when they had visited Télimélé and that he had worked as an interpreter during previous elections. I briefly discussed the matter with Marie and we agreed to accept him as our STO assistant/interpreter. After all, we were total strangers there.

Mamadou turned out to be a likeable chap. And he was especially useful in directing Yaya, our driver. I noted that Mamadou had only one arm, but I was too chicken too ask him if that had happened at birth or if it had been an accident. Why am I always so chicken? He was quite handy with his one remaining arm, though.

We set out to introduce ourselves to the local and electoral authorities. And we started to plan our observation route for E-Day. Which wasn't complicated: there was only one real road passing through the town and we could not risk going too far, because if it started to rain, the dirt road would become impassable, even for a four-wheel drive.

But we did visit a little hamlet called Fanta, where people apparently expected some problems on E-Day. We spotted no problems at all, to the contrary: we were kindly invited to attend a funeral, which we politely declined.

During our briefings, the Core Team had made it very clear that we were not allowed to go anywhere near a hospital or a funeral, because of the ebola threat. The weird thing was that I have never been invited to any funeral on any of my missions, but on this mission I was invited to a funeral.

There were apparently two little restaurants in Télimélé, but one looked rather uninviting, so we went to Le Gousta for lunch. Inside, it was cramped with a few small tables and uncomfortable wooden chairs. Outside there were two plastic chairs and one plastic table, with an unobstructed view of the town's main dirt road.

We had lunch there everyday. The moment they saw our car coming, they chased the youngsters away from 'our' table. They had a limited choice every day, but the food was surprisingly good and very cheap: we paid only three euros for a meal, including an icecold coca cola. The restaurant had a fridge and a generator. And the view was great.

For the first time in my life, I had brought hygienical napkins with me from the Netherlands. Before every meal I cleaned my hands with it and gave one to Marie too. I have never had stomach problems in Africa and I was not particularly afraid of ebola, but still: better safe than sorry. In Africa, you are obliged to shake hands all the time. It's unavoidable.

There were hardly any cars, but there were lots of noisy, old-fashioned motorbikes. After three days, everybody in the town had gotten so used to us, the only two westerners, that they hardly paid any attention to us anymore.

In fact, during the eight days that we spent there, everyone was nice to us. In other countries, it happens that followers of certain parties don't like western observers. Or that westerners are not welcome because of religious or political believes. But in Télimélé we were warmly welcomed by everyone. It was also a very safe place.

On E-Day, Sunday 11 October 2015, we did what observers always do on E-Day. We got up at 05.00 hours. Marie, with all her African experience, had asked the hotel 'mamam' to serve our breakfast at this early hour. Breakfast was very simple: a tiny omelette, served with slices of French bread, and nescafé.

In my country, Holland, nescafé is not considered to be coffee. It is considered to be a substitute for coffee, that you drink only during a World War, when real coffee is not available. But the good news was: because of the nescafé, 'mamam' put a large thermos flask filled with boiled water at our table.

With this boiled water I made my own, real filter coffee in my unbreakable aluminium thermos flask, that I kept with me in the car all day. Coffee is important to me. In 1992, while in Vietnam on the train from Hanoi to Saigon, I realized that I was addicted to caffeine.

There was no coffee on the train, only tea and soft drinks. After 24 hours, when we reached the imperial city of Hue, I had a splitting headache. I decided to get off the train, even though it was 05.00 hours in the morning. I took a taxi to a hotel and asked for a large pot of coffee. My headache disappeared instantly.

So on E-Day my thermos was filled with good, Dutch filter coffee. That was all I needed. I don't need food. I'll survive on bananas. As usual, we were the first persons to arrive at the Polling Station that we had selected for our Opening.

Finally, the sun was already coming up, several polling staff arrived, only to find the gate locked. Then someone arrived with a key to open the gate of the school. This is Africa: organization is a problem.

Guinea is one of the poorest countries in the world, thanks to the communist dictator Sekou Touré, whose name I knew well, since one of the main avenues in Maputo, the capital of Mozambique, was named after him.

In 1958, Charles de Gaulle invited all French speaking African countries to join the French African Community after independence. All accepted, except Guinea. De Gaulle tried to change Sekou Touré's mind and even visited Conakry, but Sekou Touré told him bluntly: 'We'd rather be poor in freedom than rich in slavery'.

A great line that went well with western leftist intellectuals, but for the Guinean people it heralded an era of extreme poverty: all the French immediately left the country, thus draining it of expertice and leadership. To make matters worse: Guinea could not join the CFA monetary union.

The CFA was linked to the French franc by 50 to 1, thus guaranteeing the value of the CFA as a hard currency. Sekou Touré remained in power until his death in 1984. He tried to convert the economy to communism. As a result, there was hardly any production of anything.

In his later years, Sekou Touré became more and more obsessed with the idea that the largest tribe in the country, the Peul/Fulani, were scheming against him, since he was a Malinké. Thousands of Peul/Fulani were executed, imprisoned or exiled. Some were hanged from bridges in Conakry. The Peul/Fulani hate the Malinké ever since.

After the communist dictator Sekou Touré came a capitalist dictator, Lansana Conté, whose policies worked out slightly better for the country, but the damage had already been done: the roads and railways, originally built by the French, deteriorated or disappeared all together. Hospitals and schools lacked everything.

Marie and I noticed that Guinean schools are amongst the most basic on the continent. We visited 18 school rooms during the day (the largest number of all STO teams, as we found out later) and all of them were without electricity.

Some school rooms were without windows and a few did not even have a door, just an opening. I wondered if the pupils could read their notes, because even when the sun was high in the sky, it was quite dark inside. The furniture was truly spartan.

It was a pitiful sight. On top of all that, grass and weeds were growing all over the school yards, since the schools had been closed for a year by now, to prevent the spread of the ebola virus.

Since Marie liked to talk to people and I did not, we authomatically fell into an efficient working relationship, whereby she would fill in the paper forms (with more than 70 questions in French!) and after that I would transmit them to our mission's computer in Conakry with our tablet. So both of us were happy.

We had only one problem during the day: sometime in the afternoon, our car wouldn't start. Apparently, the battery had been sucked dry, since all four of us were charging our mobile phones, plus the tablet and the satphone, from the vehicle's cigarette lighter. Luckily, we were in Africa, where a little problem like this is easily solved: the villagers joined forces to push our car until Yaya got it started.

Alberto was based as an LTO in Kissidougou in Guinée Forestiere. His partner was a Spanish male observer. One evening, when I was sitting at the balcony of hotel , I had a long telephone conversation with Alberto. He told me that his partner had told him that Alberto would be the number two in their team, since Alberto had no previous LTO experience.

I was trulyk flabbergasted. I had never heard of anything like this, since the EU is adamant that the two observers within a team are equally responsible for everything that happens with the team. I told him that if he had told this to the Core Team, the CT would have been furious at his Spanish partner.

But in the end Alberto probably did well in keeping things low key. It doesn't look good on your evaluation when you've had serious conflicts with your partner. Apparently, his relationship with the Spaniard improved later on. And when their STOs arrived, he had some other observers to talk to.

On our last day we took a little time for sightseeing: Mamadou insisted that we should visit the 'dam'. Well, we soon found out that he himself had never been there. Yaya had to ask three times to find the right path, leading to it. Then, abruptly, the path ended at a little concrete bridge.

It continued on the other side of the stream as a footpath. It was an isolated spot. Yaya stayed with the car and, with our little E-Day problem in mind, I instructed him to keep the engine running.

The three of us went on, on foot. I was sweating in the blazing sun as I had to carry my heavy mission bag with the satphone and all the other stuff. At a T-junction, Mamadou schose the wrong route. All of a sudden we bumped into a hunter, with a rather menacing rifle on his back.

But the hunter was OK. He lead us to an old generator at the end of a small pipeline that carried water from the dam above. We never saw the dam, but the generator looked very old and fragile to me. The old man working there turned out to have raised Mamadou as a child. Mamadou must have had a rather difficult childhood, since he had only one arm.

A day earlier I received a call from my Flamish friend Rudy, our security liaison officer, with whom I spoke Dutch. Rudy told me that the LTOs had made a reservation at their hotel in Kindia for us. I panicked. This meant that I would have to spend an entire evening with Claude.

Not that I disliked him that much, but he would speak rapid French all the time, in a rather low voice. Apart from that, it was a noisy, expensive hotel and there were lots of mosquitoes, since it was located at sea level.

I conferred with Marie and told her that I would definitely prefer to sleep the last night in our own hotel in Télimélé. She agreed, probably also since the hotel in Kindia would cost her twice as much for the night.

I talked to Rudy again and explained to him that we had come up from Conakry in just one day, after having started our journey at 06.00 hours. So we could also return in one day.

He agreed, but a few hours later he called Marie, to my surprise, since he had never called her before. He was not sure if she had agreed with me, since all other STO teams were desperate to travel back to the 'civilized world'. We were the only team that prefered to stay where we were!

Marie assured Rudy that she fully agreed with me. She even exchanged a few words in Dutch with Rudy. She told me later that she was quite embarrassed by the fact that many French speaking Belgians hardly speak any Dutch, while the Dutch speaking Belgians usually speak quite decent French. ,,We are a bilingual nation; everyone should speak both languages."

On the way back, Yaya was by now so used to the dirt road to Kindia, that he drove much faster. In Kindia, we drove on an asphalt road for the first time in eight days. We arrived one hour early at the hotel where the LTOs were staying. The regional debriefing went well. To my relieve, both Marie and I received a positive evaluation.

We reached Conakry before dark, just in time for the farewell reception of our Chief Observer, Frank Streng, a member of the European Parliament for Luxemburg. At some point, Marcell, the Observer Coordinator from Hungary, who had been my colleague LTO in Egypt, took me apart.

Marcell asked me if I had noticed any problems within our LTO team, adding that 'Claude and Anne have rather different personalities'. Since Claude and Anne had given Marie and myself a positive evaluation, I decided to play the dummy.

I told Marcell that we had only seen them for a total of three hours, so it was difficult for me to have an opinion on them. I did not tell him that one evening Anne had called me, for our daily security check. I told her that Télimélé was as safe as could be.

Two hours later, Claude called Marie to ask about the security situation in Télimélé. This meant, obviously, that Claude and Anne were not communicating with each other, even though they were staying at the same hotel.

We flew to Paris with Air France. Two of our group of 26 STOs stayed behind in the hotel. They were sick, not with ebola, but because of stomach problems. One of them was Michal, who had been my STO in Mozambique.

Since there were elaborate ebola checks at Conakry airport and just before boarding also by four Air France medical staff, it was decided that the two sick STOs should wait until their health had improved. Every traveller's temperature was checked with a *pistolette*. If your temperature was too high, they would immediately put you in isolation, for fear of ebola.

At Paris airport, Marie helped me to find the metro to Gare du Nord in Paris, where I had to board the Thalys to Amsterdam. The metro, above ground, took me past the France Stadium where four weeks later three bomb belts would be detonad by terrorists.

At Gare du Nord, four police patrolled the station, armed with automatic guns. I had never seen such a display of force in the Netherlands. But the French were right: the Thalys would be targeted by a terrorist. The terrorist was overpowered by American and French travelers. Clint Eastwood later made a film about it.

We were still hopeful that there would be a second round, but the second round never materialized. The incumbent president of Guinea, Alpha Condé, won the first round with 58 percent.

A pity, since I had told Marcell: 'I want to come back for the second round, but only if you give me the same partner, the same driver, the same interpreter and the same duty station'.

On 24 November 2015, Alberto and I were debriefed by two country experts of the Dutch Ministry of Foreign Affairs. They had been very interested in our mission, also since Joost, of the Dutch embassy in Dakar, had participated as an LSTO. They were also very interested in ebola.

It was only then that I realized that in Télimélé nobody had ever talked to us ebout ebola. In Conakry, every visitor of a big hotel or company was obliged to clean his hands with a disinfectant fluid. And they put a *pistolette* against your forehead, to measure your temperature.

In the provinces, no special measures were taken against ebola, apart from the nationwide closing of the schools. Apparently, for most Guineans ebola was not much of an issue, while for the rest of the world it was the one thing that characterized Guinea.

My lasting impression of Guinea was that it was one of the poorest countries I had ever visited. And, like many African leaders, Alpha Condé did not appear to be interested in doing anything about this.

Chapter 20

PERU - First Round - 2016

'There are two Peru's; one above the table and one below the table'

After my STO mission to Guinea, I was really afraid that I would be offered another French speaking mission. Since there are not enough French speaking observers in The Netherlands, I was worried that the ministry should reason: 'You went to Guinea and it went well, that means that you can do other French speaking missions'.

To my relief, Peru came up and I was selected as an LTO. My Spanish is much better than my French; I do not even have to practice it, before I leave home. In a Spanish speaking country I can easily communicate with anyone, without an interpreter.

It was going to be a rather peculiar mission, without STOs, but with a full-fledged Core Team and no less than 50 LTOs, most of them seasoned observers. I had met at least 30 of them on previous missions: they looked like a good bunch.

The Netherlands provided only two LTOs, one of whom was not even one hundred per cent Dutch: I met Elena during the briefings at the Ministry of Foreign Affairs. She was born in Madrid, Spain, but had been living in Amsterdam for ten years with her Dutch husband and two children.

Luckily, KLM operates a direct, daily flight to Lima. At Amsterdam's Schiphol airport I came across Elena and a number of LTOs. Finally, I could talk about observation missions. In my home region, I am the only observer, so I cannot talk to anyone about my experiences.

Back home, people don't have a clue as to what I am doing during those missions. Most people believe that an observer is a kind of overpaid tourist. I can explain a million times that I've never worked so hard in my life, seven stressful days a week and also seven evenings a week, but that doesn't change people's opinions.

With other observers, though, I do connect. Elena had done nine missions as an STO. It was to be her first mission as an LTO and it must have dizzied her, the way the experienced LTOs talked about mission after mission.

Twelve hours later, at Lima airport, something happened to me that had never happened before: I could not open my suitcase! It dawned on me that it might not be my suitcase. Since most passengers had already left the airport, I feared that some Peruvian would arrive home, only to find out that he could not open his suitcase, since it was mine. How in the world would I get my suitcase back?

Then, to my infinite relief, at the other side of the baggage belt I spotted the Peruvian woman who had been sitting next to me in the plane. She looked bewildered at her suitcase, which was identical to mine. I hurried over to her and yes: she could not open her suitcase either. I tried my code on her suitcase and it sprang open instantly!

So she had my suitcase and I had hers! I made a mental note to make a mark on my suitcase, so that I can easily recognize it. And I will make sure that I hurry to the baggage belt as quickly as possible, instead of wasting my time with slow walking female LTOs.

So there we were, all fifty of us, in the five-star hotel Delfines, where the hotel and also all the buffet meals were paid for us, which was actually to our disadvantage, since the EU deducted 30 per cent of our daily allowance for the hotel and also 30 per cent for the meals, leaving us with only 30 per cent (90 euros).

That the EU paid the hotel was fine with me, but they also deducted 90 euros for 3 meals, of which I could eat only two, since it was too much food for me. And breakfast is normally included in hotel rates anyway, so I was in fact paying a hefty 90 euros for just one buffet meal.

To make matters worse: these five-star hotels always seem to be situated miles away from any decent shop, where you can buy day-to-day necessities like shampoo and shaving cream. We could not carry all these items in our suitcases because of the weight limit in the aircraft and the security arrangements vis-à-vis liquids.

But even if there was a shop nearby, we could not buy anything, since the hotel did not change money. And at the airport we did not have time to change money, since our transport was waiting for us. Anyway: we had no choice. It was only for a few days of briefings.

And maybe I should not complain about the fact that I was obliged to stay in a five-star hotel. The three days of briefings went well. The Core Team was headed by Deputy Chief Observer Domenico from Italy. He had been my trainer in 2009 in Brussels, when I joined the 5-day course for Legal/Election Experts.

I liked him. He was good, as were the others in the Core Team. The Service Provider was also good, headed by Miguel. When Miguel is in charge, there are no problems. It all depends on the people: good people means a good mission.

My partner on this mission would be Agnieszka from Poland. I had never met her, nor heard about her. When someone pointed her out, she appeared to be very young. In reality, she was forty years of age, which is not that young anymore, but still a younger generation compared to me, since I was 61 by now.

It was obvious that she was disappointed to have such an old idiot as her partner. We were obliged to sit together, but she did not utter one word to me. Instead, she chatted all the time with younger LTOs on her other side and behind her. It was not a promising start to our relationship, but after we started working in our province, things improved considerably.

In fact, Agnieszka would turn out to be one of my best partners. Her husband was a Chilean diplomat. They lived in Brussels. I also learned that she was a friend of Alejandra, my much appreciated Belgian/Chilean partner from the Nicaragua mission. Alejandra told Agnieszka that she should consider herself lucky to have me as her partner. After that, Agnieszka and I had a very good mission together.

During the briefings, the mission doctor, a Peruvian, held his obligatory speech on the health situation in his country. In front of a room full of pale-faced Europeans, fresh from the European winter, he explained all the health hazards of a developing country to us.

Little did the good doctor know that most of us had worked for extended periods under difficult conditions in horrible countries like Afghanistan, Pakistan, Nigeria, Sudan, and so on. Countries that are much more difficult than Peru! Since all of us have worked and lived in difficult countries, our stomachs were better adapted to Third World conditions than the stomachs of the average Peruvian.

But the doctor insisted that we should not eat the most famous of all Peruvian dishes: *ceviche*. When he said this, the observers laughed. We were looking forward to eating *ceviche* and a scary speech by a Peruvian doctor was not going to deter any of us.

It's a bit strange that we, observers, are extensively trained to deal with all kinds of dangers, from health hazards to terrorist attacks, but the one thing that is most dangerous to us receives little attention: the traffic in Third World countries.

At least four LTO teams would be involved in accidents in Peru, of which one very seriously. One car was hit by a truck. Our colleagues Andrea and Heike, based in Arequipa, were lucky that they escaped unharmed. They sent us a photograph of their destroyed car: it looked horrible.

It turned out that our driver, Jaír, was a very nice guy of 36 years old, but he was not the best driver in the world. Like most drivers, he had a police or a security background. I don't know why. Quite possibly, the EU in Brussels had the idea that our drivers should be able to double up as our bodyguards.

To me, it seems that it is quite dangerous to have a bad driver. To be honest, Jaír was not the worst driver in the world, but he was a real Peruvian macho driver. Agnieszka and I tried to slow him down many times, but to no avail. Like all other Peruvians, Jaír would aggressively take over other cars and use his horn at every turn.

He especially hated taxis, of which there were many in Chiclayo, and he hated the thousands of rickshaw taxis (*moto taxis*) even more. On top of that, he could not find his way around Chiclayo, a city with 600.000 inhabitants. Even after three weeks he could hardly find our hotel back.

He could not read maps, but he used his GPS, to find the address we wanted to go to. Then he would stop the car and type in the street name, which took him five minutes. Several times he was obliged to call his ex-girlfriend Gloria, who lived in Chiclayo and knew the city very well. But we never had a real accident and Jaír was always positive and willing to help us, so we liked him nevertheless.

The good news was that we were staying in a fantastic hotel: Casa Andina. Initially, the mission had reserved a horrible hotel for us: hotel *Casa de la Luna*, the House of the Moon. A nice name, but there was no elevator, so we had to carry our suitcases all the way to the fourth floor. Outside it was 38 degrees Celsius; inside it was even hotter. I sweated profusely.

My room was very small and there was no water coming from the tap. I could not find an air conditioner, even though the receptionist had assured me that it was behind the curtain. The hotel did not have a garden, just a tiny swimming pool at the rooftop.

Agnieszka and I decided to check out other hotels. There were quite a few, but we both immediately liked Casa Andina. It had originally been built by the Peruvian government as a *Hotel Turismo*. Those hotels were especially commissioned to provide tourists with decent hotels at reasonable prices, in order to promote tourism to the country.

Hotel Casa Andina had by now been privatized, but they were still good value for money, especially after Agnieszka managed to negotiate our room rates down to just 50 euros per day. A great buffet breakfast was included. The EU paid us 280 euros per day, of which I spent only 50 on the hotel, about 15 for lunch and a few euros on beer.

I couldn't eat three meals a day, but since Agnieszka got hungry every day around lunch time, I joined her for lunch. In the evenings, I just ate some bread and cheese or cold hotdogs from the supermarket. I purchased my beers at the petrol station, just across the road from the hotel.

I had been afraid that Agnieszka, as an eastern European, would prefer a cheaper hotel, but luckily she was married to a Chilean diplomat and she lived in Brussels. She was westernized. And she was not poor.

Thanks to the great hotel, a good partner and the fact that no STOs would take part on this mission, it was clear that it was going to be an easy going mission for me. Every evening I sat down at one of the tables at the back of the hotel, next to the swimming pool.

I was usually the only person there. A cool breeze came in continuously from the west, where the Pacific Ocean was only fifteen kilometres away. Thanks to the cool and constant breeze, there were no mosquitoes there.

The only problem was the constant honking of cars. Because of the high walls, I could not see the traffic, but the noise was rather irritating. But as Johan Cruijff used to say: you can't win them all. Some things you just have to endure.

Our very first visit was to the police commandant. Just before the police headquarters, Jaír drove against the traffic on a small roundabout. We were stopped by the traffic police.

As usual, I sat at the left-back side of the car, behind the driver. A police man and a police woman came up to my side of the car. Both Jaír and I opened our windows. Agnieszka hissed at me not to interfere. I just told them that we were on our way to their highest boss.

Jaír did not have to pay a fine, but he lost ten points on his driver's licence. A good lesson. Jaír obviously believed that, since we had EU visibility attached to the sides of our car, he was above the law. He clearly was not. EU observers don't enjoy a full diplomatic status.

On a Monday morning, just one week before E-Day, my hotel phone rang loudly. The hotel staff had always been very friendly and helpful towards us. Now, the guy from the reception desk told me that I had to go to a hospital with Agnieszka.

I hurried down to the lobby, where Agnieszka was sitting, surrounded by three receptionists waving air at her. She looked bad and she felt bad. I took her arm and we walked into the hot sun to one of the taxis. It would take too long to wait for Jaír, who stayed at the house of some relatives, at one hour from Chiclayo.

The clinic was supposed to be the best in town, but to me it looked like a real Third World hospital: no air conditioning, just a few fans, so it was very hot inside. Because of this, there were lots of mosquitoes. I got bitten several times. I had not been bitten by any mosquitoes, until I entered that bloody hospital.

There is no malaria in the area, but only 30 kilometres from Chiclayo there are huge irrigation projects. Mosquitoes need water, so dozens of cases of dengue had been reported there, as well as a few cases of yellow fever.

It's a bit weird that you don't get sick as long as you are not in the hospital, but that you are at risk of getting a mosquito-based disease while you are inside the hospital. Inside, dozens of patients were desperately trying to get the attention of the medical and administrative staff.

We joined the queue. It was quite chaotic, like the traffic in Peru. Agnieszka had to pay 30 euros. After that, a doctor examined her behind a curtain. Apparently, she had some kind of infection. Agnieszka had to buy medication.

Unfortunately, the medication didn't help much. Two days later, we had to return to the hospital. Again, I was bitten by mosquitoes. And I received several phone calls from the Core Team and the security expert, who were worried about Agnieszka.

Luckily, I always carry a headphone with me. Since the hospital had no air conditioning, all the doors and windows were open and the horning of the traffic was deafening. I explained on the phone that I would stay with Agnieszka and that we would report back if we knew what caused her distress.

This time, Agnieszka had to go to the pharmacy, inside the hospital, and buy intravenous needles and a drip. A nurse applied it to her, while Agnieszka was sitting on a bed in a hallway. After about an hour we walked back to our hotel in the cool evening air.

The good thing about being an LTO is that you stay around for a relatively long period. As an STO, you fly into a country and before you know it you're on the plane back home. But an LTO usually stays about six weeks in a province, which means that you have time to get to know local people really well and gain their trust.

This happened to Agnieska and me in Chiclayo. People told us things that you would normally never hear. How to become a member of the Peruvian Congress, for example. As was explained to us, it comes at a price, a very high price.

You have to pay for it, not only above the table, but also under the table. Above the table, you would pay the, rather low, officially allowed amounts. Under the table, you would have to pay much more, usually in cash dollars, that could not be traced. As our interlocutors explained: 'There are two Peru's; one above the table and one below the table'.

This is how it works in Peru: political parties exist only on paper. They don't exist in reality. They don't have political programs. But if you want to become a member of Congress, you are obliged to join one of the large political parties.

That's the only way, because the electoral law states that only parties who obtain more than 5 per cent of the vote can have representation in Congress. This is a recipe for corruption. It's no use to start your own political party. You would never obtain more than 5 per cent of the national vote.

Peru is divided into 25 electoral districts, which are roughly the same as the country's 25 provinces (called *departamentos*). Each province elects between one and seven members of Congress, depending on the population of the province, but here is the trick: Peruvians can cast preferential votes.

This means that people appearing on the list of one party are in fact each other's competitors: if you want to obtain preferential votes, you have to beat your own party members. The funny thing is that, because of this, political parties don't have offices in the provincial capitals, but individual candidates do, since they are fighting each other.

There are only 130 seats in Congress. Now the best bet in obtaining a seat in Congress is to be the number one candidate of one of the larger parties in an electoral district. If you are number two, you can forget it. And if you appear on the list of a smaller party, you can also forget it, because of the 5 per cent threshold.

Parties have no ideology, in reality, so you can shop around for any political party. But here is the trick: if you want to be the number one of a large party, you have to pay the party leader, usually the (ex) presidential candidate. Officially, all parties are required to be democratic internally. In reality, the party leader decides.

Since Peru is trying to do something about corruption, your 'donation' to the party leader has to be carried out in secrecy. So you have to pay the party leader under the table, anywhere between 50.000 dollars and 200.000 dollars in cash.

The only thing you obtained for these large sums of money was a place high on the party's list in your province. Apart from this, you also had to spent a lot of money for your personal campaign: for billboards, murals, ads in newspapers and on local TV and radio, and the most important thing: hand outs to your prospected voters.

These hand outs are sometimes in cash, sometimes in bags of rice or even fish. Hand outs are forbidden by law, but without hand outs you would never obtain enough votes. Since nowadays everyone can make photographs with their mobile phones, you cannot risk doing the hand outs yourself. You have to hire people to do the dirty deeds for you.

That costs money. In Peru, everything has a price. When we asked people in Chiclayo if they ever drove a car after they had been drinking alcohol, they would invariably answer: 'Yes, of course. When I'm stopped by the police, I know exactly how much I have to pay them'.

An article in a newspaper can be purchased. An interview on local TV or radio can be purchased. When you have to appear in court, you have to hand a nice sum of money to the judge, after which all charges are miraculously dropped. And so on. All you need is money.

To Europeans this may seem horrible corruption, but to Peruvians it is the only way. It is like winning the Tour de France. We know now that, during the 1980s, the 1990s and 2000s, all cyclists who ended in the top-ten of the Tour de France took doping.

If a cyclist decided to stay clean and not take doping, that would have been a noble undertaking, but this cyclist would never have made it into the top-ten of the Tour de France. If you wanted to win it, you simply had to take doping. In other words: if you decided to be honest and not take doping, you were considered to be an idiot.

As a prominent Peruvian scholar commented about corruption in his country: 'If you are honest in Peru, you are considered to be a leper'. The reason why people are willing to pay large amounts to party leaders under the table is, of course, that they expect to earn back their money, with a handsome profit, once they are members of Congress.

So, once in Congress, you have to earn back all that money. No one explained to us how this is done, but it seems to me that there is only one answer to this question: you sell your vote to the highest bidder. Either criminals, like drug traffickers, or large legitimate enterprises.

As a result, Peruvian parliamentarians have no interest in national or regional development; they only think about filling their own pockets as quickly as possible, since there are no guarantees that they will be re-elected.

At the same time, all Peruvians we met in the city of Chiclayo and the province of Lambayeque were very proud of their country and their own region. People can be corrupt and nice at the same time.

Every day, people asked us if we liked it over there. Did we like the food? Did we visit the Lord of Sipán museum? They even asked me several times if I liked Peruvian women. Apparently, they are a proud people, but there is also a hint of insecurity. The Peruvians appear to be a bit embarrassed about the state their country is in.

Certainly, Chiclayo is not a tourist destination. In the local newspaper, *La Industria*, a study was published about tourists' opinions on the city and the results were invariably negative. Tourists complain about the dirt that lies strewn around the city (in spite of a Swiss project to provide garbage collection trucks) and they also complain about the incessant horning of the vehicles on the streets.

Chiclayo is a very noisy place. The horning, by the way, is totally useless, since everyone does it, but it appears to be the national sport, apart from the diplomatic enclave in Lima, where horning is explicitly forbidden.

La Industria is by far the best newspaper in Chiclayo. But even this quality newspaper could go terribly wrong, as Agnieszka and I would find out. One morning I was reading the newspaper at the buffet breakfast, when I noticed our names in an article about the strike at the sugarcane factory in the nearby town of Pomalca.

Since the strikers had been blocking the main road to the east for weeks on end, Agnieszka and I had never been near that factory. Yet, in the article it was stated that we supported the strikers. It was the most unbelievable bunch of lies I had ever read in any newspaper. Fake news *avant la lettre*.

The article was signed by a female journalist, whom we had never met. She had clearly been paid money by someone who hoped to involve the EU on behalf of the strikers. We immediately informed our mission's press officer, who requested an explanation from *La Industria*.

The explanation was ambiguous, to say the least. A few weeks later we met the young female journalist and confronted her with her fake news. She walked away as fast as she could. This incident shows that many journalists in Third World countries sell themselves to the highest bidder. Can you blame them for it?

All people we met invariably asked us the same questions: 'Where do you come from?' I knew what was coming next, since I had lived in Bolivia and Ecuador, countries with similar cultures as Peru. The moment I told them that I was Dutch, all Peruvians of a certain age would exclaim: 'Ah, the Clockwork Orange'.

At first, Agnieszka thought that they meant the famous book written by Anthony Burgess or the even more famous movie by Stanley Kubrick, but I knew that the Peruvians meant the Dutch national soccer team of 1974. All the more so since the team's most legendary player, Johan Cruijff, died during our mission in Peru.

In the final of that World Cup, Holland lost 2-1 against West-Germany, yet the German players are all but forgotten, while any South American taxi driver older than fifty years can still name all the Dutch players.

It gets a bit boring when you hear the same thing over and over again, but that's the way it is. The moment Agnieszka told them that she came from Poland, every Peruvian would acclaim: 'Ah, Pope John Paul II'. That's all they know about Poland.

Most Latin Americans are Catholics and Pope John Paul II is a well-known pope of recent times. One guy told us that his son was presently in Poland, namely in its capital, Prague. We gently explained that Prague was the capital of the Czech Republic. Most Peruvians have never been abroad and speak only Spanish.

Agnieszka kept sending photographs of us to Sylvia, the Press Officer of our mission. As a result, Agnieszka and I appeared more on the mission's Facebook page than any other LTO team. Because of this, it appeared to the outside world that we were very active. In reality, it was an easy going mission for me.

Agnieszka had a little problem with one of the electoral judges. We visited their office quite regularly, to check if any complaints had been filed. One of the younger judges, Yuri, had been very helpful.

But after a couple of weeks, Agnieszka confided to me that Yuri kept sending her SMSs, with a rather sexual undertone. She had asked him to stop, but he just kept sending them. ,,What shall I do?" she asked me.

I didn't know. I had never experienced this. ,,Send him a text that, if he doesn't stop, we are going to forward his texts to his boss", I suggested to her. This worked. Problem solved. When we visited him later on, he was as friendly as always. His co-workers probably never suspected anything.

I had by now become accustomed to spending my evenings at the swimming pool, at the back of the hotel. I smoked a few of my Dutch factory cigars and I drank a few Peruvian Cusqueña beers. Thanks to new technologies, I was now able to read the Core Team's Daily Brief on my smart phone.

Agnieszka regularly visited the workout room at the pool side. After exercising, she would briefly join me for a beer. Since she was not comfortable with English, we always talked Spanish amongst ourselves. I really enjoyed my quiet time alone in the evenings, in the cool sea breeze besides the swimming pool. I'm not a very social person.

Just a few days before E-Day, I realized that the *Ley Seca* would be imposed. I hurried over to my favourite little shop, at the petrol station just across the road. I did not need to be worried, though. The lady of the shop told me simply: ,,You're a foreigner and a regular costumer. The *Ley Seca* does not apply to you. Don't worry: you can always get your beers here."

The Finance Officer of our mission sent us a message that he had wired some money for our Petty Cash to a bank in Chiclayo. We just had to go to the bank and cash it. I always prefer to just pay petty cash expenses from my own pocket, which would be reimbursed to me by the end of the mission.

But the FO replied that he had already wired the money and that we were obliged to go to the bank. So, on Saturday morning at 11.00 hours, we were waiting in line outside the bank. There were about 30 people waiting in front of us and the sun was already burning on our heads.

Then something extraordinary happened. A bank official approached me and said that elderly people, like me, were legally allowed to jump the queue. I looked at him in utter surprise. I explained: ,,But I'm not 65 years old yet." The official persisted: ,,Every person older than 55 is allowed to jump the line."

He pointed at a sign that was posted next to the door, pinpointing all the people who were allowed to jump the line: pictures of a pregnant woman, someone in a wheelchair, a person carrying a baby and an old man with a bent back, walking with a stick.

I was that old man. I was duly allowed inside, followed by Agnieszka, who said that she was with me. Once inside, I felt embarrassed, while Agnieszka couldn't stop laughing. ,,It's the first time this has ever happened to me," I told her sternly.

E-Day went fine. For the closing, we had to observe in a polling station that would transmit the results by computer. This polling station, about twenty kilometres from Chiclayo, had no air conditioning. It remained stifling hot inside, while outside the air became pleasantly cool, thanks to the sea breeze.

In the department of Lambayeque, the party of the Fujimori family (Fuerza Popular) obtained 3 out of the 5 available seats for Congress. Because of this, I believed that Keiko Fujimori would be elected president, but it turned out that not one candidate had obtained more than 50 per cent of the vote. A second round of presidential was to be held between Keiko and Pedro Pablo Kuczynski.

Agnieszka had still not fully recovered from her illness. The oppressive heat was bothering her. She had brought an Indonesian paper fan with her. I took it over from her and waved warm air into her face. The members of the polling station saw it and laughed. It probably confirmed what they already believed: that all Europeans are crazy.

At about 22.00 hours they finished transmitting the results to Lima and we headed to the departmental election headquarters in Chiclayo. The small room was cramped with observers and journalists. At 23.00 hours, Agnieszka felt really bad and called Marcell, the Observer Coordinator, to ask permission to return to our hotel.

At first, Marcell declined, but half an hour later Agnieszka called him again. This time, we were allowed to return to our hotel, from where I transmitted the last forms to our Core Team.

After E-Day, Agnieszka and I wanted to visit the world famous dig site, where the 'Lord of Sipán' had been discovered, but this turned out to be impossible, since the only road leading there was still blocked by strikers of the sugarcane factory in Pomalca. Instead, we visited the museum in Lambayeque.

After the discovery of the 'Lord of Sipán' in the 1980s, just about ten kilometres west of Chiclayo, the leading archaeologist at the dig site, Walter Alva, managed to collect funds to build a completely new museum in Lambayeque town. The brand new museum exhibited the most important finds of the dig site of the 'Lord of Sipán', also known as the South American Tutankhamun.

It's a fascinating museum and fortunately it stood next to the Lambayeque district electoral office, so the tracking system of our security expert would show our car parked in front of the electoral office. We were indeed hardworking observers!

The last couple of days we went around to say goodbye to our interlocutors. At the airport of Chiclayo we said goodbye to Jaír. He was going to drive the car back to Lima that same day.

When the passengers were called to board the airplane to Lima, yet again I joined the short, separate line for 55+ ancients. No one even asked me if I was really older than 55. It dawned on me that I had definitely entered the ranks of old folks.

A minibus took us to our hotel Delfines. At least: that's what I expected. To my surprise, the driver halted a few hundred meters before the hotel. I told him to continue to the hotel, but he simply stepped out of the car, that had halted at the back entrance of the Service Provider's offices at the Country Club.

The other LTOs stepped out of the car, but I remained seated. To no avail, because at the back of the car all suitcases were placed on the pavement, including mine. I was furious. Than Pedro, our mission's Logistics Officer, arrived. He was from Portugal, like the other massive Pedro, whom I disliked fiercely.

But this Pedro was slim and he was actually OK. He explained that nearly all 50 LTOs were expected to arrive during the day, so they could not afford to waste time with the handover of the materials and the settling of the petty cash.

I was furious at him, which I regretted later. Pedro was right and I was being childish. I later apologized to him. The problem was that no one had told us about this procedure.

Since we were obliged to travel by plane, I had distributed our mission materials over my big and small suitcases. Now I had to open both my suitcases in front of everybody. All of them had a good look at my dirty underwear. But that's the life of an observer: it's not all oranges and sunshine.

On the last day of our mission, Marie-Therese approached me. It had been her first mission as an LTO, so she did not know most of the other LTOs, but since she had been my STO in Nicaragua in 2011, she confided in me. We had a rough start in Nicaragua, but after that we related very well to each other.

She still maintained contact with my partner of Nicaragua, Alejandra, who also happened to be a friend of my current partner in Peru, Agnieszka. The observers world is a small world. Marie-Therese had shocking news for me. She told me that her LTO partner in Peru was nice to everybody, except to her.

Worse than that, he treated her like shit, especially the first weeks that they spent together in Ica province, south of Lima. He was a Danish guy, a journalist, with lots of election mission experience, and both his Spanish and his English were very good.

His disdain of Marie-Therese was obvious. But the EU EOMs operate according to a holy principle: within a team, both observers are equals. It is absolutely forbidden to treat your partner like shit. In fact, the perpetrator can expect to be sent home on the first available airplane and then to be blacklisted for five years.

I really felt for Marie-Therese. She did not deserve this. I advised her to tell everything to Soraya, her Observer Coordinator, who had a British passport but came from Spanish origins and whom, as far as I could tell, was good at her job.

But Marie-Therese was hesitant. Since it was her first mission, she did not want to be known as someone who always created problems. Which made some sense: within the observers community it is important to build a good reputation.

But in the end, fortunately, she did tell Soraya. It is important that the Core Team are informed when an observer misbehaves. In a group of fifty, inevitably there are one or two horrible persons. My Dutch colleague LTO, Elena, had also been extremely unfortunate.

At the beginning of the mission she thought that her partner George, a very old Rumanian guy, was deaf in one ear, since he did not seem to understand many things.

But it turned out that George suffered from something much more serious: he did not speak one word of Spanish! So she had to do all the talking during the interviews. And it was her very first mission as an LTO!

How is it possible that the EU selects someone who does not speak Spanish, when in the TOR it is stated clearly that all LTO should be fluent in the working language, Spanish, as well as in the reporting language, English? Apparently, there was yet another LTO who hardly spoke Spanish, a young guy from Austria.

Within a week after our return to Holland, Elena and I were debriefed at the Ministry of Foreign Affairs in The Hague. As usual, the country experts at the ministry were curious at what observers like us were doing all those weeks in a country like Peru.

I explained that 80 per cent of our work consisted of interviewing anybody who had anything to do with elections. I also told them that we conducted the interviews in Spanish and wrote our Weekly Reports in English, and that we directed the remaining 20 per cent of our time to our STOs.

I explained that we had worked 39 days in a row, including the weekends and all evenings. During these election observation missions I worked harder than at any other time in my life!

In the train back to Amsterdam, Elena told me that one LTO, Slaveena from Bulgaria, had been very sick on the plane, when we returned from Lima. Slaveena had been deployed to Iquitos, in the vast Peruvian Amazon region, and apparently she had contracted malaria. Several LTOs had helped her to arrange an ambulance to a medical facility, near Schiphol airport.

Chapter 21

PERU - Second Round - 2016

'Peruvians are nice and corrupt, all at the same time'

After the first round, I spent one month at home. I was looking forward to the second round, because I had a good partner, a good Core Team and a good Service Provider. On top of that, the people in our province were very nice to us, the hotel was great, I was in a Spanish speaking country and the money was good.

But I wasn't sure if the second round would materialize. Several things could go wrong: the EU could decide not to send a mission after all, because of budget constraints or political considerations. In Peru the military could step in and take over the country. It has happened before in Latin America.

There were personal risks involved: one of the two candidates, Keiko Fujimori and Pablo Kuczynski, could get an accident or get sick. Or one of them or both of them could be prohibited from running by the Peruvian Electoral Judiciary (JNE, in Spanish), because of art.42.

I myself could get an accident, my wife could get an accident, my parents could get an accident: in all of these cases I could not go on a mission. But nothing happened. So on Friday 20 May 2016, once again, I stepped on board of the direct KLM flight to Lima.

Already at Schiphol Airport I met a number of observers. My partner, Agnieszka, had managed to persuade the Service Provider that it was much more convenient for her to fly via Amsterdam, instead of via the horrible airport of Madrid, since she lived in Brussels.

Agnieszka was very happy to see me and she gave me a present: a book with short stories by the Polish Nobel Prize winner Isaac Bashevis Singer. Rather embarrassed I told her that—as a Dutchman—I was not accustomed to giving presents to people.

Then I remembered that I had recorded two CDs with Andean music from the Kjarkas from Bolivia—to be played in the car, since our driver only played horrible Peruvian salsa.

I don't hate salsa as much as I hate jazz, but after nine weeks non-stop salsa I vowed not to listen to any salsa any more for the next ten years. I promised Agnieszka one of my Kjarkas CDs.

This time I picked up my own suitcase at Lima Airport. The flight from Madrid had also arrived. I greeted the other observers as if they were old friends. Which in fact they were, to some extent. The Observer Coordinators, Marcel and Soraya, were waiting for us. So were Miguel and Pedro of the Service Provider. Off we went in the bus to hotel Delfines in the affluent embassy district of Lima.

Check-in took quite a while, with so many observers. On top of that, our old smart phones were handed out to us, as well as new mission jackets. All of this took time and I was anxious to go the small shop, two blocks behind the hotel, to buy a some beers.

Finally I got my key-card, went to my room, chained my big and small suitcases to a seat and left for the shop. It was 20.45 by now, but thank God it was still open. Back at the hotel I took two beers with me to the buffet-dinner.

The buffet was paid by the mission, but alcoholic drinks were not included. You can order a beer, but then you have to pay from your own pocket. And in this five-star hotel, the same Cusqueňa beer would cost me five times more than in the shop.

I gave one beer to Slaveena from Bulgaria. We emptied the beer into plastic cups that were supposed to be filled with lemonade or alcohol free *chicha*. I hid the empty cans in my bag. My wife and I used to do this in Pakistan, so I had previous experience of the evil deed.

After this, I enjoyed a few Dutch factory-made cigars and a few more beers at the terrace beside the swimming pool, on the third floor. It was much cooler now than during the first round.

And it was quiet there, since in the embassy area of Lima it is forbidden to use the horn of your car. Anyone who did use the horn, would have to pay a hefty fine. The next day we were briefed by the Service Provider and we were handed our IT equipment. All the same as during the first round.

We found out that our driver was still the same old Jaír, thank God. He is one of the worst drivers in the world, but he is a very nice guy, always willing to help and even to protect us, as a kind of bodyguard. And we did not have an accident during the first round, so we preferred to keep him on.

We also found out that Jaír would leave the next morning, very early, in our car to Chiclayo. We asked Pedro, the Portuguese Logistics Officer, if we could put some of our heavy office materials in the car with Jaír, to avoid having to pay for excess luggage in the airplane. Pedro agreed immediately and even handed us a large bag.

Of the 50 LTOs, 48 had returned. Only two were new: my good old Hungarian friend Sándor was going to be the new partner of Elena, my Dutch colleague. Her first partner did not speak Spanish. I knew from Pedro, my partner in Bolivia, that Sándor's Spanish was very good, but that his English was poor.

The other newcomer was Gregorio, a Spanish guy. I remembered him from another mission, but at first I didn't recall which one. He told me that he remembered me from the Venezuela mission in 2006. Gregorio replaced Markella from Greece, who had been my STO in Honduras.

To our chagrin, we had to change hotels. At 17.00 hours, all 50 of us were hoarded into a big bus and driven to hotel Costa del Sol Wyndham. This was not the fault of the mission. Hotel Delfines had booked another big group for that same night, so the hotel was double booked.

The hotel dutifully acknowledged their mistake, but still: we had to move to another hotel. My new room was much smaller, but what was worse: I had no beer. So out I went, in search of a shop. I walked several blocks around the hotel, but it was a residential area. No shops.

It was already getting dark and I decided to return to the hotel, since Lima is not as safe as Chiclayo. I noticed several groups of young men hanging around. And I was alone, an old man of 61, in a strange city. Then, out of the blue, someone called my name. It was Agnieszka, also on her own.

I asked her where on earth she was going to and she replied: 'To the Salaverry Mall'. I could not let her venture out all by herself, so I decided to join her. I bought my six-pack and then I had to wait half an hour for her. She had finally managed to buy the same book by Singer that she had given to me, but this time in Spanish. Very few Peruvians speak English.

The next morning I had to get up at 05.00 hours, only to find out that there was no warm water. But observers are tough cookies: I washed myself with ice-cold water. The flight to Chiclayo went well. The moment we stepped out onto the tarmac, I had an odd sensation: I felt at home!

Jaír was waiting for us in the same Toyota land-cruiser as during the first round. We drove through familiar streets to our familiar hotel Casa Andina. The staff were still the same and greeted us wholeheartedly.

Was it because of the eternal sunshine, that people in Chiclayo were much more friendly and outgoing than people in Lima, who have to live in depressing fog for months on end? To make things even better, both of us would be staying in spacious suites, at the very end of the hallways, far away from the elevators. For the same price: I love Chiclayo!

The next day we started visiting the offices of ODPE, the electoral commission and JEE, the electoral judiciary. The offices were still the same and the people were still the same.

Obviously, the second round would be a routine exercise, not only for us, but also for them. A bit boring perhaps, but at the same time devoid of stress or tension. Every advantage has his disadvantage, as Johan Cruijff used to say.

In the evenings, as usual, I sat next to the swimming pool at the back of the hotel with my favorite Dutch factory cigars and my beloved Peruvian Cusqueña beer. It was much colder now and there was an eternal wind blowing from the west, where the Pacific was only fifteen kilometres away.

I had not brought a jacket, since we had to travel by plane, so I put on two shirts. As an observer you have to be inventive. All the cars were horning again, the noise was deafening, but strangely enough this didn't bother me anymore: to the contrary, it made me feel at home. I was becoming a Chiclayo boy.

The first round of the Peruvian elections had been a relaxed mission for Agnieszka and me. The second round was even more relaxed. There were no more candidates for congress, no more candidates for the Andean parliament and only two, instead of the original nineteen, presidential candidates. There was hardly any campaign.

In the car I showed Agnieszka my Kjarkas CD, that I had recorded especially for her (or so I told her). Jaír possessed only one CD with salsa, that he played over and over again. I asked him to play the Kjarkas CD for a change. Just like I had done in Cochabamba and Oruro, I sang the first lines of 'Munas Quechay' in Quechua.

Unlike my previous partners, Agnieszka was not impressed. ,,You just learned a few lines, didn't you", she sneered at me in English, which Jaír could not understand. ,,What language is this?" Jaír asked. ,,It's your language", I replied. ,,It's Quechua: the language of the original Peruvians."

Add to this that we were extremely lucky that on this mission there would not be STOs, only a few LTSOs from the European embassies, who only observed E-Day in Lima, Cusco and Arequipa. Of course there were also some Euro parliamentarians, but they also preferred Lima and Cusco.

No one came to Chiclayo. We were completely forgotten by everybody, which was great: we did not have to write an STO manual, we did not have to make all kinds of arrangements for STOs and we did not have to supervise them.

We were even more lucky that none of the Core Team experts came to visit us. They too preferred Cusco and Arequipa, but some visited also other departments, like La Libertad (with Trujillo as its capital, where the ancient city of Chan Chan and the pyramids of the sun and the moon are located) and Piura. Thank God no one came to us.

We did get some visitors in the end, but they were our colleague LTOs. They were Marianna from Hungary and Søren from Norway. As LTO06 they were responsible for Cajamarca, a vast department up in the mountains, where the winding roads make progress slow.

Therefore, to travel from Cajamarca city to Jaen City, it would be faster and more comfortable for them to travel via Chiclayo, since the Peruvian coastal desert roads are straight and of reasonable quality.

They spent Monday and Friday night in our hotel, since they had to travel back the same way. We had a good time by the swimming pool. Luckily, I had enough cigars and beer for everyone. On Monday evening one of the two presidential candidates, Kuczynski, held a rally in the centre of town.

Agnieszka and I observed it from the first floor of restaurant Hebron, just ten meters from the stage. Kuczynski, whose father was a Polish Jew, apparently didn't speak Polish himself. He was 77 years old, had no charisma and was a poor speaker.

I wondered how on earth such a man could have ended up in second place during the first round. Other presidential candidates, like twice ex-president Alan García and Barnechea, possessed much more charisma.

Marianna and Søren also observed the rally, at a safe distance. We all met again at the swimming pool. At 23.00 hours, the three of them decided to go out to a discotheque. I can't dance and I am too old for these frivolous things anyway, so I stayed at home.

When we approached the elevators of the hotel, a man was standing there. It was Kuczynski! Agnieszka and I shook his hands. He shook our hands reluctantly. Not a pleasant man. Little did I know that he would ultimately beat Keiko Fujimori with 50,11 per cent against 49,89 per cent of the vote. We had shaken the hand of Peru's new president!

Agnieszka and I had gone to the rally on foot, since our driver needs to rest in the evenings and in any case: it is not a good idea to go by car into the congested city centre, especially when a rally is held there. It was only eight blocks to the centre, but we found out soon enough that Peruvian traffic is a force to be reckoned with.

Drivers don't stop for pedestrians, not even when they are walking on a zebra crossing. They do stop for the red light, though, but Peru remains a chaotic society: the traffic is chaotic, the bureaucracy is chaotic and the football is chaotic. They have good individual players, but they never win anything, since they are not able to organize themselves decently.

During the first round, Agnieszka and I had visited the museum in the town of Lambayeque that had been built in 2002, exclusively for the archaeological treasures found in the grave of the Lord of Sipán. During the second round, we had more time on our hands, so we visited the site where the Lord of Sipán had been discovered in 1987 by the Peruvian archaeologist Walter Alva.

By now, the road through Pomalca was passable. The strike at the sugarcane factory had finally ended. My wife and I had passed by here in 1987, when we moved from La Paz, Bolivia, to Quito, Ecuador, with our land cruiser filled with personal belongings.

We had visited Chan Chan and the adobe brick pyramids of the Sun and the Moon, near Trujillo. From there, we followed the Pan American Highway that ran straight through Chiclayo.

Little did we know that in that same year grave robbers had been active near the hamlet of Sipán. The police had informed Walter Alva about some incredible artefacts that had been offered for sale on the black market.

Alva and his fellow archaeologists started digging and discovered the most important archaeological finds of the South Americas. The site itself is not spectacular, but it is a historic site, like the tomb of Tutankhamen in Egypt, which is also an empty tomb, but at least has world famous mural paintings.

The tombs at Sipán contain replicas, but still: it fills you with awe. Next to the site was a small museum, with minor artefacts. All the major finds were exhibited in the large museum in the town of Lambayeque.

It was determined that the graves dated back to the time when the Moche ruled this part of northern Peru, nearly 2,000 years ago. They were considered to have been the best metal workers of South America. The artefacts were made of gold, silver, copper and semi-precious stones. Some strange ornaments had been hanging from noses and ears.

All these ornaments had been depicted on paintings on pottery, that had been discovered decades earlier. Since these paintings appeared to be totally weird, it was believed that they depicted dreams or trance situations. Now, after the finds at Sipán, it turned out that the paintings depicted real events, like the carving out of the hearts from living victims.

A week later we visited the pyramids at Túcume, where Thor Heyerdahl had been working from 1988-94. Obviously, he had hoped to become as famous as Walter Alva, but to his disappointed no major artefacts were found at Túcume.

Yet, the site covers an enormous area, with a total of 26 adobe pyramids, built by the Lambayequans, just before they were conquered by the Chimú, who themselves were later conquered by the Incas. The tomb of the Lord of Sipán was a thousand years older!

Túcume also has a small museum, but you have to walk long distances to visit all the pyramids. And even though it was much cooler now than a few months ago, the sun was still burning mercilessly above our heads. Even so, Agnieszka and I decided to climb the stairs to the top of the mountain at the centre of the site.

At the beginning of each mission I always tell my new partner that my family, from both my father's and my mother's side, had been Dutch peasants. And peasants, I explained, were tough cookies.

Many partners, like Agnieszka, were considerably younger than me, and they would look at me with an expression on their face that said: 'I hope this old fool is not going to faint'. But I always tell them, in earnest: 'I will hold out longer than you. Mark my words.'

I actually did hold out longer than any of my partners, of which four had fainted due to the tropical heat or exhaustion. At Túcume, I reached the top before young Agnieszka. We were both sweating profusely, but the view was breath-taking.

Archaeologists were still digging at about five sites, under canvas canopies against the brutal sun. Every now and then work stops for a few years, due to a lack of funds. Sometimes I wish I had studied archaeology, instead of economics.

What good comes from studying economics, anyway? I've never heard of an economist who has become rich. Economists never buy shares, since they know that shares can go down as well as up.

E-Day turned out to be a routine exercise for us. Since Agnieszka was not feeling well, I visited most of the polling stations, while she remained in the car to transmit the results. We observed no major problems in our Area of Observation.

A few days later, at 10.30 hours, we were supposed to leave for the Electoral Judiciary, but there was no Jaír and no Agnieszka. I called Jaír, who told me that he was still 15 minutes away, so I took a taxi to the Judiciary, where Agnieszka arrived a little bit later.

The three senior judges held a public hearing, to rule on three 'observed' ballot papers. The hearing went very fast, since the intention of the three voters was absolutely clear after all.

I told Agnieszka to quickly take a photograph of the judges and also my back, with the mission's logo, with her smartphone. Just in time she shot a photo and sent it to Sylvia, our mission's press officer. The photo was instantly published on the mission's Facebook page.

Thanks to Agnieszka's numerous excellent photo's—and my small advice on how to take them—the Core Team must have had the impression that we worked really hard. In reality, this had been the most relaxed mission I had ever done.

We took a taxi back to our hotel. The driver turned out to be a lawyer! And not only that: he had been studying law with Yuri, the lawyer who had been sending double-meaning SMSs to Agnieszka during the first round. We didn't tell the taxi driver this; instead, we told him that Yuri was a lovely guy. Just a year later, a worldwide 'Me Too' discussion would dominate the headlines all over the world.

Jaír was waiting for us at the hotel. He had sent us an SMS, pleading not to inform Lima about the fact that he had been late and that I had to take a taxi. 'I need the employment', he wrote. The good news for him is that I always try to avoid contact with our Core Team and Service Provider, since it only gives me a lot of hassles.

The day came to say goodbye to Chiclayo. We were booked on the very first flight to Lima. Luckily, Jaír arrived punctually at 06.00 hours at our hotel. It was an emotional goodbye to Chiclayo. I had come to like the cheerful, sunny attitude of the people there.

Lima is either covered in mist or low-hanging clouds. This must have long-term effects on the minds of the inhabitants: the people in Lima appear to be downtrodden all the time.

This time I was totally prepared that we would have to go the offices of the Service Provider first, before we could drop off our luggage at hotel Delfines, but we were told that we were allowed to go to hotel Delfines first and bring the mission materials to the SP after that. When Agnieszka and I entered the offices of the SP, Pedro asked me if I was happy that this time I was allowed to get rid of my suitcases first.

I was a bit embarrassed that he remembered my outburst of the first round. I told him that, actually, I regretted my unprofessional outburst. Pedro smiled. This slim Pedro from Portugal was a much nicer and better organized guy than the other, massive Pedro from Portugal. In general, I like the Portuguese.

When I walked the streets near our hotel Delfines, I had a strange feeling. Something was wrong. Then I spotted a large sign saying: 'Honking is strictly forbidden'. I had gotten used to the constant honking of cars in Chiclayo. In the embassy district of Lima, drivers had to pay a hefty fine if they honked. It was eerily quiet. I missed the honking!

There was another difference with Chiclayo: when I crossed the street at a zebra crossing in Lima, cars actually stopped. In my beloved Chiclayo, this would never happen. To the contrary.

When a car driver approached a zebra crossing in Chiclayo, he would accelerate the car, to try to kill as many pedestrians as possible. That was the first thing I learned in Chiclayo: avoid zebra crossings, like the plague.

The debriefings by the Core Team had a pleasant surprise in store for Agnieszka and me. Rosa, our mission's expert on political party's finances, showed excerpts from ten (out of 25) weekly reports. Our WR was the first to appear on the big screen.

I had told Agnieszka, after we finished our latest WR, that my lines on 'The two Peru's, one above the table and one below the table', would catch the attention of the CT. Like many of my partners, Agnieszka had not been all too happy with my textual contributions, which were seen as 'too journalistic'.

On many occasions, my partners had a point, but in this case my gut feeling had been quite right: not only did my lines appear on the big screen, but also a photograph of Agnieszka and me. Alas: my little moment of triumph.

The last days of the mission I smoked my remaining cigars on the terrace at the third floor, beside the swimming pool. I was joined quite often by Sándor, Elena's new Hungarian partner, who had turned out, as I had predicted, a great partner for her. He's an old hand and a bit of a legend among the Spanish speaking observers. He still smoked incessantly.

I also talked to Marie-Therese, whose Danish partner was still the same asshole as he had been during the first round. No improvement there. When we were with a small group of LTOs, out of the blue, Marie-Therese suddenly exclaimed: „All Dutchmen are horrible pigs, except him."

She pointed at me. I thought it was a funny remark. It didn't bother me at all, knowing who said it, but Elena reacted furiously. „That's not true. I should know, because I am married to a Dutchman and I have lived in Holland for ten years."

Roger, from Sweden, joined me a few times, as did Søren and Marianna, who had been with us in Chiclayo for two nights. Marianna was depressed. She had to stay an extra day in hotel Delfines, because the pilots of Air France were on strike. Her flight had been cancelled. I explained to her that KLM pilots would never go on strike, since it would only harm their company.

At the same time, French train operators were also on strike. Just at the time when the European Football Championship 2016 had started in France. Can you believe that? Rowan Atkinson had been right about the French: along with criminals, rapists, burglars and murderers, the French will go straight to hell.

After arriving at Schiphol Amsterdam Airport, a weird thing happened to me: I was halted by a man in civilian clothes, who showed me some kind of ID. He asked for my passport. I was flabbergasted and tired from sitting cramped in economy class for twelve hours.

I asked why anyone would work in civilian clothes inside an airport: what's the use of that? While he was busy looking at my passport, all Peruvian passengers entered The Netherlands unobtrusively. No wonder you can buy cocaine at every street corner!

When I finally picked up my suitcase, Elena said she hoped that we would not have to go to the ministry yet again, for a debriefing. Her words turned out to be prophetic: the next day I received an email that there would not be a debriefing, but instead Elena and I were required to file a short report on our findings during the second round.

The report took me only half an hour to write. It was the first time ever, that I had to write a report for my ministry, which is strange, since nearly all observers from other countries are required by their ministries to write extensive reports after each mission.

But no matter what: Peru had been a very good mission for me. A very long mission also, so I made a lot of money. There was only one problem left: my next mission would surely not be as good.

In December 2017, president Kuczinsky ordered the release from prison of ex-president Fujimori. Kuczinsky was facing an impeachment vote by Parliament, but he struck a deal with Kenji Fujimori, who apparently agreed to sway a number of Fuerza Popular parliamentarians to vote in favour of Kuczinsky.

Strangely enough, during the 2016 congressional elections, the party of the Fujimori family (Fuerza Popular) obtained 73 out of 130 seats. An absolute majority, but Keiko was not elected president.

Kenji acted against the orders of his sister Keiko, who had wanted to replace Kuczinsky as president. In March 2018, Kuczinsky was forced to step down anyway, after the Brazilian construction company Odebrecht revealed that it had handed nearly 800,000 dollars to Kuczinsky's engineering company, some ten years previously.

Kuczinsky even had to hand over his passport: he was not allowed to leave Peru before the investigation into these corruption charges had been finished. Several ex-presidents were either imprisoned or under investigation on corruption charges.

Ollanta Humala spent nine months in prison in 2018. Alejandro Toledo fought his extradition in California. And on 17 April 2019 Alan García killed himself. When police officers arrived at his door to arrest him, García retreated to a room and pulled a bullet into his own head.

García had been president from 1985-1990 and from 2006-2011. During his first period he was an ardent leftist, while Peru's economy was hit hard by hyperinflation. During his second period he had become a populist, advocating free markets. He was accused of having accepted 100,000 euro's from Odebrecht. García denied the charges, but committed suicide nonetheless.

Kuczynski was succeeded as president by Martín Viczarra, who like all presidents before him, vowed to root out corruption in Peru. Yet again, without success. To give just one example: in November 2019 Keiko Fujimori was released from prison. She had been detained for one year on (guess what) corruption charges. She had been charged, but not convicted, of having received 1,2 million euro's by the same Odebrecht.

I cannot judge if these allegations were true or false, but one thing is certain: In Peru, everyone is corrupt. It's endemic to the system. Everyone believes that public money is there to fill private pockets. As John le Carré formulated it, in 'The Tailor of Panama': 'Corruption is not part of the problem; corruption is the problem'.

Chapter 22

HEAT
(Hostile Environment Awareness Training) - THE NETHERLANDS - 2018

'The military do not use diplomatic language'

I had not done any missions in 2017. I had been selected by the Dutch Ministry of Foreign Affairs three times, but I was not selected by the EU afterwards. Since I was 63 years of age, my wife thought that I was becoming too old. I explained to her that many observers were in their late sixties and that the EU cherished experience.

The problem was that these three missions had been small missions, with around 20 LTOs each. A total of 31 countries (28 EU countries plus Norway, Switzerland and Canada) were providing observers for EU EOMs and each country was allowed to submit three observers.

So for each mission a maximum of 93 observers could be submitted, while only 20 were needed. This meant that out of every five observers submitted, only one would ultimately be selected. I am not so arrogant to think that I am the best observer on the planet.

On top of that: since there were usually less women than men proposed by their countries, I would lose out if The Netherlands had proposed a female observer besides me. Because, let's face it, the other Dutch observers were my main competitors, especially Dutch women.

In April 2018 I was yet again selected by my own country, this time for a mission to Tunisia. I was not keen on being an LTO on a French-speaking mission, but by now I was so desperate that I would accept a mission straight into hell. Actually: a French-speaking mission comes close to hell, because in a French-speaking mission there are, by definition, lots of French. Who speak very fast French, without consideration for basic French speakers, like me.

Anyway, even for the Tunisia mission I was ultimately not selected by the EU. How low can you get? A few days later another query from the Dutch Ministry of Foreign Affairs arrived in my inbox: was

I interested in a mission to Colombia? Yes, I was. But history repeated itself.

Then, a few months later, I was offered an LTO job in Mali. By now I had been practicing my French for three years, so I was confident that my French was—at long last--good enough. So I replied: 'Yes, I'm interested in Mali'.

The next email from the Ministry of Foreign Affairs came as a bit of a surprise to me. Mali was considered to be a 'conflict area'. In fact, Dutch military had been based in Mali for several years, ever since Islamic extremists had occupied the northern part of the country in 2012, including legendary Timbuktu.

Since Mali was a 'conflict area', it was obligatory for me to attend the 4-day HEAT Training: Hostile Environment Awareness Training. I replied to the ministry that I had already done three HEAT trainings: two by the Italian special forces in Pisa, Italy, and one by the UN Peace Keeping Force in Khartoum, Sudan. Furthermore, I had been working and living in 'conflict areas' on numerous occasions.

The reply was: 'All of that is very useful, but you still need the official Dutch HEAT Certificate, which will be valid for five years'. I was not really in the mood to follow a four-day training course which was of little use to me, but the ministry was adamant: 'It's obligatory for the Mali mission'.

In the end, as always, my wife talked me into attending the training course. 'It's only four days and it's free of charge', she said. So I agreed. I knew that the HEAT training had been developed especially for Dutch military personnel who would be deployed to countries like Iraq, Afghanistan and Mali.

I also knew that the Ministry of Foreign Affairs was entitled to send some of its staff to these training courses, which were provided by the Dutch army. So I expected to do the HEAT training together with a few diplomats and young soldiers, who had most probably never set foot in Africa.

Since I had lived in 25 African countries, these young soldiers would certainly ask me all kinds of questions about life in Africa. That was fine. The only problem was: I had never visited Mali. I therefore decided to buy a guide book on Mali. In Dutch.

I knew that it was a good guide book, since it had been published as part of the Dominicus travel series. Jo Dominicus had been my history teacher at secondary school in Alkmaar. Thanks to him, I had developed an interest in history and archaeology.

I would have loved to study history, but I dreaded that in that case I would have to work as a teacher for the rest of my life. Therefore, I decided to study development economics, so that I could spend a part of my life in the Third World. In later years I realized that I would have loved to spend my entire life working at dig sites in Egypt as an archaeologist. Instead, I became an election observer. How low can you get?

Anyway, I learned a lot about Mali. The terrorist threat is mainly apparent in the northern part of the country, north of the Niger river, which for the most part is empty desert. Only one per cent of the population lives there.

The southern part of the country, where 99 per cent of the population lives, appeared to be quite a normal African country, with quite normal African challenges. But the Dutch soldiers lived in army barracks near the town of Gao, north of the river, where terrorist attacks were part of life.

For election observers, on the other hand, there did not seem to be major problems in the southern part of Mali. I have worked in countries and regions that were much more dangerous. But who am I, to question the wisdom of the Ministry of Foreign Affairs, when it comes to HEAT trainings?

So on Tuesday 15 May 2018, at 06.00 hours, I drove over the dyke across Lake IJsselmeer to Lelystad and further onto the Veluwe national park. The Dutch army still occupies huge stretches of land there, even though the army is much smaller than it once was.

In fact, all the tanks had been sold to countries like Indonesia. Who needs tanks anyway, when the Soviets are not coming anymore? And if they decided to come, the Russians would have to cross Ukraine, Poland and Germany first, in order to reach Holland. That means that, for the time being, we're quite safe.

I had never been a soldier. When I was young, the army still employed conscripts, but I went to university and therefore I was excused. In fact, none of my five younger brothers had been soldiers either, but my father made good for all of us: he had served in the Dutch Indies (nowadays: Indonesia) as a conscript soldier in 1949-51, when Indonesia gained its independence.

So here I was, for the first time in my life, at age 63, at the gate of Dutch army barracks. It took me some time to find the correct building. I was too early, of course, but I saw some people who were probably there for the same training. They were too old to be soldiers, for sure. And, like me, they were not built like athletes.

As it turned out, we were a group of sixteen ministry staff: nine men and seven women. Most were full-time diplomats. A few were consultants, like me. To my surprise, there were no soldiers in our group.

We were briefed by five military training experts. They told us that they would not reveal the training program to us, so it would be four days filled with surprises. I stood up and said that I had already done three of these trainings, so I knew what kind of surprises we could expect. I added that I would not utter a word to the other trainees. Only one of them had attended a HEAT training previously.

But the military trainers had some surprises in store for me. First of all, we had to leave our mobile phones in storage. The same for our photo cameras. It was forbidden to take photos. The training had to remain a surprise party for future trainees. The army would take some photos and mail them to us, after the training had been finished.

They explained that we could leave all our electrical equipment, like hairdryers, in storage, since we were going to a place where there was no electricity. I was puzzled by this, since during my previous HEAT trainings, in Pisa and Khartoum, I was driven back to my comfortable five-star hotel at the end of each day.

I was afraid the Dutch military had other ideas. Well: they had. We had to enter an army truck and we were driven to a forested area in the middle of nowhere. Not my idea of a nice time. When my wife and I were students, we were forced to go camping on our holidays, since we did not have money. That was the last time I went camping. I don't care much for luxury, but I certainly prefer to sleep in a decent hotel bed.

We had to erect our own tents: two huge, green army tents, with eight field beds in each. Erecting such a huge tent for the first time, together with seven men and women you have never met in your life, is a challenge, to put it nicely. It took us quite a while to figure out how to put all the parts together.

Thank God, it was not raining. To the contrary: I was sweating, since the sun was burning on our heads. I claimed the field bed that was closest to the opening in the tent. We slept with five men and three women in our tent.

I was only wearing a light jacket. Normally, around half May, the nights are not really cold any more in Holland, but we were unlucky: it turned out to be only five degrees Celsius at night. I was shivering from the cold. I slept with all my clothes on in my army sleeping bag.

The program was not revealed to us, but the trainers had explained that the first day would be relatively easy for us. The second day would be tougher. And so on until the fourth day. I didn't trust the trainers very much, but this turned out to be true.

The first afternoon we practiced first aid, in an open space in the forest. At 17.00 hours we were all handed army rations and small army stoves. I have to admit: the army rations were much better than the ones I had consumed in 1994 in Mozambique.

The chilli con carne really tasted—more or less—like chilli con carne. I still hated camping out, though. In the evening we all sat down in yet another army tent. Several guest lecturers arrived, to inform us about land mines, booby traps and embassy security measures.

There was no running water in our encampment, but several jerry cans were kept filled with potable water at all times. If we really wanted it, we could wash ourselves in a separate 'washing tent', but the water was ice cold.

As it turned out, none of us washed him or herself for four days. It didn't matter, really. We all smelled the same. I did brush my teeth, though. And, on the last morning, I even shaved, after I noted that the other men had shaved as well.

There was no electricity, except for a few lamps and—most important—a coffee machine. I later stumbled upon a generator that was humming on top of an army truck, out of sight, just beyond a small hill. A mobile toilet stood a hundred meters away, along a dirt road. I hate camping. That first night I slept only four hours.

The next morning we were divided into four teams of four. My teammates were a male consultant of my age, a slightly younger Afghan refugee who had lived in Holland for a number of years and a young women who had been born in Holland, but whose parents were originally from Turkey.

They asked us who of us wanted to be the driver. I did not know what that meant. On EU or OSCE missions I had never been allowed to drive myself. Were the trainers planning a practical joke with our 'driver'?

I was expecting the worst, but it turned out that driver literally meant driver: each team was provided with an army jeep. The consultant volunteered to be our team's driver.

The four teams drove out in their jeeps to yet another army training ground. Here, we were abducted and tortured for the first time. I knew what lay in store for us. And I knew what to do: do exactly what your captors tell you to do. The objective is not to play the hero: the objective is to stay alive.

After our abduction, we observed another team approach the road block. The bad guys were actually seven young actors, who were paid to abduct and rape us multiple times. They acted convincingly, though. It was quite funny to watch ministry officials being subjected to rough treatment.

One of them, Floor, immediately started negotiating with her captors. She had a lot of experience, since she worked in Palestine but lived in East Jerusalem and therefore had to pass an Israeli checkpoint twice a day. But these guys were not government officials. They were either criminals—in it for the money—or terrorists.

,,Why are you doing this to us?" Floor pleaded. As a result, one of the bad guys dragged one of Floor's female colleagues behind a truck, where he raped her (the actor actually told her to shriek, so it seemed quite real). A male colleague was also dragged behind the truck. He also shrieked after a shot rang out; he then returned with his hand covered in red lipstick.

It may seem funny, but when you experience for the first time that you are totally powerless in the hands of bad guys, it has quite an impact. The actors make it seem real. They force you on your knees and put a hood over your head. Then one of them puts his Kalashnikov between you shoulder blades and shouts abuse (in pigeon English!) in your ear.

The second night I only slept four hours again. The trainers had hinted at a very early start of the day, so yet again I slept with all my clothes on, including my jacket. Better safe than sorry, but they let us sleep until the sun came up. They then instructed us to break down the huge army tents.

I was delighted: the last night they would surely allow us to sleep in proper beds. No such luck, though. In fact, the third night would be the worst of all. But first we were all hoarded into a bus. The bus took us to Gilze-Rijen in the far south of The Netherlands, near the border with Belgium.

Our good friends Erick and Marianne de Mul possessed a house in Gilze. Erick had been my boss at UNDP in Mozambique for three years in the 1980s. My wife and I kept visiting Marianne in Gilze, even after Erick had passed away in 2006. I knew therefore that the Dutch special forces had an airfield there.

Now, for the first time, I was about to enter that airfield. Which was far from easy, as it turned out. Our bus was parked just outside the main entrance gate. Our trainer entered into a lively discussion with the guards at the gate.

We learned later that the list with our names had not been dispatched properly to the guards, so they did not know who we were, nor who we were supposed to meet at the airfield.

I always believed that The Netherlands was the best organized country in the world, but that believe was now severely put to the test. We had to wait for 45 minutes at that bloody gate, while hundreds of cars with workers were allowed entrance without much ado.

Finally, someone from the training unit arrived and we were allowed inside. On foot. In jeeps we were driven to the training facility. The rest of the day we were informed on how to survive after having been captured. The trainers were real professionals. They used examples of people who had really been captured, either by criminals or by terrorists.

Yet again, we were captured by bad guys. It was much more comfortable, though. Instead of lying on a moist forest floor, the captors entered our classroom. Even so, they put hoods over our heads and 'tortured' a few of us. These bad guys were not actors, but trainers, who knew exactly what they were doing.

At 17.00 hours we boarded the bus again and drove back. I was expecting the bus to be driven to army barracks, with proper beds and an army cantina with coffee, beer and cigars, but to my surprise the bus drove back to the exact same spot in the forest where our tents had stood.

What now? Well, the answer came immediately. We were handed army raincoats and some rope. We were told to make our own makeshift cover with a camouflaged raincoat between two trees. It would be a half-open cover against wind and rain. Not my idea of having a nice time.

I admit that I watch survival programs on TV sometimes, but I do that with the happy knowledge that I don't really have to live like that. Now I had to. Thank God, the army sleeping bag kept me warm. And by now I was so tired that I slept even better than in the eight-persons tent.

We would spend the last day of our HEAT training driving around in teams of four. We were expected to bring everything we had learned into practice. Yet again, we were captured several times.

We had to lie face down on the floor of a house for ten minutes. My army helmet was not bothering me, but my heavy bullet-proof vest was burying itself painfully into my chest. I decided to hold out, nevertheless.

The good news: I am a very patient man. And I am flexible. As an observer, you have to be. We received our HEAT certificates in the army barracks where we had started. Before we departed, the trainers warned those of us who were driving themselves.

,,You have probably slept less hours than you normally do. So be careful when driving." I thought about these wise words while driving back home. Imagine I would be involved in an accident, just after having received a four day training to arm myself against accidents!

But I arrived home safely. I was very tired, indeed, but at least I would possess some nice photographs of myself. I had never been in the army, so it would be great fun to possess a photograph of myself with an army helmet on and wearing a bullet-proof vest.

And it had been very interesting, for me as a journalist, to observe the interactions between down-to-earth military men and ever cautious diplomats. The military trainers had lived in difficult countries like Afghanistan and Mali, so there was some common ground with the diplomats.

But the military are used to communicate differently. They use dirty words all the time and some of them utter political views that are leaning towards the far right. Soldiers use plain, straightforward language, while diplomats always remain diplomatic when speaking in public.

Two groups with very different cultural backgrounds. It was quite funny for me to observe. Yet, we all had a good time together, out there in the woods. And the HEAT certificate would be valid for five years. That meant no more camping for me.

The only regret I have is that I lost my photographs: the military had posted our photographs on a website, where they would be available for just a few weeks. Just after I had downloaded them, my computer at home crashed! It had never happened to me before.

It simply did not occur to me that a computer could crash. But it did. By the time our new computer was operational, the photographs had been removed from the website. And I had lost the list with the names of the participants as well, so I could not ask them for copies of the photographs. Such a loss!

A few weeks later, I was selected by the EU for the Mali mission. But then I realized that I had misread the email from the EU. I was so delighted that I had been selected, that I had missed the very last word: 'reserve'.

I wondered what it meant, but then I remembered that I had been a 'reserve' before, some ten years earlier. It meant that I had to be available, in case another LTO would drop out of the mission. In the meantime, I was not permitted to apply for other missions.

Even though I was just a reserve, I had been selected, so I was invited to the ministry for a briefing on Mali. A male Dutch LTO and a female Dutch STO were also attending the briefing by the ministry's 'country expert'.

The LTO explained that he had been an LTO in Mali previously, as well as in three other French-speaking countries. I therefore understood why he had been selected, instead of me. Sometimes you graciously have to accept defeat. You can't win them all.

The LTO told us that during the previous elections in Mali two of the twenty LTOs were evacuated after they had caught malaria. That meant that there was a good chance that I would be called upon, to replace an unfortunate LTO. I was more than ready for Mali. So was the ministry.

They explained that, apart from the HEAT certificate, I also needed an elaborate health check. During the HEAT training some fellow trainees had talked about a 'KLM Health Check'.

I believed this only applied to diplomats, since I had never heard of it, but then the ministry ordered me to undergo an extensive health check at the KLM (Royal Dutch Airlines) premises at Schiphol Amsterdam airport. All of this, because Mali had been designated a 'conflict area'.

So on a hot day in early June 2018 I took the train to the airport. Health checks are always scary. You never know what they might find. On the other hand, it is good to know that you do not suffer from diabetes or prostate cancer or any other horrible disease.

In fact, I appeared to be just fine, except that my blood pressure was way to high. I explained to the KLM doctor that I already took an Irbesartan tablet every morning. „You need to see your general practitioner", the KLM doctor replied briskly.

In all truth, I did not worry about my blood pressure at all, but I worried very much about my ability to go on election observation missions. I therefore went to see my doctor immediately. I was prescribed Amlodipine as well.

Still, these two pills were not enough, as I found out. I checked my blood pressure every day, with my own device. I went to see my doctor again. This time, Hydrochloorthiazide was added to my daily medication. A few days later I noted a significant decrease in my blood pressure. Combined, the three tablets worked!

After that, all I had to do was wait for a phone call for Mali. But it never came. A few months later, I was invited by the ministry to go to Georgia as an LTO. I expected that I needed to be selected by the OSCE, but apparently that was merely a formality. Just a few days later, the ministry mailed me my E-ticket with Georgian Airways. ,,It looks as if this time you are really going", my wife told me.

Chapter 23

GEORGIA - First Round - 2008

'Amongst themselves, the Georgians are even more rude than the Dutch'

I had never visited the Caucasus and the only thing I knew about Georgia were four Georgians, two of whom were dead: Stalin and Shevardnadze. The other two were ex-footballer Shota Arveladze and ex-president Mikheil Saakashvili.

The latter had been exiled from Georgia and therefore lived abroad with his Dutch wife Sandra Roelofs. She was still allowed to enter Georgia. She had even been elected as a Georgian member of parliament in 2016, but she had declined to take her seat.

Thank God I found a well-written guide book on Georgia and Armenia in a bookstore. Like the book on Mali, it was published under the Dominicus series. Jo Dominicus, my old history teacher, had died in 1989, but the series had been continued by others.

In this case, the author was Karel Onwijn, a Dutch journalist who had lived in Georgia. He was wel informed. Georgia is a curious country. It is twice the sice of The Netherlands, but where my country has 17 million inhabitants, they only have 4,5 million.

In spite of their limited numbers they have their own language and their own scripture, which differs from the Russian cyrillic script. They even have their own religion: the Georgian Orthodox Church. Georgians are very proud of their history and they are extremely emotional people, very much like Italians.

I took the book to the ministry in The Hague for the briefing. I was the only observer there. The Dutch STOs had not been selected yet. The book started by stating that the Georgians are the most hospitable people in the world. The ministry's country expert said the same: he was also country expert for Armenia and Azerbeijan, but he liked Georgia better. A lot better.

That sounded good. Interestingly, the book contained a page that was fully dedicated to the Georgian uprising against their German masters on the Dutch island of Texel, which had happened during the last months of the second world war.

This was especially interesting to me, since my surname is Tesselaar, meaning someone from the island of Texel. I have to explain here that the name 'Texel' is pronounced with an 'x' in all of Holland, but not on the island itself. The 15,000 people who live on the island pronounce it as 'Tessel'.

In any case: my surname is spelled with two 'ss', so there cannot be any misunderstanding here. I am quite certain that my ancestors left the island more than three centuries ago, during the religious 'troubles' in Holland. Proof of this is that all Tesselaars were originally catholics, while most of the current islanders are descendants of protestant families.

And, curiously, there are no Tesselaars living on Texel. Every other year on 2 December, my birthday, my wife and I take the ferry to Texel. We visited the Georgian cemetary several times.

I later found out that ex-professional footballer Gia, who would be our driver in Tbilisi for eleven weeks, knew the story of the Georgian uprising by heart. He had even seen the movie *De Vliegenierster van Kazbek*.

The movie, made by the Dutch female filmer Ineke Smits, who had lived in Georgia, came out in 2010. It tells about the interaction of the islanders with the Georgians against the Germans.

The story of the Georgian uprising tells a lot about the Georgians in general. A Georgian batallion of 800 men had been fighting on behalf of the Soviet Union, but in 1943 the entire batallion was captured by the Germans. They were given a choice by the Germans: either fight for us or perish in prison camps.

Since the Georgians hated the Russians anyway, this was an easy choice them. They saw the Soviets as occupiers of their country. So they changed sides and fought for the Germans.

But the Germans never trusted the Georgians fully, so during the spring of 1945 the Georgians were transfered from the mainland of Holland to the island of Texel, where they could do little harm, or so the Germans believed. How wrong they would be!

In april 1945 it became apparent that Germany was losing the war. The Georgians feared the wrath of the Soviets and therefore the entire batallion decided to change sides yet again. They hoped to take over the island of Texel from the Germans, aided by local Dutch resistance fighters, but the plan failed miserably.

After the Georgians had captured a part of the island, the Germans quickly transfered extra troops and heavy weaponry to Texel. In the end, around 500 Georgians were killed or captured. The Germans lost nearly the same number and about 100 islanders also lost their lives. The Georgian cemetary is now the final resting place for 476 Georgian soldiers. The cemetery has been kept neat by the islanders.

On Sunday 23 September 2018 my wife and I celebrated my mother's 88 birthday, together with my brothers and sisters and their spouses. Just a few months earlier, in April 2018, my youngest brother Ivan and his wife Wendy had been succesful in persuading my parents to move to a rented appartment in an old folks home in Warmenhuizen, the village in north-west Holland where my mother had been born and where we had lived as a family.

At some point my mother asked me when I would leave for Georgia. ,,Tomorrow", I replied. And to the astonishment of my brothers and sisters I added: ,,At 06.00 hours." For them, to travel to a faraway country was still quite an enterprise. To me, it was like stepping on a bus to the next village.

On the plane I looked around, because I expected to see other observers. But I did not see anyone. Upon arrival at Tbilisi airport the OSCE driver told me that I was indeed the only observer on this particular plane.

I sat down next to him in the front seat and while driving along the George W. Bush Highway towards the center of Tbilisi, he recited the names of all the Dutch players of the 1974 national football squad, that lost in the final of the World Cup against the West-Germans in West-Germany.

That sounded good: like Latin Americans, Georgians apparently loved Dutch football. That gives common ground for conversation. As I would find out later, Georgians are also passionate about history. Like me. Even more common ground. I liked them already.

It was getting dark when he dropped me off at the Moxy Hotel, at the eastern bank of the Mtkvari river that divides Tbilisi into two parts. On some maps the river is still called Koera, the old Persian name. After dropping off my suitcases in my room, I went for a walk.

It was a pleasant evening. Just fifty meters from the hotel I purchased a six-pack of cold beers at a small family supermarket. That first evening, I sat down, just outside the hotel entrance, with a cold beer and a Dutch cigar.

My last moment of peace. The briefings would start the next day. After that, there would be no avoiding the other observers. I would have to be social. Not an easy thing for someone like me, but I've learned to consider it as part of my job to be social. I'm a professional socializer. Let's be honest: they pay me very well for the job.

On Tuesday 25 September the briefings started in the Blu Radisson Hotel, on the westbank of the river. I saw the other 27 LTOs. The great majority I had never met. I greeted my new partner, Nina. She was a 47 years old Norwegian, but she lived in London. She explained to me that her family came originally from Holland. They had moved to Norway some three centuries ago.

Nina told me that she had just arrived from Palestine, where she had lived for a year. She said that she really needed a break after that, since living in Palestine is extremely stressful. I told her what I had read about Georgia and that I believed Georgia would be just the right place for her to recuperate from the stress.

We were based in Tbilisi, the capital city with 1,5 million inhabitants. As LTO1 we would be responsible for the westside of the river, while two other LTO teams would cover the eastside of the river. Thank God, our westside was by far the most interesting part of the city. The old city center is situated on the westside, as is Rustaveli Avenue, the city's main street. The eastside consists mainly of residential areas.

The next day, Wednesday 26 September, was my wife's birthday. I had promised myself not to forget her birthday this time, as I had done several times before. After arriving in a completely new country, with new colleagues and all the briefings, I am so busy the first couple of days, that I tend to forget other important things.

Nina and I first had to find a hotel or apartment. In my case, a hotel would be fine, since my ministry would reimburse the hotel costs to me, regardless of how much I had paid. But I needed official hotel receipts, to show to the ministry at the end of the mission. Nina, however, preferred an apartment.

We called our new driver. His name was Giorgio, but everyone called him affectionately Gia, which was also his numberplate. Thank God, Gia spoke fluent English. He told us that he had worked for the Americans in Afghanistan for six years.

He also told us that he had been a professional football player. He had played in Georgia's national football team. This was an advantage, since every Georgian knew his name. We were allowed to park anywhere we wanted. Like the other driver, Gia also knew all the Dutch players of the 1974 Dutch squad by name.

In fact, Gia knew more about the current Dutch football competition than I did, since I watched the English Premier League every weekend. He told me that he was a Liverpool fan. I used to be an Arsenal fan, but because of Gia I switched to Liverpool.

We visited a few apartments. Nina spoke basic Russian, so she could communicate with the owners. Nina decided that she liked the one on the sixth floor of the building right behind the Courtyard Marriott hotel at Freedom Square. There were two large bedrooms. Nina said she preferred the one next to the kitchen. ,,That's OK", I replied. ,,Then I'll take the one at the far end of the apartment."

She looked at me in surprise. ,,I'm staying here all by myself", she said sternly. And she added: ,,I need the kitchen to myself." I was taken aback by this. On EU missions, both observers are usually required to stay in the same hotel or in the same apartment. The security experts insist on this.

As long as they are together, both observers can keep an eye on each other. You never know what calamities might happen out there in the provinces. And if it is necessary to evacuate the observers, it comes in handy when they can be picked up at the same place.

But on OSCE missions, apparently, it is quite common for the observers of one team to stay in separate places. Nina explained that it took her quite some time every morning to prepare her special muesli. She said she was a vegetarian and into health foods. That did not sound good.

People who are into health foods or superfoods do so for a good reason. They are usually quite sickly. This turned out to be true. A few weeks later, Nina got sick. She texted me that she had even lost her voice. Just before E-Day!

During the second round, she got sick again. It lasted only a few days, but still: isn't it funny that I haven't been to the doctor for the last thirty years, even though I am not a vegetarian and I drink beer and smoke cigars?

It dawned on me that it would probably be better for my mental health if I had some privacy. It takes a lot of energy on my side to act as if I'm social. In any case: now that Nina had found her apartment, I still needed a place to stay for myself.

I called our interpreter. We agreed that Gia and I would drive over to her place, to pick her up. Upon telling Gia that our interpreter's name was Brigita, he exclaimed: ,,That's great. I've worked with her before. She's very good, you'll see."

As it would turn out, Gia was right: Nina and I were lucky to have Gia and Brigita in our team. In later weeks we would find out that the driver of LTO2 did not speak one word of English. And their interpreter, an elderly man, was quite hopeless as well.

Back home in Holland I had googled a number of small hotels in Tbilisi's old city center. There were lots of them. I had noted one hotel that was called Terrace Garden Boutique Hotel. I had learned over the years that names can be misleading, but when Brigita and I visited the little roof terrace, I did not need to look any further.

It was a small terrace, filled with plants and several outdoors tables and chairs of different sizes and colours. And it had one big 'easy chair', next to the entrance door. That would be my chair in the evenings, I decided. I didn't care about the cost of the room, since my ministry would reimburse me the full amount anyway.

With Brigita translating, Nana, the owner, asked if I wanted to see the 'Blue Room' that she had in mind for me. It turned out that a Danish medical doctor was taking an afternoon nap in the room, but Nana reached for the door anyway.

Just in time, I stopped her. ,,Let him sleep. I don't need to see the room. The terrace is much more important. I will spend most of my evenings on your terrace anyway." When we drove back tot he Moxy hotel to pick up my suitcases, Brigita told me that she liked Nana.

In the coming days and weeks I would in fact be treated by Nana's family as a kind of uncle from far away. In the evenings, Nana's granddaughters would noisily play around me on the terrace, chasing each other or the dog. It felt as if I had been adopted by an Italian family, like I had been in Nairobi.

Nana spoke just a few words of English and I did not speak Russian, but we still managed to hold some sort of conversation. I asked her if she had ever heard of Nana Mouskouri. She said no. Nana's two daughters could translate, since they spoke decent English, but they lived elsewhere with their husbands. It didn't matter to me. I'm not a very social person, so the less conversation, the better.

So the easy chair was mine. It happened a few times that I arrived at the terrace and one of Nana's sons in laws was sitting in 'my' chair. The guy would jump up instantly and move to one of the other chairs.

I thoroughly enjoyed sitting in my chair in the evenings, with a Dutch cigar and a Georgian Dark Lion beer, that had been recommended to me by Nana. In October, the weather was still fine nearly every day.

On 'my' terrace I would read the mission's Daily Brief on my mission smartphone and I would whatsapp with my wife. The good news of being in a country where you cannot communicate with the locals is that nobody will ever call you on your phone. The only people who would call me were my colleagues. That gave me peace of mind.

The view was not extremely spectacular. To the far right I could see Mtatsminda Park, with the colourful lights of the TV-tower and the Furnicular going up and down the mountain side. To the left I spotted a curious steel-and-glass building, constructed near the top of a mountainous slope.

It looked like the ominous building of one of those bad guys in the early James Bond movies. Weeks later, I found out that it was the home of multi-billionaire Bidzina Ivanishvili, Georgia's strong man.

He was the leader of the country's ruling party called Georgian Dream and, according to many people, he was the owner of practically everything in Georgia.

Before Georgian Dream came to power, the country was ruled by Saakashvili's UNM. These two parties contested the current presidential elections. It was a bitter struggle, since the two parties hated each others guts.

We installed our team's printer in Nina's spacious apartment. That would be our base. The first two days, I instructed Gia to pick me up at the OSCE office at Afkhazi Street, since that was the only place I knew in the whole of Tbilisi.

It was only a five minute walk from my hotel, but I found out that it took Gia 45 minutes additional time to get there, since he had to drive all around the old city center, where the small cobblestoned streets were one-direction streets.

Since Nina's apartment was straight behind the Courtyard Marriott Hotel, at Tbilisi's main Freedom Square, I asked Gia if he could park there. This was a ten minute walk from my hotel.

Having been an ex-footballer for the national team, Gia managed to obtain permission to enter the parking lot behind the Courtyard Marriott Hotel at all times. So that became our base. From there, we would venture out every morning with our team.

Nina turned out to be a reasonably good partner for me. We did not have much in common and she kept her distance, but she was easy going and not an overachiever, thank God. She was also easy going on our Weekly Reports.

Instead of sitting down together, as I was used to, we each wrote a number of chapters and then just added them. I didn't bother to check all the details written by Nina. I guess I was becoming too old for that.

So it was a relaxed mission for me. Not too much stress. The interviews went fine. Even though the Georgians were divided into two camps, bitterly opposing one another, to us nearly everyone was very friendly.

I quickly fell into a daily routine. At the end of our working day, I let Gia drop me off at the Courtyard Marriott. I then walked over to the Galleria, the huge mall at only 200 meters distance at Rustaveli

Avenue.

I did my shopping at the Goodwill Supermarket, situated at the lowest floor of the Galleria, where I could choose from 25 fresh salad bowls. Very reasonably priced, very tasty and most importantly: I did not have to wait. Georgians are never in a hurry, so whenever I visited a restaurant, I had to wait at least half an hour, before the food arrived at my table.

I hated waiting in restaurants. I preferred to buy two or three fresh salads from the supermarket. I took them to my room and ate them in front of my Russian sports channels. Or I ate them on the terrace, where Nana would order her maid to bring me a plate, a knife and a fork.

Nina, on the other hand, loved restaurants. When we drove out to the outlying districts of Tbilisi, she would ask Brigita what the best restaurant was over there. I asked Nina if it was OK with her that the two of us paid lunch for Gia and Brigita as well. Luckily, Norway pays its observers very well, like The Netherlands, so Nina agreed.

Af first, Gia and Brigita objected. Georgians are extremely proud people and they considered Nina and me to be guests in their country, so they should actually pay for us. But I explained that Nina and I were paid eight times more than they and that we did not want them to spend their entire daily allowage on expensive meals.

They were still not convinced, until I added: ,,Listen: Gia does all the work when we sit in the car and Brigita does all the translating when we interview people. So Brigita and Gia do all the work and Nina and I get all the payments; that's not fair. Just let Nina and me pay for lunch and don't discuss it anymore."

At just thirty meters from my hotel I discovered a small, family supermarket, where I could buy beer, yoghurt, cheese and soft drinks. Live was good. At the beginning of each evening I took a stroll along the cobblestoned streets towards the river. Thanks to the tourists, there were lots of shops, restaurants, terraces and colourful lights.

I found out that the 'Peace Bridge', the ultra-modern pedestrian bridge built by Saakashvili, was only ten minutes from my hotel. At the east side of the river was Rike Park, where the cable cars started their voyage towards the top of the ridge on the westside of the river.

I crossed the Metekhi Bridge at the foot of the statue of King Gorgasali, who had founded Tbilisi in the fifth century. On the west side of the river was Meidan Square, a popular spot for tourists and Georgians alike. From there, I simply followed Afkhazi Street back to my hotel.

I normally don't like to work in the capital city, close to the Core Team, but in this case I realized that I had been very lucky. Some observers later told me that they had been based in provincial towns where there was absolutely nothing to do in the evenings. In a place without tourists, there are no restaurants, so they had to eat in their hotel every evening. I felt blessed.

We worked quite close together with the other two LTO teams, who covered the eastside of the river. We decided to visit the Police Headquarters and national party headquarters together. It went well. Marie-Therese from Switzerland and Khatchig from France formed LTO2, while Justyna from Poland and Mats from Sweden formed LTO3.

Nina and I covered four electoral districts. Three directors were friendly towards us and always made time to talk to us, even though we usually bumped in without having made an appointment. The fourth, of Mtatsminda district, was less friendly at the beginning, but became slightly friendlier as time went by. The Vale and Saburtalo districts had their offices in the same building.

Tamaz, the Vale director, had lived in Portugal for six years. To Nina and Brigita's annoyment, I talked Portuguese with him for extended periods of time. He seemed like a nice guy to me, but after E-Day he was widely accused of having sided with the ruling party.

Nina and Brigita were even more annoyed whenever we had lunch at our favourite vegetarian restaurant: Mama Terra. The owner/cook was a young Mexican woman. After I had told the waitress that I had lived in Mexico, the owner came to our table. We talked in fast Spanish about Frida Kahlo and other Mexican topics. After ten minutes, Nina instructed me briskly to switch to English.

One Saturday evening we decided to have dinner with all three teams. Mats had lived in Tbilisi, so he led us to a hidden restaurant, at a short distance from Rustaveli Avenue. Unfortanely, Marie-Therese and Khatchig had not been able to join us, so we were just four people.

After we had ordered, draft beers arrived, as well a coca cola for Justyna. Then something strange happened. Nina, sitting net to Justyna, asked Justyna a question. Justyna didn't answer, but just stared in front of her.

Nina repeated her question. No reaction at all from Justyna, who was sitting straight in front of me. Nina touched Justyna's shoulder. Still no reaction. Something was terribly wrong.

Justyna's upper body started shaking. I had never witnessed an epileptic attack in my life, except on television. Both Mats and I leaped up. We each grabbed one of Justyna's shoulders. She was shaking ever more violently.

The restaurant staff came to our aid. They asked the guests who were sitting on a nearby couch to move away. With four people we then lifted Justyna up and lowered her onto the couch. An English speaking woman said that it appeared to be an epileptic attack, but Mats explained that Justyna was a diabetic.

While we held Justyna down, Mats reached for her glass of coca cola. He put a straw in it and held it to her mouth. ,,She needs sugar", he explained. It took a few minutes, but the sugar water apparently helped Justyna to calm down.

Everything went so fast and we were all so busy, that I never noticed that Nina had done a great job as well. She had gone outside the restaurant, to a quiet spot, where she had informed Silke, the Observer Coordinator of our mission. Silke had immediately called our security expert, who in turn had called for medical assistance.

Within twenty minutes, two medics arrived. They examined Justyna and gave her some medication. Merab, the Georgian security assistant of our mission, also arrived. All of this worked very well. We sat down at our table again and continued our meal as if nothing had happened. Justyna was also eating. She appeared to be reasonably OK.

Justyna explained what had happened. She was indeed a diabetic and she possessed an advanced computerized device to moniture her diabetics. Earlier that day, however, the device had fallen onto the floor.

It could not be repaired in Georgia, so Justyna would have to wait for a new device, to be sent to her from her native Poland. That would take a few days and during those days she would have to monitor her diabetics by hand.

The next day I ran into Silke at the OSCE office. ,,All three of you did great last night", Silke complimented me. ,,You coordinated very well." I replied that everything happened so fast that there had not been time for any coordination. Each of us had just done what seemed to be necessary at the time. Luckily, it worked out fine. And Justyna was fine during the rest of the mission. No more seizures.

I called the Dutch embassy and made an appointment with Jos Douma, the ambassador and two embassy staff: Loes and Floris, who during E-Day would join our mission as locally recruited STOs. I explained to them that we were all Dutch, since Nina's family had originated in The Netherlands.

The Dutch ambassador explained that Georgian Dream exploited their position as ruling party quite shamelessly, but that UNM had done exactly the same when they had been in power. It's what ruling parties do all over the world.

During the briefing at the Dutch ministry in The Hague, the country expert had told me that Sandra Roelofs, the Dutch wife of ex-president Saakashvili, had won a seat in the Georgian parliament. The Dutch ambassador now explained to me that UNM, Saakashvili's party, had assigned a constituency to Sandra that had always been won by UNM. So victory was guaranteed.

Regardless of this, wherever we went, the moment I mentioned that I came from Holland always resulted in the same remark: 'Ah, the land of our Sandra'. She was much more popular in Georgia than her Georgian husband, who was widely seen as a womanizer. Sandra mastered the language very well. She even sang songs in Georgian on Georgian television!

I started typing our STO manual. As usual, I added some interesting historical information about Georgia, but then the Core Team warned us not to include any sensitive information. This was a bit strange, since the STO manual is not an official OSCE report. It's for our own internal use only.

Anyway, I had typed about twenty pages, when I mailed it to Nina. She resolutely took out five pages. ,,Sensitive stuff is not allowed", she told me briskly. I accepted. It's not the end of the world, when someone edits your text.

I had a good partner, a good interpreter, a good driver, a good Core Team and a good hotel in the old city center, amidst thousands of tourists. Why would I create a fuss about a stupid manual?

EU missions deploy relatively small numbers of STOs, since long-term observation is considered to be more important, but OSCE still emphasizes the importance of short-term observation around E-Day. Therefore, in addition to the Core Team and 28 LTOs, there would be a whopping 320 STOs, of which 16 were assigned to Nina and me.

In addition, we were assigned 15 parliamantarians, belonging to four parliaments: EU, OSCE, NATO and the Council of Europe. I realized that, during E-Day, Nina and I would be so busy coordinating these 31 observers, that we would not have time to visit polling stations ourselves.

Our 16 STOs would stay the first and last nights at the Hualing Hotel, a relavitely new hotel at the eastern outskirts of Tbilisi, close to the Tbilisi Reservoir, that provided the city with fresh water. The STOs were briefed by the Core Team in the great hall of the Hualing Sea Palace Shopping Mall, at a short distance from the hotel.

I had never seen so many STOs in my life! It looked like a rock concert, with two giant TV-screens at either side of the stage, where the CT was seated. But it was well organized. To show the STOs how how the elections would be organized in Georgia, a fake polling station would be operational at the back of the hall.

The three Tbilisi LTO teams were requested to act as polling staff. The STOs would act as voters. I immediately proposed to be the PS member who would administer invisible ink to each voter's index finger.

This proved to be great fun. I had administered the ink to my own finger and then showed it to each voter under a fluorescent flash light. It was clearly visible.

Kyle, our mission's sympathetical logistical expert from the USA, had been so nice as to book rooms for all our 16 STOs at the Holiday Inn, conveniently situated at 'our' westbank of the river, albeit around five kilometers from the center of Tbilisi.

A few days before our STOs would arrive, I visited the Holiday Inn, to book a conference room, where Nina and I could brief our STOs. A woman from the hotel's management showed me two of the conference rooms. Both of which were empty.

,,We have five conference rooms", she explained. ,,What time do you need them?" I told her that I did not know exactly what time the STOs would arrive in the Holiday Inn. And I added: ,,Can I just ask for a conference room after the STOs have arrived here? You have five conference rooms. They will never be occupied all five of them." She concurred.

This would be my biggest mistake of the entire mission. It turned out that all five conference rooms were actually occupied by the time the STOs arrived. Nina and I had to do our briefing in the lobby on the first floor. During my first visit to the Holiday Inn, the lobby had been totally deserted. Now, on a Friday afternoon at 15.00 hours, it was packed with people.

So the briefing was a disaster. And it was my fault. I realized that our debriefing had to be better organized. I visited the Best Western hotel, just 500 meters from the Holiday Inn. They had a nice, small, affordable conference room. I immediately booked it. As we say in Holland: not even a donkey bangs his head twice against the same stone.

Luckily, the welcome dinner with 9 of the 16 STOs, was a great succes, even though Nina did not join us. She went her own separate ways with her old STO friend Erika, from Sweden. I explained to Nina that it was important to dine with the STOs, since they would, at the end of their mission, give their opinion about us to the CT. Nina did not listen to me.

But we had a nice dinner at restaurant Tabla at Chavchavadze Avenue. One of the STOs, Karin from Germany, would a year later again be my STO in Mozambique. I was so pleased with the evening that I paid the bill for Gia, Brigita and her husband Mikko from Finland. And we took 4 STOs in our car back to the Holiday Inn, so they did not have to spend money on a taxi. Always be nice to your STOs!

Nina and I were supposed to brief our parliamentarians together with LTO2 and LTO3. It was decided that Mats would speak for all six of us, since he had lived in Tbilisi. The parliamentarians would only be in the country for two or three days, so the briefing was held on Saturday afternoon, just before E-Day.

By then, the parliamentarians had already been briefed by the Core Team for half a day, so they had reached the limits of their endurance. Most of them walked away. The few that remained seemed not the least interested in Mats's speech. Thank God I did not have to hold that speech. It's my greatest nightmare, to hold a speech in front a non-interested audience.

Towards the end of Saturday afternoon I received a call from Silke, the observer coordinator. She said that she was sick and therefore worked from her apartment. She asked me to point out a good polling station for ambassador Geert-Henrich Ahrens, our Head of Mission, and Thomas Rymer, the OSCE/ODIHR spokesperson, who had just arrived from Warsaw.

It had to be a polling station close to the OSCE office, it had to be easily accessible and it had to be hidden from the media. I went to the OSCE office and told Thomas to just follow me, as I knew a polling station at only twenty meters from the office. ,,There's a cold wind blowing, so put on a jacket", I advised him. ,,Don't worry", Thomas replied. ,,I'm Canadian. I'm used to it."

I showed it to him and he agreed that the polling station was ideally situated, the more so since it was listed under a wrong address. It was listed at Afkhazi Street, while in reality the entrance was at the back, at Iveria Street.

We walked back to the OSCE office, where everyone was surprised that I, a lowly LTO, was talking amiably to a high-up OSCE person from Warsaw. Thomas thanked me. ,,That's what they pay me for", I said. ,,I hope they pay you well", he replied. Canadians have a good sense of humor.

E-Day went fine, except for the fact that Nina was sick. She could work her phone, though, since she had most of her voice back. One of our STOs was also sick, so I decided to take her place for a few hours. STO Erika was doing very well on her own, aided by a good interpreter, but she was happy that I joined her.

We observed a polling station at the outskirsts of the city, an area whose inhabitants were mainly Azeris, from Azerbaijan. After that, Erika told me that she had received information about the polling station where presidential candidate Salome Zurabishvili was going to vote at 13.00 hours.

Salome was officially an independent candidate, but she was supported by Georgian Dream, Ivanishvili's ruling party and she was considered to be the frontrunner. Gia and I followed Erika's car.

To my horror, she drove straight to the polling station that I had selected for our Chief of Mission and the ODIHR spokesperson. I had promised them that it would have been hidden from the media, but when we went inside at least fifteen TV camera's were waiting at one side of the class room.

A few minutes later, Salome arrived and voted, just three meters in front of Erika and me. It was all over in minutes. The camera crews left and Erika received a phone call. It was her Italian partner. She felt better now and was coming over to join Erika. I thanked Erika and bid her farewell.

I walked over to the Goodwill supermarket to buy a few salads, which I ate in my room, with my headphone at the ready at my side. There were no major problems with any of our STO teams.

The only problem was that I had to stay awake until the very last team had returned to their hotel. When I could finally lay down in my bed, the sun was almost coming up. The next day Silke told me that I had been the very last LTO to go to sleep.

To everyone's surprise, Salome did not win with more than 50 per cent, which meant that there would be a second round. The UNM candidate, Grigol Vashadze, did remarkably well. Both he and Salome received 39 per cent of the vote.

The third candidate, David Bakradze of European Georgia (a spin-off of UNM), received ten per cent. The other 22 candidates received next to nothing. I always wondered why someone would run as a candidate, when you know that you don't stand any chance at all.

The LTOs had been contracted for six weeks, so each LTO was free to decide if they wanted to stay on for the second round or not. Out of 28 LTOs, 21 decided to stay on, including myself. One extra LTO was contracted, so for the second round, there would be 11 LTO teams.

The number of LTO teams for Tbilisi was reduced from three to two, which meant that we would have to cover one additional electoral district at the eastern side of the river.

Chapter 24

GEORGIA - Second Round - 2018

'You'll find the Stalin Museum at the end of the Stalin Avenue'

According to the electoral law, the second round had to be held within two weeks after the results of the first round had been published officially. For some reason, the electoral authorities delayed the decision on a date for the second round for several weeks. This lead to speculation. Was there a secret agenda?

While Nina, Brigita and I were interviewing the electoral chief of Saburtalo district, he received a text message, stating that Sunday 2 December would most probably be the date of the second round. ,,That's my birthday", I exclaimed spontaneously. Not very smart, from my side, as I realized soon after.

,,Then I will give you a bottle of wine", the district chief said with typical Georgian hospitality. I remembered what I had read in my guide book, that Georgians are the most hospitable people in the world. For a Georgian, a guest is a gift from God.

Not so for Norwegians. When we drove away, Nina told me briskly that, as observers, we were not allowed to accept presents. ,,Why did you not tell me this during the meeting?" I asked her. ,,Now I cannot refuse his bottle of wine, without insulting him."

As a result, I did not dare to meet this district chief again for a number of days. And from this moment on, both Brigita and Gia did not like Nina very much anymore. They believed she was a bit nuts or, in any case, not a very nice person.

Obviously, Brigita had talked about this incident at home, because a few days later her sympathetic husband, Mikko from Finland, told me he was afraid to do a mission for OSCE as an LTO, since there was a chance that Nina would then be his partner. I tried to convince him that she was not really a bad partner, but Mikko said that the risk was too great.

Mikko had been an STO twice and therefore had been forced to work close together with people whom he had never met before in his life. Apparently, there had been some problems. As Forrest Gump's mama used to say: „Life is like a box of chocolats; you never know what you gonna get."

It was a few days after my birthday when we finally went back to meet the district chief. He reached under his desk and pulled out the biggest bottle of wine I had ever seen in my life. It must have contain-ded five liters.

But I came prepared: I had purchased two big birthday cakes, one for the staff of the Saburtalo office and one for the people of the Vake office, next door. All of this with Nina's full permission. Everybody happy.

During the first round there had been 25 presidential candidates. Now there were only two left, of which one, Salome, was not campaigning at all. The strong man of Georgian Dream, multi billionaire Bidzina Ivanishvili, had decided that it was better to let his party do the campaigning. Salome had estranged many voters during the first round, because of her rather clumsy performance as a candidate.

Salome's picture was everywhere in Tbilisi. Enormous banners showed an attractive woman in her fifties. But she had a problem: she had lived the first 32 years of her life in Paris. Even though her parents had been Georgians, she spoke better French than Georgian. In a country where everybody was fiercely nationalistic, this was a serious setback.

In between the first and second rounds, Nina and I had nothing to do for one and a half weeks. When I was an LTO in Sudan, the LTOs were allowed to return home for ten days between two rounds. In Peru, we were allowed to return home for a full month. But in this case, for some reason, it was decided that the LTOs would not return home.

So for ten days, I had nothing to do. Surely, I still received our Core Team's Daily Brief every evening at 19.00 hours, but there was nothing to report. There were no attachments. Apparently, the Core Team had also switched off completely. I decided to take two long walks every day, one in the early afternoon and one in the early evening.

I visited the national museum twice and I went to the movies a few times. I purchased a metro ticket and visited the central train station, as well as the huge market nearby. There was supposed to be a Pirosmani museum, just north of the station, but I couldn't find it.

I'm not much of an art lover, but I liked Pirosmani's rather primitive looking paintings. Niko Pirosmani (1862-1918) means to the Georgians what Vincent van Gogh means to the Dutch.

I sat down at Rike Park to smoke a cigar and watch locals and tourists walk by. I took the cable car to the medieval Narakala castle on top of the cliff. It turned out to be just a façade: only the outer wall was still standing. In the evenings, it was nicely lighted though. From below, it looked great.

I walked around the twenty meter aluminium statue of Kartlis Deda, which means Mother Gergia. The statue is visible from the entire center of Tbilisi. She holds a sword in one hand and a glass of wine in another, meaning: when you arrive as an enemy, we will kill you, but as a friend we'll offer you wine.

I like the Georgians, but they are a curious people. They are frequently shouting at one another. The first couple of times this happened, I froze. When someone shouts in Holland, this means that something really serious is going on. In Georgia, they shout all the time. After a while I got used to it.

Georgians are very hospitable, but they have a rather peculiar idea about what's private and what's public. In western Europe, no one would enter someone else's hotelroom without knocking on the door first. In Georgia, they just open the door of any hotelroom, whether there's a guest inside or not.

It happened to me several times that one of Nana's daughters tried to open my door, to check if the hot water in my bathroom was functioning properly. Luckily, I had barricaded my door with my telescopic walking stick, that I always carry in my suitcase for precisely this purpose.

Another curious aspect of life in Georgia: it happened quite a few times that I was walking behind someone on the pavewalk, when this person suddenly stopped dead in his/her tracks. In Holland, we would first look behind us, before standing still on a busy pavewalk, but Georgians do not do this.

The same applies to cars: a driver would suddenly stop his car, without checking if anyone was driving behind him. Another remarkable thing is that many drivers don't fill their tanks at official petrol stations, but instead buy their car fuel from black market vendors. The fuel is imported from South Ossetia, where the Russian ruble is still in use. Obviously, this is cheap, tax-free Russian car fuel.

The Georgians are very emotional and fiercely nationalistic. I quickly learned not to mention any historic events anymore, since the Georgians would not, or could not, stop talking about it. Admittedly: they know a lot more about their own history than any of my neighbours in Holland know about our Dutch history.

Georgians are very proud of the history of their motherland. They get emotional when they talk about it. Like Italians, they will raise their voices and make wide gestures with their hands. And they don't like it when you criticise them.

I once mentioned that Georgia could never become a member of Nato, because the risk is too great that the Georgians might attack their mighty neigbour, Russia, on impulse. And then the other Nato members would be forced to attack Russia as well. I never mentioned this again, for fear of being lynched on the spot.

Unfortunately, in Tbilisi the weather is much worse in November than in October. It was raining quite often and the temperature became so low that my summer jacket was hardly protecting me from the cold. I purchased a shawl and an umbrella. It became too cold and too wet to smoke a cigar on my beloved terrace.

Which was rather good news in a country where cigars are unbelievably expensive. My wife really hated to be alone for so long, but I encouraged myself by repeating to myself, over and over again, that I was making a lot of extra money.

I was, in fact, doing a second mission, which meant that I would not have do another mission for the entire next year! As Johan Cruijff used to say: 'Every disadvantage has its advantage'

And the old centre of Tbilisi is a very pleasant place. Thanks to the tourists. In the evenings most shops and restaurants are brightly lit.

You never get bored in the old centre. But all things must pass. After ten days I received a call from Brigita, our interpreter: she wondered if I was still alive.

So we went around again, interviewing the electoral authorities, human rights groups, women's groups and the remaining two political parties. Even though Salome herself was quite invisible, apart from hundreds of billboards with her photograph, her campaign office remained in function.

One late afternoon we entered her office, opposite the Blu Radisson hotel at Rustaveli Avenue. The female spokesperon immediately took us to Salome's room, but just before she opened the door, I stopped her.

I explained that our Core Team would maintain contact with the presidential candidate. We, as lowly LTOs, were only allowed to talk to the lower echelons of Salome's campaign.

The spokesperson told us to wait a few minutes. She then returned with a bunch of copies of exchanges between the two campaigns, that had been translated into English for the international media. Interesting stuff.

I always explained to foreigners that Dutch people are extremely direct, even rude, when talking among themselves in Dutch. Now it turned out that Georgians were even worse than the Dutch. Much worse! I could hardly believe what I read. Was this all true?

Of course, you have to be careful, when a political party provides you with information about their opponents, but the texts appeared to be authentic. To summarize: the two camps, Georgian Dream and UNM, insulted one another with words that I cannot repeat here.

Even Saakashvili, who in The Netherlands was considered to be a decent guy, joined enthousiasticallly in the dirty fights, as was the director-in-chief of the private Rustavi 2 TV-station, which supported UNM.

In the end, the insults from both sides became so bad, that the Swiss embassy drafted a 'Code of Conduct'. Both sides signed it, but continued with the insults nevertheless in their native language.

Georgians like to stage protests. In front of the parliament building, at Rustaveli Avenue, there were always people protesting against something or someone. Two fathers, whose teenage suns had apparently been killed by the security forces, had been staging a protest for weeks on end.

They even slept there. When it became colder, supporters erected tents for them in front of the parliament building. It did not harm democracy, since the Georgian parliament had in 2012 been moved to Koetaisi, the ancient capital, situated in the mid-west of the country.

The parliament building in Tbilisi, now in use as government offices, is destined to become a luxury hotel. It's the most notable building at Rustaveli Avenue. It has the look of an old classic building, but was in fact constructed after the Second World War by German prisoners of war.

Nina and I started preparing for the arrival of our new STOs. The donor countries were getting tired of the electoral process in Georgia. They were not willing to finance as many as during the first round. This meant that we would have to supervise only four STO teams. We were also assigned one LSTO team and six teams of parliamentarians.

But it was routine for us by now. We just had to modify our STO manual a bit and print it again. I had found a much better map of Tbilisi in the shop of the national museum. And by now I had figured out how to pinpoint all the polling stations by using the digital system of the Electoral Commission.

The new group of eight STOs was OK. I was so happy with them, that after our joint welcome dinner at the Sakhli restaurant, I told them that I would pay the entire bill. There was a reason fort his: it was 26 November, the day my parents celebrated their 65 marriage anniversary.

I had missed their 60th marriage anniversary, when I was on a mission in Honduras. Now I missed this one as well. That is the price you have to pay as an election observer. The STOs and Nina were surprised that I paid the entire bill, but I explained my reasons to them.

To be honest, restaurants are not expensive in Georgia. And we were only seven strong, since the two Swedes were invited by their embassy and Bujar, the Italian, was staying with friends in Tbilisi.

Little did I know that Bujar, who was of Albanese descent but possessed an Italian passport, would first be Nina's LTO partner in Khazakstan and after that my STO in Mozambique, where he would create a stink for my partner there. Thank God, I cannot look into the future.

E-Day was finally set at 28 November 2018. The day went fine. So much so that Nina and I decided to go out and visit polling stations ourselves. As it turned out, we went around Tbilisi for a full four hours, but we did not enter one polling station. The situation outside the polling stations was much more interesting.

Outside each polling station a car was parked with the doors open. Men with tattoos and dark sunglasses were hanging around these cars. They were called 'coordinators', but it was not clear what they were coordinating. They looked like gangsters in old-fashioned Hollywood movies.

The voters must have felt intimidated when they entered the polling stations. We asked several of these men what they were doing there, but they were evasive. We noted that some of them had lists with names and telephone numbers. Democracy, Georgia style.

Loes, of the Dutch embassy, who had been an LSTO for the other Tbilisi team, later told me that she had had the same impression of these 'coordinators': they were there to intimidate the voters. Obviously, they were paid by Georgian Dream, the ruling party. That's the advantage, when your party leader is a billionaire.

As was to be expected, Salome won with 59 per cent of the vote. After E-Day, there were several large rallies held in Tbilisi, by both coalition and opposition parties. Nina and I were asked to observe them, assisted by Merab, the security assistant of the mission, in case irregularities would break out.

I asked Brigita to literally write down what was being said in Georgian during those rallies, including all insults. After the rally was finished, Brigita and I sat down and she translated the quotes into English. As I expected, the CT was very happy with my elaborate rally reports.

That Georgians are emotional became obvious when they were foolish enough to invade South-Ossetia on 8 August 2008. This provoked

Russia to intervene. Tiny Georgia against mighty Russia: any sensible human being would not start a war against such a giant neighbour.

But once Georgians get emotional, they quickly go from bad to worse. The war broke out because the Georgian provinces South-Ossetia and Abchazia declared themselves independent.

In effect, the inhabitants decided that they would be better off under Russian domination than under Georgian domination. There are Georgian minorities living in both provinces, but also Russian minorities and, of course, the indigenous population.

At some point, the Georgian city of Gori was bombed by the Russians. On 12 August 2008, a (forbidden) cluster bomb fell onto Gori's central square, killing the Dutch cameraman Stan Storimans and four Georgian civilians.

The Russians claimed that Storimans had died after a car accident, but a research committee from the Dutch Ministry of Foreign Affairs travelled to Georgia and concluded that Storimans had died from a 5 millimeter bullet, one of 20 bullets that had been released by a Russian SS-26 cluster bomb.

Gori, the birthplace of Stalin, would be occupied by the Russians for several weeks. After the population had fled, the Russians allowed militants from South-Ossatia to enter the city and sistematically rob the houses. It proved to be Saakashvili's Armageddon. He was blamed for the military disaster and was, a few years later, exiled from his own country.

The end result of all this was that many Georgians had to leave their houses in South-Ossetia and Abchazia, to be resettled in Georgia. The independence of the two provinces was only recognized by Russia, Venezuela and Nicaragua. The provinces became in effect Russian provinces.

On 2 December 2018 yet another big rally was scheduled to be held in Tbilisi. Since Nina and I had reported extensively on previous rallies, Silke, our mision's Observer Coordinator, asked if I was willing to observe this rally yet again, even though it was on a Sunday. On EU missions, observers work seven days a week, but on OSCE missions it is quite customary to take the Sundays off.

I replied to Silke that I had been working in Tbilisi for ten weeks on end and that I had never set foot outside the city. I told her that it would be my 64th birthday and that I had planned to visit the Stalin museum in Gori, in order to see a bit of the rest of Georgia as well.

Silke understood this, especially after I quoted a few lines from a Beatles song: 'Will you still need me, will you still feed me, when I'm 64?' She asked me why I was so interested in the Stalin museum.

,,First of all, back home in The Netherlands, it will be great fun to tell people that I visited the Stalin museum. After all: why would anyone devote a museum to a dictator who was hated by everyone? And secondly, I don't believe in reincarnation, but I was born nine months after Stalin's death."

Silke was fully convinced now. After consulting with Davor, our security expert, she told me that I was allowed to visit Gori, but I was not allowed to take a *Mazurka* minibus, since these were frequently involved in accidents and sometimes tourists were assaulted in them. I told her that I had already planned to travel by train.

Thankfully, the electronic signs at the Central Station provided arrival and department information in both Georgian and English. And I was lucky: the young woman who sold me my train tickets spoke English. She explained the proceedings to me. I love old trains. It was only one hour to Gori. And for the first time I saw something of the countryside.

For the first time in ten weeks I saw cows and goats. And snow-capped mountains. Very few passengers stepped off the train at Gori's station. Thanks to Google Maps I knew that I had to follow the Stalin Avenue straight up to the Stalin museum. Only one road. It could not go wrong.

But it did go wrong. Where the hell was the Stalin Avenue? It turned out that the exit of the train station is situated at the opposite side of where the Stalin Avenue started. And the sign pointed in the wrong direction: away from the city center. I had to walk several hundred meters to a bridge across the railway lines and then to another bridge across the river.

It was cold, even colder than in Tbilisi, and I was only wearing a thin summer coat. It was also windy. It gave the central square, where

Stan Storimans was killed, an eary feeling. It was a typical Soviet square: very large and desolate, since it was a Sunday. Not a nice place for your last minutes on planet earth.

To warm up, I ordered a pizza and a capuccino at the Champs Elysée restaurant straight opposite the square. I was the only customer. An hour later I entered the Stalin museum. Lots of Stalin memorabilia and Stalin photographs. I could not find any critical remarks anywhere in the museum.

Apparently, the inhabitants of Gori have mixed feelings about the Soviet dictator. 'He was one of us, so he could not be wrong', they seem to think. While in the rest of Georgia all statues of Stalin have been removed, in Gori the main avenue is still called Stalin Avenue.

In front of the museum Stalin's birth house stands prominently, under a protective roof. Months later, when I was in Holland again, my best friend remarked: ,,How could you visit a museum that is dedicated to the worst dictator the world has ever seen?"

But Stalin has been a historic figure, whether you like it or not. He gave orders from behind his desk. The head of the KGB, Beria, on the other hand, had personally raped, tortured and killed many people. After Beria's death, the corpses of several women were found buried in Beria's garden.

Curiously, Beria was also a Georgian, that is to say: he was born in Abchazia from Georgian parents. During Stalin's days, more Georgian than Russian was spoken in the Kremlin. Tiny Georgia dominated the giant Soviet Union.

The day after my birthday, Nina invited me and Mats and Justyna to our favorite vegetarian restaurant Mama Terra. They gave me a bottle of Georgian cognac as a birthday present.

To my surprise, Silke joined us after we had finished our meals. Silke told us that on my birthday, 2 December, her parents had celebrated their 65th marriage anniversary.

Did I find a Goofy? You bet I did. It took me some time, but I found one in a toyshop inside the Galleria Mall, where also my favorite Goodwill supermarket was located. A small, plastic Goofy driving a Formula One race car, like Max Verstappen. In the end, it had been my longest mission and my smallest Goofy.

The return flight back to Holland went fine. For me, at least. My colleagues were not so lucky. For some reason, many flights depart from Tbilisi in the middle of the night. I had to leave my guesthouse at 02.00 hours, so I did not get any sleep at all.

Even at this unruly hour, Nana, the owner of my guesthouse, was up and waiting for me with a farewell present: a bottle of Georgian wine. Unfortunately, I could not take the heavy bottle with me, so I left it with Gia. We picked up Nina and drove over to the airport, which was covered in thick fog. This came as a surprise, since there had not been any fog at all in the center of Tbilisi.

It became apparent that this was posing a problem for my colleagues, who were scheduled to fly to Istanbul in two different Turkish Airways planes. Because of the fog, these planes were not able to land in Tbilisi. The passengers were waiting in front of the Turkish Airways counter in long queues.

Nina decided to book a seat on a Lufthansa flight to Frankfurt and pay from her own pocket. I was luckier: I was flying with Georgian Airways, and this plane was already waiting at the airport. Ever since I obtained my flying licence in 1986, I know that it's a problem to land in thick fog, but taking off is not really a hazard. And it was a direct flight to Amsterdam as well. Lucky me.

I took the train back to Enkhuizen. At the train station I stepped out with my two suitcases and who was the first of my townsmen I came across? My own boss, Stef Blok, the Minister of Foreign Affairs. There was no one else on the street, so I greeted him and he greeted me back, but he did not know who I was, nor that I was in fact working for him!

Chapter 25

MOZAMBIQUE - 2019

'You're suffering from the Stockholm Syndrome'

I knew that, one day, my luck would change. Thus far, I had been blessed with my 20 partners. This could not go on for ever. Little did I know that I would encounter the most problematic of all my partners in my beloved Mozambique.

I had promised my wife that, after my 11 week to mission to Georgia, I would not do any missions in 2019. Unless an extraordinary mission would come up. Well, it did. The moment I saw the email inviting me to go to Mozambique as an LTO, I felt exhilarated.

I know the country, I like the people, I speak Portuguese. On top of that: I thought: „If I don't go to Mozambique now, I will probably have to go later to some horrible country like Afghanistan, Somalia, Nigeria. Or even worse!"

The only thing I was afraid of was having to spend seven weeks in Tete yet again: the hottest provincial capital of the country. I was lucky: this time they were sending me to the—literary—coolest provincial capital: Lichinga.

Lichinga is situated on top of a 1,400 meter high plateau in faraway north-western Niassa province, often referred to as 'The Forgotten Province'. I remembered the pleasant climate from my very first mission in 1994.

Another advantage was that no CT-member would visit us in this remote and totally unimportant place, bordering Lake Malawi. Little did I know that something far more horrible did lay in store for me: the worst partner of all my twenty missions.

Her name was—officially—Marie-Helene, but she insisted on being called Mahé: „I did not choose that horrible Marie-Helene", she explained. „My parents did that." Her father was Greek, her mother French.

Her father had passed away. He had been born in Khartoum, but grew up in Alexandria. Mahé was 60 years old and lived with her 92-year old mother in Athens. Mahé had a dog and a cat. A bad omen. I had always believed that you are either a dog-person or a cat-person, but not both.

She had done thirteen missions, so she was experienced. No problem there. But already during the briefings in Maputo I noticed something worrying. She told me sternly that we should hire an assistant/interpreter. ,,We don't need an interpreter", I replied. ,,We both speak decent Portuguese. I didn't have an interpreter in Tete in 2014."

But Mahé insisted. I explained that an extra team member would mean extra organizational complications, like the planning of our trips and having to wait for someone to arrive. And all of this for no reason at all, since we didn't need an interpreter.

But she remained adamant. I decided to give in. What's the use of fighting over such a trivial matter? Little did I know that she would insist on doing pretty much everything her way.

Mahé told me that her brother had been my colleague observer in Khartoum, back in 2011. I could not remember him, not even his name, but I later learned that he had indeed been with me in Khadaffi's hotel over there, as a member of the CT.

,,But I hate my brother", Mahé said. And she added: ,,I don't want to talk about him." This was strange. Since they had talked about me, she must have spoken with her brother just before she travelled to Mozambique. Weird.

Back in The Netherlands, the Ministry of Foreign Affairs had decided not to brief me, since the 3 Dutch STOs had not yet been identified. Instead, I would be briefed at the Dutch Embassy in Maputo. The Dutch ambassador, Henny de Vries, was occupied with the expatriation of the deceased wife of one of her ambassy staff.

I remembered the hassles UNDP had to face in Mozambique in 1984, after my close friend and colleague Jean-Paul Langlois (a French speaking Canadian) had died in a motorcycle accident. His family wanted to bury him in Canada, but to transport a corpse across borders is not an easy undertaking. It took weeks to get all the paper work in order.

The ambassador was replaced by Guus, a young diplomat, who had arrived in Mozambique just one month earlier. As was to be expected, I ended up briefing him on Mozambique, instead of the other way around. But he was a likable guy and a quick learner.

We had to get up at 03.00 hours, to catch our LAM flight to Lichinga. Five years earlier, the UN forbade us to fly with LAM, but apparently the airline had improved over the years. I hoped so.

I was reassured, to some extent, by hearing an unmistakable American accent in the pilot's announcements. I am not a racist, but I prefer a decent pilot, if possible. This guy was probably using an African airline to increase his flying hours.

The plane landed first at Nampula, where most of the passengers stepped out. Only a handful people remained on board, which provides you with a feeling of connectedness to the few remaining passengers, but it makes you also realize that you're going to a really remote place.

At Lichinga's charming little airport, our driver, Chaibo, was waiting for us. He seemed to be a decent chap and the car was a decent four-wheel drive. Without any discussion, Mahé claimed the left front seat.

I took the left back seat, which was fine with me. Much safer, in case of an accident. And it gave me a bit of privacy, since it would be more of an effort for Mahé to turn around and talk to me.

In Portugal, the traffic drives on the right side of the road, but since Mozambique is surrounded by left-driving English-speaking countries, the Portuguese had decided that Mozambique should drive at the left side as well.

After all, when you bought a car in South Africa, the wheel would be on the right side. And when driving, the wheel should always be at the middle of the road, as I had learned from the movie 'The World's Fastest Indian'.

The most urgent matter was to find a decent place to stay. Mahé and I agreed that it would be convenient to find a place close to the town center, so that we didn't need the driver at all times.

The hotel where I staid in 1994 is close to the center, but it was now part of the Girassol chain and therefore quite expensive. Guesthouses were much cheaper, but most of them were quite hopeless or too far away from the center. Then we found a nice place, called Residencial Bendiak.

Chaibo knew where the owners lived. He drove us to a ranch in the sprawled-out suburbs of Lichinga. To my surprise, the owner was not Mozambican. He came from Guinea in West-Africa. I told him that I had worked in Guinea in 2015 as an observer.

,,Where?" he asked. ,,In a small town that nobody has ever heard of", I replied. ,,What's it called?" he insisted. ,,It's called Telimélé". He smiled. ,,That's a nice place. I've been there. It sits on top of a plateau, like Lichinga."

As usual I left the negotitiatons to my partner. Mahé spoke French with the owner. He clearly liked the idea of having two westerners staying longtime at his guesthouse. It's good PR. Mahé explained that we had to pay for the rooms from our own pockets. The price went down and down. Then he became a bit nervous. ,,I'm not the sole owner," he said. ,,I have to consult my partner."

We quickly realized that his partner was actually his wife and she was a tough cookie. She was Mozambican, but she came from Maputo, which was situated 2,500 kilometers to the south. I wondered how this rather odd couple ended up in Lichinga, of all places, but I didn't dare to intervene in the negotiations. It would only make the price go up.

Eventually, a very decent price was agreed. We would pay only 22 euros per day. We agreed to skip breakfast, since those breakfasts are usually very basic and you had to be present at the little restaurant at a certain time. I preferred to buy my own fruit juice and make my own coffee in my own room in my own time.

When we drove back to our guesthouse, I told Mahé that there was one little thing that I absolutely needed: Laurentina Preta, the best dark beer in the world. By now, it was early evening and it was a Saturday. Shops were closing. Chaibo took us to a sort of primitive dancing hall. To my delight, they indeed sold Laurentina Preta there.

Chaibo took me apart and told me that the price was double the normal price, but I bought two six-packs anyway. ,,Next week we'll go to the normal shops", I explained to him. ,,Right now, I need these beers and they sell these beers."

That evening, Mahé and I had our first meal in the little guesthouse restaurant. A simple meal, with some chicken and vegetables. From then on, Mahé would supervise our meals in cooperation with Arnaldo, the cook.

Arnaldo was a good cook, but his tiny kitchen was extremely primitive. It contained just one light bulb and an old-fashioned wood stove. The owners of the guesthouse, like every body else in Mozambique, were always short on money and spending money on an electric stove was simply inconceivable.

The food was served by either Eusebio or Jolinda, both young and cheerful. The first days I handed them the money, which was only 2 euros, but in Mozambique that's a lot of money. It dawned on me that they would probably keep most of it themselves, instead of handing Arnaldo his fair share.

Mahé agreed that from then on I would go to the kitchen and give the money directly to Arnaldo. The cook received a salary of only about 50 euros per month, so Mahé and I decided to pay him directly from our pockets for the evening meals.

We either gave Arnaldo money to buy food at the market or Mahé bought beans and vegetables herself at the market, to be prepared by Arnaldo. This was very cheap. All in all, we ate well every evening. And the cook was happy with the little extra money.

There were a few restaurants in Lichinga, but they were very basic and in the evening it was not really pleasant to go out on foot. It was not dangerous, but the roads, especially the pavewalks, were littered with potholes and the street lights were not really up to standards.

Add to this that the few passing cars and motorbikes had either no lights at all or one blazing headlight. It was simply more comfortable to remain at our guesthouse, where I offered Mahé a Laurentina Preta every evening during dinner.

There was, as we discovered later, one decent restaurant in Lichinga. It was called 'O Chambo', which means tilapia in the local language. The tilapia fish came fresh from Lake Malawi, just 15 kilometers from Lichinga. Mahé and I went a few times to O Chambo and I have to admit: that really was the best tilapia I had ever tasted.

The restaurant is situated next to the central market, in an unobtrusive building. The O Chambo restaurant and the owner/cook, Dona Argentina, had been mentioned in LAMs monthly flight bulletin, after which people flew from Maputo to Lichinga, just to eat tilapia at the O Chambo. It may sound weird, but that fantastic tilapia made it really worth while.

The CT had identified an assistant/interpreter for us, but this Americo turned out to be a total nitwit. We visited the usual suspects: CPE, STAE, the political parties. While presenting ourselves to the provincial chief of police, Mahé mentioned that we needed an interpreter. A day later, the chief's aide called us. He knew an interpreter.

I was afraid that we would hire a Frelimo supporter, since most government officials supported the ruling party. But Nito appeared to be a reasonably bright fellow. Much better than Americo, in any case. Nito was 30 years of age, unmarried, but he had a girl friend.

Mahé suggested that at the end of each day the three of us would sit down in Mahé's room, to work on our Weekly Reports. I liked the idea of typing the reports on a daily basis, since this would reduce the stress levels by the time it came to sending the WRs to the Core Team. But I had never typed a WR in the presence of an interpreter. What if Nito really was a Frelimo supporter?

On the other hand: Frelimo was probably not interested in our EU EOM, since Frelimo would win the elections in any case. They always did. So Nito joined us and added to our notes. The only problem was that the WRs had to be written in English and Nito's English was rather basic.

Our CT mailed us the names and telephone numbers of the two EISA observers in Lichinga. EISA stands for Electoral Institute for Southern Africa. It has a good observational reputation. The next morning Jimbo and Carla came to our guesthouse.

Jimbo was a very pleasant chap from Angola. He provided us with lots of contacts in Niassa province. He was very smart and outgoing. He would become our best friend. He told us that back home in Angola people called him Kandangongo.

I wrote it down on a piece of paper that I kept ready at hand. Whenever we met, I called him Kandangongo. It always made him laugh, since not even Mozambicans could remember that name.

Jimbo/Kandangongo made himself even more useful by telling me where I could buy coffee. Back in Maputo, in the big supermarket near the Southern Sun hotel, I had noted coffee in a black paper bag that was called '*Café de Niassa*'.

I showed it to Mahé. ,,Niassa is our province", I told her. ,,This must mean that we can buy this real coffee over there, right?" Mahé agreed. Since on an airplane every kilogram counts, I decided to gamble that I could buy it in Lichinga.

But after ten days I was still drinking instant coffee. Then Jimbo took me to a little shop, only 300 meters from our guesthouse. Curiously, they sold only two things: yoghurt and *Café de Niassa*.

The shopowner explained that indeed there was a coffee factory, situated at the far north-east of Niassa province, close to Cabo Delgado province. He said that nearly all the coffee was exported.

Carla was very nice, but she did not speak one word of Portuguese. She was Kenyan and had ordered food for her from nearby Tanzania, since she did not like the Mozambican food. She was happy to meet us, though, since we spoke English.

We met Jimbo and Carla a few days later in a suburb, where people were climbing onto trucks. Jimbo, who loved to talk to everyone around him, explained that the trucks were hired by Frelimo to transport 8,000 people to the football stadium, where president Felipe Nyusi would hold a speech later that afternoon in his capacity as Frelimo candidate.

,,The people will have to remain at least four hours in the stadium, in the blazing sun and without water", Jimbo explained to us. ,,Then, after the presidents' speech, some of them will be transported back to their suburbs, but since there are not enough trucks for all 8,000 of them, most of them will have to walk back many hours in the dark."

We observed the president's rally in the stadium. At first Mahé and I stood in the middle of the pitch, but then Jimbo approached us. He took us to the tiny tribune, where the dignitaries sat comfortably in the shade.

We should not profit from our privileged position, as EU observers, but to stand in the hot sun for several hours was not an attractive prospect. My nose was already getting sunburned.

The rally was a typical African rally, with speeches and music. The spectators were quite enthusiastic, but it is hard to say if that is because they love Frelimo or because it is the only exciting thing that happened in Lichinga.

Mozambique is a very hierarchical country. I noticed this when we had to visit the garage of our car company. Whenever our driver, Chaibo, talked to one of his superiors, Chaibo lowered his voice to a whisper and lowered his shoulders in a submissive gesture.

At one point, the owner of the car company arrived. Chaibo was even more submissive. The owner seemed to be of Indian origine, but spoke the formal Portuguese of Portugal. He treated his garage workers with dedain, as if they were second-hand citizens.

On top of that, company owners often pay their personnel several months too late. If they pay at all. But what can the workers do? If they go on strike, they will be fired instantly. Thousands are waiting to take their places. It's like Europe in the 19th century.

Even within our little team the hierarchy was obvious. Nito received more payment than Chaibo, so Nito felt superior. One morning, Chaibo approached Mahé and me and said that Nito had called him. Nito told Chaibo to drive over to Nito's home and pick him up. We sternly told Chaibo, and later Nito, that Nito was not in a position to give orders to Chaibo.

After having interviewed all possible interlocutors in Lichinga, we planned to travel to Cuamba, the second town in Niassa province, at about five hours south of Lichinga. One of our STO teams would be based there, so we needed to check the place out for our STO manual.

Unfortunately, we received a message from our Security Officer that a 20 ton truck had wrecked an iron bridge, about halfway between the two towns. The road was blocked. We decided to visit the nearby districts first.

Most district capitals were within two hours drive from Lichinga, so we could visit one or two and return that same day to our guesthouse. These visits quickly became boring, since there was hardly any interesting information for our Weekly Reports.

The town of Mandimba was about three hours drive, so we decided to stay overnight there. To my surprise we found a nice, recently constructed small hotel, with airconditiong and a nice little open air restaurant. I started talking to two Pakistani businessmen, who had lived in Mozambique for many years.

Mahé joined us briefly. She asked the Pakistani's where we could buy beer, but I said: „It's OK. I can live without beer for a day." Mahé didn't know that I had smuggled six Laurentina Preta's in my medical kit. In my room, I poured the beer in a plastic yoghurt bottle. Both Mahé and the Pakistani's must have thought that I drank a lot of yoghurt.

A week later, the road to Cuamba was passable again. About halfway on the road to Cuamba I noticed a rusted sign, half hidden by bushes, with a picture of an elephant. 'Beware of crossing elephants', it meant, apparently.

„Where there elephants here, in the old days?" I asked our driver. „Probably", Chaibo answered. „But it must have been a very long time ago. I have never seen an elephant here."

A bit further down the road, we drove along the border with Malawi for a short while. The border is actually a wooden fence, just half a meter high. You can simply step over it and then you are in Malawi. No border guards anywhere in sight. The local people cross the border every day at will.

Just before we reached Cuamba, we drove past a concentration camp. It looked like Auschwitz, with high fences all around, cameras everywhere and strong lamps to make sure no one would escape during the night. „That's where the Chinese live," Chaibo explained.

Many of the Chinese road constructors are actually Chinese convicts. Some of them are real criminals, others are political prisoners. In any case, they have to work for two or three years and then they are cleared of all charges. The Chinese are hard workers; they only stop to eat and sleep.

In their concentration camp, the Chinese have their own Chinese food, prepared by Chinese cooks. They watch Chinese TV and they speak exclusively Chinese, since they do not have any social contacts with Africans.

They have no contacts with Africans for two reasons: firstly, they don't have time, since they work all the time and secondly they are afraid to become infected with HIV or tropical diseases. It's a new form of apartheid.

It's also a new form of colonialism: in exchange for the construction of roads, the Chinese receive concessions from the Frelimo government. The Chinese reap the riches of Mozambique. They dig out a diamond mine and load the diamond-rich soil onto a ship to China, where the diamonds will be extracted.

The Mozambican people are happy with the asphalt roads, constructed by the Chinese, but the Mozambicans don't realize that they pay a heavy price for this. One thing is certain, though: the Mozambicans don't like the Chinese. „*Os novos colonizadores*", Nito called them.

Vitor, the security assisant of our EU EOM, had passed through Cuamba and reported that there was only one hotel: Hotel Vision. It was not a nice place. On top of that, Mahé had a big row with Nito, our assistant. To my surprise, Nito came out of his room dressed in a T-shirt with short pants and wearing slippers. He looked like a tourist.

Since I'm a bit laid back, I did not react immediately, but Mahé started screaming and shouting at him. Nito returned to his room and put on his normal clothes. He was very upset. A bit later, in the car, tears were streaming down his face, but Mahé refused to apologize to him. „Those are crocodile tears", she said.

We soon found out that there were other guesthouses in Cuamba. We checked them out and they looked much better than the hotel. We moved into a very nice guesthouse called Residencial Zezinha.

Just two blocks away, the female owner, Dona Maria José, owned yet another guesthouse called Villa Verde, with a pleasant terrace. Mahé and I enjoyed our evening meals there, accompanied by a large bottle of Laurentina Preta beer.

As long as we were not arguing, Mahé was decent company. By now, I had decided to do everything exactly the way she wanted it to be done. This meant that Mahé was happy and whenever she was happy I was happy.

„It's only six weeks", my wife had told me via WhatsApp. „After that, you'll never see her again. Just keep in mind that the EU pays you 280 euros per day, just for being obedient."

An interesting thing happened the second morning at the nice, simple buffet breakfast in Residencial Zezinha. Mahé sat at a round table with Nito and Chaibo. She pointed at the only other table that was occupied. ,,That woman speaks your language", Mahé told me.

I walked over to the other table. To my surprise, the young black woman indeed spoke perfect Dutch. She explained that she came from Suriname, our old colony in South America. The Dutch socialist government of the 1970s had forced Suriname to become independent, since 'Colonialism should not exist anymore, in our present day and time'.

The 600,000 people of Suriname, however, had other ideas. They did not want to be independent, since they feared political and economic chaos. Therefore, within just a few years, half the population of Suriname moved to the Netherlands, where they automatically received Dutch passports.

The other half remained in Suriname, but they were obviously not the best and brightest. A few years later, the country suffered a coup d'etate by a handful of military men. Their leader, Desi Bouterse, would many years later be elected as president, after he had been convicted by international courts for murder and drug trafficking.

The economy of Suriname went down the drain. Those 300,000 who had moved to the Netherlands were glad that they had escaped just in time. The young woman from Suriname explained that she had been studying in Rotterdam for three years.

,,So you have a Dutch passport?" I asked her. She said no. ,,Then you're passport is most probably the very first passport from Suriname that the Mozambican customs people have ever seen", I replied. ,,I bet most Mozambicans have never even heard of Suriname."

She was in Mozambique to work on water projects. Her partner was a Mozambican, who spoke a bit of English. ,,Do you speak Portuguese?" I asked her. She said no, but she added that she could follow most of the conversations. ,,In Suriname we speak both Dutch and Sranantongo, which is a mix of English, Spanish, Portuguese and Creole. And Brazil, our neighbouringing country, is a Portuguese speaking country."

In Cuamba we interviewed the usual suspects. At one point, we drove by a cotton factory. We decided to pay it a visit. We were allowed to pass the gate and we were led into the administration building. A young, energetic Portuguese offered us an espresso and explained everything about the factory. His name was Manuel Delgado and he was the general manager.

He showed us the factory. It was fascinating. I had always believed that cotton in Mozambique was grown on giant plantations, like the one I had visited in 1985 near Nampula, but this factory received cotton from tens of thousands of small farmers!

Since my family were small farmers in the Netherlands, I am of course very simpathetic towards them. The João Ferreira dos Santos Factory existed 123 years and had more than one million hectares of cotton under concession, spread out over three provinces.

Most farmers owned just one or two hectares. Since many small farmers were not accustomed to handling money, the factory did not pay them cash but credits, with wich the farmers were able to obtain seeds or farm tools.

The factory, in fact, appeared to be more like an aid project, distributing micro credits to the farmers. Manuel took us to the offices, where the thousands of small farmers were administered. An enormous and complicated undertaking, but with the help of computers all these farmers and their cotton crops were listed one by one.

A few days later our STO team arrived in Lichinga. Amongst the twenty or so passengers that stepped out of the plane I immediately recognized Bujar, who had been my STO in Tbilisi, Georgia, during the second phase. Over there, he always wore a gypsy hat and a gypsy long coat. This time, he wore neither, but I recognized him because he is a full head taller than the people around him.

Beside him walked Karin, whom I also recognized vaguely. It dawned on me that she had been my STO in Georgia during the first phase. I'm getting old. I forget faces and she was one of a staggering 16 STOs. Behind her walked Luís Kandangongo Jimbo, our EISA observer-friend from Angola.

Bujar is 47, has an Italian passport and lives in Toscane, but had been born in Albania. In the mid nineteen ninetees he escaped to Greece. He and his friend crossed the mountains for two days.

At the other side of the border, they surrendered to the Greek army, who tortured them for twelve hours, according to him. This surprised me. I asked my partner Mahé, who lives in Athens, if it is customary in Greece to torture visitors. She did not reply, but instead looked away angrily.

Karin was fifty years old and born in a small German town, just across the border from the Dutch town of Venlo. She spoke a bit of Dutch. She asked me if I remembered her from that nice restaurant in Tbilisi. Honest to God, I did not. We had so many STOs over there, during the first and second round.

We took them to our Residencial Bendiak, where I served all four of us fresh coffee in our 'garden'. Both of them told long, boring stories, probably because they were a bit nervous, being in a totally new place with new people. They were both tired, of course, since they had to get up in the middle of the night to catch the early plane.

We took them for lunch to Safeera, 'our' buffet restaurant at the central roundabout of Lichinga. Karin enjoyed the food, but Bujar ate nothing at all. I remembered him as a good observer, but also that he was easily agitated. I therefore made no comments.

For Mahé, however, it was not possible not to make comments. She asked him if he had eaten already. In reply, he grumbled something. I later realized that he was extremely economical. Like all eastern Europeans, he wanted to bring home as much money as he could from his missions.

The four of us observed first a Renamo rally and then a Frelimo rally. This was the last day that campaigning was permitted, so these were the closing rallies. At the Frelimo rally several districts of Niassa province played football against one another. There were also a few female teams.

The teams wore orange, grey and white shirts, but all players had written the same name on their backs: Filipe Nyusi, the president, who was also the presidential candidate for Frelimo. So Nyusi played against Nyusi. This guaranteed that Nyusi would always win.

The four of us sat down at the far side of the podium, where the current and future governors of Niassa province were going to speak. The TVM camera was also there, so we would be on TV again, sitting perilously close to the Frelimo provincial leadership. The Core Team would not like this.

On top of this, Mahé sent a photo of the four of us to Sylvie, the Observer Coordinator. I was on the verge of advising her not to transmit that photo, but decided not to risk another argument with her. After all: why create a fuss? This would probably be my last mission anyway.

In the early evening we briefed our STOs in our hotel's restaurant. After that the three of us ate a lovely vegetable soup, made by Arnaldo, the hotel's talented cook. Bujar did not eat soup, but instead pealed an apple.

At one point, Mahé, who was always observing other people intently, asked if he felt allright. ,,What do you mean?" he asked. His face changed from friendly to angry. When he looked angry, he looked like Rasputin.

The next morning, I first had a row with Mahé and then with Nito, our rather useless assistant. Mahé told me that she had slept only two hours, because of the Saturday evening discotheque, just across from our hotel. ,,Don't you have earplugs?" I asked her. ,,Yes, I do, but they didn't help."

Then she told me what was probably the real reason for her not sleeping. ,,Do you remember Bujar's face yesterday evening?" Mahé asked me. She added: ,,I'm going to call Sylvie, to explain what happened, because I'm afraid Bujar will talk negatively about me to the Core Team, once he's back in Maputo."

I wanted to tell her that it seemed not a good idea to me to alert Sylvie about a possible problem, since in that case Sylvie would certainly ask Bujar what happened. Most probably, Bujar would not have mentioned it to Sylvie in any case. But when I go against Mahé, she starts shouting and screaming at me. So I just nodded: 'Do whatever you want to do'.

We would not meet our other STO team face to face. From Maputo they flew to Nampula and from there traveled by car to Cuamba, which actually took them twice as long as the road between Lichinga and Cuamba. About halfway between Nampula and Cuamba, they had to stay overnight at a roadside guesthouse.

It would have been much more convenient for all of us if they had passed through Lichinga. In the end, we never saw them face to face. We briefed them via WhatsApp, which worked quite nicely. They seemed to be doing OK.

Just one day before E-Day, our LSTO team arrived. They checked into the Girassol Hotel, about 500 meters from our Residencial Bendiak. This was the hotel I stayed in in 1994. By then, it had beeen a run-down communist hotel. Now, it was a 4-star place, quite fancy.

We briefed them in the restaurant of our guesthouse. They were pleasant embassy staff, both of them Irish, though—to my surprise—one of them came from Northern Ireland. ,,I thought that Northern Ireland was part of the UK", I told them. But apparently, ever since the 1998 peace agreement, Northern Irish can opt for an Irish passport.

I realized—but didn't dare to mention it to them, because religion is such a sensitive topic in Northern Ireland—that the Northern Irish guy was catholic, since he told us that he came from Derry, which is called Londonderry by the protestants.

In my country, Holland, there are catholics and protestants, but they haven't kill each other for centuries. It's hard for Dutch people to understand why different religious groups hate each other so much.

After the two Irish had left, Mahé started shouting at me about our E-Day route. A week earlier, we had driven past 18 PSs and I had typed them all. To my horror, I realized that Mahé had been thinking, the entire week, that this was to be our route.

In truth, it was just a random list of PSs, without any logical coherence. Sometimes you just cannot imagine what other, unorganized people, are thinking. Anyway, I would go out with Nito to map a proper route.

Since both Mahé and I and STO1502 would observe on E-Day in Lichinga District, I explained to the STOs that the first two pages of the official PS-list were for us and the last two pages were for them. It could not be simpler. The only problem was that, unknown to me, Mahé had also given them the PS list that I had typed.

I walked to our car, where Nito was already sitting in the front seat, where Mahé always sits. ,,Please come with me on the back seat, where you always sit", I told him. He refused. I told him again. He started talking about a traffic cop who had stopped us the other day and told us that the front seat should not be vacant.

I told him: ,,Listen, Nito: a traffic cop does not determine who sits where in our car. We determine that. But if you don't go to your backseat immediately, I will go alone with Chaibo." He grimassed towards me. That was the drop that caused the bucket to spill over.

Nito opened the backdoor of the car, but by this time I sat down on the front seat. I turned my head towards him and said: ,,Stay out of the car; I'm going alone." He said that he would inform Mahé. Chaibo, our driver, was paralized after all this, but I sternly told him: ,,Let's go, Chaibo. Right now."

Chaibo and I did a good job. We planned a decent route for our E-Day observations. Mostly, we would only have to drive 5 minutes between PSs. I even found two rural PSs, just behind the runway of the airport. While on the road, my phone rang twice. I knew it was Mahé.

Chaibo looked at me, but I didn't answer her calls. Then Chaibo's phone rang. He was so afraid of me, that—wisely—he didn't answer it. But then we arrived at the Ceramics School. They were playing football at the central school square, so Chaibo parked his car next to a classroom wall.

He stepped out of the car, presumably to ask confirmation if it was indeed the Ceramics School. But he stayed away for a full ten minutes, while there were people standing at just twenty meters away. I noted that he had taken his mobile phone. I stepped out and waited for him.

He came towards me with a guilty grin on his face. Later, Mahé told me that Chaibo had called her and told her the same bullshit story about the—alleged—cultural habit in Mozambique that one person should occupy the front seat. So Chaibo, whom I had always treated correctly, had betrayed me. I was not going to forget this.

When Chaibo and I returned to the hotel, I called Mahé, to ask her if Chaibo could go home for lunch. She did not pick up the phone. Obviously, she was pissed off. So I sent Chaibo to his lunch anyway. Five minutes later he came back and asked me for the car keys. ,,Mahé is at the market and wants me to pick her up", Chaibo explained. I handed him the keys.

I ate bread and cheese in my room, with the door open. That afternoon, Mahé walked passed my room at least three times. She didn't even look at me. At 17.30 hrs I met Karin at the parking lot. She told me that she was going to eat at what she called the 'Kilo Restaurant', the buffet-restaurant Safeera. I offered to join her, since Bujar was not going with her.

While I was eating at the restaurant, Mahé called me. ,,Where are you? You should have told me where you were going." I answered: ,,But you were not on speaking terms with me, the entire afternoon." Mahé said: ,,Let's not argue in front of Karin. Come back to the hotel."

I went to Mahé's room. She screamed that I should offer my apologies to Nito. I bluntly told her that I would never speak to Nito again. This was actually my third major fight with Mahé. The first one occurred when we started writing our first Weekly Report.

The CT had prepared questions for every section of the WR. These questions are there to help us, to guide us. However, Mahé believed that we should answer each and every question one by one. She's not very smart and she honestly believed this.

I panicked, because I believed that our WR would be considered amateuristic. At the NEEDS course for Legal/Election Experts in Brussels, in 2009, I had learned to start every chapter with the most important information and then continue with the less important information.

I called Alex, the very experienced Electoral Expert from Ireland. He agreed with me. Mahé was furious. She called Dora, the young Political Expert from Belgium, who agreed with Mahé.

In the end I decided: 'What the hell; I do it her way. After all: what can I do when even our own CT is divided on the issue? Let's face it: as long as I can sit peacefully on my porch every evening with a cigar and a beer in the cool evening air, and as long as they pay me 280 euros per day, I'm a happy man'.

My second major fight with Mahé was about the printer. I wanted to print the official list of PSs in Lichinga District. Only four pages, in black and white. I reached for the printer, when Mahé shouted: „What are you printing?" I was flabbergasted. Never before had any of my partners asked me what I was printing.

„Is this your printer or is this our team printer?", I asked her. „What are you printing?" she insisted. „Just the PSs in Lichinga District", I replied. „I already printed that", she said. „But I need a list for myself", I told her. „I already printed that list", she repeated.

„That's your list, now I need my list", I replied. She walked over to the cupboard, took the list and threw it in front of me on the table. „Here, take it", she said. Several days later I asked her why she was so obsessed with printing. „People print too much", she replied rather vaguely.

She tells every Mozambican that she loves trees. In Niassa province, most trees have been burned to produce charcoal, which is sold along road sides everywhere. One sack of charcoal costs around two euros. To produce one sack of charcoal, three trees need to be destroyed.

There are hardly any trees left. When we drove back from Cuamba, Mahé asked Chaibo and Nito why Mozambicans were destroying their own country. The two of them just laughed about it. Mozambicans don't really care about the future of their country. They have other imminent problems, mainly financially.

I was not the only one who had problems with Mahé. The first evening after the arrival of our STOs I sat down with them in the 'jardim' of our guesthouse, where Mahé could not hear us. Out of the blue, Karin told me that Mahé had entered Karin's room and threatened Karin that she would receive a negative recommendation, if Karin supported Bujar.

I was perplexed. Karin had done nothing wrong and was quite new on the job. Why did Mahé scare her like this? The problem was, of course, that there had been no witnesses, but Karin looked so shaken that I absolutely believed her.

One evening, Bujar showed me a Whatsapp exchange with Gert from Austria, who was our colleague LTO now, but had been my Observer Coordinator in 2014. Gert also exchanged Whatsapp's with Mahé, in which he was diplomatically correct and therefore Mahé thought that he was her friend. However, Gert confided to Bujar that he really hated her guts.

E-Day went fine. No major problems. As always, Frelimo won the elections. Our two STO teams and the LSTO team performed properly. So did Mahé and I. We observed the closing and counting at the nearby Escola Khankombo. Our Polling Station had only 360 voters, so we were back in our guesthouse at 23.00 hours.

A bit later, while I was sitting on my pouch waiting for Bujar and Karin to return to our guesthouse, I received a Whatsapp from Marta from Portugal, my old partner from Tete, who was now in Chimoio with John from Denmark.

Marta asked me if I had survived my partner thus far. I answered: ,,Every day she says that all men are idiots, but my wife has been doing the same for the last 47 years, so I'm quite used to it."

Her partner John, a likeable Danish guy who had been my colleague LTO on many missions, then whatsapped me that Mahé had been his STO and that he had wanted to give her a 'not-recommended', because Mahé had lied to him. ,,Unfortunately, I had already given her a 'recommended' and I could not change it anymore", John added.

It was quite funny for me to look at Bujar and Mahé when they were together. They looked at each other with such mutual hatred on their faces, that I couldn't stop myself from laughing. On their last evening in Lichinga, I took Bujar and Karin to the O Chambo restaurant, to eat the best tilapia in the world.

During the dinner in O Chambo, Bujar asked me: ,,When did you realize that Mahé was crazy?" I replied that it had dawned bit by bit after a few days. ,,But why do you do everything that she asks you to do? She yells at you from her room and you oblige by running towards her."

That was true. I replied that, after consulting with my wife, I had decided to keep the peace and simply do everything Mahé's way. To avoid conflicts. Bujar could not understand this. ,,But how do you cope? It must hurt." I replied with a quotation from Lawrence of Arabia: ,,The trick is not minding that it hurts."

I explained that I was used to being bullied by a woman, since back home I was in the same situation. ,,My wife loves the dog, but she hates walking the dog, so I walk the dog three times a day. Still: my wife tells me how to walk the dog. She tells me to go there and there, so the dog can run and swim and play with other dogs."

Bujar looked at me with a face that showed both pity and disbelief. ,,But once you're away with the dog, do you still do what she says?" I laughed. ,,Of course not. Once I'm away from home, I do whatever I want to do." Karin said that she quite understood that I preferred not to quarrel with Mahé on a daily basis.

The next morning, Mahé asked me why she had not been invited to the dinner. ,,Because you and Bujar hate each other so much, that it would have ended in a terrible fight", I answered. I thought she would explode in anger, but nothing happened. She probably agreed with me.

I was afraid Mahé would give Bujar a 'not-recommended', because then I would have refused to sign it. Thank God she gave him a 'recommended'. We both signed it and she handed it to him with the words: ,,You need improvement". The next morning, when our STOs said goodbye to us, Bujar told her: ,,I hope you receive what you give!"

Funnily, Mahé believed that our Observer Coordinator, Sylvie, was on her side, but it had actually been Sylvie who had given Mahé a 'recommended-but' during a previous mission, when Mahé was an STO and Sylvie was her LTO, together with Rumiana from Bulgaria, a well-respected LTO.

So, obviously, Sylvie was not fond of Mahé. Therefore, I found it strange that Mahé chatted nearly every day in rapid French with Sylvie on the phone. Sylvie only once called me, but didn't ask me anything about my relationship with Mahé.

One evening at dinner Mahé had confided to me that she had had serious problems with at least two of her previous partners. She referred to one of her partners as 'The Nazi'. She refused to reveal his name, but she admitted that the CT had decided to split the two of them and reassign both Mahé and her 'Nazi' to other partners.

The Core Team was probably happy that I took care of Mahé, without major headaches. The truth is: in the end, I had an easy going mission. Mahé was very energetic, very pro-active and she took good care of me. She asked my opinion on everything (expecting me to always agree with her; otherwise she would explode in anger).

Every day Mahé went to the market to buy vegetables or beans. She then handed them to Arnaldo, our cook at the hotel, who prepared a delicious meal under Mahé's direct supervision.

After that, I had the rest of the evening to myself, since Mahé ran out of steam after 19.00 hours. I would sit happily on my pouch with a beer and a cigar, watching the one or two other guests arriving or simply looking up at the stars.

A few days after E-Day, Mahé and I were observing at the office of CPE, the provincial electoral authority, where the results of all the districts were delivered. Out of the blue I received a call from Tania, our Deputy Chief Observer. This was the first time in 25 years that I received a direct call from a DCO!

They are usually too busy with meeting ambassadors and ministers, giving press conferences and pleasing their own direct boss, our mission's Chief Observer. I immediately realized what that call meant: Bujar had indeed written a complaint about Mahé. I quickly walked over to the toilet, at the far end of the back garden. ,,Are you alone?" Tania asked me.

It appeared that Karin had also signed the complaint, since Tania talked about 'The STOs'. This meant it was serious business: a complaint from a single person could mean that two persons just disliked each other, but a complaint signed by two persons could only mean that something had been seriously wrong.

I was cautious. I did not want to betray my partner. ,,I can only respond to allegations when I see them in front of me", I told Tania. ,,If you text them to me, I will answer them one by one. Maybe it's better to do this when we return to Maputo?" I suggested to her.

The next day I received a call from Sylvie. ,,Can you speak freely?" she asked. I locked the door of my room. We spoke about ten minutes. After that, Mahé was shouting at me to open my door. ,,What was that about?" Mahé wanted to know. ,,My father was taken to the hospital in an ambulance", I told her.

,,That's not true", Mahé said. ,,I heard you talking English and I heard you calling my name. What's up?" I repeated that my father had been taken to hospital, that my mother was in a state of panic, being all by herself in the apartment for the first time in her life. I added that I didn't like it that she had been eavesdropping at my door.

Half an hour later, Mahé appeared in front of my open door yet again. ,,I know about the complaint", she said. It turned out that Sylvie had sent it to Mahé, who had already printed it. She threw the complaint on my table. ,,I never saw this", I told her feebly. Which was true.

Bujar and Karin had indeed signed it, both of them. They had formulated five major accusations, against Mahé. A bit later, Sylvie asked me to comment on each accusation in writing. Which I did, even though it felt like betraying my partner.

But what could I do? All accusations were accurate. I knew then that my last week with Mahé would be even more hellish than the previous six weeks. How could I escape? Well: luckily, it was true that my 90-year old father had just been taken to hospital in an ambulance, with possibly a fractured hip.

And my 89-year old mother was now all alone, for the very first time in her life. She was panicking. Apparently she had entered the first stage of dementia. My five brothers and two sisters were taking shifts to support both our parents at two different locations.

I called Sylvie again and asked her if I could go home one week earlier than originally planned, to support my family. ,,Can you put it in writing?" she asked. I did. Sylvie forwarded it to the CT and the SP. ,,I will come back to you", she said. To my surprise I was granted to go back home the very next morning 'because of special circumstances'.

That evening, Mahé and I still ate together, but in total silence. Pedro had sent me my air ticket by email. I was afraid that Mahé would not print it for me, so I asked him to sent me my ticket by Whatsapp as well. He did, but an hour later Mahé handed me my printed ticket after all.

She entered my room. Obviously, she was afraid that I would betray her, once I was in Maputo. I told her that I would not file a complaint about her, but that I was forced to answer questions by the CT and that I would answer truthfully.

„What is the truth?" Mahé asked. I replied with an enigmatic quote from Johan Cruijff: 'The truth is never exactly what you think it should be'. She started crying. „I'm afraid they'll put me on the black list", she snottered, tears falling down her cheeks. In spite of everything, I felt pity for her.

The next morning I set out for the airport. Through the glass doors of the departure lounge I saw Vitor, the mission's security assistant, leave the airplane. He would take my place for a couple of days.

In Lichinga, I had hardly seen any rain at all, but in Maputo it was raining and the clouds were very low. With my nose against the window, I saw the 737 approach the runway.

Then, at the very last moment, the pilot gave his plane full throttle and pulled the nose up. 'Overshooting the Field', this is called, as I remembered from my pilot training back in 1986. Five minutes later, the captain confirmed this over the speakers.

Funnily, the people behind me had no incling at all to what had just happened. They were blisfully unaware. But the captain did the right thing: when a pilot is not sure that he can land his plane at the beginning of the runway, the correct procedure is 'Overshooting the Field': bring the plane up in the air again and circle around, to try to land properly.

In Maputo's Southern Sun hotel, where the CT had its offices, Sylvie took me to Tania's room. They wanted me to confirm what I had already put into writing: answering the five complaints regarding Mahé, that our STOs had put to paper. I did as requested.

They told me one thing that was very funny: when a complaint is filed against a person, this person has the right to read the complaint. In this case, Tania had ordered Sylvie to send the complaint to 'Marie-Helene'.

Tania did not know that Mahé wanted to be called Mahé, and not 'Marie-Helene'. „I only know her by her full passport name", Tania explained to us. But as it turned out, there was another 'Marie-Helene'.

This other Marie-Helene was working for the EU in Brussels. Sylvie had accidentily sent the complaint to the wrong Marie-Helene!

Tania also read parts to me of the reply (three pages!) that Mahé had written with regards to the complaints made by Bujar and Karin. In it, Mahé wrote that I was old and getting deaf and that I did not know how to use a smartphone.

Tania did not make a point of this: ,,We are all getting old", she said. ,,And by now you probably know your smartphone better than most of the CT members."

Tania and Sylvie wanted to know when the animosities between Mahé and Bujar had started. I could not remember a clear starting point. ,,Probably after Bujar told us that he had been tortured by the Greek military", I said. ,,Mahé told me that there are many Albanians working in Greece, in lowly paid jobs.

The Greeks and the Albanians apparently don't like one another. As Mahé said: 'They steal like the ravens'." Tania said that she herself had experienced a negative incident with Bujar, nine years previously. ,,So, admittedly, he is not the easiest person in the world", she concluded.

When I left Tania's room, I repeated what I had said earlier: ,,All in all, I did not have a bad mission." Tania replied—and I thought this was very funny—that I was suffering from the Stockholm Syndrome.

I had to admit that Mahé was a bit of a character. Indeed, Mahé had been the most problematic of my 21 partners, but to compare her to kidnappers was a bit overdone. After that, I was free. I walked through the drizzling rain towards the supermarket, where I bought a sixpack of Laurentina Preta beer.

In the evening, I treated myself to a full buffet in my hotel Southern Sun. It cost me 2.200 méticais (30 euros), fifteen times more than an average dinner in Lichinga, but I still had lots of méticais in my pocket, so I didn't care.

I also had plenty of cigars left, since I had left a week earlier than expected. Unfortunately, the rain was slamming onto the open terrace of the hotel, so no cigar smoking for me. But in my room I had a TV that worked. For the first time in six weeks I watched CNN, BBC World and a few more English channels.

The next morning I checked out and left my suit cases in the room that Sylvie shared with Carlo, the other Observer Coordinator, who had been my OC in Kenya. I had to see the SP people for my Time Sheets and my air ticket back home. I handed Pedro my keys for the metal box and my medical kit, that I had forgotten to give to Mahé.

I had a short meeting yet again with Tania and Sylvie. Tania read her report on Mahé to me. I fully agreed to everything she had written. ,,I am not sure yet if we will give her a 'Recommended-But' or a 'Not-Recommended', Tania said.

,,But one thing is certain: she needs to be checked by a medical expert, since I am not sure about her mental state of mind. I talked to her on the phone, this morning, and she did not sound right."

Then Tania confided another interesting bit of information to me: she said that another LTO team had faced such severe internal problems that the two LTOs had been split. An extraordinary measure, that the EU doesn't take lightly. Unfortunately, Tania did not reveal which team it had been.

After that, Sylvie took me to a deserted conference room and handed me my 'Recommended'. There was nothing left to say. She told me that she had studied in Utrecht, the Netherlands, and that she had liked my country very much.

Since Sylvie had been nice to me, I replied that in Dutch we use many French words, albeit pronounced in our own way. Maybe the French are not so bad after all. After that, I visited the SP staff one by one, to thank them for their support.

The flight back home, via Addis Ababa and Frankfurt, was uneventful. My wife told me that my father's situation was stabilized by now: he was lying flat on his back in a special hospital bed, in his own private room. He was scheduled to receive an artificial hip on 10 December 2019, provided he was strong enough to survive the operation.

My brothers and sisters continued to visit my parents in shifts, which by now included me as well. When we were young, our parents cared for us. Now, we cared for our parents. I was glad that I had returned home one week earlier than originally foreseen. In all the confusion, I had totally forgotten to look for a Goofy.

Two weeks later, I received an email from Mahé. She had indeed received a 'Not Recommended' and was blacklisted by the EU for five years. ,,I expected to receive some support", she wrote me. And she added: ,,Especially from you."

I look back at Mahé with mixed feelings. On one side, I profited from her energy. On the other side, she was a pain in the neck. But that is what you get as an election observer: each mission is an adventure. As Forrest Gump's mother used to say: 'Life is like a box of chocolates: you never know what you gonna get'.

LIST OF ACRONYMS:

AU:	African Union
BGAN:	Apparatus that links a laptop to a satellite/internet
CT:	Core Team
CO:	Chief Observer
COC:	Code of Conduct
DCO:	Deputy Chief Observer
EB:	Electoral Body
ECG:	Electro Cardiogram
E-Day:	Election Day
EISA:	Electoral Institute for Southern Africa
EMB:	Electoral Management Body
EU EOM:	European Union Election Observation Mission
IDPs:	Internally Displaced Persons
IOM:	UN International Office for Migration
LEU EOM:	Limited European Union Election Observation Mission
LO:	Liaison Security Officer
LTO:	Long-Term Observer
LROM:	Limited Referendum Observation Mission
LSTO:	Locally Recruited Short-Term Observer (i.e. EU embassy staff)
MEP:	Member of European Parliament
MOSS:	Minimal Operational Security Standards (UN)
MOU:	Memorandum of Understanding
NEEDS:	Network of Europeans for Electoral and Democracy Support
OAS:	Organization of American States
OC:	Observer Coordinator
OSCE/ODIHR:	Organization for Security and Cooperation in Europe/Office for Democratic Institutions and Human Rights (Warsaw)
PACE:	Parliamentary Assembly of the Council of Europe
PC:	Polling Center
PS:	Polling Station

PVT:	Parallel Vote Tabulation
Sat Phone:	Satellite Telephone
SE:	Security Expert
SP:	Service Provider (responsible for admin/logistics of a mission)
SLO:	Security Liaison Officer
STO:	Short-Term Observer
TA:	Technical Assistance
TOR:	Terms of Reference
UNDP:	United Nations Development Programme
VL:	Voter List
VR:	Voter Register
WR:	Weekly Report